INTERNATIONAL COOPERATION IN COUNTER-TERRORISM

This book has been published with a financial contribution from the Department of Legal Sciences of the University of Trento and the Italian Ministry of the University and Scientific Research, in the framework of the interuniversity research COFIN 2002 – Cooperation between United Nations and European Regional Organizations in the Fight Against Terrorism (Trento Unit).

International Cooperation in Counter-terrorism

Counter-terrorism

The United Nations and Regional Organizations in the Fight Against Terrorism

Edited by

GIUSEPPE NESI
University of Trento, Italy

ASHGATE

Published by
Ashgate Publishing Limited
Gower House
Croft Road
Aldershot
Hampshire GU11 3HR
England

Ashgate Publishing Company
Suite 420
101 Cherry Street
Burlington, VT 05401-4405
USA

Ashgate website: http://www.ashgate.com

British Library Cataloguing in Publication Data
International cooperation in counter-terrorism : the United
  Nations and regional organizations in the fight against
  terrorism
  1. United Nations 2. Terrorism - Law and legislation
  3. Terrorism - Prevention - International co-operation
  I. Nesi, Giuseppe
  345'.02

Library of Congress Cataloging-in-Publication Data
International cooperation in counter-terrorism : the United Nations and regional
organizations in the fight against terrorism / [edited] by Giuseppe Nesi.
        p. cm.
    Contains proceedings of a meeting held at the University of Trento on 27 and 28 May
2004.
    ISBN 0-7546-4755-2
    1. Terrorism--Prevention--International cooperation--Congresses. 2. War on
Terrorism, 2001--Law and legislation--Congresses. 3. United Nations. Security
Council. I. Nesi, Giuseppe.

  K5256.A6I58 2006
  345'.02--dc22
                                                                    2005031653
ISBN 0 7546 4755 2

Printed and bound in Great Britain by MPG Books Ltd. Bodmin, Cornwall.

Contents

Part I   The United Nations and the Fight Against International Terrorism

Part II Prevention and Suppression of International Terrorism in the Regional Framework

Part III Terrorism, International Security and the Use of Force

List of Participants

Professor Georges ABI-SAAB, Graduate Institute of International Studies, University of Geneva, and Member of the WTO Appellate Body

Ms. Roberta ARNOLD, Ministry of Defence, Berne

Mr. Roberto BELLELLI, President of the Military Tribunal of Turin

Professor Patrizia DE CESARI, University of Trento

Mr. Michael DE FEO, United Nations Office on Drugs and Crime, Vienna

Professor Luigi FERRARI BRAVO, University of Rome, 'La Sapienza', former Judge of the European Court of Human Rights

Professor Andrea GIOIA, University of Modena and Reggio Emilia

Professor Pietro GARGIULO, University of Teramo

Professor Gerhard HAFNER, University of Vienna

Professor Matthias HARTWIG, Max Plank Institute, Heidelberg

Mr. Mahmoud HMOUD, Legal Adviser, Permanent Mission of Jordan to the UN – New York

Ambassador Allieu Ibrahim KANU, Deputy Permanent Representative of Sierra Leone to the UN – New York

Professor Kalliopi KOUFA, University of Thessaloniki, Rapporteur of the UN Sub-Commission on the Promotion and Protection of Human Rights

Mr. Alexander MARSCHIK, Deputy Permanent Representative of Austria to the UN – New York

Ms. Egeria NALIN, Research Fellow, University of Bari

Professor Giuseppe NESI, University of Trento

Professor Jordan J. PAUST, University of Houston

Mr. Marco PERTILE, Research Fellow, University of Trento

Mr. Eric ROSAND, Deputy Legal Adviser, Permanent Mission of the US to the UN – New York

Mr. Mahmoud SAMY, Legal Adviser, Permanent Mission of Egypt to the UN – New York

Ms. Valeria SANTORI, Research Fellow, University of Teramo

Professor Tullio TREVES, University of Milan – Judge of the International Tribunal for the Law of the Sea

Mr. Renan VILLACIS, UN Secretariat, Office of Legal Affairs, Codification Division – New York

Professor Ugo VILLANI, University of Rome 'La Sapienza'

Ms. Elizabeth WILMSHURST, Chatham House, The Royal Institute of International Affairs, London

Foreword

The United Nations' response to acts of terrorism on such a grand scale as those committed on September 11, 2001 and thereafter, has essentially been determined by exigency. Immediate and unwavering action was necessary. Today, a more comprehensive approach must be found. Upon some reflection and with critical distance, future action must be grounded on a solid and sustainable basis. In this connection, the law must play an essential role. We will only be able to adopt measures that will ultimately endure, if the rule of law, democracy and human rights are strengthened in this struggle. Law strengthens security. Security cannot be achieved in the absence of a strong legal framework. Today's efforts to reconcile law and security require, however, flexibility and creativity. This tome, published under the able leadership of Professor Giuseppe Nesi with the participation of eminent contributors, provides valuable guidance for those efforts.

Collaboration between academic circles and practitioners is essential to enrich this debate and to provide it with the profoundness and substance it requires. This is why I warmly welcome the publication of this book and would like to take this opportunity to express to all who helped in making it possible my congratulations and gratitude.

Professor Nicolas Michel
Under-Secretary-General for Legal Affairs
The Legal Counsel of the United Nations

Preface

The terrorist attacks of 2001 brought about a sea change in the way terrorism as a global phenomenon was perceived by international institutions, States, and individuals.

After 9/11 there was a multiplication of efforts to develop a coordinated response to terrorism at the global and regional levels. At the global level, the United Nations assumed a leading role in the fight against terrorism, which was perceived as 'one of the most serious threats to international peace and security.' In this context, it appeared natural that – while the General Assembly continued (amid many difficulties) its efforts to set up a normative framework that by the end of 1999 included 12 international conventions – the Security Council exercised its institutional competences in the maintenance of international peace and security.

After the attacks of 2001, the Security Council acted in a manner that seemed to be somehow 'frenetic' by comparison to its previous behaviour. In the first 55 years of its existence it had only adopted a handful of resolutions condemning terrorist acts. By contrast, in the four years after 9/11 it has adopted almost twenty resolutions on the topic: some of these resolutions were immediate reactions by the Security Council to specific terrorist attacks; others framed a coordinated international response to terrorism in a substantive way. In the fight against terrorism Security Council resolutions adopted under Chapter VII of the UN Charter placed legal obligations on Member States that went beyond the conclusion of an international convention.

Security Council resolutions also created mechanisms and subsidiary bodies such as the Counter-Terrorism Committee (CTC), whose task is to help States to adopt internal counter-terrorism measures as well as monitoring States' conduct in the struggle against terrorism. Some States that had ignored the issue of terrorism in their internal legal order before 2001 were obliged to adopt measures to define it, at the same time creating the basis for concrete internal action against terrorism and the promotion of international cooperation in the prevention and suppression of terrorism.

The system created by the Security Council was recently improved when a series of resolutions were adopted, including Resolution 1535 (2004), which set up the Counter-Terrorism Executive Directorate to enhance the Counter-Terrorism Committee's ability to monitor the implementation of Resolution 1373 (2001) and continue its capacity building. On the other hand, Resolution 1540 (2004) broadened the Council's attention to the fact that terrorists acquire weapons of mass destruction. In all those resolutions the Security Council reiterated the crucial role played by international cooperation in the fight against terrorism.

Regional organizations put the struggle against terrorism at the very core of their activities. They adopted normative or quasi-normative instruments such as Conventions, Protocols, Plans of Action, often recalling relevant Security Council's counter-terrorism resolutions as the main 'trigger mechanisms' for their action. At the same time, various pragmatic initiatives were adopted at the regional level, mainly to better define, in that context, the crime of terrorism, the conditions for the exercise of criminal jurisdiction by States and regional judicial bodies, and the instruments of intergovernmental coordination and cooperation. Special emphasis was given, in some cases, to the need for respect for human rights in the fight against terrorism.

The global and the regional responses to international terrorism are examined in the present volume that collects the proceedings of a meeting held at the University of Trento on 27 and 28 May 2004. Scholars, diplomats, and representatives of international organizations met to analyse various legal aspects of the international cooperation in the fight against terrorism. They also examined whether counter-terrorism activities (or other types of activities presented as such) ended up affecting some fundamental principles of international law, such as the international protection of human rights or the use of force.

The different backgrounds of the contributors to the conference explains the twofold approach of this volume: (i) a more practical one, focused on the problems and policy options that States and practitioners face in their everyday in-the-field activity; and (ii) a more academic/theoretical one, aimed at studying the broader legal implications of the global counter-terrorism effort.

In the period following the Trento meeting, there have been further important developments in counter-terrorism, both within the UN and beyond:

- Resolution 1566 (2004) was adopted in October 2004. According to some practitioners, it contains a 'rough' definition of terrorist acts and establishes a new Working Group of the Security Council to, *inter alia*, review the Council's Chapter VII counter-terrorism measures;
- The UN reform process suddenly accelerated with the issuance of the High-level Panel's Report and the subsequent Secretary-General's Report *In Larger Freedom*. These crucial documents both make important recommendations in the field of international cooperation in the fight against terrorism. The Secretary-General further clarified his proposals for a global counter-terrorism strategy that became known as the '5 D strategy', presented in Madrid on 11 March 2005;
- In April 2005 the General Assembly, overcoming the difficulties that had blocked for seven years any development on the draft Convention on the Suppression of Acts of Nuclear Terrorism, decided that the Convention shall be open for signature at the UN Summit, in September 2005.

These developments and their possible legal and political consequences were analysed in a workshop at Columbia University in June 2005, whose proceedings will, it is hoped, be published in a separate volume.

This volume opens with an analysis of the role of the United Nations in the fight against terrorism that encompasses the activities of the various organs of the UN (in particular, the General Assembly and the Security Council) and the main legal questions that have arisen in that framework. The second part of the volume is devoted to the activity of regional organizations, both in their 'individuality' and in their connection with the United Nations' counter-terrorism efforts. The book then ends with the results of a panel discussion on whether, to what extent and how the fight against terrorism encroaches upon some fundamental international law rules affecting the use of force among States and international security. The appendix includes a list of relevant international documents of universal and regional character on counter-terrorism prepared by Marco Pertile, and an updated bibliography prepared by Valerie Santori.

This volume is one of the products of a research project started in January 2002 and co-financed by the Italian Ministry of University and Scientific Research and the University of Trento.

The most recent developments indicate that international cooperation will remain at the core of the struggle against terrorism in the years to come. This volume aims to provide a point of reference on the achievements made so far in this field.

Giuseppe Nesi
New York, 17 July 2005

Acknowledgements

My sincere thanks go first of all to the participants in the Trento Meeting together with the students who attended, especially those who helped to organize the meeting. Many thanks to the University of Trento, which hosted the meeting, and its former Rector, Massimo Egidi, to the Director of the Department of Legal Sciences, Luca Nogler, and to the Law School and its Dean, Roberto Toniatti. Special thanks also to the Autonomous Province of Trento and its Governor, Lorenzo Dellai, for their generous support of the initiative.

From the scholarly point of view I would like to thank Pietro Gargiulo, Marco Pertile and Valeria Santori. All of them contributed actively to organizing the meeting and were extremely helpful with their suggestions and support. The distance between Trento and New York was bridged thanks to the extroadinary efforts of the personnel of the Department of Legal Sciences, Ornella Bernardi, Carla Boninsegna, Valentina Lucatti and, last but not least, Stefano Talassi. To all of them my warmest thanks.

PART I
The United Nations and the Fight Against International Terrorism

Chapter 1

The UN Conventions on the Prevention and Suppression of International Terrorism

ANDREA GIOIA[1]

The 1937 Geneva Convention on the Prevention and Punishment of Terrorism

The first attempt to articulate a definition of terrorist acts for the purposes of international criminal law is represented by the Geneva Convention on the Prevention and Punishment of Terrorism,[2] which was adopted, on 16 November 1937, on the initiative of the League of Nations (LN), the predecessor of the United Nations, following the assassination in Marseilles, on 9 October 1934, of the King of Yugoslavia and of the French Minister of Foreign Affairs by a Croatian exile. The 1937 Convention was intended, *inter alia*, to oblige parties thereto to establish as offences in their national criminal legislation certain specific acts listed in Article 2 thereof, as well as to prosecute, or extradite, the alleged offenders if certain conditions were met.[3] Without going into unnecessary details, it may be interesting to recall that the acts listed in Article 2 of the convention were: (a) intentional acts directed against the life, bodily integrity, health or freedom of Heads of State, or members of their families, or other persons exercising governmental functions; (b) intentional acts resulting in the destruction of, or in damage to, foreign state property; (c) intentional acts of a nature to endanger human life through the creation of a collective danger; (d) attempts to perform any such acts; (e) the manufacture, acquisition, detention or transfer of arms, ammunition, explosive products or noxious substances with a view to committing in any country any such acts.

However, the acts in question were only covered by the convention if they were directed against a party thereto and, more crucially, if they constituted 'acts of terrorism'. Article 1, paragraph 2, of the convention gave a general definition of 'acts

---

1   University of Modena and Reggio Emilia.

2   LN Doc. C.546.M.383.1937.V; *International Legislation, A Collection of the Texts of Multipartite International Instruments of General Interest*, Edited by Manley O. Hudson, 9 volumes. Originally Published: Washington; Carnegie Endowment for International Peace; 1931-1949, Reprinted: Buffalo; William S. Hein & Co., Inc.; 2000.

3   See: Articles 8-10.

of terrorism' as 'criminal acts directed against a State and *intended or calculated* to create a state of terror in the minds of particular persons, or groups of persons, or the general public' (emphasis added). Thus, at least the English text of the convention appeared to make it clear that what turned the acts therein listed into terrorist acts was the existence of a special intent on the part of the offender; in other words, that of creating a state of terror.

On the other hand, if the French text of the convention is examined, the picture appears to change: acts of terrorism are therein defined as 'faits criminels dirigés contre un Etat et *dont le but ou la nature* est de provoquer la terreur chez des personnalités déterminées, des groupes de personnes ou dans le public' (emphasis added). It may well be that the drafters' intention was, indeed, to signify that, whereas some acts can only be regarded as terrorist acts if there is a specific intent on the part of the offender, others can in themselves be so regarded, irrespective of such intent.[4] The fact that this is, in principle, a reasonable assumption has, indeed, been confirmed by later practice. However, there is little guidance in the 1937 Convention as to which of the offences specifically covered in Article 2 are in themselves of a terrorist nature.

The conventions adopted under the auspices of UN specialized agencies and other world organizations

The 1937 Convention never entered into force, partly as a result of the outbreak, only two years after its adoption, of the Second World War.[5] Although it undoubtedly served as a model for later conventions dealing with the prevention and suppression of terrorism, most of these conventions were adopted on the basis of a different approach; this so-called 'sectoral' approach aimed at identifying offences which were seen as belonging to the activities of terrorists and working out treaties in order to deal with specific categories thereof.

This step by step approach has been followed, in the first place, by the UN specialized agencies. The way was opened by the International Civil Aviation Organization (ICAO), under whose auspices a number of conventions have been adopted dealing with acts directed at, or undermining, the safety of civil aviation, a phenomenon which had not been envisaged by the drafters of the 1937 Convention and which became of special concern to the international community as from the

---

4   This would seem to be the interpretation given by Y. Sandoz, 'Lutte contre le terrorisme et droit international: risques et opportunités', *Swiss Review of International and European Law*, vol. 12, 2002, pp. 319 ff., at p. 325.

5   In addition, there appears to be some indication that the definition of terrorism therein contained was considered as too wide by some states: see, for example, T.M. Franck, B.B. Lockwood, 'Preliminary Thoughts Towards an International Convention on Terrorism', *American Journal of International Law*, vol. 68, 1974, pp. 69 ff., at p.70.

1960s. These conventions are:[6] the 1963 Tokyo Convention on Offences and Certain Other Acts Committed on Board Aircraft;[7] the 1970 Hague Convention for the Suppression of the Unlawful Seizure of Aircraft;[8] the 1971 Montreal Convention for the Suppression of Unlawful Acts Against the Safety of Civil Aviation;[9] and the 1988 Montreal Protocol for the Suppression of Unlawful Acts of Violence at Airports Serving International Civil Aviation.[10]

The conventions dealing with aerial terrorism – more particularly, the 1970 Hague Convention and the 1971 Montreal Convention – served as models for the adoption, under the auspices of the International Maritime Organization (IMO), of the 1988 Rome Convention for the Suppression of Unlawful Acts Against the Safety of Maritime Navigation,[11] following the seizure, in October 1985, of the Italian cruise ship *Achille Lauro* by a group of Palestinian terrorists. At the same time, the 1988 Rome Protocol for the Suppression of Unlawful Acts Against the Safety of Fixed Platforms Located on the Continental Shelf[12] was adopted also.

Another specific sector which had certainly not been envisaged by the drafters of the 1937 Geneva Convention is that of acts of 'nuclear' terrorism. In this field, one important treaty adopted under the auspices of the International Atomic Energy Agency (IAEA) has to be recalled: the 1980 Vienna Convention on the Physical Protection of Nuclear Material,[13] which deals with offences relating to nuclear material both in international transport and in domestic use, storage, and transport.

The UN conventions following a 'sectoral' approach

But the 'sectoral' approach followed by these specialized organizations has also been followed, until recently, within the United Nations. Three important conventions have so far been adopted under the auspices of the United Nations: the 1973 New York Convention on the Prevention and Punishment of Crimes Against Internationally Protected Persons;[14] the 1979 New York Convention Against the

---

6 In addition to the conventions mentioned in the text, another ICAO Convention is usually listed among international conventions on the prevention and suppression of terrorism, namely the 1991 Montreal Convention on the Marking of Plastic Explosives for the Purpose of Identification. This convention, is, however, not relevant for purposes of international criminal law.

7 United Nations, *Treaty Series*, Vol. 704, pp. 219 ff.

8 United Nations, *Treaty Series*, Vol. 860, pp. 105 ff.

9 United Nations, *Treaty Series*, Vol. 974, pp. 177 ff.

10 United Nations, *Treaty Series*, Vol. 1589, pp. 474 ff.

11 United Nations, *Treaty Series*, Vol. 1678, pp. 221 ff.

12 United Nations, *Treaty Series*, Vol. 1678, pp. 304 ff.

13 United Nations, *Treaty Series*, Vol. 1456, pp. 124 ff. As will be alluded to in the section headed 'The UN Convention' below, a draft convention on the suppression of acts of nuclear terrorism is currently being elaborated within an Ad Hoc Committee established by the UN General Assembly.

14 United Nations, *Treaty Series*, Vol. 1035, pp. 167 ff.

Taking of Hostages;[15] and the 1997 New York Convention for the Suppression of Terrorist Bombing.[16] In addition, although it is not usually listed among the anti-terrorist conventions,[17] mention must be made of the 1994 Convention on the Safety of UN and Associated Personnel.[18] On the other hand, as will be explained later, the 1999 New York Convention for the Suppression of the Financing of Terrorism falls into a different category, and requires separate consideration, since it contains a general, if indirect, definition of terrorist acts.[19]

The Convention on the Prevention and Punishment of Crimes Against Internationally Protected Persons, including Diplomatic Agents, was opened for signature in New York on 14 December 1973; it entered into force on 20 January 1977 and has at present[20] 147 Parties, including all Permanent Members of the UN Security Council. Under Article 2, the Contracting Parties are obliged to criminalize under their domestic law the intentional commission of a murder, kidnapping or other attack upon the person or liberty of an 'internationally protected person',[21] a violent attack upon the official premises, the private accommodation or the means of transport of such a person likely to endanger his person or liberty, as well as a threat or an attempt to commit any such attack and an act constituting participation as an accomplice in any such attack.

Whereas the 1973 Convention is principally designed to suppress attacks against diplomatic agents and certain other persons which enjoy a similar status under international law, the more recent Convention on the Safety of United Nations and Associated Personnel – which, however, does not exclusively deal with issues of international criminal law and procedure[22] – obliges the Contracting parties to criminalize similar attacks when committed against forces performing non-combat peace-keeping operations.[23] This latter convention was adopted by the General

---

15 United Nations, *Treaty Series*, Vol. 1316, pp. 205 ff.

16 United Nations, Doc. A/RES/52/164 of 15 December 1997. To be published in United Nations, *Treaty Series*, Vol. 2149.

17 See, for example, the list annexed to the 1999 Convention for the Suppression of the Financing of Terrorism, which will be referred to in note 38 below.

18 United Nations, *Treaty Series*, Vol. 2051, pp. 363 ff.

19 See the section headed 'The UN Convention' below.

20 Data for this and other UN conventions have been updated as of 15 August 2004.

21 Article 1 defines an 'internationally protected person' as including: (a) a Head of State, a Head of Government or a Minister of Foreign Affairs, when in a foreign State, as well as accompanying members of his family; and (b) any representative or official of a State or any official or other agent of an international intergovernmental organization who is entitled to 'a special protection from attack on his person, freedom or dignity', as well as members of his family forming part of his household.

22 In addition to creating a regime for prosecution or extradition of persons accused of attacking UN peace-keepers and other persons associated with operations under UN mandates, the Convention also contains provisions concerning the relationship of peace-keepers and others with host and transit States.

23 The scope of application of the Convention was a politically sensitive issue during the negotiations and, as is pointed out in the text, is currently under review within the UN.

Assembly on 9 December 1994 and entered into force on 15 January 1999; it has at present 74 Parties, including the Permanent Members of the Security Council, but its scope is currently under review within an Ad Hoc Committee established by the General Assembly in 2001.[24]

The International Convention Against the Taking of Hostages was adopted by the General Assembly on 17 December 1979; it entered into force on 3 June 1983 and has at present 138 Parties, including all Permanent Members of the Security Council. Under Article 1, any person commits the offence of 'taking of hostages' within the meaning of the Convention if he (or she) 'seizes or detains and threatens to kill, to injure or to continue to detain another person ... in order to compel a third party, namely, a state, an international intergovernmental organization, a natural or juridical person, or a group of persons, to do or abstain from doing any act as an explicit or implicit condition for their release of the hostage'; moreover, the attempt to commit hostage-taking, as well as the participation as an accomplice in such an act (or attempt thereto) are also considered as offences.

Finally, in the aftermath of the deadly truck bombing attack on US military personnel in Dharam, Saudi Arabia, on 25 June 1996, it was realized that existing anti-terrorist conventions did not deal with the problem of attacks in public places such

---

At present, Article 2(1) provides that 'the Convention applies in respect of United Nations and associated personnel and United Nations operations, as defined in Article 1', but Article 2(2) specifies that the Convention does not apply 'to a United Nations operation authorized by the Security Council as an enforcement action under Chapter VII of the Charter of the United Nations in which any of the personnel are engaged as combatants against organized armed forces and to which the law of international armed conflict applies'. 'United Nations operations' are defined in Article 1 as 'operations' established by the 'competent organ of the United Nations in accordance with the Charter of the United Nations and conducted under United Nations authority and control'. These operations are covered if: (a) they are for the purpose of maintaining or restoring international peace and security, or (b) if the Security Council or the General Assembly has declared, for the purposes of the Convention, that 'there exists an exceptional risk to the safety of the personnel participating in the operation'. Thus, even operations not involving peace-keeping activities can be covered, as long as there is a declaration of risk. As for coverage of 'personnel', the Convention covers two types of personnel who carry out activities 'in support of the fulfilment of the mandate of a United Nations operation': (a) 'United Nations personnel', which includes persons engaged or deployed by the UN Secretary-General as members of the military, police or civilian components of a UN operation, as well as other officials and experts on mission of the United Nations or its specialized agencies (or the IAEA) who are present in an official capacity in the area where a UN operation is being conducted; (b) 'associated personnel', which includes: (i) persons assigned by the UN Secretary-General or by an intergovernmental organization (such as, for example, NATO) with the agreement of the competent organ of the United Nations; (ii) persons 'engaged' by the UN Secretary-General or a specialized agency (or the IAEA); (iii) persons deployed by a humanitarian non-governmental organization or agency under an agreement with the UN Secretary-General or a specialized agency (or the IAEA).

24 See United Nations, Doc. A/RES/56/89 of 12 December 2001. The latest report of the Ad Hoc Committee (third session) is in United Nations, Doc. A/59/52.

as the Dharam bombing and similar acts in the mid-1990s. Thus, the International Convention on Terrorist Bombing was adopted by the General Assembly on 15 December 1997; it entered into force on 23 May 2001 and has at present 123 Parties, including all Permanent Members of the Security Council. Under Article 2(1), 'any person commits an offence within the meaning of the Convention if that person unlawfully and intentionally delivers, places, discharges or detonates an explosive or other lethal device in, into or against a place of public use, a State or government facility, a public transportation system or an infrastructure facility: (a) with the intent to cause death or serious bodily injury; or (b) with the intent to cause extensive destruction of such a place, facility or system, where such destruction results or is likely to result in major economic loss'. In addition, ancillary offences are very comprehensively defined in Article 2(2) and (3) as including, in addition to the attempt to commit the principal offence and the participation as an accomplice in its commission, the fact of organizing or directing others to commit such offence or 'in any other way' contributing to its commission by a group of persons acting with a common purpose.[25]

The merits of the 'sectoral' approach

All of these 'sectoral' conventions follow, with minor variations, a common normative standard for the prevention and punishment of the various acts they contemplate, based, at least in part, on the 1937 Geneva model: more specifically, the punishment of such acts is based on the Parties' obligation to establish them as offences in their national criminal legislation, to establish their jurisdiction over such offences in specified cases, and to prosecute or extradite the alleged offender (on the basis of the well-known principle *aut dedere aut judicare*).[26] There are, moreover, obligations relating to international cooperation in the investigation and prosecution of these offences.

As for the criminal acts therein contemplated, it is often underlined that all of these conventions exclusively deal with conduct that has an international element, such as where the perpetrators and victims are from two different countries. But in fact that is not always the case and, at least as far as the obligation to prosecute

---

25 Such a contribution must be 'intentional and either made with the aim of furthering the general criminal activity or purpose of the group or be made in the knowledge of the intention of the group to commit the offence or offences concerned'.

26 A special case is constituted by the 1963 Tokyo Convention on Offences and Certain Other Acts Committed on Board Aircraft, which contains no obligation to prosecute or extradite the offenders. For different reasons, a special case is also constituted by the 1997 Convention on Terrorist Bombing, which, in an innovation over the prior counterterrorism conventions, includes a provision in Article 8(2) to the effect that the obligation to extradite or prosecute can be discharged by the temporary transfer of nationals for trial by those States that could not otherwise extradite their nationals, provided that both Parties agree to such arrangements.

or extradite is concerned, it must be stressed that, even where all elements of the criminal conduct are purely domestic, it is sufficient that the perpetrator has escaped from the country where the conduct took place and is located in another Contracting Party in order to trigger the application of these conventions.

Moreover, it seems interesting to point out that the earlier treaties do not even refer to the need to suppress 'terrorism' or 'terrorist acts' as (one of) the motive(s) leading to their adoption. Even the later treaties which do make that reference, in their title and/or preamble, confine themselves, in their operative part, to defining the offences to which they specifically relate, and little or no explanation is given of why these offences are considered to be manifestations of international terrorism. The implication is clearly that these offences have to be punished irrespective of whether or not they are committed for a specific 'terrorist' purpose, on the assumption that they are commonly committed by 'terrorists', as these are perceived by the general public, and/or they cause concern to the international community as a whole.

An exception is constituted by the 1979 Convention on the Taking of Hostages, which, as seen above, refers to acts of hostage-taking intended to compel a third party, namely, a State, an international intergovernmental organization, a natural or juridical person, or a group of persons, to do or abstain from doing any act. A similar special intent on the part of the perpetrator is also required by other 'sectoral' treaties, but exclusively in respect of the threat to commit one of the 'primary' offences therein contemplated.[27]

A somewhat special case is constituted by the 1997 Convention on Terrorist Bombing, whose Article 5 imposes upon the Contracting Parties an obligation to adopt measures necessary to ensure that criminal acts within the scope of the convention are punished by appropriate penalties and are not justifiable by political, philosophical, ideological, racial, ethnic, religious or other similar considerations, 'in particular where they are intended or calculated to provoke a state of terror in the general public or in a group of persons or particular persons'. Indeed, the language used in this provision, which has no parallel in prior counter-terrorism conventions, is strikingly similar to that used in the 1937 Geneva definition of 'terrorist acts'. But, whereas Article 5 emphasizes that the offences outlined in Article 2 should be universally condemned and criminalized regardless of the motivations of the perpetrators, Article 2 defines the offences covered by the convention without making any reference to such motivations.

On the whole, therefore, the 'sectoral' conventions confirm the assumption that some offences can be considered *in themselves* as offences of international concern, irrespective of any specific 'terrorist' intent or purpose. Indeed, the principal merit

---

27 See: Article 6(1)(e) of the 1980 IAEA Convention on the Physical Protection of Nuclear Material; Article 3(2)(c) of the 1988 IMO Convention for the Suppression of Unlawful Acts Against the Safety of Maritime Navigation; Article 2(2)(c) of the 1988 IMO Protocol for the Suppression of Unlawful Acts Against the Safety of Fixed Platforms Located on the Continental Shelf; Article 10(1)(c) of the 1994 UN Convention on the Safety of United Nations and Associated Personnel.

of the 'sectoral approach' is that it avoids the need to define 'terrorism' or 'terrorist acts'; it is a well-known fact that the definition of terrorism has proved to be a very difficult task at the world level, notably because it raises the issue of the relation of terrorism and wars of national liberation, on the one hand, and so-called 'state terrorism', on the other.[28] So long as the 'sectoral' approach is followed, there is no need to define terrorism; a definition would only be necessary if the punishment of the relevant offences were made conditional on the existence of a specific 'terrorist' intent; but this would be counter-productive, inasmuch as it would result in unduly restricting their suppression. On the other hand, the mere labelling of these offences as 'terrorist' offences serves no operative legal purpose, and leaves the door open for new treaties to put the same label on other categories of offences.

It is only when the 'sectoral' approach is abandoned in favour of a comprehensive approach that a (residual) definition of terrorism or of terrorist acts becomes essential, inasmuch as it is probably inevitable to include a specific 'terrorist' intent or purpose as an element of the crime. This seems to be proven by an examination of the various comprehensive conventions which have been adopted at the regional level,[29] as well as by the ongoing efforts to adopt a comprehensive convention on international terrorism at the world level. But, of course, it is precisely here that the political and ideological difficulties which were alluded to above arise.

The UN Convention for the Suppression of the Financing of Terrorism

From 1972 to 1979, within an *ad hoc* committee established by the General Assembly,[30] all efforts to elaborate a global convention on the suppression of international terrorism were frustrated by the insistence on the part of some States on the need to differentiate terrorism from national liberation struggles and to address the causes underlying terrorism, which, in their opinion, were to be found in the policy of 'state terrorism' inherent in colonial, racist and alien régimes.

---

28 The kidnapping and killing at Munich, on 6 September 1972, of eleven Israeli Olympic competitors by Arab terrorists, as well as a number of other acts of terrorism, resulted in the introduction by the United States, on 25 September 1972, of a Draft Convention on the Prevention and Punishment of certain Acts of International Terrorism (United Nations, Doc. A/C.6/L.850), but the US initiative failed, mainly because of concerns on the part of some States that it was directed against wars of national liberation. By resolution 3034 (XXVII), of 18 December 1972, the General Assembly decided to establish an *ad hoc* committee, which, however, reported to the 28th Session of the Assembly that it was unable to agree on any recommendations dealing with the problem. On the more recent efforts to adopt a comprehensive convention on the suppression of terrorism, see this and the following sections.

29 Regional counterterrorism conventions are dealt with elsewhere in this book and are outside the scope of this report. The present writer has dealt with such conventions in A. Gioia, 'Terrorismo internazionale, crimini di guerra e crimini contro l'umanità', *Rivista di diritto internazionale*, vol. 87, 2004, pp. 5 ff., at pp. 19-26.

30 See note 26 above.

On 9 December 1994, an important development was the adoption of a General Assembly Declaration on Measures to Eliminate International Terrorism,[31] since when the General Assembly has repeatedly stated that 'criminal acts intended or calculated to provoke a state of terror in the general public, a group of persons or particular persons for political purposes are in any circumstance unjustifiable, whatever the considerations of a political, philosophical, ideological, racial, ethnic, religious or any other nature that may be invoked to justify them'. In the post-cold war climate, the idea seemed thus to emerge that international terrorism has no justification; in fact, unlike previous resolutions, the 1994 Declaration makes no reservation in respect of wars of national liberation.

By Resolution 51/210 of 17 December 1996, the General Assembly established a new Ad Hoc Committee, open to all Member States, with the task, *inter alia*, of addressing 'means of further developing a comprehensive legal framework of conventions dealing with international terrorism'. Within this Committee, the 1997 Convention for the Suppression of Terrorist Bombing was elaborated and work is currently going on for the elaboration of a draft convention on the suppression of acts of nuclear terrorism and of a draft comprehensive convention on international terrorism.

But before examining the latest outcome of negotiations aimed at the adoption of a comprehensive convention on the suppression of terrorism, it seems necessary first to refer to another important convention elaborated within the Ad Hoc Committee, which has been described as a 'cornerstone' of the struggle against terrorism: the International Convention for the Suppression of the Financing of Terrorism,[32] which was adopted by the General Assembly on 9 December 1999. This convention entered into force on 10 April 2002 and has at present 117 Parties, including all Permanent Members of the Security Council except China.

As was pointed out earlier, this convention cannot be put in the same category as the other UN conventions following the 'sectoral' approach, inasmuch as it does not deal with specific acts of terrorism, but is rather intended to suppress the financing of terrorism from a general point of view. In addition to establishing a distinct offence of terrorist financing, which is defined in Article 2, the 1999 Convention obliges the Contracting Parties to take appropriate measures to identify, detect, freeze or seize terrorist-related funds, as well as the proceeds derived from the offences defined in Article 2.[33] Moreover, Parties are obliged to monitor and license money transmission agencies, as well as cross-border transportation of cash and bearer-negotiable instruments.[34]

As far as international criminal law and procedure are concerned, apart from the definition of the offence of terrorist financing, an important feature of the

---

31 United Nations, Doc. A/RES/49/60.

32 United Nations, Doc. A/RES/54/109, of 9 December 1999. To be published in United Nations, *Treaty Series*, Vol. 2178.

33 See Article 8(1).

34 See Article 18(2).

1999 Convention is that it obliges States to hold a legal person liable 'when a person responsible for the management or control of that legal entity has, in that capacity, committed' an offence described in Article 2.[35] Moreover, in addition to the usual provisions contained in the other counter-terrorism conventions, the 1999 Convention, like the 1997 Convention on Terrorist Bombing, appears to remove the political-offence exception by obliging the Contracting Parties to ensure that criminal acts within its scope are 'under no circumstances justifiable by considerations of a political, philosophical, ideological, racial, ethnic, religious or other nature'.[36] Finally, using less ambiguous language, the Convention also obliges the Contracting Parties not to refuse a request for extradition or for mutual legal assistance on the basis that it concerns a 'fiscal' offence.[37]

As for the definition of the offence of terrorist financing, Article 2(1) envisages two categories of offences. The first category, enumerated under (a) is constituted by the financing of acts constituting offences within the scope of, and as defined in, nine existing treaties listed in an annexe to the Convention,[38] and broadly corresponding to the 'sectoral' treaties which were referred to in the preceding paragraphs. While the criminalization of the funding of such acts does not necessarily require ratification of the relevant 'primary' treaties, the Contracting Parties to the 1999 Convention which are not party to any of those treaties may declare that they shall be excluded from the application of the Convention.[39] But, irrespective of whether or not the 'primary' offence is criminalized under an applicable treaty, the second category of offences covered by the 1999 Convention, which is enumerated under Article 2(1)(b), consists of the financing of 'any other act intended to cause death or serious bodily injury to a civilian, or to any other person not taking an active part in the hostilities in a situation of armed conflict, when the purpose of such act, by its nature or context, is to intimidate a population, or to compel a Government or an international organization to do or to abstain from doing any act'.[40]

---

35 See Article 5(1).

36 See Article 6.

37 See Article 13.

38 These treaties are: (1) The 1970 Hague Convention for the Suppression of Unlawful Seizure of Aircraft; (2) The 1971 Montreal Convention for the Suppression of Unlawful Acts against the Safety of Civil Aviation; (3) The 1973 UN Convention on the Prevention and Punishment of Crimes against Internationally Protected Persons, including Diplomatic Agents; (4) The 1979 UN International Convention against the Taking of Hostages; (5) The 1980 Vienna Convention on the Physical Protection of Nuclear Material; (6) The 1988 Montreal Protocol for the Suppression of Unlawful Acts of Violence at Airports Serving International Civil Aviation; (7) The 1988 Rome Convention for the Suppression of Unlawful Acts Against the Safety of Civil Aviation; (8) The 1988 Rome Protocol for the Suppression of Unlawful Acts against the Safety of Fixed Platforms located on the Continental Shelf; (9) The 1997 UN International Convention for the Suppression of Terrorist Bombing.

39 See Article 2(2).

40 In addition, Article 2(4) and (5) also criminalize participation as an accomplice in terrorist financing, as well as the fact of organizing or directing others to commit an offence

The 1999 Convention is, therefore, the first treaty in force at the world level which contains a general definition of acts of terrorism. This definition confirms the assumption that, in order to distinguish terrorist acts from ordinary offences, it is inevitable to include a specific 'terrorist' intent or purpose as an element of the crime; as will be pointed out in the next paragraph, this specific 'terrorist' intent is described in identical terms in the draft comprehensive convention on the suppression of terrorism which is currently being elaborated within the UN Ad Hoc Committee. On the other hand, the 1999 definition is rather narrow in the description of the relevant conduct, since it relates to acts intended to cause death or serious bodily injury to a person, thus excluding all damage to property, and it refers to damage caused to 'civilians' or 'other persons not taking an active part in the hostilities in a situation of armed conflict'.

Moreover, the 1999 definition is an indirect definition, which exclusively serves the purpose of defining a 'secondary' (accessory) offence related to certain 'primary' activities which are implicitly deemed to be acts of terrorism. The very existence of this definition makes the need to adopt a general definition of the 'primary' offence even more evident. In fact, is seems paradoxical that the financing of terrorism as a whole is considered to be an offence, whereas terrorism itself is only criminalized if it consists of specific acts covered by the 'sectoral' treaties.

Ongoing efforts to elaborate a comprehensive convention on the suppression of terrorism

As was alluded to in the preceding section, work has been going on for some time within the Ad Hoc Committee established by the General Assembly in 1996 in order to elaborate a draft comprehensive convention on international terrorism; moreover, when the Ad Hoc Committee is not in session, negotiations usually continue within an ad hoc working group of the Sixth Committee. Within these bodies, consideration is also being given to the elaboration of a draft convention for the suppression of acts of nuclear terrorism, as well as to the convening of a high-level conference to formulate 'a joint organized response of the international community to terrorism in all its forms and manifestations'.[41]

The events of 11 September 2001 have undoubtedly underlined the importance of this effort. However, although the negotiations on the draft comprehensive convention are almost completed, there remain some outstanding issues which have so far prevented the adoption of the convention. In particular, one such issue is the precise relation of the comprehensive convention with the existing 'sectoral' treaties. Another outstanding issue is the relation of terrorism and wars of national liberation, on the one hand, and state terrorism, on the other; more specifically, discussion centres around the application of the comprehensive convention to acts committed

---

of terrorist financing or of otherwise contributing to the commission of such an offence.

41 See the report of the latest (eighth) session of the Ad Hoc Committee: United Nations, Doc. A/59/37.

in times of armed conflict, as well as its application to acts committed by the military forces of a State in situations not governed by the laws of armed conflict.[42] Only a few brief remarks on these issues will be made here.

The elaboration of a comprehensive convention on international terrorism is not designed to replace the existing 'sectoral' treaties dealing with specific categories of acts of terrorism, but rather to complement them in order to fill existing gaps; the comprehensive convention is expected to oblige States to consider as offences certain acts, defined in Article 2[43] and thus implicitly deemed to be terrorist acts, even if they are not covered by existing treaties. On the other hand, the question arises of which treaty would apply in the event that the same offence is covered both by the comprehensive convention and an existing 'sectoral' treaty.

Article 2 *bis* of the draft comprehensive convention states that: 'Where this Convention and a treaty dealing with a specific category of terrorist offence would be applicable in relation to the same act as between States that are parties to both treaties, the provisions of the latter shall prevail'.[44] This provision is intended to give the comprehensive convention a merely residual character, which is perhaps unfortunate in view of the fact that the draft convention contains several important provisions which cannot be found in the existing 'sectoral' treaties. For example, an obligation not to grant refugee status to persons accused of acts of terrorism (Article 7), as well as a clear-cut obligation not to refuse a request for extradition or for mutual legal assistance on the sole ground that it concerns a political offence (Article 14); following the precedent of the 1999 Convention for the Suppression of the Financing of terrorism, there is also a provision on the liability of legal entities (Article 9). [45]

As for the (residual) definition of terrorist offences, Article 2(1) of the draft comprehensive convention states that: 'any person commits an offence within the meaning of this Convention if that person, by any means, unlawfully and intentionally, causes: (a) death or serious bodily injury to any person; or (b) serious damage to public or private property, including a place of public use, a State or government facility, a public transportation system, an infrastructure facility or the environment; or (c) damage to property, places, facilities or systems referred to in paragraph 1(b) of this article resulting or likely to result in major economic loss'. But such acts are only covered 'when the purpose of the conduct, by its nature or context, is to intimidate a population, or to compel a Government or an international organization to do or abstain from doing any act'. In addition, under Article 2(2)

---

42 See the report of the eighth session of the Ad Hoc Committee: United Nations, Doc. A/59/37, Annex I, paras 14 ff.

43 The 'informal' text of Article 2 is reproduced in Annex II to the Report of the sixth session of the Ad Hoc Committee: see United Nations, Doc. A/57/37, at p. 6.

44 The 'informal' text of Article 2 *bis* is reproduced in Annex II to the Report of the sixth session of the Ad Hoc Committee: see United Nations, Doc. A/57/37, at p. 7.

45 The texts of Articles 3 to 17 *bis* and 20 to 27 *bis* of the draft comprehensive convention, which appear to pose no special problem, are reproduced in Annex III to the Report of the sixth session of the Ad Hoc Committee: see United Nations, Doc. A/57/37, at pp. 8 ff.

to (4), the threat or attempt to commit a terrorist act, as well as participation as an accomplice in the commission of such an act and the fact of organizing or directing others to commit such an act or of otherwise contributing to its commission, are also considered as offences.

If this provision is compared with the corresponding provision in Article 2(1)(b) of the 1999 UN Convention on the Suppression of the Financing of Terrorism (leaving aside, for a moment, the question of acts performed in situations of armed conflict), the major difference appears to lie in the description of the relevant conduct (the *actus reus*): unlike the 1999 Convention, the draft comprehensive convention contemplates acts intended to cause death or serious bodily injury to *any* person, as opposed to *a civilian*; moreover, it also includes acts intended to cause damage to property, places, facilities or systems (which, as seen above, are also covered by the 1997 UN Convention on Terrorist Bombing), as well as serious damage to the environment.

But if we look at the state of mind of the author of that conduct (the *mens rea*), this is defined in terms identical to the ones employed in the 1999 Convention on the financing of terrorism. In addition to the need for a general wrongful intent, a specific intent is required, consisting in the intent to intimidate a population or to compel a government or an international organization to do, or abstain from doing, something. As seen above, the 1979 UN Convention on the Taking of Hostages also requires a similar intent on the part of the perpetrator, but this is defined in much wider terms; indeed, the 1979 Convention does not refer to the intent to 'intimidate a population' but then refers to the intent to compel 'a third party' to do or abstain from doing any act, and the term 'third party' includes, in addition to a State and an international intergovernmental organization, a natural or juridical person and a group of persons.

In any case, it appears that the specific 'terrorist' intent is defined in the UN conventions as something more specific than the mere intent to provoke a state of terror in the general public or in particular persons, which was required by the 1937 LN Convention. As seen above, General Assembly resolutions do refer to the intention to provoke a state of terror, but they also make reference to the political purpose of terrorist acts. In fact it is precisely this political purpose that usually distinguishes 'terrorist' offences from 'ordinary' crimes; the spreading of terror is a means used by terrorists in order to attain a more specific objective, which is indeed usually a political one. Leaving aside the somewhat wider scope of the 1979 Convention on the Taking of Hostages, the political purpose of terrorist acts appears to be implicitly recognized both in the indirect definition of terrorist offences contained in the 1999 Convention on the Suppression of the Financing of Terrorism and in the direct definition of such offences contained in the draft comprehensive convention on terrorism.

On the other hand, both definitions describe terrorist intent in a way more restrictive than do the definitions contained in some existing regional instruments relating to the prevention and suppression of terrorism. Some such instruments confuse the rights that may be breached by terrorist conduct with the specific terrorist intent and, as a consequence, define such intent in a way so wide that almost any criminal act might be deemed to be an act of terrorism.[46] But there can be no doubt that at least another intent, which is specifically covered in some regional instruments, might reasonably be considered as a terrorist intent: this consists, according, for example, to the 2002 EU Council Framework Decision on combating terrorism, in 'seriously destabilising or destroying the fundamental political, constitutional, economic or social structures of a country or an international organization'.[47]

Although it could be argued that this additional intent can sometimes be considered as subsumed under the intent to intimidate a population or under the intent to compel a government or an international organization to do, or abstain from doing, something, this is certainly not always the case; the fact remains that States are not prepared, at the world level, to accept a clear-cut obligation to prosecute or extradite terrorists who have acted in order to bring about a change of political or social régime within another State, for example because that State is not politically friendly or, perhaps more nobly, because it does not abide by some minimum standards of democracy and human rights.

The problem of acts to be excluded from the definition of terrorist offences

Apparently, the text so far arrived at of Article 2 of the draft comprehensive convention, which was prepared by the Coordinator of informal consultations, has attracted a large measure of support. But in fact, its final adoption is closely linked to the resolution of some outstanding issues within the negotiating bodies: these are expected to be dealt with in Article 18 of the draft convention, a provision intended to provide for a savings clause as well as for two exclusions from the scope of application of the convention.

As was alluded to above, the main obstacle to an agreement is the legal assessment of the 'struggle' of peoples for liberation against foreign occupation, colonialism, and the like; whereas some States believe that such a 'struggle' can never be equated to terrorism, others retort that even an undoubtedly legitimate 'struggle' cannot be

---

46 As was pointed out above, regional instruments dealing with the suppression of international terrorism are outside the scope of this report. However, a reference can be made here, for example, to Article 1(2) of the 1999 Convention of the Organization of the Islamic Conference on Combating Terrorism: '"Terrorism" means any act of violence or threat thereof notwithstanding its motives or intentions perpetrated to carry out an individual or collective criminal plan with the aim of terrorizing people or threatening to harm them or imperilling their lives, honour, freedoms, security or rights or exposing the environment or any facility or public or private property to hazards or occupying or seizing them, or endangering a national resource, or international facilities, or threatening the stability, territorial integrity, political unity or sovereignty of independent States'. This very wide definition of terrorism is in marked contrast with the exclusion of all acts committed in the context of a national liberation 'struggle': in this respect, see note 49 below.

47 Council Framework Decision of 13 June 2002 on combating terrorism (2002/475/ JHA), in *Official Journal of the European Communities*, 22 June 2002, L 164/3, Article 1(1).

carried out by any means whatever. Another obstacle is represented by the relation of 'private terrorism' and 'State terrorism'. More specifically, the controversial nature of these issues is well represented by the existence of two alternative drafts of Article 18,[48] one circulated by the Coordinator of informal consultations, and the other by the Member States of the Organization of the Islamic Conference (OIC).[49]

As far as the savings clause is concerned, both drafts provide that nothing in the convention 'shall affect other rights, obligations and responsibilities of States, peoples and individuals under international law, in particular the purposes and principles of the Charter of the United Nations, and international humanitarian law'; thus, the legitimacy or otherwise of peoples' 'struggles', as well as of States' reactions to insurgency and, more generally, of their activities designed to maintain law and order, remain unaffected. But when it comes to the exclusions, the two drafts differ significantly.

The first exclusion refers to acts performed during an armed conflict. It seems to be agreed, as a matter of principle, that acts governed by international humanitarian law should not be covered by the convention, irrespective of the internal or international nature of the conflict. However, the Coordinator's draft would exclude from the scope of the convention 'the activities of armed forces during an armed conflict, as those terms are understood under international humanitarian law, which are governed by that law'. The OIC draft, on the other hand, would exclude 'the activities of the *parties* during an armed conflict, *including in situations of foreign occupation*, as those terms are understood under international humanitarian law, which are governed by that law' (emphasis added).

The second exclusion refers to 'the activities undertaken by the military forces of a State in the exercise of their official duties. 'Military forces of a State' are defined in Article 1(2) of the draft comprehensive convention as 'the armed forces of a State which are organized, trained and equipped under its internal law for the primary purpose of national defence or security and persons acting in support of those armed forces who are under their formal command, control and responsibility'. However, the Coordinator's draft text of Article 18 would exclude these activities 'inasmuch as they are governed by other rules of international law', whereas the OIC draft would exclude them 'inasmuch as they are in conformity with international law'.

---

48 The alternative texts relating to Article 18 of the draft comprehensive convention are reproduced in Annex IV to the Report of the sixth session of the Ad Hoc Committee: see United Nations, Doc. A/57/37, at p. 17.

49 It may be interesting to mention here that Article 2(1) of the 1999 Convention of the Organization of the Islamic Conference on Combating Terrorism, which was referred to in note 46 above, clearly states that: 'Peoples' struggle including armed struggle against foreign occupation, aggression, colonialism, and hegemony, aimed at liberation and self-determination in accordance with the principles of international law shall not be considered as a terrorist crime'.

It is not my intention here to deal with these issues in any detail.[50] In this context, I shall confine myself to a few remarks relating to the Coordinator's draft text of Article 18, which appears to reflect the prevailing view within the Ad Hoc Committee.

As far as the relation of terrorism and armed conflicts is concerned, the Coordinator's draft text follows *à la lettre* the precedent of the 1998 Convention on Terrorist Bombings, whose Article 19(1) already excludes from the scope of application of that convention 'the activities of armed forces during an armed conflict, as those terms are understood under international humanitarian law, which are governed by that law'. A similar exclusion clause can be found, at the regional level, in the 2002 EU Council Framework Decision on combating terrorism,[51] which was referred to in the preceding paragraph.

The fact that acts of terrorism can be committed in the context of an armed conflict also is implicitly recognized by the indirect definition of terrorist offences contained in the 1999 Convention for the Suppression of the Financing of Terrorism, which, as seen above, covers the financing of any act intended to cause death or serious bodily injury to any 'person not taking an active part in the hostilities in a situation of armed conflict'. The exclusion of such acts from the scope of the 'primary' definition of terrorist crimes only relates to acts committed by members of the 'armed forces'[52] of

---

50　I have tried to deal with both exceptions in: Gioia, *supra* note 29, at pp. 35 ff. and, in English, in A. Gioia, 'The Definition of Terrorism in International Criminal Law', to be published in the Proceedings of the 2003 Hague Joint Conference on 'Contemporary Issues of International Law', organized by the American Society of International Law and the Dutch Society of International Law.

51　Preamble, Point No. 11.

52　Since the exclusion is meant to apply equally to both international and non-international armed conflicts, the term 'armed forces' cannot, in my opinion, be taken to apply exclusively to the so-called 'lawful' combatants, namely to those persons who have a 'right' to participate directly in the hostilities and who, as a consequence, cannot be punished by the enemy for the mere fact of having taken part in those hostilities; in fact, the concept of 'lawful' combatant is exclusively relevant in the context of international armed conflicts. In other words, the clause excludes the activities of the 'armed forces' of all parties to the armed conflict, be these the armed forces of a State, an insurgent organization or a national liberation movement. From this point of view, therefore, the old dispute as to the internal or international nature of so-called 'wars of national liberation' appears to be irrelevant. However, the fact remains that the exclusion exclusively refers to the activities of the 'armed forces' of a party to the conflict and not simply to those of the 'parties' thereto (as in the draft proposed by OIC Members). In this respect, reference can be made to the definition of 'armed forces' contained in Article 43(1) of the 1977 Geneva Protocol I Additional to the Geneva Conventions of 12 August 1949 and Relating to the Protection of Victims of International Armed Conflicts. Of course, that definition relates to international armed conflicts and, consequently, Article 43(2) adds that all members of the 'armed forces' of a party to the conflict are 'combatants'; however, it is a well-known fact that Protocol I includes wars of national liberation in the category of international armed conflicts. Therefore, even if that inclusion is not considered as part of existing customary law, the definition of 'armed forces' contained in Article 43(1) can be

the parties to an 'armed conflict'[53] and is partly compensated by the fact that, in case such acts gravely violate the international laws of armed conflict, they constitute war crimes and entail the individual criminal responsibility of the author.

On the other hand, the clause excludes all activities which are 'governed by international humanitarian law', quite irrespective of whether or not they amount to war crimes;[54] moreover, a conventional obligation to prosecute or extradite war criminals only exists at present in respect of crimes committed in a situation of international armed conflict. It is significant, in this respect, that Article 12 of the 1979 Convention on the Taking of Hostages, which is also intended to exclude from the scope of application of that convention acts of hostage-taking committed in the course of armed conflicts,[55] exclusively refers to acts in respect of which States

---

taken as a general definition which may be applied irrespective of the international or internal nature of the conflict and, consequently, of the 'combatant' status of the members of those forces.

53 As was alluded to in the preceding note, the term 'armed conflict' is used in modern international humanitarian law to refer to both international and non-international armed conflicts. However, at least as far as non-international armed conflicts are concerned, there is a threshold which distinguishes 'armed conflicts' governed by international humanitarian law and mere 'situations of internal disturbances and tensions, such as riots, isolated and sporadic acts of violence and other acts of a similar nature' (Article 1(2) of Geneva Protocol II Additional to the Geneva Conventions of 12 August 1949 and Relating to the Protection of Victims of Non-International Armed Conflicts). As for situations of 'foreign occupation', which the OIC Member States would like to be explicitly mentioned in the exclusion clause, it would seem that, if an armed conflict has resulted in the military occupation of a territory, that occupation continues to be governed by international humanitarian law even after the end of active hostilities. As the Appeals Chamber of the International Criminal Tribunal for the Former Yugoslavia put it in a famous decision of 1995, 'international humanitarian law applies from the initiation of [...] armed conflicts and extends beyond the cessation of hostilities until a general conclusion of peace is reached; or, in the case of internal conflicts, a peaceful settlement is achieved. Until that moment, international humanitarian law continues to apply in the whole territory of the warring States or, in the case of an internal conflict, the whole territory under the control of a party, whether or not actual combat takes place there' (*The Prosecutor v. Dusko Tadic, Decision on the Defence Motion for Interlocutory Appeal on Jurisdiction,* Case No. IT-94-1-AR72, *International Legal Materials,* vol. 35, 1996, pp. 32 ff., para. 70).

54 As was pointed out above, the clause only excludes the activities of members of the 'armed forces' of a party to the conflict; it does not exclude the activities of 'civilians'. In other words, whereas the activities of the 'armed forces' are excluded, in so far as they are 'governed by international humanitarian law', even if they do not amount to war crimes, the activities of 'civilians' are never excluded, even if they are 'governed by international humanitarian law' and amount to war crimes (because there is a link or connection between the offence and the armed conflict, even if the offence is committed against other civilians).

55 Article 12 expressly includes 'armed conflicts mentioned in article 1, para. 4, of Additional Protocol I of 1977, in which peoples are fighting against colonial domination and alien occupation and against racist regimes in the exercise of their right of self-determination, as enshrined in the Charter of the United Nations and the Declaration on Principles of

are bound, under the 1949 Geneva Conventions or the 1977 Additional Protocols thereto, 'to prosecute or hand over the hostage-taker'.

As for the relation of 'private' and 'State' terrorism in situations not governed by international humanitarian law, the Coordinator's text of Article 18 again follows *à la lettre* the precedent of the 1998 Terrorist Bombing Convention, whose Article 19(2) already excludes from the scope of application of that convention 'the activities undertaken by the military forces of a State in the exercise of their official duties, inasmuch as they are governed by other rules of international law'. In this respect also, an identical exclusion clause has been inserted in the 2002 EU Council Framework Decision.[56]

The exclusion of such activities from the scope of the definition of terrorist acts is partly compensated for by the fact that they are governed by other rules of international law, both customary and conventional, such as the rules on the protection of human rights or, in respect of activities carried out abroad, the rules on respect of other States' territorial sovereignty or on the prohibition on the use of armed force in international relations. But it cannot be taken for granted that the violation of these rules necessarily entails the individual criminal responsibility of the authors, let alone an obligation to prosecute or extradite him (or her) on the part of the State where that person has found refuge. Under customary law, individual criminal responsibility only arises if the conduct in question can be characterized as a crime against humanity, but at the present state of development of international law, there seems to be a mere faculty to prosecute the authors of such crimes on the basis of the universality principle, not an obligation to prosecute or extradite them.

As for treaty law, it is true that most of the 'sectoral' treaties do not expressly exclude from their scope the activities of State organs – or, more specifically, of the military forces of a State – in the exercise of their official duties. However, the *Lockerbie* case has made it clear, in my opinion, that their application to such activities can certainly not be taken for granted.[57]

International Law concerning Friendly Relations and Co-operation among States in accordance with international law'.

56 Preamble, Point No. 11.

57 That case centred on alleged violations of the 1971 Montreal Convention for the Suppression of Unlawful Acts Against the Safety of Civil Aviation on the part of the UK and the US for trying to impair Libya's right to exercise jurisdiction over the persons accused of the Lockerbie 'incident' under Article 7 of that convention. In its 1992 order denying Libya's request for interim measures, the International Court of Justice exclusively relied on UN Security Council Resolution 740(1982), adopted under Chapter VII of the UN Charter, which, in accordance with Article 103 of the Charter, prevailed over Member States' obligations under other international conventions, including the Montreal Convention (*ICJ Reports 1992*, pp. 3 ff. and 114 ff.). However, it is interesting to recall that, during the oral hearings on 20 March 1992, Judge Schwebel pointed out that the persons accused of the Lockerbie 'incident' were persons 'claimed to be ...officers of the Libyan Intelligence Services', and he appeared to cast doubt on the application of the Montreal Convention to 'acts of persons in official service carrying out official purposes', despite the fact that the Convention refers to acts committed

Conclusions

The events of 11 September 2001 have tragically reminded world public opinion that international terrorism imperils the entire fabric of the international community. It is important to recall that, since the adoption of the Declaration on Measures to Eliminate International Terrorism in Resolution 49/60 of 9 December 1994, and most recently in Resolution 58/81 of 9 December 2003, adopted without a vote, the UN General Assembly has reiterated that 'criminal acts intended or calculated to provoke a state of terror in the general public, a group of persons, or particular persons for political purposes, are in any circumstances unjustifiable, whatever the considerations of a political, philosophical, ideological, racial, ethnic, religious or other nature that may be invoked to justify them'. However, the ongoing negotiations on the elaboration of a comprehensive convention on terrorism have made it quite clear that States find it easier to reach agreement on the text of non-binding General Assembly resolutions than on binding international criminal law treaties.

Given that existing treaties following the 'sectoral' approach have already given birth to a world network of legal obligations covering the most important aspects of international terrorism, and that acts of terrorism can sometimes qualify as war crimes or as crimes against humanity, the final question remains of whether a new comprehensive convention on terrorism is really needed. Indeed, especially since the adoption of the 1997 Convention for the Suppression of Terrorist Bombing, it is not easy to think of a terrorist act that would not be covered by one of the existing 'sectoral' treaties. A good case could be made that measures designed to enhance compliance with existing treaties are more urgently needed than a new comprehensive treaty on terrorism.

I believe, however, that the adoption of the comprehensive convention giving a generally agreed definition of terrorist acts would still be an improvement on the present situation. It is true that an indirect definition has already been agreed in the 1999 Convention for the Suppression of the Financing of Terrorism. But whereas the 1999 definition is rather restrictive, there continue to exist regional definitions which appear to be inordinately wide and to make it very difficult to distinguish acts of terrorism from 'ordinary' offences. The adoption of an agreed definition at the world level would, therefore, not only fill all possible gaps and thus further reduce the risk that some States may serve as safe havens or shelters for terrorist activities; it could also serve as a basis for reducing the negative effects of some excessive regional definitions.

It is important to recall that obligations to deny safe haven to terrorists, to ensure that they are brought to justice, and to ensure that 'terrorist acts' are established as 'serious criminal offences' in domestic law and punished in a way that reflects their 'seriousness' have already been imposed upon all UN Member States by Security

---

by 'any person' without expressly excluding the activities of State officials. See: A. Ciampi, 'Questioni concernenti l'applicabilità della Convenzione di Montreal nel caso *Lockerbie*', *Rivista di diritto internazionale*, vol. 86, 2003, pp. 1043 ff., at p. 1062.

Council Resolution 1373(2001) of 28 September 2001, which was adopted under Chapter VII of the UN Charter. But this resolution does not give a general definition of terrorist acts, and there is a danger that, in the absence of a generally agreed definition at world level, States may apply their own, or a regional, definition, which may appear too restrictive or too wide.[58]

Secondly, the adoption of an agreed definition at a world level could serve as a basis for the development of a customary rule for the prosecution of terrorist acts under the principle of 'universal jurisdiction', irrespective of whether or not they amount to war crimes or to crimes against humanity. The view that terrorism as such *does* amount to a discrete crime under customary international law and that a customary definition of terrorism already exists has been authoritatively put forward in the legal literature.[59] But national courts often tend to deny that customary international law currently provides for the prosecution of 'terrorist' acts under the universality principle, in part due to the failure of States to achieve anything like consensus on the definition of terrorism.[60]

That said, there is no doubt that measures to enhance compliance with existing treaties are urgently needed, and will continue to be needed even if UN Member States succeed in adopting a new comprehensive treaty on the prevention and suppression of terrorism. One such measure could be the adoption of a mechanism for the international prosecution of terrorist offences, irrespective of whether or not they qualify as war crimes or as crimes against humanity. It may be interesting to recall in this respect that, when the 1937 LN Convention on the Prevention and Punishment of Terrorism was adopted, another convention designed to establish an International Criminal Court was adopted at the same time, precisely in order to provide for the international prosecution of terrorists.[61] But, of course, that convention, like the convention on terrorism, never entered into force.

I personally share the view that, despite its flaws, the recent adoption and entry into force of the Rome Statute of the International Criminal Court represents a major step forward in the effort to bring international criminals to justice. It is a well-known fact that the inclusion of treaty crimes, including those covered by the 'sectoral' treaties dealing with terrorist acts, among the crimes falling within

---

58 In this respect, see: E. Rosand, 'Security Council Resolution 1373, the Counter-Terrorism Committee, and the Fight Against Terrorism', *American Journal of International Law*, vol. 97, 2003, pp. 333 ff., at p. 340.

59 See, for example: A. Cassese, *International Criminal Law*, Oxford: Oxford University Press, 2003, at pp. 120 ff.

60 See, for example, the decision of the US Court of Appeals for the Second Circuit (*United States* v. *Yousef et al.*, 4 April 2003), which held that 'customary international law currently does not provide for the prosecution of 'terrorist' acts under the universality principle, in part due to the failure of States to achieve anything like consensus on the definition of terrorism'. The text of the decision is available through a link provided by the American Society of International Law's electronic publication *International Law in Brief*, of 21 May 2003: http://www.asil.org/ilib/ilib0689.htm.

61 LN Doc. C.546.M.383.1937.V.

the Court's 'complementary' jurisdiction had been envisaged by some States, but, because of opposition on the part of a majority of States, it was eventually left for future decisions by a review conference.[62] A decision to that effect would be a step in the right direction.

---

62 See: D. Robinson, 'The Missing Crimes', in A. Cassese, P. Gaeta, J.R.W.D. Jones (eds), *The Rome Statute of the International Criminal Court. A Commentary*, Oxford: Oxford University Press, 2002, pp. 510 ff.

Chapter 2

Terrorism as an International Crime

JORDAN J. PAUST[1]

I want to address a few themes that were developed recently. I see certain UN conventions created by state elites as being part of the problem. The definition of terrorism in some of the conventions is part of the problem. For example, if acts of war are excluded, it is not that state actors who engage in terrorism during an armed conflict are not going to be subject to the laws of war, but what are the state elites telling us? They are telling us that what they do should not be called terrorism. Why not? Why should it not be called terrorism if it is terrorism? That raises the problem of course as to what is 'terrorism'.

There is a possibility that the international community can identify a shared content of the meaning of 'terrorism' or, if you prefer, elements of terrorism and a shared understanding, a core area of understanding of what are the elements of terrorism. We should not play the game of exclusion; for example, 'what *we* do is *not* terrorism, what *you* do *is* terrorism'. That has been part of the problem for some 200 years, and it plays into the hands of the non-state terrorists who are going to be very unimpressed that state elites have agreed to a convention that excludes their terroristic activities from the label of terrorism. I think it is not going to be helpful in terms of actually shaping attitudes and the behaviour of others. We need a descriptive, objective, definitional focus without exclusions for certain actors or contexts, precisely because we cannot simplistically associate permissibility or impermissibility of a war, revolution, or a self-determination struggle with 'terrorism'. Terrorism is a tactic or, if you wish, a strategy that various people (individuals and groups of various sorts) use, and we should approach the question of permissibility as a separate question, one divorced from the question of the legitimacy of the overall struggle; for example, whether or not a State uses military force in permissible self-defence, or whether or not NATO permissibly engages in 'regional action' in Kosovo that is not proscribed under articles 52 and 53 of the UN Charter, certain tactics are impermissible under international law. The issue of permissibility should be divorced from a description of a particular tactic that a NATO soldier uses in Kosovo. If it is terrorism, let us call it what it is and not have these types of exclusions. I think it would also be helpful to identify certain types of terroristic tactics. By the way, one

1 Law Foundation Professor, University of Houston. The following pages constitute a transcript of what was said by Professor Paust on 27 May 2004, and subsequently reviewed by him.

thing the US Executive could do to stop some forms of terrorism at Guantanamo and in Afghanistan and Iraq would be to ban the use of dogs for interrogation purposes, but that depends on how you define terrorism.

Actually, we have some indicia of objective and generally agreed-upon factors, even in the United Nations' General Assembly resolutions. I would like to go back just a little in time. In 1985, we had the first sweeping general condemnation of terrorism as an international crime and this sweeping condemnation has been reiterated in several resolutions of the General Assembly (such as in 1989, 1991, 1993 and 1994). Importantly, these involve sweeping, unequivocal, unlimited condemnations of terrorism.

I think we should start with that: no limitations, no exceptions. The language of the 1985 General Assembly resolution provides *opinio juris*, or juristic opinion, that is relevant to the interpretation of international law. It unequivocally condemns 'as criminal all acts, methods and practices of terrorism wherever and by whomever committed'.[2] Thus, we should not make distinctions on the bases of the status of the actor. Both state terrorism and non-state actor terrorism are terrorism, and we could not have exclusions for military forces or other state actors from the reach of the General Assembly resolutions or from the reach of an objective definition of terrorism. The problem is that the international community in general has been unable to articulate exactly what it is that is universally condemned in every form by whomever and wherever practiced. The 1985 resolution recognizes that there is an international crime of terrorism (that terrorism is 'criminal') and unequivocally condemns all forms of terrorism, but we are not sure exactly what is criminally proscribed. I would like to point out, however, that some of the definitional elements do exist in a 1994 General Assembly resolution, UN Res. 49/60 (9 Dec. 1994), UN Doc. A/RES/49/60. In paragraph 1 of the annex to the resolution, it sets forth the same sweeping condemnation that exists in other resolutions. In paragraph 3, we can recognize certain elements that are based in the resolution and, thus, that are based in the consensus or *opinio juris* lying behind acceptance of the resolution. These include the following elements: (1) intended or calculated, (2) to provoke a state of terror, (3) in the general public, a group of persons or particular persons, and (4) for political purposes. Another criterion in paragraph 3 is unhelpful – the requirement that acts be 'criminal acts'.

I think that the *mens rea* element set forth in the phrase 'intended or calculated' is an important element. Most would agree that terrorism is an intentional tactic or strategy. The crime of terrorism, in terms of *mens rea*, should involve a specific criminal intent to engage in terrorism – as opposed to mere wanton or reckless disregard or criminal negligence, which are *mens rea* standards regarding certain other types of international criminal activity. Intended or calculated to do what? An intent to produce terror or to terrorize. I think that part of the problem in the past, in terms of manipulated definitions and overly broad definitions as well as definitions

---

2   UN GA Res. 40/61, 40 UN GAOR, Supp. No. 53, at 301, UN Doc. A/RES/40/61 (9 Dec. 1985).

that are too limited and unhelpful, is that some of the definitional orientations exclude a terror outcome and a terror purpose or the intent to produce terror. As an international lawyer, your first effort will be to find what the generally shared expectations of the community are in terms of what is terror and what is terrorism. If you are interpreting a treaty, you use article 31 of the Vienna Convention on the Law of Treaties, so you are looking for the ordinary meaning of a term or phrase; that is, the core of generally shared meaning (even if at the outer edges of the core there is some disagreement). I think the objective meaning should guide us in terms of customary international law and treaty-based definitional orientations.

We can look up the objective, generally shared human meaning of terms or phrases in a dictionary. For example, 'terrorism' is often defined as a tactic or strategy involving an intent to produce intense fear or anxiety. Lawyers know these new words (such as 'fear' or 'anxiety') are still, what we call in the US, 'question beggars', which means that these additional words also have to be defined. What is intense, what is fear, what is anxiety? But we can identify objective elements of the definition and can build a list of these. Moreover, the identification of objective elements can be helpful to overcome efforts of others to exclude certain forms of terrorism as if they are not terrorism. We can identify an objective definition that can guide further inquiry concerning effective efforts at proscription and prosecution of terrorism and other responses to terrorism, including the combating of terrorism and terrorists and lawsuits against terrorists. Terror outcome and terror intent are objective elements that should be part of an objective and policy-oriented definition. It is very unhelpful that new UN conventions consider terrorism to be 'serious' damage. That approach to definition is completely overly broad. Serious bodily injury, without a terror purpose? If the definitional approach in a particular convention does not include a terror purpose as well as a terror outcome, such an approach is not realistic and it is not a descriptive or objective approach to what is actually 'terrorism'. Such an approach can either be over- or under-inclusive and quite unhelpful. Overly broad definitions can deflate the efficacy of the prohibition of terrorism.

Another element identifiable in some General Assembly resolutions involves the need for a political purpose; for example, the 1994 GA resolution. One might disagree that a tactic of terrorism must involve use of the tactic for a political purpose, but this seems to be what the community generally expects. For example, one might think that organized crime, which sometimes involves use of internal terrorism for the purpose of controlling its own actors, should be excluded from the crime of international terrorism. Of course, sometimes organized criminals engage in politically motivated terroristic tactics (for example, against state actors for political ends), and these should fit within the definition of terrorism. It appears that the community has often looked for political purpose as opposed to other types of purposes, so that might be something that we should think about for an objective definitional orientation. In any event, important elements exist in the 1994 resolution (for example, terror purpose and political purpose) but the element of terror outcome is missing.

Also missing is an element of violence or a threat of violence. A number of textwriters had been focusing on terrorism as an intentional tactic utilizing violence, like aircraft sabotage, terrorist bombings, and assassinations. Then we had the anthrax scare in the US, and now we have a scare in the US and abroad concerning use of bacteriologic or biological weaponry. In my own definitional orientation in the 1970s, I included the element of violence or threat of violence and defined terrorism as the use of violence or threat of violence by a precipitator against an instrumental target in order to communicate to a primary target a threat of future violence, so as to coerce the primary target through intense fear or anxiety (that is, terror) in connection with a demanded political outcome.[3] The primary target could be the same as the instrumental target or it could be a different target. Today, I am having second thoughts about a requirement of the use of violence. Perhaps the element in this case should be something like 'violence or the use of weapons'. Then the next question would be 'what is a weapon?'. I want to cover use of bacteriologic or biologic weaponry in the definition of terrorism, so I have come up with these types of elements: (1) intent, (2) tactic or strategy; that is, an intentional tactic or strategy, (3) to produce terror, or intense fear or anxiety, (4) in a primary target, (5) by using violence or a weapon, (6) against an instrumental target, (7) for a political purpose, (8) with a terror outcome. By the way, an instrumental target could be human or non-human. For example, when a bomb is set off in front of a door of a bank, the bank is the instrumental target, but the intent is to produce intense fear or anxiety in a primary human target that could be governmental, non-governmental, civilian or other individuals or groups – we should not limit it here; it could be any type of individual or group of primary targets. The definition using these elements can be complex, but complexity is unavoidable if we wish to identify an objective definition of terrorism and, thus, one that is not manipulated to exclude certain actors, tactics, or contexts and one that is not overly broad.

What should be excluded from an objective definition? Again, I think you have to have a terror outcome. Anything less would be under-inclusive and would not really be 'terrorism'. Should the term 'subversive' be used? Sometimes a definitional orientation considers terrorism to involve merely acts that are subversive against a government. Such definitions often do not include acts of the government against their own people or against other persons, and such an approach is not helpful. 'Illegal' acts or 'criminal' acts? The UN apparently favours this type of criterion, but it has its own problems: criminal acts under international law, criminal acts under domestic law? We have some 200 countries in the world today. Are we limiting the definition to whatever happens to be in the laws of these 200 countries? What is 'criminal' in terms of international or domestic law? We should avoid use of that word in order to have an objective definition of terrorism, especially one that is neither over- nor under-inclusive. 'Perpetrated by sub-national groups'? Of course, that criterion would exclude state-actor terrorism or nations that engage in terrorism. We know that there are groups of people that are called nations, like a Palestinian nation, whether or not the Palestinians have a State. The US has treaties with certain

---

3   See, for example, J. J. Paust, 'An Introduction to and Commentary on Terrorism and the Law', *Connecticut Law Review*, vol. 19, 1987, p. 697.

Indian nations. There are actors participating in the international legal process other than States. We do not want to exclude any particular actor if we are going to reach an objective consensus on an objective definition of terrorism. 'Perpetrated by state-agents'? Of course, that criterion would leave out non-state actors. Terror perpetrated by acts 'dangerous to human life'? Sometimes when I drive on the freeway I suppose I am dangerous to human life, but I do not have a terror intent and I do not engage in speeding as a tactic for political purposes. You can understand that some of the definitional orientations are potentially too broad. 'To intimidate'? In my country, we intimidated the heck out of the British oppressors of our people in the 1700s during legitimate revolution. We should not confuse the question of the permissibility of a revolution with the question of permissibility of particular tactics, but 'intimidate'? There must be some forms of permissible social violence during a revolution or a self-determination struggle, but 'intimidate' the heck out of those who are your oppressors, or those you are at war with? 'Intimidate' seems far too broad, especially if we are missing the terror outcome and terror purpose elements that are needed to objectively define terrorism.

A tactic to 'affect conduct of a government' by a listed set of acts? I hope I affect the government of the US by some of my writings, but writings are not in the list. Nonetheless, 'affect' a government is far too over-inclusive. We should all be affecting and intimidating governments from time to time, but not necessarily by violence. Yet, there might be some forms of social violence that are permissible self-defence for groups that do not involve terrorism as objectively defined. 'Innocence' or 'innocent victims'? Some people load their definition with another set of questions, but who is completely innocent in a particular social context? Innocence could be a relative criterion; for example, relatively innocent, non-innocent, more innocent, less innocent. We do not use that word with respect to the laws of war, nor should we do so. If you have somebody who is detained during an armed conflict, regardless of their status, you cannot interrogate them in certain ways that we see are occurring at Guantanamo and in Afghanistan with the approval of the administration in my country. These are war crimes and lawyers who wrote secret memos as part of a common plan to do so can be reasonably accused of aiding and abetting such crimes. It does not matter that the person is innocent, guilty, a former combatant, an enemy combatant, or a terrorist. It simply does not matter because you have a human being in your control and you do not do certain things to human beings that you control without violating the laws of war and human rights law. That is quite preferable as we attempt to regulate terrorism and the putative criteria of innocence and non-innocence are not helpful.

Other types of exclusions were actually mentioned indirectly. With respect to 'just wars', can you use terrorism in a just war? No, unless possibly against enemy combatants who are still fighting. Can you use terrorism as a tactic if you are rightly engaged in self-defence operations? No, unless the same combatant exception applies. Can you use terrorism to promote a legitimate self-determination struggle? No, unless the laws of war apply as well as the same combatant exception. We have to objectively define what terrorism is as a tactic. My own government has overreacted quite a bit after 9/11. In many ways, 9/11 is not so new. It is rather new that you fly an aircraft into a building instead of missiles, but if you think about it even the loss of life, although significant and terrible, is not new when compared to other times of social violence. But after 9/11 some argue that everything has changed, perhaps as part of a scheme to avoid legal restraints. I do not agree that international law has changed, especially concerning the treatment of human beings who have been captured and detained. Of course, you cannot be at 'war' with 'terrorism' and you cannot be at 'war' with a group of non-state actors who do not have the status of an insurgent, belligerent, nation, or State.

One of the problems we are facing in my country is that the so-called 'war' against Al Qaeda has no basis in international law. You simply cannot be at war with Al Qaeda as such because they do not meet the criteria for insurgent status, much less any of the others necessary for labels such as war or armed conflict to apply. Of course, you could find Al Qaeda persons in Afghanistan or Iraq during a war there, but you cannot be at war with a non-state terrorist organization that does not meet even the lowest level for armed conflict, an insurgent. I do not think that bin Laden intends to represent a nation or a State, and Al Qaeda certainly does not meet the criteria for belligerency or insurgence status (for example, involving (at a minimum) control of significant territory as its own and having some form of government). What would happen if you are at war with Al Qaeda or some other non-state terrorist organization? You might enhance their status politically and in terms of international law as different governments and entities interact with this newly created process of 'war', and it muddies up the approach to questions about prisoner of war status, combatant status, legitimate targeting, and such. If you are at war with Al Qaeda, they could rightly target the Pentagon and they could rightly target the USS *Cole*, although not the US embassies in Tanzania or Kenya and not the World Trade Centre. The latter would be illegal even during war and most likely a crime against humanity. In any event, under international law there are certain things that might follow if you are at 'war' with a non-state terrorist group.

The claim of some within my government who chose to authorize illegal interrogation tactics and denials of law of war protections of human beings is that we are in a new era after 9/11 and the laws of war were not developed with respect to terrorism or that terrorism was not in the minds of anyone when the laws of war were developed. That is really nonsensical. In 1919, the Paris Peace Conference's Responsibilities Commission looking into certain war crimes committed during World War I created a list of customary war crimes. One of the war crimes identified was 'systematic terrorism', so at least, whether or not it is defined, there was some attention in 1919 to terrorism committed during war. Moreover, article 33 of the 1949 Geneva Civilian Convention contains a prohibition of 'all measures of intimidation or of terrorism', so obviously some of the laws of war were created with terrorism in mind. The 1977 Protocols to the Geneva Conventions have specific references to terrorism as well.

I have been struggling with the issue concerning the permissibility of terrorism. I think we should separate out the description of terrorism as a tactic or a strategy from the question of whether or not it is permissible under international law. If you are trying to objectively define something, do not build into your definition a value-loaded conclusion that it is impermissible or criminal at the beginning. Are there some forms of terrorism that are permissible? That question will be shocking to some and apparently most consider that there are no permissible forms of terrorism, given the General Assembly's unequivocal condemnation of all forms of terrorism. However, I still believe that patterns of practice reflect the permissibility of the tactic of terrorism in war engaged in by combatants against enemy combatants that are not in the control of those who engage in the tactic. I see the practice and the permissibility of combatant terrorist tactics against other combatants being retained. Of course, you cannot lawfully terrorize those who are detainees, or those who are not combatants. So if you are engaged in lawful targeting during a war (that is, targeting a lawful combatant still engaged in combat) and use terroristic tactics to do so, we should continue to view that as an exception to impermissible terrorism. In any event, you might have others in mind. I could not come up with others myself, but it might be useful to consider the one exception as we attempt to objectify what is terrorism and to separate out the independent question of permissibility versus impermissibility.

Chapter 3

The Definition of the Crime of Terrorism

GERHARD HAFNER[1]

The problem of the definition of terrorism[2] has long bothered the General Assembly. It had come up already when the now existing conventions dealing with various special forms of terrorism (such as, for example, the 1988 Convention for the Suppression of Unlawful Acts against the Safety of Maritime Navigation[3]) were being negotiated. There is now a long list of such international agreements: the United Nations recognizes 19 such global or regional conventions:

- Convention on Offences and Certain Other Acts Committed on Board Aircraft, signed at Tokyo on 14 September 1963 (entered into force on 4 December 1969);
- Convention for the Suppression of Unlawful Seizure of Aircraft, signed at The Hague on 16 December 1970 (entered into force on 14 October 1971);
- Convention for the Suppression of Unlawful Acts against the Safety of Civil Aviation, signed at Montreal on 23 September 1971 (entered into force on 26 January 1973);
- Convention on the Prevention and Punishment of Crimes against Internationally Protected Persons, including Diplomatic Agents, adopted by the General Assembly of the United Nations on 14 December 1973 (entered into force on 20 February 1977);
- International Convention against the Taking of Hostages, adopted by the General Assembly of the United Nations on 17 December 1979 (entered into force on 3 June 1983);
- Convention on the Physical Protection of Nuclear Material, signed at Vienna on 3 March 1980 (entered into force on 8 February 1987);
- Protocol for the Suppression of Unlawful Acts of Violence at Airports Serving International Civil Aviation, supplementary to the Convention for the

---

1   University of Vienna.

2   The restriction to the international nature of terrorist acts derives from the exclusion of offences which were committed within a single State and in relation to which no other State has any ground to exercise jurisdiction from the future convention.

3   IMO Doc. SUA/CONF/15/Rev. 1; the texts of these conventions are also reproduced in: United Nations, *International Instruments related to the Prevention and Suppression of International Terrorism*, New York, 2001.

Suppression of Unlawful Acts against the Safety of Civil Aviation, signed at Montreal on 24 February 1988 (entered into force on 6 August 1989);

- Convention for the Suppression of Unlawful Acts against the Safety of Maritime Navigation, signed at Rome on 10 March 1988 (entered into force on 1 March 1992);
- Protocol for the Suppression of Unlawful Acts against the Safety of Fixed Platforms Located on the Continental Shelf, signed at Rome on 10 March 1988 (entered into force on 1 March 1992);
- Convention on the Marking of Plastic Explosives for the Purpose of Detection, signed at Montreal on 1 March 1991 (entered into force on 21 June 1998);
- International Convention for the Suppression of Terrorist Bombings, adopted by the General Assembly of the United Nations on 15 December 1997 (opened for signature on 12 January 1998 until 31 December 1999);
- International Convention for the Suppression of the Financing of Terrorism, adopted by the General Assembly of the United Nations on 9 December 1999 (opened for signature on 10 January 2000 until 31 December 2001);
- Arab Convention on the Suppression of Terrorism, signed at a meeting held at the General Secretariat of the League of Arab States in Cairo on 22 April 1998 (entered into force on 7 May 1999);
- Convention of the Organization of the Islamic Conference on Combating International Terrorism, adopted at Ouagadougou on 1 July 1999;
- European Convention on the Suppression of Terrorism, concluded at Strasbourg on 27 January 1977 (entered into force on 4 August 1978);
- OAS Convention to Prevent and Punish Acts of Terrorism Taking the Form of Crimes against Persons and Related Extortion that are of International Significance, concluded at Washington, D.C., on 2 February 1971 (entered into force on 16 October 1973);
- OAU Convention on the Prevention and Combating of Terrorism, adopted at Algiers on 14 July 1999;
- SAARC Regional Convention on Suppression of Terrorism, signed at Kathmandu on 4 November 1987 (entered into force on 22 August 1988);
- Treaty on Cooperation among States Members of the Commonwealth of Independent States in Combating Terrorism, done at Minsk on 4 June 1999.

It is interesting to note that even this long list is not exhaustive since even on the brink of World War II the first attempt was made to get to grips with the phenomenon of terrorism by the Convention on the Prevention and Punishment of Terrorist Activities of 1937. Triggered by alleged activities of Yugoslav terrorists in Hungary, the assassination of King Alexander of Yugoslavia in France in 1934, and the appeal of Yugoslavia to the League of Nations in 1934, the Council came to the conclusion that the rules of international law concerning the repression of terrorist activity were not sufficiently precise to guarantee efficient international cooperation in this matter. As a result, the Convention for the International Prevention and Punishment of Terrorism and the Convention for the Creation of an International Criminal Court were opened for signature in 1937; the first was signed by 23 States, the second by ten States, so neither really become effective.

The need for a definition?

But none of these global conventions provide a satisfactory generic definition; only the 1999 International Convention for the Suppression of the Financing of Terrorism[4] includes a definition in its article 2 para. 1 subpara. (b) which goes beyond the reference to the definitions of special conduct provided by other conventions.[5]

One can therefore easily ask whether a definition is necessary at all. Would it not be possible to proceed like Wittgenstein, saying that the definition results from the usage?

But such an approach is hardly possible: the problem is that the usage in the various States is different so that a common usage cannot be established. Not only does the domestic legislation on terrorism vary considerably, but also the definitions in the various international conventions are very diverse.

Nevertheless, a common definition is necessary and indispensable to any serious attempt to combat terrorism. Without such a definition, a coordinated fight against international terrorism can never really get anywhere. This was stated in the opinion of the League of Nations Council: namely that the definition is needed in order to enable international cooperation.

Terrorism has always shown an international dimension: for instance the assassination of the Yugoslav King occurred in France. Even the assassination of Empress Elizabeth (Sisi) of Austria in 1889 – if it falls under the definition of terrorist acts – occurred in Geneva, and the attack in Sarajevo in 1914 on Franz Ferdinand, the Austrian successor to the throne, was performed by a Serb nationalist supported by a criminal organization in Serbia, the Crna Ruka. The present situation and the facility to move across boundaries by various technical means, including the Internet, strengthen the international dimension of terrorism.

The international or transboundary cooperation to combat such events, however, was impeded by the restriction in extradition laws, namely the exemption of political

---

4   UN Doc. A/RES/54/109, Annex.

5   Article 2 para. 1 reads:

'Any person commits an offence within the meaning of this Convention if that person by any means, directly or indirectly, unlawfully and wilfully, provides or collects funds with the intention that they should be used or in the knowledge that they are to be used, in full or in part, in order to carry out:

(a) An act which constitutes an offence within the scope of and as defined in one of the treaties listed in the annex; or

(b) Any other act intended to cause death or serious bodily injury to a civilian, or to any other person not taking an active part in the hostilities in a situation of armed conflict, when the purpose of such act, by its nature or context, is to intimidate a population, or to compel a government or an international organization to do or to abstain from doing any act.'

crimes. It is in particular this exemption that reflects the limits to international cooperation in criminal matters; it is still the last reminder of the fact that criminal jurisdiction is considered as the core of sovereignty and that criminal jurisdiction has been conceived as a means to pursue political ends within a specific population. Already Grotius asserted the duty of a State under international law to cooperate with other States in the prosecution of common crimes; although this duty came into existence by means of extradition treaties only in the course of the nineteenth century, the States did not want to assist other States to pursue their political objectives.

Only before the outbreak of the Second World War, in view of obvious terrorist acts, did the State community start to think about any common definition and the combat of such acts as a common goal. But it must not be overlooked that, even at that time, quite a number of States were not prepared to steer this course; in particular those States which observed the policy of non-extradition for political crimes. This development reflects the political nature of the definition of terrorism.

The political nature of terrorism

As the Working Group in the United Nations stated quite clearly:

> Terrorism is, in most cases, essentially a political act. It is meant to inflict dramatic and deadly injury on civilians and to create an atmosphere of fear, generally for a political or ideological (whether secular or religious) purpose. Terrorism is a criminal act, but it is more than mere criminality. To overcome the problem of terrorism it is necessary to understand its political nature as well as its basic criminality and psychology.

The difficulty of reaching an agreement on a generally acceptable definition results from the old saying that one state's 'terrorist' is another state's 'freedom fighter.' The general acceptability of a definition of terrorism obviously depends on a certain political homogeneity or at least ideological vicinity of the participating countries since those conventions which include a generic definition are of a regional nature. One might cite groupings such as the Convention of the Organization of the Islamic Conference on Combating International Terrorism of 1999,[6] the OAU Convention on the Prevention and Combating of Terrorism of 1999,[7] the Treaty on Cooperation among the States Members of the Commonwealth of Independent States in Combating Terrorism of 1999[8] or the Arab Convention on the Suppression of Terrorism of 1998.[9]

The particular difficulty to achieve this homogeneity has clearly been demonstrated by the fact that, despite the events of 11 September, the States represented in the UN were not able to arrive at such a definition in the course of the discussions of the

6   The Organization of the Islamic Conference; The Twenty-Sixth Session of the Islamic Conference of Foreign Ministers, July 1999, Annex to Resolution No: 59/26-P.
7   Text in *International Instruments, supra* note 63, p. 210.
8   *Ibid.*, p. 174.
9   *Ibid.*, p. 152.

Sixth Committee, including the Working Group.[10] At the same time, the definitions contained in the various regional conventions illustrates the wide gap existing between them: whereas, for instance, the OAS Convention only refers to the crimes against internationally protected persons, the Islamic Convention (unlike the OAS Convention) includes 'certain intent' as an element of the crime in its definition of terrorism.[11] Like the relevant resolutions relating to terrorism and adopted earlier by the General Assembly,[12] the proposal presented by the Chairman of the Working Group of the Sixth Committee opts for the second approach by defining the purpose of the activity as a necessary element, namely the 'purpose of the conduct, by its nature or context, … to intimidate a population, or to compel a Government or an international organization to do or abstain from doing any act'.[13]

The difficulties of definition

Irrespective of whether or not this definition will turn out to be workable in the course of further negotiations, the political dimension (and consequently the field of disagreement) is reflected in the exceptions to it, namely the definition of those acts which do *not* fall under the qualification of terrorism. Thus, the general definition in Article 2 is intrinsically linked with the exemption addressed in draft Article 18 which still remains a divisive issue.[14]

---

10 Even further discussions in the Security Council failed in this regard.

11 The intent of 'terrorizing people or threatening to harm them or imperilling their lives, honour, freedoms, security or rights or exposing the environment or any facility or public or private property to hazards or occupying or seizing them, or endangering a national resource, or international facilities, or threatening the stability, territorial integrity, political unity or sovereignty of independent States'.

12 So for instance the Declaration on Measures to Eliminate International Terrorism, UN Doc. A/RES/49/60, Annex; or the Declaration to Supplement the Declaration on Measures to Eliminate International Terrorism, UN Doc. A/RES/51/210, Annex.

13 UN Doc. A/C.6/57/L.9 of 16 October 2002: Measures to eliminate international terrorism. Report of the Working Group, p. 16.

'Any person commits an offence within the meaning of this Convention if that person, by any means, unlawfully and intentionally, causes:

(a) Death or serious bodily injury to any person; or

(b) Serious damage to public or private property, including a place of public use, a State or government facility, a public transportation system, an infrastructure facility or the environment; or

(c) Damage to property, places, facilities, or systems referred to in paragraph 1 (b) of this article, resulting or likely to result in major economic loss, when the purpose of the conduct, by its nature or context, is to intimidate a population, or to compel a Government or an international organization to do or abstain from doing any act.'

14 This draft article, for which no formulation was proposed by the Chairman, should contain an exemption clause relating, *inter alia*, to activities covered by humanitarian law.

This problem of the exception results from the vicinity of terrorist acts to other acts which have a violent character but are generally or sometimes to be considered as lawful or falling under different legal regimes: on the one hand acts of self-determination, on the other military acts.

Acts of self-determination

In the discussion on this issue the legal assessment of the armed people's struggle (including armed struggle against foreign occupation, aggression, colonialism and hegemony), aimed at liberation and self-determination in accordance with the principles of international law, again formed a substantial obstacle to an agreement. Some States did not consider such acts as constituting terrorist crimes.[15] Similarly, the Islamic Convention exempts '(p)eoples' struggle including armed struggle against foreign occupation, aggression, colonialism, and hegemony, aimed at liberation and self-determination in accordance with the principles of international law' from the definition of terrorist crimes.[16] According to a different reasoning, the undoubtedly legitimate people's struggle could not be carried out by whatever means available but had to remain subject to the rules of the armed conflicts, so that there was no need to refer to this matter in the comprehensive convention.[17]

This discussion reflects some aspects of present international relations: self-determination is seen by some as possible only if achieved by acts of violence. Only such acts are deemed to be able to exercise a conclusive influence on the political decision-maker of a State. Only after World War II did international law start to refer to such acts outside international conflicts, through the well-known Common Article 3 of the Geneva Conventions and Additional Protocol No. 2 of 1977. But, despite these efforts, the international community now faces an increase in non-international conflicts where unbelievable atrocities are still being committed. Even such international regulations are not yet able to address all possible situations where terrorist acts may occur.

Other issues coming up in this context are the qualification of guerrilla warfare or 'levée en masse' which already reaches into the field of military acts.

Military acts

The other side of the coin in this definition is the vicinity of terrorist acts to those acts occurring within a military combat. Overlapping of such activities with terrorist acts could occur: in particular, military activities may end up being assessed as war crimes, as may guerrilla warfare.

The present definitions raise in particular the question of the limits between terrorist acts and acts which can be defined as war crimes. The reluctance to subsume

---

15 WG Report, *supra* note 13, p. 34.
16 See *supra* note 6.
17 Ad Hoc Report, *supra* note 15, p. 12.

war crimes under terrorist acts stems from the presently highly debated issue of the immunity of military forces from any international or foreign jurisdiction.

Nevertheless, it seems generally agreed that acts governed by international humanitarian law would not be considered as terrorist acts. This exemption includes activities of armed forces during armed conflicts, whether of international or non-international nature, as conceived by Common Article III of the Geneva Conventions 1949[18] or the Second Additional Protocol 1977 to the Geneva Conventions.[19] Such a general reference to armed conflicts without further distinction as to their nature corresponds to a modern tendency which is reflected also in the Statute of the International Criminal Court; here Article 8 likewise brings crimes committed during a non-international conflict within war crimes.[20]

The political side

The political issue behind this discussion is not the duty of States to prosecute acts committed on their territories, but the question of how far a State could serve as a safe haven or shelter for activities which were committed in other States and which are considered by the latter as terrorist acts. This aspect is clearly reflected in the discussion of the treatment of war crimes.

In legal terms this issue amounts to a question of State responsibility. Although these conventions regularly oblige States to establish their jurisdiction over such crimes, the politically more sensitive objective of such conventions is to confirm the duty under international law for prosecution, extradition or, generally, for State-to-State cooperation with relation to acts committed in a foreign State. A broad exemption to this duty would reduce the scope of obligations and, consequently, of international responsibility for non-compliance. However, this matter of the scope of the convention is one of legal politics which escapes any purely legal argumentation and evaluation, but requires instead a political decision by the States involved.

The different legal regimes

Law on terrorism and international humanitarian law

Although it seems commonly agreed that acts governed by international humanitarian law would not be considered as terrorist acts, this apparent consensus concerns only certain elements of the exemption clause: its final formulation will still have to overcome gaps between the basic conceptualizations of the means to settle existing

---

18 See also the commentary prepared by the ICRC in: <http://www.icrc.org/ihl.nsf>.

19 Protocol Additional to the Geneva Conventions of 12 August 1949, and Relating to the Protection of Victims of Non-International Armed Conflicts (Protocol II), *International Legal Materials*, vol. 16, 1977, p. 1442.

20 UN Doc. A/CONF.183/9.

and foreseeable conflicts among States where persons in their individual capacity are conducting combat activities against the State.

The necessity of an explicit clause that would settle the relation between a comprehensive convention and humanitarian law, of course, could be disputed insofar as the relation between humanitarian law and the comprehensive convention could be decided on the basis of the *lex specialis derogat legi generali* principle. However, the VCLT (Vienna Convention on the Law of Treaties) is rather silent on this issue[21] and the precise delimitation of the application of special rules of humanitarian law against that of general rules is hard to assess. The risk of a fuzzy formulation was clearly revealed by the ICRC (International Committee of the Red Cross) in the context of the elaboration of the Convention on Nuclear Terrorism since it made quite clear that a very vague formulation of the exception clause could lead to a negative solution where activities would fall under neither of the two legal regimes.[22] A precise definition of the application of the *lex specialis* rule will therefore be needed in order to exclude legal loopholes in the combat of terrorism.

The relation between the different conventions

That it will be extremely difficult to find a generally agreeable solution for the exemption clause is demonstrated by the sectoral conventions: as far as they contain exemptions, they are differently formulated so that they could hardly serve as a useful model for such a clause in the comprehensive convention.

The relation between a comprehensive convention and the existing special conventions has to take into account the various universal conventions dealing with specific acts of terrorism.[23]

---

21 See J. Mus, 'Conflicts between treaties in international law', *Netherlands International Law Review*, vol. 45, 1998, pp. 208 ff., at p. 213.

22 UN Doc. A/C.6/53/WG.1/INF/1.

23 The following conventions are normally quoted in this context: the 1963 Convention on Offences and Certain Other Acts Committed On Board Aircraft (Tokyo Convention; UNTS vol. 704, 220); the 1970 Convention for the Suppression of Unlawful Seizure of Aircraft (Hague Convention; UNTS vol. 860, 106); the 1971 Convention for the Suppression of Unlawful Acts Against the Safety of Civil Aviation (Montreal Convention; UNTS vol. 974, 178) and its 1988 Protocol for the Suppression of Unlawful Acts of Violence at Airports Serving International Civil Aviation (ICAO Doc. 9518, UNTS vol. 1589, 474); the 1973 Convention on the Prevention and Punishment of Crimes Against Internationally Protected Persons (UNTS, vol. 1035, p. 168); the 1979 Convention on the Physical Protection of Nuclear Material (Nuclear Materials Convention; UNTS vol. 1456, 125); the 1979 International Convention Against the Taking of Hostages (Hostages Convention; UNTS, vol. 1316, p. 206); the 1988 Convention for the Suppression of Unlawful Acts Against the Safety of Maritime Navigation (UNTS, vol. 1678, p. 222) and its 1988 Protocol for the Suppression of Unlawful Acts Against the Safety of Fixed Platforms Located on the Continental Shelf (UNTS, vol. 1678, p. 304); the 1991 Convention on the Marking of Plastic Explosives for the Purpose of Identification (UN Doc. S/22393); the 1997 International Convention for the Suppression of Terrorist Bombing (UN

The existence of these numerous sectoral conventions has already prompted the question of whether the special conventions should have priority over the comprehensive or whether the latter should supersede the special ones.[24] The legal arguments put forward in this respect resorted to the *lex posterior* rule according to Article 30 (VCLT).[25] In order to accord priority to the comprehensive convention the contrary argument relied again on the *lex specialis* rule which would make the comprehensive convention complementary to the special conventions.

Although both arguments have their merits, the *lex specialis* argument nevertheless better reflects the evolution and history of the elaboration of the various instruments aimed at combating the different forms of terrorism. In particular, the sectoral conventions better suit the different contexts and characteristics of the special acts of terrorism; it is doubtful that a comprehensive convention could also address the particular features of acts committed in the context of maritime navigation where, for example, the particular legal and factual characteristics of the different maritime zones have to be reflected. Accordingly, the sectoral conventions should receive priority. In such a case, the application of the *lex specialis* rule as part of the general rules on international treaties could make a specific clause to this effect redundant; however, in view of the existing imprecision of this rule a specific clause would be preferable in order to evade further difficulties of interpretation.[26]

But, whatever the outcome of this question of priority, it has also to be taken into account that the effect of these instruments will necessarily depend on the number of States party to each of them. The more States are party to the sectoral conventions in comparison to the comprehensive one, the less significant the comprehensive will be and *vice versa*. Hence, irrespective of the regulation of the legal relations between the sectoral conventions and the comprehensive, the scope of the application of those conventions will only be relative, since the comprehensive convention will be of major importance for only those States which have not ratified any of the sectoral conventions. A further inconvenience resulting from the existing variety of relevant conventions rests in the fact that different legal regimes will apply to the same activities. These divergences illustrate the difficulties under which a code of international criminal law emerges, where the first steps are taken in a casuistic manner which necessarily leads to certain inconsistencies. In this area, international law has not yet reached the stage of completeness which is generally ascribed to it.[27]

But despite the difficulties of reaching a commonly acceptable definition, the resolution adopted without a vote in the Sixth Committee seems to make a first

---

Doc. A/RES/52/164, Annex); and the 1999 International Convention for the Suppression of the Financing of Terrorism (UN Doc. A/RES/54/109, Annex).

24 Ad Hoc Report, *supra* note 13, p. 14.

25 UNTS, vol. 1155, p. 331.

26 Cf. *supra* note 21.

27 V. Lowe, 'The Politics of Law-Making: Are the Method and Character of Norm Creation Changing?', in M. Byers (ed.), *The Role of Law in International Politics*, Oxford: Oxford University Press, 2000, pp. 207 ff., at p. 209.

step by condemning 'all acts, methods and practices of terrorism as criminal and unjustifiable, wherever and by whomsoever committed'.[28] As to the acts addressed as terrorism the resolution reiterates the definition already included in the Declaration on Measures to Eliminate International Terrorism of 1994,[29] namely 'criminal acts intended or calculated to provoke a state of terror in the general public, a group of persons or particular persons for political purposes are in any circumstances unjustifiable, whatever the considerations of a political, philosophical, ideological, racial, ethnic, religious or other nature that may be invoked to justify them'.[30]

In the course of the explanation of votes the resolution was welcomed even by those who had opposite views on the definition of terrorist acts;[31] like the delegate of Lebanon speaking on behalf of the Group of Arab States[32] on the one side and the delegate of Israel on the other, the latter declaring his satisfaction with the rejection of characterizing suicide attacks as legitimate by various acts of the General Assembly as well as of the Security Council.[33]

It is interesting to note that this example proves that agreement on the definition of terrorist acts in the resolution does not suffice for the purposes of a convention. Resolutions of the General Assembly are very often seen as the model on which conventions can draw.[34] But this example of the resolution concerning terrorism clearly demonstrates that it is easier to reach agreement on the text of resolutions (which, however, are not sufficiently precise for the domestic judicial activities) than on a treaty's language. Nevertheless, this resolution illustrates emerging, if not already existing, shared interests[35] in combating terrorism, irrespective of the fact that agreement on the text of a comprehensive convention could not yet be reached.[36] In a more general perspective, such a convention imposing clear obligations of judicial cooperation of States could, in the long run, reduce the risk of unilateral forcible acts on the State-to-State level aiming at fighting terrorist activities.

---

28 UN Doc. A/RES/56/88.

29 UN Doc. A/RES/49/60 of 9 December 1994.

30 Operative para. 16.

31 Press Release GA/L/3200, 5.

32 Press Release GA/L/3200, 5.

33 Press Release GA/L/3200, 6.

34 The best example is the Treaty on Principles Governing the Activities of States in the Exploration and Use of Outer Space, including the Moon and Other Celestial Bodies 1967 (610 UNTS 205) which was based on the resolution A/RES/1963 (XVIII), containing the 'Declaration of Legal Principles Governing the Activities of States in the Exploration and Use of Outer Space'.

35 A. Hurrell, 'Conclusion, International Law and the Changing Constitution of International Society', in M. Byers (ed.), *supra* note 26, p. 327 ff., at p. 346.

36 As to the general consensus in this field and a pessimistic view on the possibility to overcome the remaining legal divergencies see A. Obote-Odora, 'Defining International Terrorism', *E Law – Murdoch University Electronic Journal of Law*, vol. 6, no. 1 (March, 1999), para. 81. < http://www.murdoch.edu.au/elaw/issues/v6n1/obote-odora61_text.html>.

Conclusion

It seems that in the present international context the violent acts of individuals cannot be eliminated. At the same time, political basic values still differ – these may result from the clash of civilizations or from the conflicts of former times which are still upheld or resurface from time to time. This conflict of basic values is even reflected in the regime of reservations to human right treaties. As long as this situation exists, a comprehensive definition seems to be impossible to find. Nevertheless, the state community must proceed in its striving for a comprehensive definition in order to make the first steps towards a world with decreasing terrorist activities.

Chapter 4

The UN, Human Rights and Counter-terrorism

KALLIOPI KOUFA[1]

Introduction

Responding to the threat of terrorism is a most significant issue for the international community – and this, of course, is the major reason for our meeting to discuss 'International cooperation and counter-terrorism'. In this framework, one of the most crucial challenges facing the international community nowadays is assuring respect for human rights in the context of the struggle to defeat or to counter terrorism.[2]

---

1 University of Thessaloniki.

2 See, for instance, the Report by the International Bar Association's Task Force on International Terrorism, entitled 'International Terrorism: Legal Challenges and Responses', Ardsley, NY: Transnational Publishers, 2003, pp. 7 ff. and pp. 53-115, and the Second Progress Report on 'Terrorism and human rights', prepared by this speaker for the UN Sub-Commission on the Promotion and Protection of Human Rights (UN doc. E/CN.4/Sub.2/2002/35, of 17 July 2002), as well as her subsequent Additional Progress Report (UN docs. E/CN.4/2003/WP.1, of 8 August 2003, pp. 19 ff. and E/CN.4/2003/WP.1/Add.2, containing a summary of the comments and information that she received from States, IGOs, NGOs and UN special procedures), and Final Report on the same topic (UN doc. E/CN.4/Sub.2/2004/40, of 25 June 2004, in particular the section containing the conclusions and recommendation of this Special Rapporteur). See also the Report of the Policy Working Group on the United Nations and Terrorism, established at the behest of the UN Secretary-General in October 2001, contained in UN doc. A/57/273 - S/2002/875, of 6 August 2002, Annex, paras 9 (c), 26-28 and 52, recommendations 4-6. Concern to reaffirm the rule of law and civil liberties while taking the necessary measures to counter terrorism has increasingly been brought to the attention of the UN Security Council, which in its declaration on the issue of combating terrorism (adopted by resolution 1456 (2003) of 20 January 2003) has stipulated in operative para. 6 that 'States must ensure that any measure taken to combat terrorism comply with all their obligations under international law, and should adopt such measures in accordance with international law, in particular international human rights, refugee, and humanitarian law'. As of this writing, see also Security Council Resolution 1566 (2004) of October 2004. And see, further, the Report of the Secretary-General on the Work of the Organization, General Assembly Official Records, Fifty-ninth Session, Supplement No. 1, UN doc. A/59/1, of 20 August 2004, para. 77, reiterating the Secretary-General's 'conviction that the struggle against terrorism must not take place at the expense of the fundamental freedoms and the basic dignity of individuals',

Terrorism, as we all know, is not a new phenomenon, in the sense that terrorists and terrorist acts can be traced far back into recorded history.[3] However, since 11 September 2001, terrorism has become an almost household word, a spectacle played out before a worldwide audience, as violent images are beamed into our homes by the mass media. Its consequences are being publicized widely, in excruciating detail, and public support for a 'world safe from terrorism' remains steadfast. Never before has there been such a wide degree of interest in terrorism, which has become in our times one of the most pressing political and legal problems, nationally and internationally.

Moreover, since 11 September 2001, responses to terrorism have themselves been dramatic, and often undertaken with a sense of panic or emergency.[4] There still exists, in fact, a 'close-to-panic' reaction in much of the political and legal activity relating to terrorism and, of course equally importantly, on the part of many of the world's people. And 'close-to-panic' reactions can have serious implications for international law and human rights law.[5]

Thus, ours is a time of heated debate over terrorism, human rights, and counter-terrorism, a time of serious concern over these issues. It is a time marked by a general feeling of increasing urgency regarding not only the manifestations of terrorism, but regarding also the adequacy and appropriateness of the responses to it, and the conformity of national and international measures adopted and/or applied while countering terrorism with international law, human rights and humanitarian law norms.[6]

---

and the more recent Report of the Secretary-General's High-level Panel on Threats, Challenges and Change, entitled 'A more secure world: Our shared responsibility', UN Doc. A/59/565, of 2 December 2004, paras 147-148 and at p. 103, Recommendation 38, proposing among other things: 'Development of better instruments for global counter-terrorism cooperation, all within a legal framework that is respectful of civil liberties and human rights, including in the areas of law enforcement; intelligence sharing, where possible; denial and interdiction, when required; and financial controls'.

3   A good historical overview of terrorism may be conveniently found in R. A. Friedlander, *Terrorism: Documents of International and Local Control*, vol. I, New York: Oceana Publications, 1979, pp. 1-197.

4   See UN doc. E/CN.4/Sub.2/2002/35, of 17 July 2002, at para. 59.

5   *Ibid.*, paras 59 and 63. An overview of the main post-September 11/2001 international anti-terrorist activity relevant to human rights and terrorism, undertaken both at the global and regional levels, may be most conveniently found in the Second Progress Report (UN doc. E/CN.4/Sub.2/2002/35, of 17 July 2002, para. 25 ff.) and in the Additional Progress Report (UN doc. E/CN.4/Sub.2/2003/WP.1/Add.1, of 8 August 2004) prepared for the UN Sub-Commission by Ms. Kalliopi K. Koufa, Special Rapporteur on 'Terrorism and human rights'.

6   See, for instance, also Human Rights Watch, 'Country Studies: The Human Rights Impact of Counter-Terrorism Measures in Ten Countries', in In the Name of Counter-Terrorism: Human Rights Abuses Worldwide, A Human Rights Watch Briefing Paper for the 59th Session of the UN Commission on Human Rights, 25 March 2003, available at http://www.hrw.org/un/chr59/counter-terrorism-bck.htm; M. Cohn, 'Human Rights: Casualty of the

To put it also in other words, nowadays the discussion of terrorism and of the ethical and legal problems of counter-terrorism (in the sense of the trade-offs between security and civil liberties, and the dilemmas posed thereof), makes the headlines. In fact, the subject of terrorism and its human rights dimensions and parameters has become of a global concern. This was not at all the case before 11 September 2001 and its *sequelae* – that is, the ensuing 'global war on terrorism,' the significant unintended consequences to human rights, and the risk of damage to the cause of justice and the rule of law as a result of the adoption or implementation of anti-terrorist legislations and policies – along with the continuing failure to resolve some 'hot spots' still fuelling the debate of 'terrorists versus freedom fighters'.

Having said all this by way of introduction, I will next proceed with my presentation by highlighting (selectively) those efforts of the United Nations to deal with the problem of terrorism, which are relevant to my topic. Then, I will speak about the nature of the relationship (or the direct and indirect links) between terrorism and human rights. I will finish with counter-terrorism and human rights in the United Nations, with references to the need to uphold human rights and the rule of law in combating terrorism, and some basic human rights delimitations and prescriptions regarding counter-terrorism legislations and measures.

The United Nations and international terrorism

It hardly need be recalled that the United Nations made no attempt to revive or resume the efforts of the League of Nations to control international terrorism, which were interrupted by the Second World War.[7] These efforts had culminated, as is well known, in the adoption of the (failed) 1937 complementary Conventions on the Prevention and Punishment of Terrorism[8] and on the Establishment of an International Criminal Court.[9] Nonetheless, the problem of international terrorism has been the subject of a number of actions in the course of the work carried out by the United Nations on the codification and progressive development of international law, since the early 1950s, and on the maintenance of international peace and security, in the early 1970s.

War on Terror', Thomas Jefferson Law Review, vol. 25, 2003, pp. 317-365; M. Sassoli, 'Use and Abuse of the Laws of War in the "War on Terrorism"', Law and Equality: A Journal of Theory and Practice, vol. 22, 2004, pp. 195-221.

7   A good account of the efforts made before the Second World War to study the problem of terrorism as a common danger to be confronted by international law is contained in the study prepared by the United Nations Secretariat for the Sixth Committee, under the title 'Measures to prevent international terrorism which endangers or takes innocent human lives or jeopardizes fundamental freedoms, and study of the underlying causes of those forms of terrorism and acts of violence which lie in misery, frustration, grievance and despair and which cause some people to sacrifice human lives, including their own, in an attempt to effect radical changes'. See UN doc. A/C.6/418 of 2 November 1972, para. 22 ff.

8   See LN Doc. C.546 (I). M.383 (I).1937.V.

9   See LN Doc. C.547 (I). M.384 (I).1937.V.

Thus, for example, the International Law Commission dealt with terrorism in its 1954 Draft Code of Offences Against the Peace and Security of Mankind, which provided that the undertaking or encouragement by the authorities of a State of terrorist activity in another State, or the toleration by the authorities of a State of organized activities calculated to carry out terrorist acts in another State was declared to be an offence against the peace and security of mankind and a crime under international law.[10] Also, the General Assembly, in its Resolution 2625 (XXV) of 24 October 1970, on the Declaration on Principles of International Law concerning Friendly Relations and Co-operation among States in accordance with the Charter of the United Nations, addressed terrorism both under the principle that States should refrain in their international relations from the threat or use of force against the territorial integrity or political independence of any State, or in any other manner inconsistent with the purposes of the UN,[11] and the principle concerning the duty not to intervene in matters within the domestic jurisdiction of any State, in accordance with the Charter.[12] Further, in its Resolution 2734 (XXV) of 16 December 1970, on the Declaration on the Strengthening of International Security, the General Assembly solemnly reaffirmed that every State has the duty to refrain from organizing, instigating, assisting or participating in acts of civil strife or terrorist acts in another State.[13]

It was not until 1972, following the spectacular kidnapping and killing of the Israeli athletes during the Olympic Games at Munich, that the issue of terrorism was included in the agenda of the General Assembly, further to the initiative of the then Secretary-General Kurt Waldheim who proposed that a new item, entitled 'measures to prevent terrorism and other forms of violence which endanger or take innocent human lives or jeopardize fundamental freedoms' be considered by the General Assembly during its twenty-seventh session.[14] Shortly after, despite considerable opposition, the General Assembly adopted the new item, and allocated it to the Sixth (Legal) Committee, under an amended (even longer) title, which included the wording: 'and study of the underlying causes of those forms of terrorism and acts of violence which lie in misery, frustration, grievance and despair and which cause some people to sacrifice human lives, including their own, in an attempt to effect

---

10 See *Yearbook of the International Law Commission*, 1954, vol. II, chap. III. See also *Yearbook of the International Law Commission*, 1951, vol. II, chap. IV.

11 'Every State has the duty to refrain from organizing, instigating, assisting or participating in acts of civil strife or terrorist acts in another State or acquiescing in organized activities within its territory directed towards the commission of such acts, when the acts referred to…involve a threat or use of force.'

12 '[n]o State shall organize, assist, foment, finance, incite or tolerate subversive, terrorist or armed activities directed towards the violent overthrow of the regime of another State, or interfere in civil strife in another State.'

13 See para. 5.

14 See UN doc. A/8791 of 8 September 1972.

radical changes'.[15] Wording which would remain in the agendas of subsequent GA sessions and the titles of its resolutions on terrorism for many years.

As a result of the work of the Sixth Committee over the next thirty-three years, the General Assembly adopted a significant number of resolutions,[16] two important Declarations on 'Measures to eliminate international terrorism',[17] and a number of important multilateral instruments addressing specific crimes of international terrorism or crimes associated with international terrorism[18] – about which we have just heard from Professor Andrea Gioia – and, thus, managed to develop a pioneering role in the global struggle against international terrorism.

A careful scrutiny of all this activity of the General Assembly, for our own purposes – that is, in order to discover (and eventually assess) any linkages of terrorism and counter-terrorism with human rights – leads us to the following two basic preliminary observations. Firstly, although there seems to be a certain awareness, of some at least, of the adverse consequences (or effects) of terrorism on the enjoyment of human rights (for example, concern is expressed about the 'growing and dangerous links between terrorist groups ... endangering the constitutional order of States

---

15 See, generally, *Yearbook of the United Nations*, 1972, vol. 26, pp.639-640.

16 See GA Res. 3034 (XXVII), of 18 December 1972; 31/102, of 15 December 1976; 32/147, of December 1977; 34/145, of 17 December 1979; 36/109, of 10 December 1981; 38/130, of 19 December 1983; 39/159, of 17 December 1984; 40/61, of 9 December 1985; 42/159, of 7 December 1987; 44/29, of 4 December 1989; 46/51, of 9 December 1991; 48/122, of 20 December 1993; 49/60, of 9 December 1994; 49/185, of 23 December 1994; 50/53, of 11 December 1995; 50/186, of 22 December 1995; 51/210, of 17 December 1996; 52/133, of 12 December 1997; 52/165, of 15 December 1997; 53/108, of 8 December 1998; 54/110, of 9 December 1999; 55/158, of 12 December 2000; 56/88, of 12 December 2001; 57/27, of 19 November 2002; 58/81, of 9 December 2003; and, as of this writing, 59/46, of 2 December 2004.

17 See Declaration on Measures to Eliminate International Terrorism annexed to GA Res. 49/60 of 9 December 1994, and Declaration to Supplement the 1994 Declaration on Measures to Eliminate International Terrorism annexed to GA Res. 51/210 of 17 December 1996.

18 These are: Convention on the Prevention and Punishment of Crimes against Internationally Protected Persons, including Diplomatic Agents, adopted by the General Assembly on 14 December 1973; International Convention against the Taking of Hostages, adopted by the General Assembly on 17 December 1979; Convention on the Safety of United Nations and Associated Personnel, adopted by the General Assembly on 9 December 1994; International Convention for the Suppression of Terrorist Bombings, adopted by the General Assembly on 15 December 1997; and International Convention for the Suppression of the Financing of Terrorism, adopted by the General Assembly on 9 December 1999. A compilation of these and other global, as well as regional, instruments on terrorism can be most conveniently found in a recent United Nations Publication entitled 'International Instruments related to the Prevention and Suppression of International Terrorism', second edition (2004), Sales No. E.03.V.9.

and violating basic human rights';[19] or about the worldwide escalation of acts of terrorism 'which endanger or take innocent human lives, jeopardize fundamental freedoms and seriously impair the dignity human beings'[20]) there is no evidence of any particular interest in the nature and content (or scope) of the relationship between human rights and terrorism.[21] Secondly, while mention is regularly made to the 'necessity of maintaining and safeguarding the basic rights of the individual in accordance with the relevant international human rights instruments and generally accepted international standards'[22] when fighting terrorism, there is scant (or rare) reference to terrorism as both a cause and effect of human rights abuses. One such rare example is General Assembly Resolution 40/61 (1985), which points out that, in some cases, perpetrators may be driven to terrorist acts by violations of human rights, and urges States and the UN organs 'to contribute to the progressive elimination of the causes underlying international terrorism'.[23]

Of course, this apparent neglect of the human rights dimension of terrorism by the General Assembly is not surprising when considering that ever since its inclusion in the agenda of the General Assembly the problem of international terrorism and of the issues related to it have been systematically developed and debated in the framework of the Sixth Committee, and in the *ad hoc* committees which the General Assembly has occasionally deemed opportune to establish, with a view to studying or dealing with specific questions and aspects (or sectors) of the fight against terrorism, envisaged from the legal perspective.[24] It is only normal that, under the

---

19 See, for instance, GA Res. 44/29, of 4 December 1989, para. 9; 46/51, of 9 December 1991, para. 9; and preamble para. 5 of the 1994 Declaration on Measures to Eliminate International Terrorism, annexed to Res. 49/60, of 9 December 1994.

20 See, for instance, GA Res. 40/61, of 9 December 1985, preamble para. 4; 32/147, of 16 December 1977, para. 1; 31/102, of 15 December 1976, para. 1; 3034 (XXVII), of 18 December 1972, para. 1; 34/145, of 17 December 1979, para. 3.

21 See also my Preliminary Report on 'Terrorism and human rights' (E/CN.4/Sub.2/1999/27), paras 16-17.

22 See, for instance, GA Res. 40/61, of 9 December 1985, preamble para. 9; 42/159, of 7 December 1987, preamble para. 16; 44/29, of 4 December 1989, preamble para. 14; 46/51, of 9 December 1991, preamble para. 13; see also para. 5 of the 1994 Declaration on Measures to Eliminate International Terrorism, annexed to Res. 49/60, of 9 December 1994.

23 See GA Res. 40/61, of 9 December 1985, at para. 9: 'Further urges all States, unilaterally and in co-operation with other States, as well as relevant United Nations organs, to contribute to the progressive elimination of the causes underlying international terrorism and to pay special attention to all situations, including colonialism, racism and situations involving mass and flagrant violations of human rights and fundamental freedoms and those involving alien occupation, that may give rise to international terrorism and may endanger international peace and security'.

24 Such *ad hoc* committees have been: the Ad Hoc Committee on International Terrorism, established by GA Res. 3034 (XXVII), of 18 December 1972; the Ad Hoc Committee established by GA Res. 31/103, of 15 December 1976, for the drafting of the International Convention against the Taking of Hostages; and the Ad Hoc Committee established by GA Res. 51/210, of 17 December 1996, for the elaboration of an international convention for the suppression

circumstances, concern about the human rights dimension of terrorism could not really have caught on in the United Nations.

It did catch on, however, after a period of more than twenty years and, in particular, following the 1993 Vienna World Conference on Human Rights. As is well known, this major international conference constitutes a milestone event in the development of human rights, for marking not only the evolution and current status, but also the new trends and visions of the United Nations in the field of human rights. It was during this World Conference that the inextricable relationship between terrorism and human rights was discussed and recognized on its own merit, and was then formally substantiated – for the first time ever – in paragraph 17 of the 1993 Vienna Declaration and Programme of Action, adopted at the end of the Conference, in the following terms: '[t]he acts, methods and practices of terrorism in all its form and manifestations as well as linkage in some countries to drug trafficking are activities aimed at the destruction of human rights, fundamental freedoms and democracy, threatening territorial integrity, security of States and destabilizing legitimately constituted Governments'.[25]

That same year, in the framework of its Third (Social, Humanitarian and Cultural) Committee the General Assembly began to debate and adopt a new type of resolutions under the title 'Human rights and terrorism' – while continuing to develop systematically its main international anti-terrorism activity within the legal framework of its Sixth Committee, under its agenda item 'Measures to eliminate international terrorism' and its resolutions bearing that same title.[26] The resolutions on 'Human rights and terrorism', adopted by the General Assembly after the 1993 Vienna World Conference on Human Rights,[27] evidence not only the broadening of its interest in the particular relationship that exists between human rights and terrorism, but also a certain evolution of its attitude towards terrorist acts committed by non-State actors.[28] In fact, while some provisions of these resolutions derive from the provisions embodied in the resolutions on 'Measures to eliminate international

---

of terrorist bombings and, subsequently, an international convention for the suppression of acts of nuclear terrorism, and other international instruments thereafter, to supplement related existing instruments and develop further a comprehensive legal framework of conventions dealing with international terrorism. The mandate of this last Ad Hoc Committee has since been annually renewed.

25 See UN doc A/CONF.157/23, of 25 June 1993, Part I, para. 17. See also *ibid.*, para. 30.

26 K. Koufa, 'Human Rights and Terrorism in the United Nations', in G. Alfredsson, M. Stavropoulou (eds), *Justice Pending: Indigenous Peoples and Other Good Causes – Essays in Honour of Erica-Irene A. Daes*, The Hague: M. Nijhoff Publishers, 2002, p. 214.

27 See GA Res. 48/122, of 20 December 1993; 49/185, of 23 December 1994; 50/186, of 22 December 1995; 52/133, of 12 December 1997; 54/164, of 17 December 1999; 56/160, of 19 December 2001; 58/174, of 22 December 2003; and, as of this writing, 59/195, of 20 December 2004.

28 See also my Working Paper on 'Terrorism and human rights' (UN doc. E/CN.4/Sub.2/1997/28), at para. 4 (f).

terrorism' which condemn all forms of terrorism, and the rest of them focuses on some of the obvious links between terrorism and human rights violations, attention is drawn to a preambular paragraph – which they all contain – expressing the 'serious' (or 'grave') concern of the General Assembly 'at the gross violations of human rights perpetrated by terrorist groups'.[29]

Now, as is well known, according to traditional international law and human rights law, human rights are protected and violated by the State because, generally speaking, human rights involve obligations of States towards individuals.[30] The whole movement for the protection of human rights arose as an attempt to redress the balance between the power of the State to impose duties on individuals and the powerlessness of the individuals to ensure correlative respect for their rights. So, the provision that I have just mentioned is extremely controversial. Because of considerable opposition to it by a significant number of States, the General Assembly resolutions on 'Human rights and terrorism' have not been always adopted by consensus but after voting, the result of the voting having yielded, at different times, either a considerable number of abstentions, or even a number of abstentions and negative votes at the same time.[31]

In any case, beginning in 1994, the UN Commission on Human Rights also began to adopt resolutions on 'Human rights and terrorism', which contained almost similar provisions to those adopted by the General Assembly on the same topic, including an identical preambular paragraph that expressed serious concern about 'the gross violations of human rights perpetrated by terrorist groups'.[32] The Commission, further, urged the UN Sub-Commission on Prevention of Discrimination and Protection of

---

29 See GA Res. 48/122, of 20 December 1993, preamble para. 5; 49/185, of 23 December 1994, preamble para. 7; 50/186, of 22 December 1995, preamble para. 10; 52/133 of 12 December 1997, preamble para. 10; 54/164, of 17 December 1999, preamble para. 11; 56/160, of 19 December 2001, preamble para. 15; 58/174, of 22 December 2003, preamble para. 16; and, as of this writing, 59/195, of 20 December 2004, preamble para. 18.

30 An excellent advocacy of the classical doctrine is provided by N. Rodley, 'Can armed opposition groups violate human rights?' in K. E. Mahoney, P. Mahoney (eds), *Human Rights in the Twenty-first Century – A Global Challenge*, Dordrecht: M. Nijhoff Publishers, 1993, pp. 298 ff. Cf., however, also A. Clapham, 'The Privatisation of Human Rights', *European Human Rights Law Review*, Launch Issue, 1995, pp. 20 ff., as well as A. Clapham, *Human Rights in the Private Sphere*, Oxford: Clarendon Press, 1998 (reprinted).

31 As of this writing, it is interesting to note that GA Res. 59/195, of 20 December 2004 (which is the latest one on 'Human rights and terrorism') was adopted by a recorded vote of 127 in favour, 50 against, and 8 abstentions. See UN Press Release GA/10321, of 20 December 2004.

32 See Commission on Human Rights Res. 1994/46, of 4 March 1994, preamble para. 6; 1995/43, of 3 March 1995, preamble para. 7; 1996/47, of 19 April 1996, preamble para. 12; 1997/42, of 11 April 1997, preamble para. 11; 1998/47, of 17 April 1998, preamble para. 13; 1999/27, of 26 April 1999, preamble para.19; 2000/30, of 20 April 2000, preamble para. 21; 2001/37, of 23 April 2001, preamble para. 23; 2002/35, of 22 April 2002, preamble para. 23; 2003/37, of 23 April 2003, preamble para. 23; and 2004/44, of 19 April 2004, preamble para. 23.

Minorities (which later took the name of Sub-Commission on the Promotion and Protection of Human Rights) to undertake a study on the issue of terrorism and human rights in the context of its procedures.[33] The same year, following suit to the urging of the Commission, the Sub-Commission, by its Resolution 1994/18, requested one of its members to prepare a working paper on this topic. When in 1996 a paper had still not been submitted, the Sub-Commission entrusted this speaker to prepare it.[34]

In 1997, following the submission to the Sub-Commission of the requested working paper,[35] your speaker was appointed as Special Rapporteur with the mandate to conduct a comprehensive study on terrorism and human rights.[36] In the course of her mandate, this Special Rapporteur has produced five annual reports and other documents,[37] containing a detailed analysis of the inextricable link between terrorism and human rights and of its broader international implications, and investigated the complex nature and the issues involved in the human rights dimensions of terrorism. This long engagement by the Sub-Commission in the study of terrorism and human rights established and strengthened significantly the interest in this topic, even prior to the events of 11 September 2001. It also provided a solid basis for the post-11 September 2001 efforts, within the United Nations and elsewhere, to eventually and in the course of time address the issue of protecting human rights and fundamental freedoms while countering and combating terrorism – an issue I will deal with in the last part of my presentation.

The link between terrorism and human rights in fact and law

There is probably not a single human right exempt from the impact of terrorism. In this part of my presentation, however, I will only indicate cursorily the three major areas in which terrorism puts under threat the social and political values that relate, either directly or indirectly, to the full enjoyment of human rights and fundamental freedoms.

The life, liberty and dignity of the individual

Terrorist acts and methods do not only violate the rights of their victims but, at the same time, provoke or give an excuse for serious breaches of human rights

---

33 See Commission on Human Rights Res. 1994/46, of 4 March 1994.

34 See Sub-Commission Res. 1996/20, of 29 August 1996.

35 UN doc. E/CN.4/Sub.2/1997/28, of 26 June 1997.

36 See Commission on Human Rights decision 1998/107, of 17 April 1998, followed by ECOSOC decision 1998/278, of 30 July 1998.

37 See UN docs. E/CN.4/Sub.2/1997/28, of 26 June 1997; E/CN.4/Sub.2/1999/27, of 7 June 1999; E/CN.4/Sub.2/2001/31, of 27 June 2001; E/CN.4/Sub.2/2002/35, of 17 July 2002; E/CN.4/Sub.2/2003/WP.1 and Add.1 and 2, of 8 August 2003; and E/CN.4/Sub.2/2004/40, of 25 June 2004.

and freedoms by overreacting State authorities that feel threatened by terrorism. Furthermore, terrorists anticipate, and will often aim to provoke the State authorities into the kind of suppressive reaction and response that will eventually involve them in a spiral of terrorist abuse and violations of human rights, in order to create fear and dissatisfaction among the general public.[38]

Clearly, then, there is a close link between terrorism and human rights. That link is seen directly when groups or individuals resort to acts of terrorism and, in so doing, kill or injure individuals, deprive them of their freedom, destroy their property, or use threats and intimidation to sow fear. It can, further, be seen indirectly when a State's response to terrorism leads to the adoption of policies and practices that exceed the bounds of what is permissible under international law and result in human rights violations, such as extra-judicial executions, torture, unfair trials, and other acts of unlawful repression, which violate the human rights not only of the terrorists but of innocent civilians. There seems to be widespread agreement on both the direct and indirect link between terrorism and respect for human rights.[39] Moreover, the devastating effects of terrorism on the life, liberty, and dignity of the individual have been clearly expressed and documented in the debates and the related pronouncements on terrorism of the competent organs and bodies of the United Nations, as well as of the regional intergovernmental organizations.[40]

Democratic society

The preceding observations point already to the second area, that of democratic society, which can also be threatened by terrorism.[41] A democratic society requires the existence and free exercise of certain basic individual and group rights and freedoms, including the liberty and security of person, equality and non-discrimination, due process of law, freedom of opinion and expression, freedom of assembly and association, judicial access and review.[42] A democratic society, moreover, is identified by certain principles and institutions, such as pluralism, the rule of law, legitimacy, political equality, popular control and public accountability of government, which, again, have their starting point in human rights and freedoms. It follows that the concept of democratic society is inseparable from fundamental human rights and freedoms, and from respect for the rights and freedoms of others.[43]

Apparently, then, terrorism is totally at odds with the concept of democratic society. Terrorist acts and methods utilized to coerce others from a free choice and

---

38 See also K. Koufa, 'Le terrorisme et les droits de l'homme", in *Le droit international face au terrorisme – Après le 11 septembre 2001*, CEDIN-Paris I, Cahiers internationaux No. 17, 2002, p. 195, as well as E/CN.4/Sub.2/1997/28, para. 8, and E/CN.4/Sub.2/1999/27, para. 24.

39 E/CN.4/Sub.2/1999/27, para. 25.

40 *Ibid.*, notes 27 and 28 and accompanying text.

41 See, more extensively, E/CN.4/Sub.2/1999/27, paras 26 ff.

42 *Ibid.*, para. 29.

43 *Ibid.*, para. 30.

full participation in the political process offend democratic society.[44] As a matter of fact, terrorism can threaten democratic society in various ways. By using violence and fear as a political tool, terrorism can undermine the legitimate authority of governments; influence ideological and political factors in order to impose its own model of society; impede citizens in their use of their rights to have a say in the decisions that affect their lives; subvert pluralism and democratic institutions through the creation of negative conditions for the functioning of the constitution; halt the democratic process and democratization; and undermine free political, economic, social and cultural development. In short, terrorism can impair the quality of democratic society for all, even when it does not actually threaten its survival, and can lead to even more terrorism and militancy.[45]

Social peace and public order

Lastly, in considering the area of social peace and public order, the effects of terrorism can also be devastating. Terrorist acts and methods involving impermissible violence and fear, whether engaged in by private individuals or in the name of the official State, will inevitably create social and political disorder and affect stability and peace.[46] In this connection, it is appropriate to consider the actual and potential threat to stability, peace and order posed by terrorism, in both its national and international dimensions.

To begin with the national dimension, the actual and potential threat to stability, peace, and order posed by terrorism will be easily deduced from what has already been said. Terrorist outrages aiming at the destruction of human rights in order to create fear and provoke conditions that are propitious to the destruction of the prevailing social order may destabilize governments.[47] The killing of innocent people, destroying property and fostering an atmosphere of alarm and terror amount not merely to a violation of the rights of the direct victims but to a solicitation of further serious breaches of human rights. In response to the terrorists' despicable conduct and the threats posed to society, the authorities of the State which is responsible for bringing the terrorist violence to an end are entitled to adopt counter-terrorist measures and may not be constrained by the normal limits of official measures for the prevention of ordinary crime.[48] As a consequence, there is a real danger that the State will overreact to the threat of terrorism and slide towards repression and violation of the human rights not only of the terrorists but of the rest of society whose rights and liberties might be diminished in the course of discovering, apprehending

---

44 *Ibid.*, para. 31.

45 *Ibid.*, para. 32.

46 *Ibid.*, para. 33.

47 See generally G. Wardlaw, *Political Terrorism: Theory, tactics and countermeasures*, Cambridge: Cambridge University Press, 1982 and P. Wilkinson, *Terrorism and the Liberal State*, London: Macmillan, 1986.

48 See C. Warbrick, 'The European Convention of Human Rights and the Prevention of Terrorism', *The International and Comparative Law Quarterly*, vol. 32, Part 1, 1983, p. 84.

and convicting the terrorists. The damaging impact and effects of terrorism on social peace and public order may, in the long run, threaten the very existence of the State.

This is particularly true in cases where terrorist activity becomes strongly linked to illicit trafficking in narcotic drugs, arms traffic, political assassinations and other international organized criminal activity,[49] as well as in cases where terrorism takes the form of violent insurgent activity – devoted to the violent overthrow of authority – that succeeds in creating a crisis which overshadows public order and destabilizes the government. In such cases, which are likely to have international repercussions, the potential danger posed by terrorism to regional and international peace and order also becomes clear. In this age of interdependence and globalization, the national and international dimensions of terrorism are but two facets of the same dangerous social phenomenon which infringes upon the interests of all States, not only as an assault against their public order and the institutions that protect the life, liberty, dignity and security of their citizens but, at the same time, as a serious danger to peaceful international relations and cooperation,[50] which in our day is clearly understood as encompassing also human rights and values.

These widely recognized prescriptions are characteristic of the general awareness within the international community of the increased role of terrorism as a catalyst for wider conflict. The involvement of States in mounting long-range terrorist activity may not only put at risk the constitutional order, the territorial integrity and the security of targeted States but may also have profound effects on regional and international balances, and jeopardize friendly relations and international peace and order.[51] International terrorism, then, evinces similar characteristics to those of terrorist acts and methods in the domestic context: arbitrariness, indiscriminateness in effects, non-recognition of any rules or conventions of war, inhumanity and barbaric cruelty.

In conclusion, there is an inescapable link between terrorism and human rights violations. Terrorism provides a severe test for the idea of fundamental rights. In this respect, it is worth recording that in all debates about the responsibilities of

49 See, for instance, N. N. Vohra, 'Democracy and management of terrorism', in G. N. Srivastava (ed.), *Democracy and Terrorism,* New Delhi: International Institute for Non-Aligned Studies, 1997, pp. 176-177; and see also International Association of Penal Law, International Society for Criminology, International Society for Social Defence and International Penal and Penitentiary Foundation, *Contribution to the Eighth United Nations Congress on the Prevention of Crime and the Treatment of Offenders (Havana, Cuba, 27 August-7 September 1990), on Effective National and International Action against: (a) Organized Crime; (b) Terrorist Criminal Activities* (Topic 3 on the Provisional Agenda), in particular the reports by C. Bassiouni, pp. 55 ff., and C. Barrantes, G. Picca, A. Beristain, pp. 76 ff.

50 See also R. H. Kupperman, D. M. Trent, *Terrorism: Threat, Reality, Response*, Stanford, California: Hoover Institution Press, 1979, pp. 140-141 and O. Schachter, *International Law in Theory and Practice*, Dordrecht: M. Nijhoff Publishers, 1991, p. 163.

51 See UN doc. E/CN.4/Sub.2/1999/27, para. 39.

governments to respond to terrorist activities within their territories, both those who argue in favour of more action against the terrorists and those who argue for limitations upon the governments' responses invoke notions of human rights in order to support their diametrically opposite claims.

Counter-terrorism measures and human rights: the necessity to uphold human rights and the rule of law in combating terrorism

Responding to the threat of terrorist actions is, as I have already said at the beginning of my presentation, a significant issue for States and the international community. There can be no doubt that every State has not only the right but also the duty to prevent and suppress crime, especially crime which by its nature, objectives, or the means employed for its commission, is considered or qualified as terrorist.[52] Furthermore, the international community should also equip itself with all the appropriate legal instruments and means that are necessary to fight this scourge.[53] There can equally be no doubt, however, that States and the international community have an obligation to perform their rights and duties within the limits of the rule of law,[54] respecting in particular the principles of international and criminal law, including international human rights and humanitarian law.[55] The responsibility of

---

52 See my Additional Progress Report on 'Terrorism and human rights' (UN doc. E/CN.4/Sub.2/2003/WP.1) para. 61. See also Human Rights Committee, *Preliminary Observations: Peru*, 25 July 1996, UN doc. CCPR/C/79/Add.67, para. 3, where the Committee affirmed the 'right and duty of the State party to take firm measures to protect its population against terror'. And see also J. J. Paust, 'The Link Between Human Rights and Terrorism and Its Implications for the Law of State Responsibility', *Hastings International and Comparative Law Review*, vol. 11, no. 1, 1987, pp. 53-54, and K. Bennoune, '"To Respect and to Ensure": Reconciling International Human Rights Obligations in a Time of Terror', *Proceedings of the American Society of International Law*, vol. 97, 2003, pp. 25-26.

53 UN doc. E/CN.4/Sub.2/2003/WP.1, para. 61. And see also the suggestions contained in the Report of the Secretary-General's High-level Panel on Threats, Challenges and Change, *supra* note 1, paras 149-156.

54 See, for instance, the *Digest of Jurisprudence of the United Nations and Regional Organizations on the Protection of Human Rights While Countering Terrorism*, compiled by the Office of the United Nations High Commissioner for Human Rights Geneva, New York and Geneva, 2003, pp. 12 ff., and the Report by the International Bar Association's Task Force on International Terrorism, *supra* note 1, pp. 53 ff. As the European Court of Human Rights has appropriately stated in *Klass and Others v. Germany* (Judgment of 6 September 1978, Series A no. 28, p. 23, para. 49): '[b]eing aware of the danger such a law poses of undermining or even destroying democracy on the ground of defending it, [the Court] affirms that the Contracting States may not, in the name of the struggle against espionage and terrorism, adopt whatever measures they deem appropriate.' See also text accompanying notes 41 and 42 in this chapter; the section headed 'Democratic society' above, and the sub-section headed 'The rule of law' later in this chapter.

55 UN doc. E/CN.4/Sub.2/2003/WP.1, para. 61.

State authorities to respect the limits of the rule of law is, unfortunately, all too often ignored by anti-terrorist legislation in the political climate generated by the fear of terrorism. In this context, it should be recalled, that not only the UN Commission on Human Rights but also the other competent organs and bodies of the United Nations system have repeatedly affirmed that all measures to counter terrorism must be in strict conformity with international law, including international human rights standards.[56]

There is a lot to be said about human rights and counter-terrorism in the framework of the United Nations, upon which focuses this last part of my presentation. Since time is running fast, however, I must confine myself to signalling only some basic human rights delimitations of counter-terrorism legislation and measures, underlining the need to refer on and apply human rights and the rule of law in all international and national instruments destined to combat terrorism. Before I do this, I must refer also to the work of the Security Council's Counter-Terrorism Committee, and to the efforts of the General Assembly and of the Commission on Human Rights to protect human rights and freedoms while countering terrorism.

The Security Council's Counter-Terrorism Committee

In the aftermath of 11 September 2001, most States have, in accordance with their obligations under Security Council Resolution 1373 of 28 September 2001 (adopted under Chapter VII of the UN Charter and, therefore, mandatory), revised their legislation regarding terrorism, either by amending the current laws or by drafting new ones, in order to address the emerging issues related to terrorism.

In very broad terms Resolution 1373 (2001)[57] requires States to attack the funding of terrorism and to deny support to, and prevent, terrorist acts. It also imposes on States the duties to deny safe haven to terrorists, to install effective border controls, to enact domestic counter-terrorism legislation, and to bring to justice those who commit terrorist acts. It further calls upon States to exchange information regarding terrorist actions, cooperate to prevent the commission of terrorist acts, and enter into the relevant international instruments relating to terrorism. Last but not least, this wide-ranging and far-reaching resolution established the Counter-Terrorism Committee (CTC) – a Committee, consisting of all the members of the Security Council – 'to monitor implementation of this resolution, with the assistance of appropriate expertise', and called upon all States to report to this Committee 'on the

---

56 See, for instance, GA Res. 58/174, of 22 December 2003, para. 7; Commission on Human Rights Res. 2004/44, of 19 April 2004, para. 5; Security Council Res. 1456 (2003), of 20 January 2003, adopting its declaration on the issue of combating terrorism, para. 6. And see also the *Digest of Jurisprudence of the United Nations and Regional Organizations on the Protection of Human Rights While Countering Terrorism*, note 53 *supra*, as well as the section headed 'The rule of law' below.

57 See also my Second Progress Report on 'Terrorism and human rights' (UN doc. E/CN.4/Sub.2/2002/35, of 17 July 2002) paras 25-29.

steps they have taken to implement this resolution'.[58] It is all well known that the CTC has played a most important role in beginning the long and critical process of building the anti-terrorism capacity of States.[59]

In my view, however, the most significant challenge still lying ahead of the performance and accomplishments of the CTC is its ability to help build also the capacity of States to protect and safeguard human rights while combating terrorism.[60] In other words (and from the human rights perspective), since upholding respect for human rights and the rule of law is imperative in countering terrorism, much of the CTC's future success in combating this scourge depends on its willingness to assist also in building the capacity of States to comply with their human rights obligations and the rule of law while strengthening their counter-terrorism legislation.

It is worth noting in this context, that the UN Office of the High Commissioner for Human Rights has exchanged views with the CTC and briefed it many times since its inception in 2001, with a view to working out an appropriate relationship and assisting it in its work with expert guidance in the area just mentioned.[61] Thus, for example, among its many efforts, particular mention should be made to a Note, entitled 'Proposals for "further guidance" for the submission of reports pursuant to paragraph 6 of Security Council Resolution 1373 (2001)' regarding 'Compliance with international human rights standards', which the High Commissioner for Human Rights submitted to the CTC, early in 2002.[62] These 'guidance' proposals were providing criteria for the balancing of human rights protection and the combating of terrorism, as well as specific instructions to the reporting States. A few months later, the High Commissioner submitted a further 'Note' to the Chair of the CTC, entitled 'A Human Rights Perspective On Counter-Terrorist Measures'.[63] This 'Note' was spelling out a number of key human rights principles (such as, legality, non-derogability, necessity and proportionality, non-discrimination, due process and rule of law, as well as the right to seek asylum and non-refoulement) for the CTC to

---

58 See UN Doc. S/RES/1373 (2001) para. 6.

59 See, for instance, J. E. Stromseth, 'The Security Council's Counter-Terrorism Role: Continuity and Innovation', *Proceedings of the American Society of International Law*, vol. 97, 2003, pp. 41 ff., as well as E. Rosand, 'Security Council Resolution 1373, the Counter-Terrorism Committee, and the Fight Against Terrorism', *American Journal of International Law*, vol. 97, 2003, pp. 333 ff.

60 Cf. Stromseth, pp. 44-45 and Rosand, p. 340, in note 59 *supra*.

61 See also *Digest of Jurisprudence of the United Nations and Regional Organizations on the Protection of Human Rights While Countering Terrorism*, *supra* note 53, p. 5.

62 The 'further guidance' proposals were included in the High Commissioner's Report entitled 'Human rights: a uniting framework', submitted to the Commission on Human Rights at its fifty-eighth session (UN Doc. E/CN.4/2002/18, of 27 February 2002, Annex).

63 The 'Note to the Chair of the Counter-Terrorism Committee: A Human Rights Perspective On Counter-Terrorist Measures' was presented by the then High Commissioner Mary Robinson to Ambassador Jeremy Greenstock (then CTC Chairperson) on 9 September 2002, in New York. It is available on the CTC website at: http://www.un.org/ docs/sc/ committees/1373/ohchr1.htm.

have continually in view in the pursuit of its struggle against terrorism. It was also suggesting a non-exhaustive list of questions applicable to all States, which could assist the CTC in assessing States' replies on their counter-terrorism action in the light of the above key principles.

For the rest, the ongoing dialogue between the CTC and the Office of the High Commissioner for Human Rights, consisting in its largest part of the regular updates submitted by the latter to the Chair of the CTC on the relevant conclusions and observations of the various UN human rights treaty bodies and special procedures, still leaves much to be desired. While welcoming dialogue with the Office of the High Commissioner for Human Rights, the CTC has been unwilling to take into consideration the human rights dimension of counter-terrorism measures in its review of State reports.[64] This review, done with the assistance of expertise coming from multiple areas, such as legislative drafting, financial law, immigration law, extradition law, police and law enforcement measures, as well as illegal arms trafficking,[65] does not include human rights expertise, even though several of these areas have a strong human rights dimension.[66] It is, therefore, expedient and not just desirable that the Counter-Terrorism Committee includes human rights expertise among the expertise it already has at its disposal.[67]

The General Assembly and the Commission on Human Rights

The danger to human rights in countering terrorism – which one has seen in many situations in our post-11 September 2001 era – has naturally alerted and troubled, over the past few years, not only the human rights organizations and all those who work to promote and protect human rights, but also the General Assembly's Third Committee, as well as the UN Commission on Human Rights.

Following an unsuccessful attempt during the fifty-eighth session of the Commission on Human Rights, in 2002, to adopt a Mexican draft resolution, entitled 'Protection of human rights in countering terrorism' – a text primarily drafted by

---

64 See Jeremy Greenstock, Address at the Symposium on Combating International Terrorism: The Contribution of the United Nations (June 3-4, 2002), pp. 3-4, available at http://www.un.org/Docs/sc/committees/1373/ViennaNotes.htm. See also 'Human Rights Committee Briefed on Work of the Counter-Terrorism Committee', United Nations Press Release, 28 March 2003, available at http://www.unhchr.ch/huricane/huricane.nsf/view01/FFB9934C2667CC3FC1256CF7.

65 See http://www.un.org/Docs/sc/committees/1373work.html.

66 See the Address by Bacre Ndiaye, Director of the New York Office of the High Commissioner for Human Rights to the Counter-Terrorism Committee of the Security Council, 11 December 2001, at p. 3.

67 As of this writing, more recent information received at the OHCHR (September 2004) from the newly-created Counter-Terrorism Committee Executive Directorate (CTED) has indicated that it is the intention of the new Executive Director, Javier Rupérez, to include among his staff an expert on human rights, humanitarian law and refugee law. See UN doc. A/59/428, of 8 October 2004.

NGOs, which would have the Commission appoint a Special Rapporteur for that topic – the issue was again promoted by Mexico a few months later – successfully this time – at the level of the Third Committee of the General Assembly, at its fifty-seventh session.[68] The new Mexican draft resolution, entitled 'Protection of Human Rights and Fundamental Freedoms while Countering Terrorism' was finally adopted by the General Assembly without a vote.[69] As to its content, this resolution affirmed, among other things, that States must ensure that any measure taken to combat terrorism complies with their obligations under international law, in particular international human rights, refugee and humanitarian law. It did not provide for the appointment of a Special Rapporteur but requested the High Commissioner for Human Rights to take a number of actions, including (a) examining the question of the protection of human rights and fundamental freedoms while countering terrorism, taking into account reliable information from all sources; (b) making general recommendations concerning the obligation of States to promote and protect human rights and fundamental freedoms while taking actions to counter terrorism; and (c) providing assistance and advice to States, upon their request, on the matter.[70]

As expected, the Commission of Human Rights immediately followed suit to this action by the General Assembly. At its fifty-ninth session, in 2003, it adopted for the first time a resolution with similar approach,[71] and continued in the same direction during its 2004 session.[72] So, there are already a number of resolutions on 'Protection of human rights and fundamental freedoms while countering terrorism', adopted by both the Commission on Human Rights and the General Assembly on a yearly basis.[73] Regarding the most recent Commission on Human Rights resolution on the subject, it is significant to note in particular the inclusion of a new provision, whereby the Commission decides to designate for the period of one year an 'independent expert' to assist the High Commissioner in the fulfilment of the mandate provided for in the resolution, and 'to submit a report, through the High Commissioner', to the Commission at its 2005 session 'on ways and means

---

68 See UN doc. A/C.3/57/L.61, of 12 November 2002. The adoption without a vote by the Third Committee of this draft resolution in the morning of 21 November 2002 was immediately acclaimed by Amnesty International and Human Rights Watch in their joint statement of the same date, in New York, entitled 'Battle for human rights in fight against terrorism one step forward', which stated, among other things, that it was the 'first step towards making sure that human rights do not become another victim of terrorism' and that '[i]f terrorism is to be successfully defeated, states must put the protection of human rights first'.

69 See GA Res. 57/219, of 18 December 2002 (UN doc. A/RES/ 57/219).

70 See para. 3.

71 See resolution 2003/68, of 25 April 2003 (UN doc. E/CN.4/RES/2003/68).

72 See resolution 2004/87, of 21 April 2004 (UN doc. E/CN.4/RES/2003/87).

73 The subsequent to GA Res. 57/219, of 18 December 2002, on 'Protection of human rights and fundamental freedoms while countering terrorism' (A/RES/57/219, of 18 December 2002) are: A/RES/58/187 of 22 December 2003; and, as of this writing, A/RES/59/191, of 20 December 2004.

of strengthening the promotion and protection of human rights and fundamental freedoms while countering terrorism'.[74] This important development is already indicative of the considerable pressure put upon the Commission, over the past two years, by human rights organizations and a number of governments, to have it finally agreed to adopt a special procedure to deal with the issue of human rights and counter-terrorism.

In this very context, it is worth noting also the position taken by the Commission's subsidiary body, the Sub-Commission on the Promotion and Protection of Human Rights, after the failure of the Commission in the years 2002 and 2003, to appoint a Special Rapporteur, or create some other special procedure regarding the issue of human rights and counter-terrorism. At its fifty-fifth session, in 2003, the Sub-Commission, approved without a vote a new resolution entitled 'Effects of measures to combat terrorism on the enjoyment of human rights',[75] in which it decided, among other things, to study the compatibility of counter-terrorism measures adopted after 11 September 2001, with international human rights standards, giving particular attention to their impact on the most vulnerable groups, with a view to elaborating detailed guidelines.[76]

For completeness, a word about all the other mechanisms and procedures created by the Commission on Human Rights. Referring to them collectively here, all I need is underline the fact that in the past few years they have attached particular attention to the issue of human rights and counter-terrorism, within their respective mandates, and also that they have taken collective positions as well on the impact of counter-terrorism measures on human rights.

The necessary human rights delimitations of counter-terrorism legislation and measures

I will now end my presentation by going into some necessary human rights delimitations of counter-terrorism legislation and measures, underscoring also the imperative need to refer on and apply the rule of law in all international and national instruments destined to combat terrorism.

---

74 See para. 10 of Commission Res. 2004/87, note 72 *supra*. As of this writing, Professor Robert Goldman (US) has been appointed by the Chair of the Commission as the independent expert.

75 See Sub-Commission Resolution 2003/15, of 13 August 2003.

76 *Ibid.*, paras 5 and 6. At the time of this writing, the new development is that the Sub-Commission, in August 2004, decided to establish at its fifty-seventh session (2005) a working group of the Sub-Commission with the mandate to elaborate detailed principles and guidelines, with relevant commentary, concerning the promotion and protection of human rights when combating terrorism. See Sub-Commission decision 2004/109, of 12 August 2004, and my Working Paper entitled 'A preliminary framework draft of principles and guidelines concerning human rights and terrorism'(UN doc. E/CN.4/Sub.2/2004/47, of 11 August 2004).

Everyone is aware that one of the most disturbing aspects of post-11 September 2001 national legislations and/or administrations of laws to combat terrorism is the establishment of legal definitions of the crime of terrorism or of terrorist acts, which can lead to the criminalization of legitimate or lawful behaviour under international law, especially as regards the exercise of fundamental rights and freedoms.[77] For example, there are certain domestic laws which actually or potentially conflict with the exercise of the right to take part in the conduct of public affairs, the right to strike, as well as freedom of expression, association and information. Further, there are definitions of terrorism which directly criminalize legitimate forms of political, ideological and social opposition, as well as definitions which simply disregard the basic principle *nullum crimen sine lege*,[78] by being either too wide and/or of such an ambiguous and imprecise nature that they leave space for the eventual criminalization of activities falling within the legitimate exercise of fundamental rights and freedoms, such as the right to freedom of assembly and of association, certain modalities of the right to strike, and other activities that fall within the legitimate exercise of trade unionism.

Of course, the phenomenon is not all that new, or only post-11 September 2001. The UN human rights system, the European Court of Human Rights, the Inter-American Commission on Human Rights, and other regional institutions have already, on several occasions in the past, dealt with issues such as the relationship between freedom of expression and terrorism, the principles of legality, presumption of innocence, and so on, in the context of anti-terrorist laws and other norms and standards of behaviour, in relation to the prosecution of persons charged for terrorism.[79] Suffice it to mention, in this context, one only important example, which is General Comment No. 29 of the Human Rights Committee, on states of emergency, issued in July 2001.[80]

Since the abhorrent turning point of 11 September 2001, however, the scale (or degree) and variety of the measures taken, which violate basic human rights and freedoms in the name of the globalized campaign against terrorism, have risen to such unprecedented dimensions as to make the difference. While concern has been growing worldwide about the 'war on terrorism' being used as a pretext for the suppression of legitimate expressions of dissent and the limitations of fundamental rights and freedoms, there is also growing general recognition worldwide that human rights cannot be set aside in striving to achieve security. Moreover, there seems to be now general worldwide consensus that violating human rights as part of the 'war on terrorism' is counter-productive, since counter-terrorism measures

---

77 See my Additional Progress Report (UN doc. E/CN.4/2003/WP.1), paras 73 ff.

78 See extensively *ibid.*, paras 62-67.

79 For some examples of relevant jurisprudence and commentary, see *ibid.*, paras 73-79.

80 See General Comment No. 29 on states of emergency (article 4 of the International Covenant on Civil and Political Rights), adopted by the Committee on 24 July 2001 (UN doc. CCPR/C/21/Rev.1/Add.11).

and legislation that fall outside the framework of the rule of law and democratic principles effectively roll back well-established norms and lay the foundations for terrorism and further insecurity.[81]

It is vital, therefore, that States' counter-terrorist legislation and measures take account of human rights and fundamental freedoms and States' international and domestic obligations in that regard. The big question, however, which still begs the answer, is how to strike the much-needed balance in accommodating the control of terrorism and the guarantee of national and international security with the protection and respect of human rights and the rule of law.

As already underscored, terrorism affects the full enjoyment of human rights and it is the duty of States to protect their citizens against this scourge. This implies, further, that the emphasis is put, in the first place, on the national (or domestic) prevention and suppression of the crime of terrorism. In the second place, that the temptation of the responsible government authorities to use their arsenal of legal weapons against terrorism indiscriminately; that is, in disregard of the general principle of legality and of the rule of law, and in violation of their international human rights obligations under customary and treaty norms and standards, triggers their international responsibility, and engages the existing mechanisms of monitoring compliance of their action with international human rights norms and standards. This said, what then are the limits of human rights and freedoms that States should not go beyond in combating terrorism? These limits (or human rights delimitations) are now examined.

The rule of law   In the words of the Universal Declaration of Human Rights, which makes preambular reference to the rule of law, 'it is essential, if man is not to be compelled to have recourse, as a last resort, to rebellion against tyranny and oppression, that human rights should be protected by the rule of law'.[82] Indeed, the general principle of the rule of law means that all persons are equal before the law, and that acts of government officials are cognizable in the ordinary courts of law; it means the supremacy of law for both the government and the governed.[83] The laws to which governments are bound are their domestic laws, as well as those international laws that have either become customary international law or those to which the government of that State has voluntarily chosen to become bound,

---

81   See Office for Democratic Institutions and Human Rights (ODIHR), 'Preventing and Combating Terrorism: The New Security Environment', Food for Thought Paper prepared for the 2nd OSCE Annual Security Review Conference, Vienna 23-24 June 2004, p. 4 (OSCE doc. ODIHR.GAL/43/04, of 22 June 2004).

82   See GA Res. 217 A (III), of 10 December 1948, preamble para. 3.

83   See, for instance, *Mozley and Whiteley's Law Dictionary*, 7th edition by J. B. Saunders, London, Butterworths, 1962, p. 329, and W. Friedmann, *Legal Theory*, 5th edition, London: Stevens & Sons, 1967, pp. 422 ff.

including international human rights treaties, refugee and humanitarian law and the UN Charter.[84]

The importance of the rule of law, at the national level, and the obligation of the government authorities to act within the limits of human rights and freedoms, has been recognized and consecrated in the constitutions of most States. At the international level, the obligation of States to act in conformity with international law, and in particular international human rights law, is recognized in several global, as well as regional conventions,[85] including some of the anti-terrorism conventions.[86] It is also consecrated in customary international law,[87] in several resolutions of the Security Council, the General Assembly and other UN human rights organs and bodies, as already mentioned.[88] The acceptance, therefore, of the limitations imposed upon the Sates by international law when combating terrorism is acceptance of the primacy (or supremacy) of the rule of law.

Derogation and states of emergency It should, further, be emphasized that international law takes into account situations in which national security is threatened – and we all know that terrorism can lead to such a situation – so, it allows States to declare a state of emergency in the given specific situation. During a state of emergency threatening the life of the nation, States may derogate from certain human rights guarantees subject, however, to specific limitations and procedural requirements strictly necessitated by the situation.[89] Rules regarding issues such as the necessity, duration scope, and manner of implementation of states of emergency

---

84 See Advisory Council of Jurists, 'Reference on the rule of law in combating terrorism', Draft Preliminary Report submitted by Justice Glazebrook, Asia Pacific Forum of National Human Rights Institutions, 2003, p. 46.

85 See, generally, *Digest of Jurisprudence of the United Nations and Regional Organizations on the Protection of Human Rights While Countering Terrorism*, note 53 *supra*.

86 See, for example, the International Convention against the Taking of Hostages (1979), preamble para. 2, which recognizes 'in particular that everyone has the right to life, liberty and security of person, as set out in the Universal Declaration of Human Rights and the International Covenant on Civil and Political Rights', and the International Convention for the Suppression of Terrorist Bombings (1997), Article 19, which stipulates that nothing in that convention 'shall affect other rights, obligations and responsibilities of States and individuals under international law, in particular the purposes and principles of the Charter of the United Nations and international humanitarian law'.

87 See, for instance the Report by the International Bar Association's Task Force on International Terrorism, *supra* note 2, p. 56, referring also to Article 38, para. 1 (b) of the Statute of the ICJ.

88 See, for instance, note 56 *supra* and accompanying text.

89 See, in general, J. Oraa, *Human Rights in States of Emergency in International Law*, Oxford: Clarendon Press, 1992; J. Fitzpatrick, *Human Rights in Conflict: the International System for Protecting Human Rights during States of Emergency*, Philadelphia: University of Pennsylvania Press, 1994.

and accompanying derogations exist in both the global and the regional systems.[90] Nonetheless, international law has also established a number of human rights that are non-derogable under any circumstances, meaning human rights that can never be suspended or restricted, not even in times of emergency.[91] Although the list of non-derogable human rights is not always identical in universal and regional instruments, a number of rights are non-derogable in both systems – thus, for example, the right not to be arbitrarily deprived of life, the right to freedom from torture and other cruel, inhuman or degrading treatment and the prohibitions on retrospective laws.[92]

Rights subject to restrictions   Additional human rights guarantees, which are particularly relevant to our discussion on how to strike the balance between the State's duty to ensure public security and protection of the lives of its citizens, on the one hand, and its duty to uphold and protect basic democratic values and the respect for human rights and freedoms, on the other, exist with regard to most individual rights that the fight against terrorism puts under pressure, or at risk,[93] through excessive restrictions or limitations which may erode the basic values they seek to protect. Special attention should be drawn, in this context, to rights and liberties such as, for example, the right to privacy, freedom of expression, freedom of assembly and association, freedom of movement, and other important clusters of rights associated with detention, due process or fair trial, penalties, the position of refugees, and so forth. [94]

As a matter of fact, most human rights and freedoms can be subject to restrictions or limitations in both national (or domestic) and in international law. In general terms, the reason for restricting or limiting human rights and freedoms is the need to accommodate and/or reconcile them with the comparable rights and freedoms of the others and of the community at large.[95] In this connection, States will normally restrict

---

90   See, generally, R. Higgins, 'Derogations Under Human Rights Treaties', British Yearbook of International Law, vol. 48, 1976-77, pp. 281 ff. And see also, the Report by the International Bar Association's Task Force on International Terrorism, supra note 2, pp. 54-55.

91   See, generally, *Digest of Jurisprudence of the United Nations and Regional Organizations on the Protection of Human Rights While Countering Terrorism*, note 53 *supra*, pp. 17 ff.

92   Ibid. See also Article 4, para. 2, of the International Covenant of Civil and Political Rights, as well as the Human Rights Committee's General Comment No. 29, note 80 supra; Article 15, para. 2, of the European Convention on Human Rights; and Article 27, para. 2, of the American Convention on Human Rights.

93   See, for instance, the ODIHR doc. on 'Preventing and Combating Terrorism: The New Security Environment', note 81 *supra*, p. 4.

94   See, extensively, the *Report by the International Bar Association's Task Force on International Terrorism*, supra note 2, pp. 66 ff., and the *Digest of Jurisprudence of the United Nations and Regional Organizations on the Protection of Human Rights While Countering Terrorism*, note 54 *supra*, pp. 39 ff. for relevant jurisprudence.

95   See, for instance, Higgins, note 90 *supra*, at pp. 281-282 and notes 4 and 5.

and delineate most human rights and freedoms – even in the absence of an emergency situation – provided, however, that the imposed restrictions and delineations do not go beyond the degree necessary in a democratic society and the limits set by customary international law and/or the relevant human rights instruments. All major human rights instruments thus provide for restrictions or limitations of rights and liberties, in order to meet, for instance, requirements such as public health, morals, public order, the rights of others, the general welfare in a democratic society, and so on.[96] In the battle against terrorism, the risk of abusing these 'built-in limitations'[97] in most human rights is all the greater because of the combined pressure of terrorist threats and public opinion, which can precipitate the adoption of legislation and measures transgressing the limits mentioned above. Moreover, when combating terrorism, the risk of abusing these 'built-in limitations' and, consequently, eroding or undermining most rights and liberties (which fall into this broad category of 'non-absolute'[98] or 'conditional'[99] rights) are enhanced by the still inadequate international scrutiny and review (meaning, international and regional monitoring) in the current institutional development of the international community.

International human rights standards   Finally, there is an abundance of relevant internationally recognized human rights standards set out in various non-treaty international instruments, including the Universal Declaration of Human Rights,[100] which must also be taken into account when taking legislative and other measures against terrorism. These international standards of human rights, which provide both substantive protection and procedural guarantees, can also come under threat when fighting against terrorism.[101] These are standards usually adopted by the United Nations and other international or regional organizations and bodies, by way

---

96 See, for instance, Articles 12, para. 3 (freedom of movement) and 19, para. 3 (freedom of expression) of the International Covenant of Civil and Political Rights that are subject to restrictions which are provided by the law and are necessary to protect, among other things, 'public health', 'morals' and 'the rights of others'. And see also Article 4 of the International Covenant on Economic, Social and Cultural Rights: '[t]he State may subject such rights only to such limitations as are determined by law only in so far as this may be compatible with the nature of these rights and solely for the purpose of promoting the general welfare in a democratic society.'

97 L. Doswald-Beck, 'Human Security: Can It Be Attained?', *Proceedings of the American Society of International Law*, vol. 97, 2003, p. 96.

98 See, for instance, R. P. Claude and B. H. Weston (eds), *Human Rights in the World Community: Issues and Action*, 2nd edition, Philadelphia: University of Pennsylvania Press, 1992, p. 18.

99 See, for instance, F. Sudre, *Droit international et européen des droits de l'homme*, Paris: Presses Universitaires de France, 1989, p. 143.

100 See also the *Report by the International Bar Association's Task Force on International Terrorism, supra* note 2, p. 57 note 21.

101 *Ibid.*, p. 58.

of declarations,[102] resolutions,[103] codes of conduct,[104] minimum rules,[105] principles and guidelines,[106] and other non-binding or 'soft law' instruments.[107] Alongside compliance with 'hard' international law, addressing and assessing the legality of counter-terrorism measures in light of internationally recognized human rights standards is also extremely valuable in the quest to achieve the much-sought after, delicate balance between firmly countering terrorism and upholding human rights; between safeguarding security and protecting freedom while combating terrorism.

In conclusion, while it cannot be overemphasized that all States have the right to defend themselves against terrorism, and to take the necessary measures to guarantee their security and integrity – including the right to incriminate behaviours that threaten their security and integrity – in so doing, they must fully respect and conform with international law, including international human rights law and other relevant international norms, principles, and generally recognized standards.

---

102 See, for example, the Declaration of Basic Principles of Justice for Victims of Crime and Abuse of Power, adopted by the General Assembly in 1985.

103 For example, the Universal Declaration of Human Rights was adopted by GA Res. 217 A (III), of 10 December 1948; see also the GA Res. on UN Rules for the Protection of Juveniles Deprived of their Liberty, adopted in 1990.

104 For example, the Code of Conduct for Law Enforcement Officials, adopted by the General Assembly in 1979.

105 For example, the Standard Minimum Rules for the Administration of Juvenile Justice (the 'Beijing Rules') adopted by the General Assembly in 1985; the European Prison Rules, adopted by the Council of Europe Committee of Ministers in 1987.

106 For example, the Body of Principles for the Protection of All Persons under Any Form of Detention or Imprisonment, adopted by the UN General Assembly in 1988; the Basic Principles on the Role of Lawyers, and the Guidelines on the Role of the Prosecutors, adopted at the Eighth UN Congress on the Prevention of Crime and the Treatment of Offenders in 1990; the Guidelines on Human Rights and the Fight Against Terrorism, adopted by the Council of Europe Committee of Ministers in 2002.

107 See further examples in the Report by the International Bar Association's Task Force on International Terrorism, *supra* note 2, p. 57 note 21.

Chapter 5

The Security Council's Role: Problems and Prospects in the Fight Against Terrorism

ALEXANDER MARSCHIK[1]

Proposals to substantially involve the United Nations in the fight against terrorism were initially greeted with much scepticism. Many Member States and experts within the UN Secretariat doubted that the global organization could provide significant added value.[2] Today, however, the UN's Security Council is recognized as the main international coordinating body and a driving force in the field of multilateral counter-terrorism. In the words of the former Chairman of the Council's Counter-Terrorism Committee, Sir Jeremy Greenstock, counter-terrorism has 'gone global, with the United Nations at the centre'.[3] Before becoming Foreign Minister, Sergei Lavrov stated (as Russia's Ambassador to the UN) that the Counter Terrorism Committee 'remains the leading element in the global anti-terrorist architecture'.[4]

This chapter will examine whether the Security Council has been able to live up to these expectations in practice. The legal and practical problems that have arisen in the last three years will be analysed to identify the areas that need to be addressed urgently by the UN's Member States to remedy existing problems and to improve the prospects of the Security Council's future role in the field of counter-terrorism.

---

1   Deputy Permanent Representative of Austria to the United Nations in New York. These remarks are made in a personal capacity and do not necessarily reflect the views of the Austrian Ministry of Foreign Affairs.

2   In October 2001 Secretary General Kofi Annan established a Policy Working Group on the United Nations and Terrorism. The Group eventually recommended a supplementary role for the UN in the fight against terrorism with three key functions: dissuade potential terrorists from embracing terrorism, deny them the means to commit terrorist acts and sustain international cooperation; Report of the Policy Working Group; Document A/57/273, S/2002/875, para 9.

3   4734th Meeting of the Security Council, on 4 April 2003; S/PV.4734 (provisional), p. 3. A month later, referring to the global coalition that had been established, Greenstock emphasized 'how uniquely placed the United Nations is to support and facilitate a global approach of that kind.'; 4752nd Meeting of the SC on 6 May 2003; S/PV.4752 (provisional), p. 5.

4   4752nd Meeting of the SC on 6 May 2003; S/PV.4752 (provisional), p. 9.

Institutional framework

In the context of this article a description of the existing counter-terrorism architecture of the UN is not necessary. It is enough to only briefly mention the two central counter-terrorism regimes of the Security Council:[5]

- The *1373 regime*, based on SC Res. 1373 (2001) of 28 September 2001, is aimed at capacity building within States and in international, regional and specialized organizations, with emphasis on terrorist financing. It requires the enactment of national counter-terrorism legislation, the freezing of assets of persons involved in terrorist activities and intensified international cooperation to prevent counter-terrorism. Implementation is monitored by a special sub-organ of the Security Council, the Counter-Terrorism Committee (CTC).
- The *1267 regime*, based on SC Res. 1267 (1999) of 15 October 1999, evolved out of sanctions against the Taliban and members of Al Qaeda and has been amended several times over the last few years. Today it relies on specific sanctions (arms embargo, travel ban, freezing of funds) directed against individuals and entities enumerated on a comprehensive list. The implementation of the regime is monitored by the 1267 Committee or 'Al Qaeda and Taliban Sanctions Committee'.

Though both are sub-organs of the Council, the regimes have different goals, structures and working methods. They are complemented by other resolutions, such as the recent SC Res. 1540[6] regarding non-proliferation of weapons of mass destruction and the prevention of their appropriation by non-state actors, especially terrorists, and they rely on the assistance of the UN Secretariat in fulfilling their mandate, for example the Terrorism Prevention Branch of the United Nations' Office for Drugs and Crime (ODC).

Both counter-terrorism regimes are confronted with many difficulties in their work. Some problems are practical, others political, legal or technical. Some originate directly from the resolutions (such as non-executable provisions, false assumptions, unrealistic goals, etc.), others result from the broader UN system (structural and institutional problems, policy implications, working methods, etc.).

---

5 See in detail E. Rosand, 'Security Council Resolution 1373, The Counter-Terrorism Committee, and the Fight against Terrorism', *American Journal of International Law*, vol. 97, 2003, p. 333; A. Marschik, 'The United Nations' Response to International Terrorism', in W.P. Heere (ed.), *From Government to Governance – The Growing Impact of Non-State Actors on the International and European System,* The Hague: TMC Asser Press, 2004, p. 301 ff. at p. 303.

6 SC Res. 1540 (2004) of 28 April 2004.

Problems originating in the Security Council Resolutions

Technical and practical problems of the 1373 regime

A report by the CTC Chairman identified the following inherent problems in SC Res. 1373:[7]

- Some States lack administrative or judicial institutions and procedures to implement an effective 'freezing of funds'.
- The monitoring of activities and financial assets and transactions of non-profit organizations in today's interconnected world is extremely difficult.
- The surge in ratifications of the Counter-terrorism Conventions after 2001 as a consequence of Resolution 1373's call on States to become parties to them did not result in adequate implementation of the Treaties on a national level.
- The lack of a definition of terrorism creates practical problems in implementing the resolution. The different interpretations of the scope and nature of terrorism has resulted in discrepancies in national legislations and regional anti-terrorism treaties, as well as in problems in the international cooperation in the fight against terrorism.

Technical and practical problems of the 1267 regime

Examples of problems arising directly out of SC Res. 1267 have been identified by a subsidiary body of the 1267 Committee, the Monitoring Group established by SC Res. 1363:[8]

- The arms embargo fails to achieve its purpose because it cannot be successfully implemented by national authorities. The experience of administrating UN embargoes against States are inapplicable to an embargo against individuals and private entities.
- The regime has no provisions to identify and deal with the new financing systems that Al Qaeda has developed to circumvent the controls established against the original financing methods.
- Without the minimum required identifiers (name, date and place of birth, nationality, etc), the 1267 list cannot be effectively used to implement the travel ban against the persons contained in the list by many States. In particular, Member States of the European Union that are parties to the Schengen Agreement have difficulties implementing the travel ban: the Schengen system envisages travel between States without border controls.

---

7 S/2004/70.
8 See the first three reports by the Group: First Report S/2002/541 of 29 April 2002; Second Report S/2002/1050 Rev. 1 of 8 January 2003; Third Report S/2002/1338 of 4 December 2002.

The 1267 regime requires the prohibition of travel from listed individuals from one State to another and this implies controls at all borders.[9]

Effects on human rights

Since their inception, the regimes' effects on human rights were at the forefront of concern. The main focus regarding SC Res. 1373 was the potential misuse of the abstract obligations to target individuals for political reasons and thereby infringing the rights of the individuals. NGOs, UN agencies and many States have requested the CTC to ensure protection of human rights, for instance, by appointing a human rights expert. The CTC repeatedly opposed this institutionalization of the monitoring of adherence to human rights obligations within the system, arguing that this function falls outside the mandate of the Committee. The Security Council included references to human rights in its later resolutions and reminded States of the need to respect their human rights obligations while applying counter-terrorism measures. This did not, however, address the concerns regarding the work of the Council itself. Even after the eventual creation of the position of Human Rights Expert within the CTC, doubts remained mainly because its mandate is far from clear.

Most concerns arose in connection with the 1267 regime, especially as regards the lack of the right to appeal decisions to include individuals and entities on the Committee's comprehensive list. Whenever the 1267 Committee places a person or an entity on its list, States are obliged to enact the sanctions against them. There are no procedural safeguards or rights to appeal the inclusion in the list by the person or entity concerned. Article 103 of the UN Charter ensures the primacy of UN law over any other international agreement. States thus could not grant due process and procedural rights of appeal to persons and entities in their jurisdiction, even if this is foreseen in their constitutional law or human rights treaties they have ratified. Under increasing public pressure the 1267 Committee adopted a 'de-listing procedure' in 2002, enabling States of residence or citizenship to request the review of the inclusion on the comprehensive list.[10] Dependent not only on the will of the requesting State but also on the will of the 1267 Committee, this procedure hardly qualifies as an improvement of the rights of the individual or entity. In particular it does not resolve the lack of legal remedies for persons whose rights a State – for whatever reason – chooses not to take up and present to the Committee. This problem can affect

---

9   The lack of a definition of terrorism does not constitute a practical problem for the 1267 regime because in that regime the Security Council decides authoritatively to which persons it is applicable. There is no need for States to determine for themselves whether the activity a person or entity is involved with is, in fact, terrorism.

10   The procedure is limited to consultations between the State asking for review and the State that had demanded the inclusion on the list. Should they not agree on a joint de-listing request, the applying State may request the de-listing alone. The decision in the CTC is taken unanimously (no-objection procedure). Should an objection be raised, the Security Council takes up the issue, which gives the five permanent members the means to veto any decision not to their liking.

dissidents or members of the political opposition, against whom a State may even welcome the possibility of implementing sanctions 'under a UN obligation'.

Another problem arose from the unspecified duty to freeze the financial assets of the individuals on the list. If all assets were frozen, the individuals would be unable to meet their primary needs. States granting material aid for persons in this situation under domestic law found themselves in violation of the 1267 regime. Later, SC Res. 1452 permitted States to make an exception for basic expenses after notification to the 1267 Committee and in the absence of a negative decision by the Committee. While this is undoubtedly an improvement, a State whose constitution obliges it to provide support could still find itself in a quandary should its notification lead to a negative decision by the 1267 Committee. Practice shows, however, that the problem is currently not significant. Since the adoption of SC Res. 1452 only two applications for exceptions were made and both were granted.

Misuse of the Resolutions

A major concern repeatedly raised by Secretary General Kofi Annan and by several UN Member States, as well as NGOs, is the potential to misuse the resolutions for political reasons. The main focus here is SC Res. 1373, which, since it is abstract, leaves significant freedom of interpretation and application, if not manipulation, to States. There is a clear danger that the activities of minorities, suppressed ethnic groups and other domestic 'trouble-makers' are branded as 'terrorist acts'. In the absence of any oversight-procedures to prevent or challenge acts of misuse the 1373 regime relies exclusively on political restraint by the States and the vigilance of other States, NGOs, the media and UN institutions.

Though to a minor degree, the 1267 regime can also be misused: States can allege terrorist connections in respect to some individual and request they be put on the 1267 list. If the Security Council Members agree (and practice shows that requests for listing are rarely questioned) the individuals will be incorporated in the list. The *de facto* non-existence of legal remedies against this decision has been explained above.

Problems originating in the UN system

Capacity to monitor implementation of Security Council Resolutions

Inadequate implementation of decisions by the Security Council is a central problem of the UN system. The lack of resources at the UN, archaic working methods and structures all but guarantee that implementation will not be monitored by the organization. As a consequence, the Council mainly relies on self-monitoring by the States in the form of reports on the domestic implementation of the resolutions. Effective monitoring thus requires rapid, full and honest cooperation by the States, a phenomenon, which – due to the absence of enforcement – is not always the norm at the UN.[11] In practice, compliance has therefore become more or less optional. Unless one of the permanent five Security Council Members (P5) brings a case of non-compliance to the attention of the Council and pursues the case, even mandatory sanctions under Chapter VII of the UN Charter are fulfilled only if the States so choose.

In the field of counter-terrorism, the Security Council also relies on reporting obligations. Though these have primarily resulted in impressive amounts of paper (by mid-2004 over 500 reports had been submitted), it is noteworthy that the 1373 regime is the sanctions regime in the history of the UN that has received the most cooperation from the Member States.[12] This may seem an irrelevant statistic. Nevertheless, the States' willingness to engage in a continuous and comprehensive follow-up process demonstrates a genuine commitment to cooperate on counter-terrorism issues with the Security Council in the framework of the 1373 regime.[13]

Against this background, the few States that still inadequately implement the obligations contained in SC Res. 1373 domestically are a particularly vexing problem. The Security Council is aware that, after nearly three years, the 1373 regime has reached a critical stage in which the discrepancy, in some States, between the reporting of the adoption of national measures and the actual application of these measures must be addressed. Any enforcement measures by the Council, however, require sound, unbiased and professional monitoring to ensure that any enforcement action will subsequently be deemed appropriate, fair and legitimate. Aware of the structural difficulties of the UN in this regard, the Council has tried to improve its monitoring capabilities: SC Res. 1535 of 26 March 2004 established a more professional structure for the 1373 regime. The CTC is now assisted by an Executive Directorate (CTED), which takes up the operational work of the Committee, in particular monitoring implementation and capacity building. The resolution recognizes the need to inspect a State in view of its implementation of the resolution, but only with the consent of the State. While this reform will undoubtedly

---

11 Some States falsely claim they are fulfilling their obligations without fear of retribution. Others admit non-compliance and blame the complexities of politics or the lack of resources.

12 By the end of May 2003, roughly 18 months after its creation, all 191 UN Member States had submitted a first report. It was the first time that a sanctions regime had achieved 100 per cent reporting response. The reasons for this unprecedented cooperation are discussed in greater detail elsewhere in this book. It should be pointed out, however, that the Member States cooperate because they see a real need to do so to achieve success, together, in the fight against terrorism and they are, on the whole, not unsatisfied with the approach adopted by the CTC, the individualized capacity building based on a bilateral dialogue between the CTC and each Member State.

13 This sustained commitment is the unique achievement of the CTC. It has resulted in a significant effort on the part of the States to improve their capacity to prevent and fight terrorism. At the same time the CTC has collected a considerable amount of information on measures being undertaken against terrorism and it is busy in sharing this information and its expertise with other regional and specialized organizations around the world.

lead to more professionalism in monitoring, time will tell whether the new tools will be effective and can be implemented against uncooperative States.

The 1267 regime initially took a different approach. The task to monitor the implementation of the sanctions was entrusted to a body of experts, the 'Monitoring Group' established by SC Res. 1363, which consulted with relevant national authorities and international institutions. The Group published reports on the impact of the sanctions on Al Qaeda, inadequacies of the resolutions and instances of non-compliance by Member States. By the end of 2002, the Group reported, more than 160 States had adopted measures under the UN's counter-terrorism regimes.[14] In 2003 the 1267 regime shifted the emphasis from the – sometimes controversial – reports of the Monitoring Group to self-reporting by Member States. In this respect, compared to the 1373 regime, the level of cooperation of States with the Al Qaeda and Taliban Committee corresponds more to the norm at the UN: in April 2004 a total of 123 reports had been submitted.

The 1267 Committee investigated the reasons why States reported to a lesser degree in its regime than in the 1373 regime and found the following reasons: lack of political will, reporting fatigue, complexity of the Committee's guidelines, lack of resources and technical capacity, as well as coordination difficulties on a national level. None of these problems are easily solved. A further important reason for the different level of cooperation is the problem of confidential information. The 1373 regime requires States to report on legislative and administrative acts. The 1267 regime requires reporting on counter-terrorism measures against individuals suspected of being connected to Al Qaeda. Even if confidential reporting is possible, confidentiality at the UN is relative. It will be difficult to persuade States to convey sensitive intelligence information to a sanctions committee of the Security Council.

The Security Council nevertheless adheres to the individual reporting technique in the context of the 1267 regime and even terminated its independent monitoring source. In early 2004 the 1373 Monitoring Group was replaced by a larger 'Analytical Support and Sanctions Monitoring Team', ostensibly to more effectively monitor implementation.[15] Following the model of the 1373 regime, this new body is technical and much more under the control of the Security Council.

Security Council enforcement and politics

With a few notable exceptions, the practice of the Security Council demonstrates a general reluctance to enforce resolutions. Effective enforcement requires not only the consent of the permanent five Council Members but also considerable involvement and commitment: a case has to be built and publicly argued, an effective enforcement strategy must be devised and a lead nation or an alliance has to accept the responsibility of implementing the strategy and of paying the costs of

---

14 Third Report of the Monitoring Group, contained in S/2002/1338 of 17 December 2002, p. 10.

15 SC Res. 1526 of 30 January 2004.

the exercise. In practice, the public pressure leading to the adoption of a resolution has often subsided by the time the question of compliance and enforcement arises. If enforcement is debated, potential targets are quick to seek protection from one of the veto-wielding Members. Geopolitical or historical alliances have often prevented the Council from acting in a decisive manner.

In the field of counter-terrorism, however, the P5 have so far demonstrated convincing unity and resolve.[16] The Security Council continued its close cooperation during the Iraq conflict in 2003, demonstrating that even a profound disagreement among the P5 on one issue is not automatically transferred to another.[17] Considering the climate of desperate harmony in the Council after the end of the crisis, it was easy to predict that the P5 would continue this cooperation.[18] After the devastating terror attack against the UN in Iraq in August 2003 the initially sceptical UN Secretariat and the wider UN Membership acknowledged the need to stay the course and intensify the fight against terrorism. As a consequence, both counter-terrorism regimes of the Security Council were strengthened in 2004: SC Res. 1526 and 1535 were devised to bring new professionalism to the Committees and to de-politicize the monitoring of the two counter-terrorism regimes. Though doubts have been expressed whether the reforms would achieve much change in practice, the recent measures enacted by the Council do suggest determination of the P5 to resolutely continue their cooperation on counter-terrorism. The near future will show whether this environment is a suitable breeding ground for coercive enforcement measures against persistent non-compliers.

---

16 After the discord in the Council following the NATO intervention in the Balkans in 1999, the need to establish an effective counter-terrorism regime united the P5. To avoid the unpredictability of a novel regime, they relied on the time-tested structure of the Security Council, which gave them ultimate control.

17 An examination of the Security Council's work on the regional and technical items on its agenda from January to June 2003 did not identify any significant backlash from the discord on Iraq. Allegedly, the French initiative of a UN mission in Côte d'Ivoire ran into difficulties due to US retaliation against the French position on Iraq but an agreement was eventually found. In early May 2003, the soon-to-depart US Ambassador John Negroponte stated in a public debate in the Council on the CTC: 'Clearly, with resolution 1373 (2001) the Security Council got something right.'; 4752nd Meeting of the SC on 6 May 2003; S/PV.4752, provisional, p. 5.

18 Cf. A. Marschik, *supra* note 5, at p. 308. The difficulties in the aftermath of the invasion reminded even strong UN sceptics of the advantages of the organization: unparalleled universality for access to States and to international media; the role as globally accepted purveyor of legitimacy; resolutions that are immediately binding and enforceable vis-à-vis all States; existing structures to facilitate quick decisions, especially for the P5; institutional experience and expertise; etc. France and UK have a primary interest in maintaining the central role of the UN in international affairs – no other global organization gives them comparable influence and power. Though some may believe that the US does not need or want the UN, the US needs and wants allies. And these allies need and want the UN.

The Security Council as lawmaker?

The obligations contained in SC Res. 1373 are not typical Security Council sanctions. States must, *inter alia*, criminalize and prevent the provision or collection of funds for terrorism and freeze funds belonging to alleged terrorists or their supporters. These provisions, directly taken from the UN Convention against Terrorist Financing,[19] go beyond the executive 'police-functions' of the Security Council.[20]

While the solidarity in the Council in the aftermath of the terrorist attacks of September 2001 certainly contributed to the adoption and acceptance of SC Res. 1373, the regime, however, also symbolizes the progression of a Council ever more determined to make use of its ability to adopt binding obligations under Chapter VII of the Charter. Arms inspection commissions such as UNSCOM and UNMOVIC and the progression of increasingly targeted sanctions regimes paved the way. The establishment of the Ad Hoc Tribunals for Yugoslavia and Rwanda as sub-organs of the Security Council indicated competences beyond narrow 'police functions'.[21] All these sanctions regimes, however, still relied on the existence of a specific situation, restricted in area and time, that the Council considered a threat to the peace. SC Res. 1373 was the defining step towards abstract lawmaking, when it deemed abstract terrorism a threat against peace and security and imposed legal obligations on States to adopt specific measures, normally prescribed by international treaties.

Paul Szasz saw SC Res. 1373 as a new tool of the Security Council to create international law that could 'enhance the UN and benefit the world community'.[22] In literature many have rejected the legislative functions the Council has assumed.[23] They point to the lack of legal basis for such competences in the UN Charter and decry the lack of democratic legitimacy in the Security Council to enact legislation.

---

19 Adopted by GA Res. 54/109 of 9 December 1999.

20 D.W. Bowett, 'Judicial and Political Functions of the Security Council and the International Court of Justice', in H. Fox (ed.), *The Changing Constitution of the United Nations*, London: British Institute of International and Comparative Law, 1997, pp. 73 ff. at pp. 79-80, 82.

21 See to the ongoing debate on the limits of the powers of the Security Council: G. Arangio-Ruiz, 'On the Security Council's Law-Making', *Rivista di Diritto Internazionale,* Vol. 83, 2000, p. 609; T. Franck, 'The 'Powers of Appreciation': Who is the Ultimate Guardian of UN Legality?', *American Journal of International Law*, vol. 86, 1992, p. 519; Lamb, Legal Limits to United Nations Security Council Powers, in G.S. Goodwin-Gill, S. Talmon (eds), *The Reality of International Law: Essays in Honour of Ian Brownlie*, Oxford: Oxford University Press, 1999, p. 361; W.M. Reisman, 'The Constitutional Crisis in the United Nations', *American Journal of International Law*, vol. 87, 1993, p. 83.

22 P. Szasz, 'The Security Council Starts Legislating', *American Journal of International Law*, vol. 96, 2002, p. 901 ff. at p. 905.

23 See as examples G. Arangio-Ruiz, *supra* note 21; B. Graefrath, 'International Crimes and Collective Security', in K. Wellens (ed.), *International Law: Theory and Practice*, The Hague: Martinus Nijhoff, 1998, p. 237; Zemanek, 'Is the Security Council the Judge of its own Legality?', in E.Yakpo, T. Boumedra (eds), *Liber Amicorum Mohammed Bedjaoui,* The Hague: Kluwer, 1999, p. 629.

Clearly, the argument that the Council acted *ultra vires* in adopting SC Res. 1373 is, by now, redundant: the UN Member States accepted the regime both in formal statements and, quite convincingly, in their close cooperation with the CTC. They thereby either accepted the resolution as an aberration or indicated that they could accept the evolution of a new legislative competence of the Security Council.

The theory of subsequent practice recognizes the emergence of powers of an organ of an international organization after recurrent practice and its acceptance by the members of the sub-system. A helpful example is the practice of abstention of the P5 in the Security Council, which – though contrary to the wording of Article 27 – is not regarded as an impediment to the validity of a decision.[24] As regards legislative powers of the Security Council, the subsequent practice to SC Res. 1373 could be SC Res. 1540. Directed against the proliferation of weapons of mass destruction to non-state actors, this resolution also focuses on a general threat as a reason to impose abstract obligations on States under Chapter VII. However, while the States welcomed and cooperated fully with the 1373 regime, the reaction to SC Res. 1540 was different. Several States, especially in the developing world, expressed substantial doubt as to the legality and legitimacy of the Council's lawmaking.[25] Interestingly enough, though, after the adoption of the resolution on 28 April 2004 only one State, India, formally protested against the legislative content of the resolution.[26] At the time of writing, it is not yet clear whether States will effectively cooperate with the Council on implementation of the resolution. Should the implementation phase give evidence of general acceptance, it could be argued that the Council has received legislative powers.

---

24 See the Judgement of the ICJ in the Namibia Case: Legal Consequences for States of the Continued Presence of South Africa in Namibia (South West Africa) Notwithstanding Security Council Resolution 276 (1970), 1971 ICJ 16, 22. There is a close affinity to the creation of customary law; M. J. Herdegen, 'The "Constitutionalization" of the UN Security System', *Vanderbilt Journal of Transnational Law*, vol. 27, 1994, pp. 135 ff. at p. 155.

25 See the statements of, *inter alia*, Indonesia, Nepal, India, Pakistan, at the 4950th meeting of the SC on 22 April 2004; UN-Doc. S/PV.4950.

26 India stated its objection in a letter circulated at the adoption of the resolution: 'India is concerned at the increasing tendency of the Security Council in recent years to assume legislative and treaty-making powers on behalf of the international community, binding on all States, a function not envisaged in the Charter of the United Nations. India has taken note of the observation of cosponsors that the draft resolution contained in document S/2004/326 does not prescribe adherence to treaties to which a State is not party. India cannot accept any obligations arising from treaties that India has not signed or ratified. This position is consistent with the fundamental principles of international law and the law of treaties. India will not accept externally prescribed norms or standards, whatever their source, on matters within the jurisdiction of its Parliament, including national legislation, regulations or arrangements, which are not consistent with India's national interests or infringe on its sovereignty'; letter dated 27 April 2004 from the Permanent Representative of India to the United Nations addressed to the President of the Security Council, UN-Doc. S/2004/329 of 28 April 2004.

The legal consequences would be significant. International law is generally understood as being 'consensual' in nature.[27] Its main sources are treaties (where States decide freely whether to become parties) and custom (where States have the possibility to opt out as persistent objectors). International legislation thus relies – in theory – on the freedom of the States to be bound and the legal equality of the subjects. A Security Council that acts as world legislator would affect not only how free States are in accepting binding norms but also – in view of the veto of the P5 – whether all States are still equal in norm creation and in suffering the consequences of norm violation.

Prospects

The experience of the past three years indicates that the success of the Security Council's counter-terrorism work rests on two pillars: (a) unity and commitment in the Council, which essentially means among the P5; and (b) acceptance and cooperation by the Member States. For the moment, both unity and resolve in the Council remain strong. The terrorist attacks in Madrid and Chechnya appear to have strengthened the determination of the delegations. The tensions resulting from the premature naming of ETA as responsible for the Madrid bombing[28] have had no lasting effect, as evidenced in the unanimous adoption of SC Res. 1535 and the decision to appoint Ambassador Ruperez from Spain as head of CTED. It remains to be seen, however, whether the unity on the issue in principle is strong enough to deal with the diverse problems of the regimes. The discussions leading to SC-1535 showed how difficult it was to even minimally increase the monitoring capabilities of the counter-terrorism regimes. To create effective mechanisms more reforms are necessary but also the commitment to use the means at the disposal of the Council. It is, at this stage, crucial that the Council Members, especially the P5, demonstrate their resolve to enforce the resolutions against States that persistently refuse to implement the obligations domestically. To avoid criticism of bias and favouritism, the Council should adopt clearly defined sanctions that would automatically be triggered if a State's non-compliance is verified by the monitoring body.

As regards acceptance and cooperation of the Member States, symptoms of reporting fatigue are becoming apparent. This is mainly due to the similar but distinct reporting obligations to the Security Council's various counter-terrorism regimes, as well as requests for information on counter-terrorism in other bodies, such as the General Assembly's Sixth Committee. At the public debate before the adoption of SC Res. 1540 much criticism was directed against the legislative tendencies in the counter-terrorism work of the Council. There is a general feeling among the wider membership that the Security Council controls the UN's counter-terrorism work too

---

27 L. Henkin, 'International Law: Politics, Values and Functions', *Recueil des Cours de l'Académie de Droit International de la Haye* ,vol. 216, 1989, p. 46.

28 Spain insisted on the naming of ETA, though this later proved erroneous; see SC Res. 1530 of 11 March 2004.

tightly, while the large majority of States is excluded from participation. It is clear, that if the Security Council wants to maintain the level of support for its counter-terrorism work, it will have to address these issues. The Council must accept that other UN organs have important roles to play in the fight against terrorism. The General Assembly must be allowed to focus with determination on addressing root causes for terrorism and on adopting a definition of terrorism. The Security Council, with the help of other UN organs, must find a way to incorporate human rights considerations into the work of the sanctions committees.

Considering the limited resources at the UN, the Security Council must also begin considering the advantages of fusing the two regimes, possibly together with the 1540 regime, into a single counter-terrorism body. The result could be a commission of the Security Council with independent experts that can investigate compliance in each State.[29] Such a reform would only find support by the wider Membership, if it is accompanied by measures that guarantee additional resources for assistance (for example, within the ODC's Global Programme against Terrorism) and a political process that enables a discussion of the problems that afflict the regimes and the sensitivities of some States regarding the definition of terrorism.

Counter-terrorism at the United Nations is – and will remain – a work in progress. The test for the sustainability of the regimes will come in the next 2–3 years. Much will depend on whether the process to implement the recommendations in the Report of the Secretary General's High Level Panel expected in early December 2004 will reach into the sensitive area of the Security Council's counter-terrorism work. Past practice raises doubts as to the Council's ability to adopt far-reaching institutional and substantial reforms. On the other hand, the field of counter-terrorism has turned out to be one in which the UN has surpassed initial expectations in various ways. Perhaps the organization has some more surprises up its many sleeves.

---

29 A model for such a commission could be UNMOVIC.

Chapter 6

Resolution 1373 and the CTC: The Security Council's Capacity-building

ERIC ROSAND[1]

The Security Council – with its global reach, primary responsibility within the UN system for maintaining international peace and security, and ability to impose obligations on all 191 UN Member States – was expected to play a leading and unique role in the global effort to combat terrorism. Because of these attributes, the Council offered countries like the US the quickest and most effective route for globalizing the fight. The Council's strategy to combat terrorism can be divided into four areas: condemnation of discrete acts of terrorism, imposition of sanctions, imposition of binding counter-terrorism obligations on all States, and capacity-building. I am going to discuss the last two areas, focusing my remarks on Security Council Resolution 1373 and the work of the Council's Counter-Terrorism Committee.

Resolution 1373 – arguably the Council's most ground-breaking resolution – imposed a series of counter-terrorism obligations on all States and established the Counter-Terrorism Committee (consisting of all 15 members of the Council) to monitor States' implementation of their obligations. The goal of the CTC, and of Resolution 1373 as a whole, is ambitious: to raise the average level of government performance against terrorism across the globe. This means upgrading the capacity of each nation's legislation and executive machinery to fight terrorism, recognizing that the international community's ability to combat terrorism is only as strong as its weakest link.

Although Resolution 1373 established the CTC, it did not provide guidance on how it should operate and what role it should play in the efforts to combat terrorism. The way it operates (transparently, through dialogue, and by consensus), the role it plays (seeking to establish a dialogue between the Security Council and Member States on how best to build global capacity against terrorism), and its focus on facilitating the provision of technical assistance and developing relationships with international, regional, and sub-regional organizations, have been shaped by both the Council and the CTC itself, largely based on direction given by the CTC's first

---

1 Deputy Legal Counsel of the US Permanent Mission to the UN in New York. These remarks are made in a personal capacity and do not necessarily reflect the views of the US Department of State.

Chairman, then British Ambassador to the United Nations, Sir Jeremy Greenstock, and by the Security Council.

One question that has often been asked, both inside and outside of the United Nations community, is whether the CTC is having a direct impact on the fight against terrorism. The answer is yes, but not in ways that grab headlines or are readily noticeable. In its more than 3½ years of work, through its capacity-building and global coordination initiatives, the CTC has become a significant element of the worldwide campaign against terrorism. It has helped energize States and organizations to pay more attention to combating terrorism, whether through the adoption of new or the improvement of existing legislation, the ratification of treaties, or the development and implementation of action plans. As a result of the some 600 reports it has received from States detailing their efforts to implement their obligations under Resolution 1373, it is conducting the first worldwide audit of States' counter-terrorism capabilities, laying the groundwork for effective capacity-building. In addition, it has galvanized more than 60 international, regional, and sub-regional organizations to become more active in combating terrorism. It has also assumed a central role in the facilitation of technical assistance to States identified by the CTC as needing capacity-building help, serving as a switch-board between donors and interested States and helping to minimize duplication and overlap among potential assistance providers.

Finally, in the process of reviewing the hundreds of States' reports, and identifying the gaps in counter-terrorism capacity, although neither required nor even addressed by the resolution, the CTC has provided States with a roadmap for what is needed to implement the resolution's different provisions. In the first stage of its work, the CTC has focused on ensuring that States have adequate legislation and effective executive machinery in place in all areas covered by Resolution 1373, including counter-terrorist financing, weapons control, early warning systems, interstate cooperation, asylum and extradition, as well as promoting the ratification and implementation of the 12 international counter-terrorism instruments.

The CTC has observed that some States argue that the existence of anti-money laundering legislation is sufficient to prevent the financing of terrorism and thus satisfies many of the counter-terrorist financing obligations under the resolution. However, as the CTC has reminded them, although often inter-related, the crimes of money laundering and the financing of terrorism are not identical and thus the existence of anti-money laundering legislation may not be sufficient to satisfy Resolution 1373's requirement to criminalize terrorist financing. In addition, the CTC has noticed that many States lack the appropriate controls over informal banking systems, such as *hawala, hundi* and the black market peso exchange, that terrorists and terrorist groups have been known to use. It has reminded States that effective implementation of Resolution 1373 requires them to regulate all banking systems, whether formal or informal, and to impose penalties on those that operate such systems without a licence or registration. The CTC has also identified a number of States that do not properly regulate charities and other non-profit organizations within their jurisdiction, stressing and prioritizing the importance of having proper controls over these organizations.

The CTC's analytical work has extended beyond the terrorist financing elements of Resolution 1373. For example, where appropriate, the CTC has asked States for a progress report on States' efforts to enact domestic legislation to implement the 12 international conventions and protocols related to terrorism. In response, some States have stated that the law ratifying the treaty is sufficient to give effect to the obligations in the instrument under domestic law: in other words, no implementing legislation is necessary. In such cases, the CTC has reminded States that in order to implement effectively many of these international instruments, they may need to enact specific implementing domestic legislation, because certain requirements of these conventions and protocols cannot be fulfilled without it.

Where States are party to a regional convention, but have yet to join all 12 international counter-terrorism instruments, the CTC has reminded them that joining regional terrorism conventions cannot be viewed as an alterative to joining the international ones. In addition, some regional conventions such as the Arab Convention against Terrorism contain provisions that may not be compatible with some of the 12 conventions to which they are not yet parties. In these situations, the CTC has expressed a particular interest in learning how these States intend to join these conventions.

As useful and effective as the CTC has been since its creation in October 2001, it became clear last fall that it had reached its limits as currently organized. The ad hoc support structure of some 10 independent experts, hired on short-term contracts, without a leader, had its limitations. These limitations became more apparent as the CTC's mandate expanded into areas of technical assistance and working with more than 60 other organizations. While the CTC has been able to assemble a large body of data based on reports by UN Member States on steps they have taken to implement the resolution, it has not had the means to verify this information independently and to assess 'ground truth'; that is, on-the-ground implementation of the resolution. While States may have become party to international conventions and enacted legislation, the CTC has had no independent information on actual implementation of laws.

In March 2004, the Security Council took an important step to address the CTC's structural limitations by establishing the Counter-Terrorism Executive Directorate – or CTED. The CTED will provide the CTC with a larger, more professional support structure, with expertise in all of the substantive areas covered by Resolution 1373. It should enable the CTC to send experts to problematic countries for the purpose of verifying their actual implementation of counter-terrorism measures and documenting any short-comings, and improve its ability to identify areas in which technical assistance is needed. As of June 2005, the CTED (with a skeleton staff) had carried out three country visits (Morocco, Kenya, and Albania) and expects to conduct a handful more before the end of 2005. In addition, this larger, more expert group should be able to be more proactive, not just in the assistance area, but in meeting the CTC's responsibility to act as the clearinghouse for information and best practices among some 60 other organizations. Perhaps the main challenge facing the

CTC in the short term is to see that the CTED becomes fully operational as soon as possible so that it can carry on with its important work. As of June 2005, more than a full year since it was established by Security Council Resolution 1535, the CTED has yet to become fully operational. Owing largely to the burdensome UN hiring procedures, only a handful of the 20 or so CTED experts had started work. The rest are scheduled to be on board by September 2005.

Allow me to conclude by highlighting what I see as some of the longer-term challenges facing the CTC. How it chooses to handle to them will, to a large extent, determine how successful it will be in fulfilling its mandate.

The first is in the area of technical assistance. As the CTC has shown during its 3½ years of existence, the UN has a pivotal role to play in helping States to develop their capacity to combat terrorism. As the Secretary-General rightly points out in his comprehensive strategy on combating terrorism, '[t]errorists exploit weak States as havens where they can hide from arrest, and train their recruits. Making all States more capable and responsible must therefore be the cornerstone of our global counter-terrorism effort'. While the CTC has sought to assume a lead coordinating role in this area, it has been slowed by its overly bureaucratic approach and lack of adequate resources, both financial and human. On the positive side, many states and organizations are ready and willing to provide assistance to States needing help. The UN, through the CTC, must do a better job of coordinating the global counter-terrorism assistance effort. States must have some assurance that when they reach out to the CTC for assistance or guidance, the CTC will be able to deliver in a timely fashion.

The CTED should enhance the CTC's ability to facilitate the provision of technical assistance to those needing help meeting their obligations under Resolution 1373. However, since the CTC does not have the resources to provide any assistance, it will still be relying on donor organizations and States to come forward to deliver the necessary aid. Thus, regardless of how successful it is in identifying the States that lack capacity to implement 1373, its ultimate success will in large part be determined by whether those States and organizations that have the resources to help are willing to do so. Unless the CTC is able to mobilize and coordinate effectively the assistance efforts to ensure there is comprehensive implementation of 1373, its efficacy will be questioned. The CTC has so far succeeded in matching the many requests for legislative drafting assistance with bilateral and multilateral assistance providers. However, it has not had similar success in finding interested donors to cover other 1373-related needs, which the CTC will begin to focus on once it moves beyond the terrorist financing and other legislative aspects of the resolution. For example, it has yet to develop strong relationships with organizations such as the World Customs Organization and the International Organization for Migration, which are capable of providing assistance in developing States' capacities to control their borders. Thus, it is by no means clear that there will be the necessary assistance available to meet the needs, which will become more apparent once the CTC begins to delve into these areas.

The CTC and its CTED also need to move beyond simply serving as a switchboard between States in need of assistance and potential donors. They need to assess States' assistance needs and share those assessments with potential donors. In April 2004, as part of its eleventh 90-day work programme, the CTC decided to do just this. More than one year later, however, due largely to staffing shortages that prevented work from beginning on this important matter until late 2004, the CTC and its CTED have only been able to share a handful of these assessments with potential donors. In general, the few assessments that have been prepared place too much emphasis on the terrorism financing-related provisions of Resolution 1373 and too little on the other provisions. It remains to be seen whether a fully-staffed CTED will allow the CTC both to expedite work on these assessments and ensure that they analyse the non-financial aspects of each State's implementation efforts with the same rigour as they currently analyse the financial aspects.

A second challenge concerns the absence of an agreed definition of terrorism among UN Member States. One of the reasons the CTC has maintained such broad support is that it has been able to avoid dealing with the divisive issue of the definition of 'terrorism'. Resolution 1373 does not include a single definition; rather, it allows each Member State to define it under its domestic system. Thus, for example, when the Security Council, under 1373, '*[d]ecide[d]* . . . that all States shall [d]eny safe haven to those who finance, plan, support, or commit terrorist acts, or provide safe havens', it allows each State to determine against whom this provision is applied. Once the CTC begins to tackle the issue, however, through site visits or otherwise, of whether States are in fact implementing their counter-terrorism laws or executive machinery against those that commit terrorist acts, it may be difficult to avoid this potentially explosive issue. Rather, it could run into a situation where a State is not prosecuting an individual or group for acts that the majority of countries on the CTC believe are terrorist acts, but the country in question does not. Does the CTC turn a blind eye to this, with the understanding that it is not for it to decide which individuals or groups are in fact 'terrorists'? If the CTC begins to broaden its focus from building technical capacity to monitoring implementation of the laws and executive machinery designed to deal with terrorism, it may find itself engaged in the same definitional debate that the General Assembly is involved in, and thus run the risk of losing the broad support and cooperation from States it has received to date.

A third challenge concerns the interplay between efforts to combat terrorism and the protection of human rights. There is the concern that implementation of 1373 not be used as an excuse to infringe upon human rights. Highlighting this risk, one commentator has written that Resolution 1373 'is now presenting opportunistic states with a ready formula for trampling upon the rights of political or other opponents in the name of the war on terrorism'. For example, the Human Rights Committee has recently expressed concern about the negative effect that some domestic counter-terrorism measures may be having on asylum seekers and other foreigners. To address this broad concern, the human rights community, and a number of CTC Members have been pressing the CTC to appoint an expert on human rights and assume responsibility for monitoring States' compliance with human rights norms in the area of counter-terrorism. The CTC, however, has so far not taken up his offer, although, it did agree to charge one of the CTED staff members with liaising with human rights organizations.

The CTC's position continues to be that while it does take human rights seriously and has engaged in a dialogue with the Office of the UN High Commissioner for Human Rights (OHCHR), the task of monitoring adherence to human rights obligations in the fight against terrorism falls outside of the CTC's mandate. This work should be left to human rights bodies and institutions. Nevertheless, the Office of the High Commissioner for Human Rights and human rights organizations such as Amnesty International will continue to press the CTC to focus more attention on human rights issues. They recognize that the Council is the only UN body with the authority to impose legally binding measures on States and are thus hoping to have the CTC recommend that the Council impose such measures on those States that fail to comply with their human rights obligations while implementing Resolution 1373. Given the current political climate and the sensitive nature of these issues, one can expect the CTC to remain seized with the human rights question for the foreseeable future.

There are two recent developments that may help mitigate the concerns of some that the CTC, and the UN more broadly, is not focusing enough attention on States' efforts to respect international human right obligations as they implement Security Council-imposed counter-terrorism measures. The first is the Security Council's decision to authorize the CTED to hire a dedicated human rights expert who will be charged with liaising with the OHCHR and other human rights organizations in matters related to terrorism. The second is the April 2005 decision of the Commission on Human Rights to approve the appointment of the first-ever Special Rapporteur on Human Rights and Terrorism, the mandate of whom is to monitor States' compliance with human rights norms in the fight against terrorism.

A fourth challenge the CTC may face in the future is whether it will be able to maintain the overwhelming support it has received from virtually all Member States as its work advances. As noted above, one of the reasons for the broad support the CTC has received to date is that States have not felt threatened by it. This feeling will likely continue so long as the CTC is simply recommending and urging adoption of rather technical measures; for example, anti-money laundering or other counter-terrorism legislation or appropriate measures to regulate charitable and non-governmental organizations. As the CTC attempts to shift its focus, however, from monitoring whether States have the necessary counter-terrorism legislation and executive machinery in place to monitoring what action States are actually taking to combat terrorism – for example, whether a State is bringing terrorists to justice or providing a safe haven to terrorists – one may wonder whether this cooperative spirit will continue. The challenge for the CTC, therefore, is to find a way to move in this direction while maintaining the broad support from UN Members.

A fifth and related challenge is whether the CTC will be able to move beyond its focus on capacity-building and agree on which States are failing to meet their obligations under Resolution 1373 and report such states to the Council for appropriate action. A prerequisite for this will be reaching agreement on a set of common standards against which to measure States' performance. Since 9/11, a number of inter-governmental bodies have adopted recommendations or guidelines for States to follow in a specific counter-terrorism field, often building upon the provisions in Resolution 1373. For example, the Financial Action Task Force has adopted its 'nine special recommendations' in the field of terrorist financing ('FATF Nine'), the International Civil Aviation Organization has adopted airline and airport security guidelines, and the World Customs Organization has adopted a set of standards related to port security. The CTC already takes these principles into account when it reviews each State's efforts to implement 1373. Thus, one possibility would be for the CTC, or even the Council, to endorse formally these guidelines, which could then serve as the formal standards by which all States would be measured. Even with an agreed set of standards, however, the CTC may find it difficult to reach agreement on which categories of States should be reported to the Council. For example, should all those who fail to meet the standards regardless of whether they are seeking technical assistance be reported or only those who are rejecting assistance in trying to meet the standards?

As a first step, the Security Council, in Resolution 1566 (October 2004), requested the CTC to prepare a set of best practices to assist States with the implementation of the provisions of Resolution 1373 related to the financing of terrorism. As of June 2005, however, the CTC's efforts to endorse the FATF Nine as CTC best practices in the area of terrorist financing had stalled because of China's objection. China is not yet a member of FATF and appears unwilling to have the CTC (and ultimately the Security Council) endorse standards or best practices of organizations to which it is not a member. Thus, it remains to be seen whether the CTC will in fact be able to borrow standards and best practices developed by technical organizations or have to embark on the time-consuming exercise of trying to develop its own.

The CTC's ability to overcome all of these challenges depends, to a large extent, on the effectiveness of its CTED. Since it was established in October 2001, the CTC has not had the necessary professional and expert support staff to enable it to carry out its mandate, which has expanded during this period. Such lack of support has often been cited as the reason for its limitations and why it was unable to carry out its mandate more effectively. The CTED was established to remedy the problem. It remains to be seen whether the CTED, once it becomes fully operational in the fall of 2005, will in fact measure up to high expectations the CTC, the Council, and the broader UN system have set for it.

In conclusion, regardless of how successful the CTC is in meeting these challenges, one thing is for certain: the monitoring of the implementation of States' counter-terrorism obligations will require a long-term and unwavering commitment – one which has faded somewhat as the memories of September 11 continue to fade – for it might take some States decades to develop their infrastructure to be ably to comply fully with the obligations of Resolution 1373. Thus, the international community may need to be prepared to continue to ensure that the CTC receives enough support, including diplomatic, financial, and human, for years to come to complete the immense task the Security Council assigned it on September 28, 2001.

Chapter 7

The UN Security Council's (Broad) Interpretation of the Notion of the Threat to Peace in Counter-terrorism

VALERIA SANTORI[1]

Introduction

Chapter VII of the United Nations (UN) Charter does not specifically deal with international terrorism. Rather, the Security Council's Chapter VII powers aim exclusively to protect international peace and security – which terrorism may well endanger. It follows that the Security Council can counter terrorism by means of Chapter VII coercive instruments only if it determines that terrorist acts amount to one of the three situations provided for in Article 39 of the Charter: a threat to the peace, a breach of the peace or an act of aggression.[2] Indeed, the Council made Article 39 determinations in connection with situations differently related to terrorist acts.[3] In particular, the Council generally determined that such situations gave rise

---

1   Ph.D. in International Organization Law. Research Fellow, University of Teramo.

2   On the other hand, no international convention exists that provides for a specific Council's role with regard to acts of terrorism. No such mechanism exists as the one provided for in Article 8 of the Convention on the Prevention and Punishment of the Crime of Genocide, Dec. 9, 1948. This provision establishes that '[a] Contracting Party may call upon the competent organs of the United Nations to take such action under the Charter of the United Nations as they consider appropriate for the prevention and suppression of acts of genocide ….' For a similar mechanism, see also Article VIII of the International Convention on the Suppression and Punishment of the Crime of Apartheid, Nov. 30, 1973.

3   The Council does not necessarily operate under Chapter VII every time that it addresses terrorism. Bearing the main responsibility for the maintenance of international peace and security (Article 24, para. 1 of the Charter), the Council can address terrorism also in the framework of its Chapter VI preventive and/or conciliatory function. The Council may well determine that an act of terrorism gives rise to a situation (Articles 34-36) or to a dispute (Articles 33-38), the continuance of which is merely 'likely to endanger the maintenance of international peace and security' (Article 33, para. 1). However, Security Council's Chapter VI action can also represent a preliminary step on the path to Chapter VII. According to Chapter VI, the Council can – both on the request of a State (also a non-UN member, see Article 35) or the ECOSOC (Article 65), and *proprio motu* – decide to investigate a certain dispute or

to a threat to the peace. Especially with its most recent counter-terrorism resolutions, the Council has definitely strengthened its post-Cold War tendency broadly to interpret the Article 39 notion of threat to the peace. This short chapter attempts some brief considerations on such practice. To do so, I will first recall the main developments in the Security Council's Article 39 practice in counter-terrorism. I will then make some remarks on this practice from the viewpoint of the Charter's relevant provisions.

The Council's Article 39 practice

In the past, the Council acted under Article 39 to address various situations arising out of discrete acts of terrorism, determining that they gave rise to a threat to the peace and adopting measures to respond to them. This happened, for example, when the Council dealt with the Lockerbie aerial disaster in 1992, when it addressed the assassination attempt on the life of the Egyptian President Hosni Mubarak in 1995 or when it dealt with the Taliban regime's support to terrorism in Afghanistan between 1998 and 2001. In this phase, whereas it generally condemned the terrorist acts considered each time, the Council did not determine that such acts amounted to a threat to the peace *per se*. The terrorist acts concerned were only indirectly relevant for the purposes of the Council's determination, as they represented the root-causes of situations that the Council considered under Article 39. According to the Council, it was rather the conducts of 'States'[4] in connections with those acts, and the tensions they produced, to cast a threat on international peace and security. (Such situations

---

situation under Article 34 with the purpose of determining whether or not its continuance 'is likely to endanger international peace and security.' Should the investigation prove that the situation or the dispute in question do not imply a mere 'danger' for international peace and security, but amount to a full-fledged threat to (or breach of) the peace, the Council will move on to Chapter VII. Article 34, therefore, represents the link between Chapter VI and Chapter VII of the UN Charter. See e.g. B. Conforti, *The Law and Practice of the United Nations*, Leiden: Martinus Nijhoff, 2000, p. 157.

4   Reference is here generally to 'States', although the question of Afghanistan, where the Taliban faction has been in control of the majority of the territory until 2001, raises various legal questions in this regard that this paper cannot properly address. On the more general issue of the status in international law of such para-statal entities, see G. Arangio-Ruiz, L. Margherita, E.T. Arangio-Ruiz, *Soggettività nel diritto internazionale*, in *Digesto delle Discipline Pubblicistiche*, vol. XIV, 1999, pp. 307-314 and G. Arangio-Ruiz, *Diritto internazionale e personalità giuridica*, Turin: UTET, 1971, pp. 99-117. With specific reference to the Council's resolutions addressing the Taliban, it can be noted that the Taliban faction appeared to be merely the target of those resolutions, irrespective of the status that that faction might have had in general international law. Although the UN did not recognize the Taliban faction as the legitimate government of Afghanistan (the seat of Afghanistan at the United Nations was held by the Government of Burhannudin Rabbani, leader of the Northern Alliance), the Council treated it as a 'government'. In many occasions it reminded the Taliban of their obligations to abide by general international law rules, particularly their obligation to desist from supporting terrorism and to comply with the relevant international conventions to

are addressed here as situations where the Council determined that an 'indirect link' existed between an act of terrorism and a threat to the peace.) It follows that, in this phase, the Council classified terrorist acts as a threat to the peace only when such acts were attributable to a 'State' either for omissions (failed prevention or repression), or for individuals or groups' conducts that were directly attributable to that 'State' as they originated from its apparatus.[5]

a) So, for example, it emerges from the combined reading of Resolution 731 and 748, of 21 January and 31 March 1992, respectively, that the Council merely condemned the destruction of Pan-Am flight 103 over the village of Lockerbie in Scotland on 21 December 1988 and the explosion, one year later, of the UTA flight 772 over Nigeria.[6] The Council did not determine that the 1988 and 1989 terrorist acts directly gave rise to a 'threat to the peace' for the purposes of Article 39. Indeed, had Resolutions 731 and 748 been adopted three years after the two aerial disasters occurred, such acts could not have, *per se*, represented a threat to the peace when the Council addressed them under Chapter VII. The results of the investigations carried out by United States and British authorities, on the one hand, and the French authorities, on the other, implicated two officials of the Libyan Government,[7] and 'several Libyan nationals',[8] respectively. The US and the UK requested Libya to extradite the two suspects and to pay appropriate compensations.[9] France, on the other hand, requested the Libyan authorities to cooperate with French justice in order to establish responsibilities for that act.[10] The three Western States further demanded that Libya 'promptly, by concrete actions, prove its renunciation of terrorism'.[11] Since the Libyan Government opposed those requests,[12] France, the UK and the US

---

which Afghanistan was a party (see Resolution 1267 of 15 October 1999, preambular para. 4 and Resolution 1333 of 19 December 2000, operational para. 8), as well as the UN Charter.

5   On the general criteria for attribution of international responsibility for terrorist acts see e.g. L. Condorelli, 'The Imputability to States of Acts of International Terrorism', *Israel Yearbook on Human Rights*, vol. 19, 1989, pp. 233 ff.

6   The Lockerbie affaire is described in M. Arcari, 'Le risoluzioni 731 e 748 e i poteri del Consiglio di sicurezza in materia di mantenimento della pace', *Rivista di Diritto internazionale*, vol. 75, 1992, p. 932 ff., G.P. McGinley, 'The ICJ's Decision in the Lockerbie Cases', *Georgia Journal of International Law*, vol. 22, 1992, pp. 577-580; J.-M. Sorel, 'Les ordonnances de la Cour internationale de justice du 14 avril 1992 dans l'affaire relative à des questions d'interprétation et d'application de la convention de Montréal de 1971 résultant de l'incident aérien de Lockerbie (Libye c. Royaume Uni et Libye c. Etats-Unis)', *Revue générale de Droit international public*, vol. 97, 1993, pp. 690-698.

7   See *UN Doc S/23307* of 31 January 1991.

8   See *UN Doc. S/23306* of 31 January 1991.

9   See *UN Doc. S/23307* cit. and *UN Doc. S23308* of 31 December 1991.

10   See *UN Doc. S/23306* cit., Annex.

11   See *UN Doc. S/23309* of 31 January 1991.

12   See *UN Doc. S/23441* of 18 January 1992, Annex, at 2. With regard to the US's and the UK's claims, Libyan authorities refused to extradite the alleged perpetrators based on a number of provisions of the 1971 Montreal Convention for the suppression of unlawful acts against the safety of civil aviation (see *UN Doc. S/23441* of 18 January 1991.) The Montreal

referred the question to the Council. The Council, incorporating these countries' requests in Resolution 731, determined, in particular in Resolution 748, that 'the failure by the Libyan Government to demonstrate by concrete actions its renunciation of terrorism and in particular its continued failure to respond fully and effectively to the requests in Resolution 731(1992) [to extradite the alleged perpetrators to the United States and the United Kingdom, to cooperate with French judicial authorities and to prove it renunciation of terrorism by concrete acts] constitutes a threat to international peace and security'.[13] According to the Council, therefore, what threatened international peace and security was not the 1988 and 1989 terrorist acts, but the Libyan government's conduct.

b) The Council classified under Article 39 similar State conduct when it addressed the assassination attempt on the life of the Egyptian President Hosni Mubarak carried out on 26 June 1995 during a meeting of the Organization for African Unity (hereinafter 'OUA') in Addis Ababa, Ethiopia.[14] Investigations by the Ethiopian authorities produced evidence indicating an implication of Sudan in the terrorist act.[15] It was alleged that the Sudanese Government had assisted, facilitated and supported the commission of the act and that it gave refuge to three of the nine alleged perpetrators.[16] Backed by the OAU, the Ethiopian Government first requested the Sudanese Government to extradite the suspects, of Egyptian nationality. Since the Sudanese authorities denied those requests, the Ethiopian Government referred the dispute to the Council.[17] Also in this case, it emerges from the combined reading of Resolutions 1044 and 1054 of 31 January and 26 April 1996, respectively, that

---

Convention applied to the Lockerbie aerial disaster and the three involved States were parties to it. In particular, Libya contended that, according to Article 7 of the said Convention, the 'contracting State in the territory of which the alleged offender is found shall, if it does not extradite him, be obliged … to submit the case to its competent authorities for the purpose of prosecution.' Libya further argued that it immediately exercised jurisdiction over the two alleged offenders in accordance with its obligations under Articles 5, para. 2, and 8, para. 2, of the Convention. (See *Provisional Verbatim Record of the 3033rd Security Council's Meeting, UN Doc. S/PV. 3033* of 21 January 1992, p. 6). See also B. Graefrath, 'Leave to the Court what Belongs to the Court. The Libyan Case', *European Journal of International Law*, vol. 4, 1993, p. 189.

13   Resolution 748, preambular para. 7.

14   See M. Arcari, 'Le risoluzioni 1044 e 1054 del Consiglio di sicurezza relative al Sudan: un nuovo caso 'Lockerbie'?', *Rivista di Diritto internazionale*, vol. 79, 1996, p. 725 ff.

15   See *UN Doc. S/1996/10* of 9 January 1996, p. 5.

16   *Ibid.*, pp. 6 ff.

17   The Sudanese Government denied Ethiopia's allegations (see *UN Doc. S/1996/22* of 11 January 1996, p. 7) and declared that it was ready to cooperate with the Ethiopian authorities as well as to extradite the suspects to the extent that they were found on Sudanese territory. Sudan further informed the Council that it had established a fact-finding commission for that purpose (*ibid.*, p. 4.) However, the Sudanese Government contended that the information provided by the Ethiopian authorities was too vague and imprecise for Sudan to verify the perpetrators' possible presence within its borders (*ibid.*, p. 5.)

the Council merely condemned the failed assassination attempt on the life of the Egyptian President without asserting that they directly gave rise to a threat to the peace.[18] Resolution 1054 determined, instead, that Sudan's failure 'to comply with the requests set out in ... resolution 1044(1996)' – to both undertake immediate action to extradite to Ethiopia for prosecution the three suspects of the assassination attempt allegedly sheltering in the Sudan and desist from engaging in activities of assisting, supporting and facilitating terrorist activities – constituted a threat to international peace and security.[19]

c) The Council, finally, followed the same path when it addressed the Taliban question before the 2001 US- and UK-led military operation *Enduring Freedom* against Afghanistan, when the Taliban were still in control of great part of the Afghan territory. The Taliban faction was held responsible for harbouring and giving logistic support to terrorists, in particular the terrorist network Al Qaeda and its leader, the Saudi, Usama bin Laden. As of 1998, the Council adopted a series of resolutions addressing the conflict in the country between the Taliban and the Northern Alliance whereby it expressed concern at the increasing presence of terrorists and terrorist camps in the area.[20] On 7 August 1998 two terrorist bombing attacks destroyed the US embassies in Nairobi, Kenya and Dar es Salaam, Tanzania. US authorities' investigations implicated Usama bin Laden and Muhammad Atef, as well as the terrorist network Al Qaeda. The Council determined in Resolution 1267 of 15 October 1999[21] that the failure by the Taliban to respond to the requests made in

---

18 Resolution 1044 generally asserts that 'the suppression of acts of international terrorism, including those in which States are involved, is an essential element for the maintenance of peace and security' (preambular para. 5) and condemns 'the terrorist assassination attempt on the life of the President of the Arab Republic of Egypt in Addis Ababa, Ethiopia, on 26 June 1995'. *Ibid.*, para. 1.

19 Resolution 1054, preambular para. 10 (referring to para. 4 of Resolution 1044).

20 Already in 1996, the Council acting under Ch. VI of the Charter indicated that 'the continuation of the conflict in Afghanistan [provided] a fertile ground for terrorism and drug trafficking which [destabilized] the region and beyond' (Resolution 1076 of 22 October 1996, para. 5).

21 Immediately after the bombings occurred, the Council adopted resolution 1189 of 13 August 1998, whereby it condemned those attacks as having a 'damaging effect on international relations and jeopardize the security of States', and generally asserted that 'the suppression of acts of international terrorism is essential for the maintenance of international peace and security' (preambular para. 2) Hence, the Council did not seem to make an Article 39 determination in that resolution: having 'damaging effects' on international relations is something different from actually 'threatening' international peace and security. On the other hand, resolution 1189 contains no reference to Chapter VII and uses, instead, a language that better matches the Council's conciliatory function under Chapter VI rather than its enforcement powers. The Council '[c]alls upon all States and international institutions to cooperate with and provide support and assistance to the ongoing investigations in Kenya, Tanzania and the United States to apprehend the perpetrators of these cowardly criminal acts and to bring them swiftly to justice', and 'to adopt, in accordance with international law and as a matter of priority, effective and practical measures for security cooperation, for the prevention of

paragraph 13 of previous Resolution 1214 to 'stop providing sanctuary and training for international terrorists and their organizations' and to cooperate with efforts to bring indicted terrorists to justice',[22] in particular Usama bin Laden, constituted a threat to international peace and security.[23]

d) It is mainly with Resolutions 1368 and 1373 (of 12 and 28 September 2001, respectively), adopted in the aftermath of the September 9, 2001 terrorist attacks occurred in the United States that the Council determined that acts of international terrorism as such constituted a threat to international peace and security.[24] Those

---

such acts of terrorism, and for the prosecution and punishment of their perpetrators.' (*ibid.*, paras 4 and 5, respectively.) It can, therefore, be concluded that Resolution 1189 was adopted under Chapter VI and that the Council determined here that the situation in Afghanistan at that time was merely likely to endanger international peace and security (*contra* C. Greenwood, 'International Law and the "War Against Terrorism"', *International Affairs*, vol. 78, 2002, p. 306, who argues that Resolution 1189 contains an Article 39 determination directly in connection with the 1998 bombings).

22 Resolution 1214 of 8 December 1998, operational paragraph 13.

23 The Council further addressed terrorist acts as referred to a State's conduct in Iraq after the first Gulf Crisis. In Resolution 687 of 3 April 1991, the Council notes that 'many Kuwaiti and third-State nationals are still not accounted for' (preambular para. 21). The Council deplores 'threats made by Iraq during the recent conflict to make use of terrorism against targets outside Iraq and the taking of hostages by Iraq' and 'requires Iraq to inform the Council that it will not commit or support any act of terrorism or allow any organization directed towards commission of such acts to operate within its territory and to condemn unequivocally ... all acts, methods and practices of terrorism' (*ibid.*, preambular paras 22-23 and operative para. 32, respectively).

24 Also when it addressed under Chapter VII terrorist acts occurring in the framework of armed conflicts the Council considered terrorism under Article 39 only indirectly, as terrorism appeared to be a means of combat of one of the parties. In those cases, whereas terrorist acts contributed to aggravate the situation, the Council did not determine that an Article 39 situation existed specifically in connection with terrorist acts. Rather, the threat to the peace was mainly caused by the situation of conflict addressed each time. In the context of the Kosovo conflict, for example, the Council condemned certain violent acts against the authorities of the Federal Republic of Yugoslavia (today 'Union of Serbia and Montenegro'), committed by the '*Ushtria Clirimtare e Kosoves*' (or 'Kosovo Liberation Army', KLA, a Kosovo-Albanian armed group), as well as by other individuals operating in the area (for a reconstruction of the Kosovo crisis, see, for example, M. Weller, *The Crisis in Kosovo 1989-1999. From the Dissolution of Yugoslavia to Rambouillet and the Outbreak of Hostilities*, Cambridge: Cambridge University Press, 1999). Belatedly intervening in the crisis, the Council adopted Resolution 1160 of 31 March 1998. This Resolution did not determine that the crisis in Kosovo amounted to one of the three Article 39 situations – neither with reference to the general situation of unrest in the area, nor with regard to the KLA's terrorist activities. The Council, however, explicitly declared that it was operating under Chapter VII and adopted a number of measures against the FRY, 'including Kosovo' (*ibid.*, para. 8.) In the third preambular paragraph of Resolution 1160, then, the Council condemned '... all acts of terrorism by the Kosovo Liberation Army or any other group or individual and all external support for terrorist activity in Kosovo, including finance, arms and training.'

resolutions, however, went further. The Council determined that not only 'the terrorist attacks which took place in New York, Washington, D.C. and Pennsylvania on 11 September 2001',[25] but also '*any act of international terrorism*, constitute a threat to international peace and security'.[26] Acts of international terrorism, therefore, are a threat to the peace whenever, wherever and by whomever committed. In fact, international terrorism constitutes a threat *per se*.[27]

Thus, on the one hand, the Council went from determining that an indirect link existed between certain terrorist acts and a threat to the peace, to determining that terrorist acts directly amounted to such a threat. On the other hand, it went from dealing each time with specific situations arising out of determined terrorist acts, to addressing the phenomenon in general.

It could be argued that the general determination in Resolutions 1368 and 1373 that any act of terrorism is a threat to the peace is a mere political statement and that

---

See also Resolution 1199 of 23 September 1998, whereby the Council determined that 'the deterioration of the situation in Kosovo, Federal Republic of Yugoslavia, constitutes a threat to the peace and security' (preambular para. 14) and reaffirmed its condemnation of 'acts of violence by any party, as well as terrorism in pursuit of political goals ...' (preambular para. 9.) The Council, then, also qualified as terrorism certain acts committed in the framework of the conflict in Tagikistan. In Resolution 1089 of 13 December 1996, the Council condemned 'the terrorist acts and other acts of violence which have resulted in the loss of life of civilians as well as members of the CIS [Commonwealth of Independent States] Peacekeeping Forces and the Russian border forces' (operative para. 4). However, it does not seem that this Resolution was adopted under Chapter VII, as the Council makes no explicit determination under Article 39. Such a determination is not contained in preceding relevant resolutions either. The Council further referred to terrorist acts in connection with acts of violence occurred in Georgia in the framework of the conflict in Abkatsia. In particular, the Council called upon the parties to the conflict to establish 'a joint mechanism for investigation and prevention of acts that represent violations of the Moscow Agreement and the terrorist acts in the zone of conflict' (Resolution 1187 of 30 July 1998, para. 10). Though, also in this case, it can be doubted that the Council acted under Chapter VII. At any rate, except for the reported wording in para. 10 of Resolution 1187, there is no mention of acts of terrorism in this or other relevant Council Resolutions. It follows that, the Council's attention to terrorism is a secondary and minor element in the framework of its action to address the conflict in Abkatsia.

25 Resolution 1373 of 28 September 2001, preambular para. 3.

26 *Ibid.*, preambular para 4. Operative paragraph 1 of Res. 1368 of 12 September 2001 similarly reads: '[the Security council] [*u*]*nequivocally condemns* in the strongest terms the horrifying terrorist attacks which took place on 11 September 2001 in New York, Washington, D.C. and Pennsylvania and *regards* such acts, like any act of international terrorism, as a threat to international peace and security'.

27 Already in Resolution 1269, adopted on 19 October 1999 under Chapter VI of the Charter, the Council began taking an all-encompassing approach to the terrorist phenomenon. Operative para. 1 of that Resolution condemns 'all acts, methods and practices of terrorism as criminal and unjustifiable, regardless of their motivation, in all their forms and manifestations, wherever and by whomever committed, in particular those which could threaten international peace and security'. The following paragraphs call upon States to take a number of measures to improve States' cooperation in countering terrorism.

the Council operated under Article 39 exclusively with regard to the 9/11 attacks. However, it is explained below that the Council subsequently enacted Chapter VII measures aimed to address not only the 9/11 events, but terrorist acts in general. The Council, then, took the same approach in subsequent resolutions. Recalling Resolution 1373 and the obligations it imposes on States, the Council qualified both the specific acts of terrorism considered each time and any act of international terrorism as a threat to the peace (see, for example, Resolution 1438 of 12 October 2002 on the bombing against the discothèque in Bali,[28] Indonesia; Resolution 1440 of 23 October 2002 on the taking of more than 600 hostages in a theatre in Moscow[29] or Resolution 1450 of 28 November 2002 on the bombing attacks at the Paradise Hotel in Kenya.[30]) The Council followed the same approach also in another area of intervention, strictly related to counter-terrorism. Resolution 1540 determined in general terms that 'that proliferation of nuclear, chemical and biological weapons, as well as their means of delivery, constitutes a threat to international peace and security', underlining, at the same time, the risk that terrorists 'may acquire, develop, traffic in or use nuclear, chemical and biological weapons and their means of delivery.'[31] It can therefore be concluded that the Council purposely determined that international terrorism (as well as the proliferation of weapons of mass destruction) are general phenomena that threaten international peace and security.

e) It stems from the determination that terrorism as such is a threat to the peace that the Council considered that private entities' conduct, irrespective of whether or not they are related to the authority of a 'State', are the core cause of situations of emergency for international peace and security. In particular with Resolution 1390, adopted after the fall of the Taliban regime in Afghanistan, the Council, on the one hand, determined that acts of international terrorism in general constitute a threat to international peace and security, and, on the other hand, condemned specific private entities (Usama bin Laden, Al Qaeda, the Taliban Group – no longer in control of Afghanistan after the 2001 US and UK-led military operation *Enduring Freedom* – and other associated organizations and individuals) for a number of terrorist activities.[32]

---

28 Para. 1.

29 Para. 1.

30 Para. 1.

31 Resolution 1540 of 28 April 2004, preambular paras. 1 and 8, respectively.

32 Resolution 1390 of 28 January 2002, preambular para. 9, and preambular paras. 5, 7 and 8. The Council's attitude toward the question of the Taliban changed as a consequence of the 9/11 events and the military operations carried out by a US and UK-led coalition of States in Afghanistan. If the 2001 operation *Enduring Freedom* resulted in the collapse of the Taliban regime in Afghanistan, it did not result in the elimination either of this group, nor of the Al Qaeda terrorist network. Whereas the latter lost its headquarters, operational bases and training camps in Afghanistan, it created cells in other parts of the world and established connections with other militant Islamic groups in Europe, Northern America, Northern Africa, Middle East and Asia (see *UN Doc. S/2002/1050* of 20 September 2002, pp. 5-7 and Annexes I, II and IV). This way, Al Qaeda, far from being eliminated, acquired

It can further be noted that, whereas in its earlier resolutions the Council generally operated under Chapter VII in order to deal with terrorist acts of an objectively *international* nature, most recently the Council also concerned itself with acts the international character of which was not so evident. An example might be Resolution 1465 of 13 February 2003 addressing the bombing of the Club Nogal in Bogotá on 7 February 2003 attributed to FARC (*Fuerzas Armadas Revolucionarias de Colombia*). This act does not seem to present any evident link with other jurisdictions as it has been perpetrated on Colombian territory, allegedly by a Colombian group, and caused almost exclusively Colombian victims.[33] In Resolution 1465, furthermore, the Council determined that not only the Bogotá event, but also any act of 'terrorism' (and not 'any act of "international terrorism"', as stated in Resolution 1373) amounts to a threat to the peace. A determination that the Council reiterated in Resolution 1516 of 20 November 2003 on the bomb attacks in Istanbul and Resolution 1530 of 11 March 2004 on the bombing in Madrid, as well as, in more general terms, in Res. 1566 of 8 October 2004.[34] It follows that, within the framework of Chapter VII Council's action the 'international' relevance of terrorist acts appears to have little to do with their objective (factual) international nature. Rather, the international relevance of terrorist acts exclusively stems from the Council's opinion that such acts threaten (or breach) international peace and security. Consequently, also acts

---

more flexibility and strength. The Taliban, on the other hand, continue to operate in both parts of the Afghan territory and neighbouring countries, in particular Pakistan (*ibid.*, p. 3) and to cross international borders undisturbed. The Council, therefore, had to modify its strategy and redirect its action against bin Laden, Al Qaeda, the Taliban and their associates wherever they are located. With regard to the latter in particular, the Council no longer addresses the Taliban as an organized group governing part of Afghanistan, but, rather, as individuals falling within the domestic jurisdiction of States on whose territory they operate. In Resolution 1390 therefore, the Council reiterated 'its support for international efforts to root out terrorism, in accordance with the Charter of the United Nations' (preambular paras. 1-3.). It then reaffirmed 'its unequivocal condemnation of the terrorist attacks ... on 11 September 2001', expressed 'its determination to prevent all such acts', noted 'the continued activities of Usama bin Laden and the Al Qaeda network in supporting international terrorism' and affirmed 'its *determination to root out this network*' (*ibid.*, para. 4 of the preamble). Following the same approach taken in Resolutions 1368 and 1373, then, the Council determined in general terms that 'acts of international terrorism constitute a threat to international peace and security' (*ibid.*, para. 9 of the preamble). What threatens the peace, therefore, is no longer the conduct of the Taliban faction as the government of Afghanistan and to which the behaviour of individuals and groups under their jurisdiction can be attributed. What threatens international peace and security is any act of terrorism that those individuals and groups plan and carry out: not only past acts but also possible future acts, wherever and whenever they occur and whatever the location of the perpetrators and the victims.

33 For this same classification of Resolution 1465, see also M. Sossai, 'The Internal Conflict in Colombia and the Fight Against Terrorism. UN Security Council Resolution 1465 (2003) and Further Developments', *Journal of International Criminal Justice*, vol. 3, 2005, pp. 253-267.

34 Preambular para. 7.

of terrorism of a 'domestic' nature acquire an international relevance consisting precisely in the fact that according to the Council they involve a threat to international peace and security.

On the other hand, the fact that the Council determines that any act of terrorism amounts to a threat to the peace, makes the Council overcome the problem of the so-called 'double-standard'. In its earlier practice, the triggering of a Council Chapter VII action to respond to a specific act of terrorism depended more on the political sensitivity and weight of its most powerful members than on the presence of an objective emergency for international peace and security. This may well explain why the Council did not address terrorist acts that objectively appeared to be susceptible, as others, to trigger a Council's intervention under Chapter VII or, at least, Chapter VI. However, as explained below, Resolution 1373 contains what seems to be a blanket provision that, by determining that *any* act of terrorism (so, even future acts) amount to a threat to the peace, implies that any such act automatically falls under the scope of Resolution 1373's measures. In other words, those measures seem to apply not only to terrorist acts that subsequent resolutions classified (or will classify) as a threat to the peace but also to any other terrorist acts for which no such determination is made (such as, for example, the May 2003 bombing in Riyadh). So, if in the past some could criticize the Council for not addressing (or not addressing as terrorism) certain acts of violence occurring in the world (why the Lockerbie disaster and not other violent acts occurred elsewhere?) the global reach of the recent Council's counter-terrorism action renders such criticism moot.

Broadening the notion of 'threat to the peace'

So, when it addressed 'international' terrorism the Council adopted a progressively broader interpretation of the Article 39 notion of threat to the peace. This is true in many respects. First the Council qualified as a threat to the peace the failure by States to extradite alleged perpetrators of terrorist acts as evidence of their support for international terrorism: a situation never addressed before under Article 39 of the Charter. The Council, then, went from operating an indirect link between terrorist acts and a threat to the peace to determine that terrorist acts directly threaten international peace and security (thus implying that private entities' conduct, irrespective of whether they act under the authority of a State, are relevant for the purposes of Article 39 determinations). On the other hand, the Council seemed to extend its attention not only to international terrorism, but also to domestic terrorism (of an international relevance). So far, the Council appeared to have done nothing much different from the past, when it made prove, especially after the Cold War, of a tendency to include in the notion of threat to the peace the most diverse situations, not only of an international character, but also of an essentially domestic one, including private entities' conduct. The Council qualified under Article 39, *inter alia*, the racial discrimination in Rhodesia[35] and South Africa,[36] various situations of humanitarian emergencies,[37] serious violations of human rights[38], serious breaches of international humanitarian law,[39] massive flows of refugees,[40] the violation of democratic principles,[41] or situations of civil strife due to the collapse of a fraudulent financial investing system.[42] What seems to be a sharp departure from the previous Council's practice, though, is that, for the first time ever, the Council, rather than linking a threat to the peace to discrete situations, determined that a general situation of emergency for international peace and security exists. At the political level, the trend in the Council's practice to extensively interpret the Article 39 notion of threat to the peace to include acts of terrorism of any nature can be explained in light of the global campaign against the 'scourge' of terrorism in all its forms. However, legal questions might arise as to this practice's conformity with the Charter. Although also the Council's earlier Article 39 practice in counter-terrorism raised concerns among States and scholars, space constraints confine this chapter particularly to focus on the Council's determination that any act of 'international' terrorism amounts to a threat to the peace.

---

35 See Resolution 217 of 20 November 1965, where the Council, 'considering that the illegal authorities in Southern Rhodesia have proclaimed independence and that the Government of the United Kingdom ... as the administering power, looks upon this as an act of rebellion' (preambular para. 2), '[d]etermines that the situation resulting from the proclamation of independence by illegal authorities in Southern Rhodesia is extremely grave, that the Government of the United Kingdom .. should put an end to it and that its continuance in time constitutes a threat to international peace and security' (operational para. 1). See M. S. McDougal, W.M. Reisman, 'Rhodesia and the United Nations: the Lawfulness of International Concern', *American Journal of International Law*, vol. 62, 1968, pp. 1 ff.

36 Resolution 418 of 4 November 1977, para. 1.

37 See, for example, Resolution 1929 of 22 June 1994 concerning the situation in Rwanda. The Council determines here that a threat to the peace is caused by the 'magnitude of the humanitarian crisis in Rwanda'. For the Council's practice in relation to humanitarian emergencies, see M. Bettati, 'Un droit d'ingérence?', *Revue générale de droit international public*, vol. 95, 1991, pp. 639 ff., and F. Lattanzi, *Assistenza umanitaria e intervento di umanità*, Turin: Giappichelli, 1997, *passim*.

38 See, in addition to the above-quoted resolutions on Rhodesia and Rwanda, Resolution 670 of 25 September 1990 concerning the mistreatments by Iraq of the Kuwaiti civilian population.

39 Resolution 955 of 8 November 1994, concerning Rwanda, whereby the Council determines that a threat to the peace is caused by the perpetration of the crime of 'genocide and other systematic, widespread and flagrant violations of international humanitarian law' (preambular paras 4 and 5).

40 See Resolution 688 of 5 April 1991 ('[g]ravely concerned at the repression of the Iraqi civilian population in many parts of Iraq, including most recently in Kurdish-populated areas, which led to a massive flow of refugees towards and across international frontiers ... which threaten international peace and security in the region': preambular para. 3).

41 Resolution 841 of 16 June 1993.

42 Resolution 1101 of 28 March 1997.

Questions of legality

This is not the place to recall in detail the extensive scholarly debate on the possible limits to the Council's powers to make Article 39 determinations. First, some argue that Article 39 determinations would not be a necessary requirement for the Council to have recourse to its Chapter VII enforcement powers as the Council could adopt binding decisions under the general powers which Article 24, read in combination with Article 25 would entrust to it.[43] Other scholars, however, believe that either the Council's powers – and in particular the power to adopt binding decisions – are grounded in one of the Chapters of the Charter referred to in Article 24 (or in other provisions providing explicitly for them), or they are *contra legem*.[44] An Article 39 determination, therefore, would always be a necessary requirement for the Council to accede to its Chapter VII powers. In any case, the Council always made Article 39 determinations before adopting binding decisions to resolve situations arising out of the terrorist acts addressed each time.

a) Suffice it, then, to recall here that no provision in the UN Charter defines the three situations addressed in Article 39 of the Charter that legitimize the Council to act under Chapter VII. Indeed, the choice was made at San Francisco to entrust the Council with a certain degree of discretion in evaluating the situations that could trigger its broadest and most important Charter powers for the maintenance and restoration of international peace and security.[45] This emerges clearly from the final Report of the Third Committee of the Third Commission of the 1945 San

---

43　L.M. Goodrich, E. Hambro, A.P. Simons, *The United Nations and the Maintenance of Peace and Security*, Washington: The Brookings Institution, 1955, pp. 204-205; S.A. Tiewul, 'Binding Decisions of the Security Council within the meaning of Article 25 of the UN Charter', *Indian Journal of International Law*, vol. 15, 1975, pp. 213-215; E. Jimenez De Aréchaga, 'International Law in the Past Third of a Century', *Recueil des Cours de l'Academie de Droit international de la Haye*, vol. 159, 1978-I, pp. 119 ff. (see also Id., 'United Nations Security Council', in Bernhardt (ed.), *Encyclopaedia of Public International Law*, Amsterdam: North Holland, 2000, pp. 1170-1171); R. Sonnenfeld, *Resolutions of the United Nations Security Council*, Dordrecht: Martinus Nijhoff, 1988, p. 21, pp. 127-141 and 143; Id., 'The Obligation of UN Member-States "to Accept and Carry Out the Decisions of the Security Council" ', *Polish Yearbook of International Law*, vol. 8, 1976, pp. 129 ff.; R. Degni-Ségui, 'Article 24, Paragraph 1 et 2', in J.-P. Cot, A. Pellet, *La Charte des Nations Unies. Commentaire article par article*, Paris/Brussels: Economica, 1992, pp. 462-464; K. Herndl, 'Reflections on the role, functions, procedures of the Security Council of the United Nations', *Recueil des Cours de l'Academie de Droit international de la Haye*, vol. 206, 1987, p. 322 ff.; Id., 'The "Forgotten" Competences of the Security Council', in A. Mock (ed.), *Verartwortung in unserer Zeit - Festschrift für Rudolf Kirchschlager*, Wien: Verl. d. Österr. Staatsdr., 1990, p. 90; J. Delbrück, Article. 24, in B. Simma (ed.), *The Charter of the United Nations*, Oxford: Oxford University Press, 2002, pp. 403-404; and S. Marchisio, *L'ONU. Il diritto delle Nazioni Unite*, Bologna: Il Mulino, 2000, p. 191.

44　H. Kelsen, *The Law of the United Nations*, London: Stevens, 1950, p. 284.

45　See G. Gaja, 'Réflexions su le rôle du Conseil de sécurité dans le nouvel ordre mondial', *Revue générale de Droit international public*, vol. 97, 1993, pp. 297 ff.

Francisco Conference dealing with Chapter VIII, section B of the Dumbarton Oaks proposals. This report explains that, notwithstanding certain States' proposals to limit the Council's discretion, the Committee 'decided to adhere to the text drawn up at Dumbarton Oaks and to leave to the Council the entire decision as to what constitutes a threat to the peace, a breach of the peace, or an act of aggression'.[46] In this context, it was also noted that if the notions of 'breach of the peace' and 'aggression' are, to a certain extent, 'more amenable to a legal determination', the 'threat to the peace' appears to be a rather 'political' notion[47] susceptible to a more flexible and elastic interpretation.

b) In light of the above, some scholars argue that Article 39's textual vagueness indicates that the Charter leaves to the Council the broadest discretion in determining what phenomena or situations can be classified, in particular, as a threat to the peace.[48] In the view of these scholars, the notion of threat to the peace would be broad enough to cover the Council's extensive Article 39 practice[49] (some arguing that such practice would be a mere return to the Charter).[50] Others, however, assert that some limitations exist to the Council's Article 39 powers. It was argued that the preliminary assessment of the existence of one of the three preconditions addressed in that provision represents a necessary step for the Council to decide, irrespective of the Article 2, paragraph 7 domestic jurisdiction limit, the application of coercive measures as well as, possibly, the recourse to armed force against one or more

---

46 *Documents of the United Nations Conference on International Organization (UNCIO)*, New York, 1945, vol. XII, p. 505. See also p. 379 and, concerning the Dumbarton Oaks proposals, p. 573 ('wide freedom of judgment is left as regards the moment [the Council] may choose to intervene and the means to be applied').

47 International Criminal Tribunal for the Former Yugoslavia, Appeals Chamber, *The Prosecutor v. Duško Tadić*, Case No. IT-94-1-AR72, *Decision on the Defence Motion for Interlocutory Appeal on Jurisdiction*, 2 October 1995, para. 28.

48 See for example, Kelsen: "[i]t is completely within the discretion of the Security Council to decide what constitutes a 'threat to the peace'", *supra* note 44, p. 727. See also, for example, the dissenting opinion of Judge C.G. Weeramantry in the Case on the *Questions of Interpretation and Application of the 1971 Montreal Convention Arising From the Aerial Incident at Lockerbie (Libyan Arab Jamahiriya v. United States), Order of 14 April 1992, Request for the Indication of Provisional Measures, I.C.J. Reports 1992*, p. 66 and T.D. Gill, 'Legal and Some Political Limitations on the Power of the UN Security Council to Exercise its Enforcement Powers under Chapter VII of the Charter', *Netherlands Yearbook of International Law*, vol. 26, 1995, pp. 40 and 42.

49 P. Picone (ed.), *Interventi delle Nazioni Unite e Diritto internazionale*, Padua: CEDAM, 1995, p. 531. See also C. Dominicé, 'Le Conseil de sécurité et l'accès aux pouvoirs qu'il reçoit du Chapitre VII de la Charte des Nations Unies', *Revue suisse de droit international et de droit européen*, vol. 5, 1995, p. 426.

50 See for example, P.-M. Dupuy, 'Sécurité collective et organisation de la paix', *Revue générale de Droit international public*, vol. 97, 1993, p. 623 and p. 626 and J.-M.Sorel, 'L'élargissement de la notion de menace contre la paix', in Société française pour le droit international, *Colloque de Rennes. Le Chapitre VII de la Charte des Nations Unies*, Paris, 1995, p. 18.

target States.[51] It is contended that, especially in light of the lack of effective review mechanisms in the United Nations system, that would not be realistic. According to this view, it would seem, rather, that the Council's determinations under Article 39 have to be evaluated against objective criteria to avoid that they are carried out as a pretext to '*atteindre des objectifs inavoués*'.[52]

c) Indeed, the fact that Article 39 grants the Council a great deal of discretion[53] may not necessarily mean that it is *legibus solutus*.[54] Scholars differently attempted to define the possible limits to the Council's powers in light of the Charter provisions. A general agreement exists, surely also on the part of those who assert the Council's broadest discretion, that, according to Article 24, paragraph 2 of the Charter, the Council must 'act in accordance with the purposes and principles of the Organization and the provisions of the Charter'.[55] This, however, seems to be too vague a reference to set specific limits on the Council's action. So, others argue that the founding fathers had intended the notion of threat to the peace restrictively as to essentially include situations characterized by the presence of armed conflicts – be they international or internal.[56] In particular Kelsen further argued that according to the Charter, '[t]he Security Council may very well decide that a situation *which has not the character of a conflict between two states is a threat to the international peace*'. This would emerge from Article 39 of the Charter that '… makes the application of the enforcement measures dependent upon the existence of 'any threat to the peace,

---

51 These considerations are Conforti's, *supra* note 3, pp. 171 ff See also G. Scotto, 'Limiti alle competenze del Consiglio di sicurezza in tema di regolamento di controversie e situazioni', unpublished Ph.D. thesis, Università degli Studi di Roma, La Sapienza, 1996, Chap. II.

52 G. Fitzmaurice, *Dissenting Opinion*, in the case *Legal Consequences for States of the Continued Presence of South Africa in Namibia (South West Africa) notwithstanding Security Council Resolution 276(1970), Advisory Opinion, ICJ Reports 1971*, p. 294. See also McDougal, Reisman, *supra* note 33, *American Journal of International Law*, 1968, p. 9 and T.M. Franck, 'The 'Powers of Appreciation': Who Is the Ultimate Guardian of UN Legality?', *American Journal of International Law*, vol. 86, 1992, pp. 519 ff.

53 This article merely provides that 'the Security Council shall determine the existence of any threat to the peace, breach of the peace, or act of aggression…'.

54 Cf. ICTY, Appeals Chamber, *The Prosecutor v. Duško Tadić, supra*, note 47, para. 28.

55 *UNCIO, supra* note 46, vol. XII, p. 519. See, for example, B. Conforti, 'Le pouvoir discrétionnaire du Conseil de sécurité en matière de constatation d'une menace contre la paix, d'une rupture de la paix ou d'un acte d'agression', in R.-J. Dupuy (ed.), *Le développement du rôle du Conseil de sécurité. Colloque, La Haye, 21-23 July 1992*, Dordrecht: Martinus Nijhoff, 1993, pp. 56-57, M. Bothe, 'Les limites au pouvoir du Conseil de sécurité', *ibid.*, p. 70. See also P. Picone, 'Interventi delle Nazioni Unite e obblighi erga omnes', in Id. (ed.), *supra* note 49, pp. 517-578. See also M. Bedjaoui, *Nouvel ordre mondial e contrôle de la légalité des actes du Conseil de sécurité*, Brussels: Bruylant, 1994.

56 Cf. J. A. Frowein, N. Krisch, *Article 39*, in Simma (ed.), *supra* note 43, p. 720. Gaja, *supra* note 45, p. 301, Picone, *supra* note 55, p. 543 and M. Koskenniemi, 'The Place of Law in Collective Security', *Michigan Journal of International Law*, vol. 17, 1996, p. 457.

breach of the peace or act of aggression'. In contradistinction to other provisions of the Charter, Article 39 does not speak of threat to, or breach of, 'international' peace. Hence the peace referred to this passage *need not necessarily be a status in the relation between states'.*[57] Indeed, in the past the Council classified as threat to the peace not only situations characterized by international armed conflicts, but also situations amounting to internal armed conflicts.[58] This practice is now generally accepted. Along the same lines, however, others contend that the concept of 'threat' evokes situations different from an outbreak of hostilities[59] and possibly immediately preceding or following them (the example was made of a post-conflict situation).[60] In this sense a threat to the peace could simply represent a first step toward a breach of the peace or toward the re-opening of hostilities.[61] Along the same lines, some argue that a threat to the peace should never be dissociated from a 'risk' of an armed conflict.[62] According to others, then, whereas the presence of an armed conflict would not represent a Charter limit, the Council always tended to make Article 39 determinations in connection with situations that all appeared to be related to at least violent clashes, even though on a small scale.[63] This assertion, however, rings untrue with respect to the Council's counter-terrorism practice.

   d) The diverse situations arising in connection with the perpetration of terrorist acts that the Council addressed under Article 39 generally took place in times of 'peace',[64] traditionally understood as the absence of armed conflict. So other scholars, who argue that the Council would act on behalf of member States to protect

---

57 Kelsen, *supra* note 44, p. 731 (emphasis added).

58 See Frowein, Krisch, *supra* note 56, pp. 723-724, fn. 52.

59 In the sense that 'action by the Security Council might be anticipatory and was not required to await the full consummation of the disaster', see McDougal, Reisman, *supra* note 35, p. 7.

60 See Frowein, Krisch, *supra* note 56, p. 722. McDougal and Reisman argued that, according to Article 39 'measures may be taken "to maintain or restore ...". While "restore" clearly refers to remedial action subsequent to a perfected breach of the peace, "maintain" refers to preliminary action aimed at removing or forestalling an imminent threat to the peace which has not yet materialized into a "breach"' (*supra* note 35, p. 8, fn. 28).

61 Frowein, Krisch, *supra* note 56, p. 722.

62 See Gaja, *supra* note 45, p. 301. Sorel believes, instead, that '[i]l serait peut être souhaitable ... de dissocier la notion de "menace" de celle de "risque" car l'histoire de la Charte renforcée par les tendances actuelles paraissent faire de la menace un concept, sinon défini, du moins identifiable, alors que le "risque" corresponderait à ce *no man's land* entre le conflit et l'objectif lointain du développement durable et équilibré' (*L'élargissement*, *supra* note 50, p. 19).

63 F. Lattanzi, 'Consiglio di sicurezza', *Enciclopedia giuridica*, Rome: Istituto della Enciclopedia italiana, 2000, p. 11. In this sense, see also B. Martenczuk, 'The Security Council, the International Court of Justice and the Judicial Review: What Lessons from Lockerbie?', *European Journal of International Law*, vol. 10, 1999, pp. 543-544 and Frowein, Krisch, *supra* note 56, pp. 722-725.

64 The Taliban question does not represent an exception to this assertion. Also in Afghanistan the Council intervened in the context of an armed conflict. However, the terrorist

the fundamental values of the 'international community' as a whole, assert that situations different from an armed conflict can imply a threat to international peace and security so long as they disrupt the fundamental values on which that community is grounded.[65] So, the Council's trend to broaden the notion of threat to the peace would be instrumental to the need to respond to breaches of essential obligations for the 'international society' (such as those outlawing genocide, apartheid, etc.)[66] and to protect its fundamental values.[67]

e) In any case, the Council itself already declared in 1992 that '[t]he absence of war and military conflicts amongst States does not in itself ensure international peace and security', as 'non-military sources of instability in the economic, social, humanitarian and ecological fields have become threats to peace and security'.[68] In particular, the subsequent paragraph on 'Commitment on collective security', expresses the Council Members' concern 'over acts of international terrorism' and stresses the need 'for the international community to deal effectively with all such acts'.[69] Also the Secretary-General more recently warned that 'we must be intensively aware of the changes in the international security environment':[70] 'there are new threats that must be faced – or, perhaps, old threats in new and dangerous combinations',[71] as 'today they are predominantly global … [and] take place in a new context and have far-reaching effects'[72] – the reference being clearly to, *inter alia*, terrorism and the new forms in which it manifests itself. This view is more broadly expressed in the Report of the Secretary-General's High-Level Panel on Threats, Challenges and Change.[73]

---

activities that took place in Afghan territory were directed against third countries and were not used as a method of combat of one of the parties, as it was the case in Kosovo.

65 For this opinion, see Picone, *supra* note 49, p. 518 ff. and *passim*, and Id., 'Obblighi reciproci e obblighi erga omnes degli Stati nel campo della protezione internazionale dell'ambiente marino', in V. Starace (ed.), *Diritto internazionale e protezione dell'ambiente marino*, Milan: Giuffré, 1983, pp. 15 ff.; G. Ziccardi-Capaldo, *Terrorismo internazionale e garanzie collettive*, Milan: Giuffré, 1990, pp. 71 ff., and 73 ff. See also P.-M. Dupuy, *supra* note 50, p. 626.

66 *Ibid.*, p. 307; Picone, *supra* note 47, p. 545.

67 Gaja, *supra* note 45, p. 307.

68 Declaration of the President of the Council on 'The responsibility of the Security Council in the maintenance of peace and security', *UN Doc. S/23500* of 31 January 1992, p. 3. In this sense, see also the considerations in B. Boutros-Ghali, *An Agenda for Peace, Preventive diplomacy, peacemaking and peace-keeping*, UN Doc. A/47/277 - S/24111 of 17 June 1992, p. 6, paras. 12-14 and p. 12, para 22. See also, Kelsen, *supra* note 44, p. 729; R. Sonnenfeld, *supra* note 43, pp. 85-86.

69 *UN Doc. S/23500*, *cit.*, p. 3.

70 See *UN Doc. A/58/323* of 2 September 2003, p. 8.

71 *Secretary-General's address to the General Assembly*, New York, 23 September 2003.

72 See *UN Doc. A/58/323* of 2 September 2003, p. 8.

73 *UN Doc. A/59/565* of 2 December 2004.

Also, it could be argued that in today's world, the concepts of peace and war have acquired a rather different meaning from the past.[74] Indeed, even possibly admitting that the presence of armed conflict represented a Charter limit for the Council to operate under Article 39, it would seem plausible that the Council addresses under that provision also new situations, different from those possibly envisaged in San Francisco 60 years ago (such as those related to terrorism and WMD), that, while not connected to an armed conflict are equally grave and require a Council's Chapter VII action.[75] As the Council bears the main responsibility for the maintenance of international peace and security, it seems admissible that it promptly reacts to situations arising in times of 'peace' taking advantage of the discretion conferred to it by Article 39.[76]

f) However, whatever the situation that the Council sets out to address under Chapter VII, it seems that the fundamental limit to the Council's Article 39 powers is that it ought to assess the presence of certain preconditions.[77] Reasoning along the line of the criteria set out by Professor Combacau,[78] it seems that, according to Article 39, the Council ought to ascertain the existence of *factual* elements existing in a given moment in time. A threat to the peace should correspond to a real, concrete and specific emergency situation that the Council must address as quickly as possible. A threat should 'exist' and it should be actual and serious at the moment when the Council makes an Article 39 determination. Accordingly, and setting aside considerations of a political or moral propriety of the broad determinations contained in Resolutions 1368 and following, one might wonder whether the Article 39 notion of threat to the peace can extend to cover also hypothetical and future situations ('any act of international terrorism'). Well, it appears that with Resolution 1373 and following, the Council engaged its future action by asserting, in a given moment in time, that any hypothetical future act of terrorism is a threat to the peace. This way, the link between the actuality of a situation considered under Article 39 and a threat to the peace would appear to be missing. Anticipating future developments, however, Tomuschat argued in 1993 that Article 39 does not prevent the Council from taking action in general terms if certain phenomena are held incompatible, as such, with

---

74 See, in this regard, the comments by F. Mégret., '"War"? Legal Semantics and the Move to Violence', *European Journal of International Law*, vol. 13, 2002, pp. 361 ff.

75 On the other hand, already at San Francisco the necessity for the Council to adapt to the changing conditions of the international security environment was acknowledged. Mention was made of the possible evolution of the situations that the Council could encounter when acting under Article 39. With reference to the determination of acts of aggression, it was decided not to accept a proposal aimed to include a list of the possible situations in which the Council could be called to intervene as, *inter alia*, '[t]he progress of technique of modern warfare renders very difficult the definition of aggression'. *UNCIO*, *supra* note 46, p. 505.

76 According to Dominicé, the Council could not 'rester inactif devant des situations qui revoltent la conscience universelle' (*supra* note 49, p. 436).

77 Scotto, *supra* note 50, Chapter II, para 31.

78 J. Combacau, *Le pouvoir de sanction de l'ONU. Étude théorique de la coercition non militaire*, Paris: Pedone, 1974, pp. 100-106.

the fundamental interests of the international community.[79] Reading Article 39 in conjunction with Article 24, this scholar argues that the Council 'could venture to develop a subject-matter-specific understanding of Article 39, determining, for instance, that certain types of armaments .... constitute *per se* a threat to international peace and security.' This on the ground that the wording 'threat to the peace' was chosen 'precisely with a view to permitting the Security Council to take precautionary action well before an armed attack occurs. If prevention is the philosophical concept underlying Article 39, then it must also be possible that the Security Council, in a more abstract manner ... outlaws certain activities' in general.[80]

Though even admitting that so broad determinations are in conformity with the Charter, it seems that the Council stretched the notion of threat to the peace to broaden the range of terrorist acts that can fall under this notion's scope and, consequently, its possibilities of intervention. The Council's Chapter VII subsequent practice seems to support this assertion.

From Article 39 determinations to enforcement measures

After making an Article 39 determination that a situation of emergency for international peace and security existed in connection with terrorist acts, the Council has enacted Chapter VII measures to resolve it. The Council adopted Chapter VII measures to address the terrorist activities of Libya and Sudan, as well as those carried out by the Taliban faction when it was in control of part of the Afghan territory. In these cases, the Council adopted, *inter alia*, arms embargoes, restrictions of diplomatic relations and assets freeze to address specific situations arising out of discrete acts of terrorism.

With Resolution 1373 the Council followed a very different approach. Having determined that any act of 'international terrorism' amounts to a threat to the peace, the Council adopted measures tailor made to address the general threat that 'international' terrorism casts on peace and security. Albeit originating from the 9-11 attacks, Resolution 1373 does not specifically address those acts, but tackles terrorism in general. This Resolution creates a broad range of (partially) new obligations for States aimed to induce them to modify, where needed, their domestic counter-terrorism legislation with a view to render their legal systems best equipped to prevent and repress terrorism, in particular its financing. Many have commented on Resolution 1373's main innovative aspects.[81] The most important feature of this Resolution, however, is that it has been conceived to apply to acts of terrorism in general, including future acts. Resolution 1373, furthermore, does not specifically

---

79 C. Tomuschat, 'Obligations Arising for States Without or Against Their Will', *Recueil des Cours de l'Académie de droit international de la Haye,* vol. 241, 1993, at p. 344.

80 *Ibid.*

81 See, for example, J. E. Alvarez, 'The Security Council's War on Terrorism: Problems and Policy Options', in E. De Wet, A. Nollkaemper (eds.), *Review of Security Council by Member States*, Antwerp/New York: Intersentia, 2003, pp. 119 ff.

focus on acts of 'international' terrorism, but addresses acts of terrorism in general (hence, possibly, also essentially domestic acts). In the preamble the Council reaffirms 'the need to combat ... threats to international peace and security caused by terrorist acts'[82] and recognizes 'the need for States to complement international cooperation by taking additional measures to prevent and suppress, in their territories, the financing and preparation of any acts of terrorism'. The operational paragraphs, then, generally refer to acts of terrorism, and not to acts of 'international' terrorism.

Therefore, Resolution 1373's scope '*ratione personarum, ratione loci* and *ratione temporis*' appears to be essentially unlimited. It applies to any individual or other private entity directly or indirectly involved in terrorist acts, whenever and wherever committed, so long as the Council decides that the threat to the peace caused by terrorism has ceased.[83]

This Council's action has been criticized as going beyond the Charter provisions.[84] As other times in the past, also with Resolution 1373 the Council created new obligations for States. Differently from the past, however, the Council did not confine itself to create new obligations with regard to discrete situations. Rather, the Council created full-fledged international law rules which 'are unilateral in form ..., create ... a legal norm, and [are] general in nature, that is, directed to indeterminate addressees and capable of repeated application in time'.[85] In doing so, the Council broadly relied (and partially incorporated) the 1999 Convention on the Suppression of the Financing of Terrorism – even though this Convention had not yet entered into force when Resolution 1373 was adopted. In this regard, it was noted that the series of obligations that Resolution 1373 creates for States seem to correspond to a sort of conventional text[86] imposed on States by means of a Chapter VII deliberation. However, according to the text of the Charter, Council's recommendations and decisions that it adopts under Articles 39-42 should be taken on a case-by-case basis, according to an evaluation of what is needed to contrast specific situations of emergency for international peace and security. Chapter VII measures ought not to present a general and indeterminate character, nor should they be structured to

---

82 Res. 1373, preambular para. 5.

83 In this sense I respectfully disagree with Condorelli, who believes that 'en réalité ladite Résolution est obligatoire pour les États ... seulement ... par rapport aux activités et aux réseaux terroristes qui sont derrière les évenements du 11 Septembre, alors qu'à l'avenir, concernant d'autres situations, les préscriptions établies par la Résolutions ne seraient applicable en tant que telles qu'après l'établissement par le Conseil qu'il y a a bien en l'espèce une nouvelle menace contre la paix engendrée par un nouvel acte de terrorisme international'. L. Condorelli, 'Les attentats du 11 septembre et leur suites: où va le droit international?', *Revue générale de Droit international public*, vol. 105, 2001, p. 835.

84 See, for example, *ibid.*

85 E. Yemin, *Legislative Powers in the United Nations and Specialized Agencies*, 1969, quoted in F.L. Kirgis, 'The Security Council's First Fifty Years', *American Journal of International Law*, vol. 89, 1995, p. 520.

86 I. Bantekas, 'The International Law of Terrorist Financing', *American Journal of International Law*, vol. 97, 2003, p. 326.

address future situations. Even admitting, against some scholars' belief,[87] that the Council can create new obligations for States, the question remains whether this also implies a more general 'international treaty making' power,[88] in substitution of States' prerogatives and, to a certain extent, the General Assembly's.[89]

On the other hand, having determined that individuals and other non State actors constitute a terrorist network that plans, supports and carries out terrorist acts against States and other targets, the Council enacted measures aimed to contrast those entities' conducts. Hence, the Council obliged States to adopt restrictive measures targeting them. Resolution 1333,[90] as amended by Resolution 1390, engages States to enact an asset-freeze, a travel ban and an arms embargo against a number of individuals and other private entities that the Council indicates by means of a list that an Article 29 Sanctions Committee established under Resolution 1267 of 15 October 1999 is entrusted to draw.[91]

Also in this regard, the Council's action raised concerns among scholars. Whereas some argue that Chapter VII measures were conceived to contrast 'States'' conducts,[92] others noted that Article 41 of the Charter says nothing in that regard.[93]

---

87 See, for example, G. Arangio-Ruiz, 'On the Security Council's "Law-Making"' in *Rivista di diritto internazionale*, vol. 83, 2000, p. 609 ff.

88 See also Y. Sandoz, 'Lutte contre le terrorisme et droit international: risques et opportunités', *Revue suisse de droit international et de droit européen*, vol. 12, 2002, pp. 330 and Condorelli, *supra* note 83, pp. 834-845.

89 See P.C. Szasz, 'The Security Council Starts Legislating', *American Journal of International Law*, vol. 96, 2002, pp. 901 ff. ('as Resolution 1373, while inspired by the attacks of September 11, 2001, is not specifically related to these (though they are mentioned in the preamble) and lacks any implicit or explicit time limitation, a significant portion of the resolution can be said to establish new binding rules of international law – rather then mere commands relating to a particular situation – and, moreover, even creates a mechanism for monitoring compliance with them', p. 902). According to A. Pellet, however, the Council would have no power to adopt 'règles générales et impersonnelles; il ne peut décider avec force obligatoire que dans des cas particuliers' ('Peut-on et doit-on dire contrôler les actions du Conseil de sécurité?', in *Le Chapitre VII de la Charte des Nations Unites*, colloque SFDI, Paris, 1995, p. 236).

90 Although Resolution 1333 of 19 December 2000 mainly targets the Taliban regime as the Government of Afghanistan, it also adopts an asset-freeze, targeting Usama bin Laden, the members of Al Qaeda and others associated with them (para. 8.).

91 So, whereas by Resolution 1373 the Council confined itself to ask States to freeze assets of persons they classify as 'terrorists' according to their domestic laws, with Resolutions 1333 and 1390 the Council went so far as to nominally indicate the private entities against which the freezing and other restrictive measures must be applied.

92 In a similar sense, see J. E. Alvarez, *International Organizations as Law Makers*, Oxford: Oxford University Press, forthcoming, p. 193.

93 See the passage by Kelsen quoted in the text *supra*. In particular, Kelsen argued that the 'Security Council may very well decide that a situation which has not the character of a conflict between two states is a threat to the international peace and take enforcement action against a state or a group of people involved in this situation, though the state is not in conflict

This provision, read together with Article 39 of the Charter, only provides that the Council adopt measures aimed to cease situations of emergency where international peace is threatened. If a threat is created by private entities' conducts, the Council should be able to address it.[94] However, the main criticism is with the fact that, when targeting private entities, the Council would fail to comply with certain guarantees for the protection of certain fundamental human rights.[95]

---

with another state and the group has not the character of a state' (Kelsen, *supra* note 43, p. 731). Although Kelsen referred to 'groups' that are not States, and not private entities, it nevertheless seemed to refer also to entities deprived of the international personality. It could therefore be argued that Kelsen's reasoning could hold with regard private entities too. On the other hand, according to a large number of scholars, the coercive nature of Article 41 measures consists precisely in the possibility for the Council to interfere in States' domestic jurisdiction, in particular by addressing measures to entities falling under their jurisdiction. See, for example, Conforti, *supra* note 51, p. 152. *Contra* G. Arangio-Ruiz, 'Le domaine réservé', *Recueil des Cours de l'Academie de Droit international de la Haye*, vol. 225, 1990, pp. 411 ff. (according to this author, the exception contained in Article 2, para. 7 of the Charter exclusively applies to Article 42 enforcement measures).

94   Indeed, it seems that the Council addresses private entities' behaviours as causing a threat to the peace and acts accordingly to counter them. This does not imply that the Council interferes with the status of the entities in regard to which it operates. The Council for example, did not consider (nor could it consider) private entities as being the addressees of international obligations that it ascertains or creates. The Council, for example, did not demand bin Laden … to surrender to the United States! Rather, the Council confines itself to ask States to apply certain restrictive measures to specific entities falling under their jurisdiction.

95   The Committee established under Resolution 1267 of 15 October 1999 to monitor States' compliance with measures targeting Usama bin Laden, the Taliban and Al Qaeda was mandated to establish and maintain an updated list of individuals and entities designated as being associated with Usama bin Laden, Al Qaeda and the Taliban. States must apply an asset-freeze, a travel ban and an arms embargo against those entities (on the activity of this Committee see E. Rosand, 'Current Development: The Security Council's Effort to Monitor the Implementation of Al Qaeda/Taliban Sanctions', *American Journal of International Law*, Vol. 98, 2004 p. 745ff.). The Committee's listing procedure, though, raised concerns among States and scholars. The Committee draws its list based on information provided by States and regional organizations. Generally, that information does not originate from criminal proceedings. It often originates directly from national governments, absent a judicial control (see, for example, the lists published by the US *Treasury Office of Foreign Assets Control* under *Executive Order 13224 – Blocking Property and Prohibiting Transactions with Persons who Commit, Threaten to Commit, or Support Terrorism*, signed by the US President on 23 September 2001 and periodically sent to the Committee for possible insertion in the list.) The listing procedure, then, does not provide for an evaluation of the information provided by States, nor does it afford individuals involved a possibility of challenging the allegations against them. A de-listing procedure was only introduced in 2002. Whereas individuals can appeal to their national State or the State where their assets are frozen, it is only for those States to trigger the de-listing procedure before the Committee. Such procedure takes place at the political inter-state level and does not involve the individual concerned. As many observed, the fact that the Committee (*rectius*, the Council) carries out its activity absent

Conclusions

The question of the possible limits to the Council's Article 39 powers, therefore, is not merely relevant *per se* as a possible parameter to assess the Council's action legality. The assessment of the existence of one of the Article 39 preconditions for the Council to have recourse to its further Chapter VII powers also determines the way in which the Council exercises those powers. Albeit it enjoys a certain discretion in determining what measures are appropriate to resolve a situation of grave emergency for international peace and security, those measures still ought to be commensurate to the gravity and characteristics of the situation concerned, as assessed under Article 39.[96] So, for example, having determined that the impunity in the former Yugoslavia and Rwanda of perpetrators of the most serious violations of human rights and international humanitarian law constituted a threat to the peace, the Council established the two *ad hoc* international criminal tribunals for the Former Yugoslavia and Rwanda.[97] Similarly, to the determination that failure by States to extradite suspect terrorists to other States constituted a threat to international peace and security, measures followed aimed at inducing those States to extradite. And having determined that any act of terrorism – whether actual or future, whether international or domestic – constitutes a threat to the peace, the Council created a number of partially new general obligations for States aimed to contrast the phenomenon as such, rather then specific terrorist acts and to target private entities.

Thus, whereas many scholars believe that there would be no point in continuing to debate around the possible limits to the Council's Article 39 action – as the Council would be perfectly free to classify under that provision whatever situation,

---

mechanisms aimed to ensure the necessary procedural guarantees (mechanisms that the Council created when it established the two *ad hoc* international criminal tribunals for the former Yugoslavia and Rwanda), raised concerns with regard to such activity's compliance with certain fundamental human rights (cf. E. de Wet, A. Nollkaemper, 'Review of Security Council Decisions by National Courts', *German Yearbook of International Law*, pp. 166 ff., *passim*, and Id. (eds), *Review of Security Council by Member States*, Antwerp: Intersentia, 2003. *Contra* J.E. Alvarez, *supra* note 81, pp. 125 ff).

96 On the proportionality as a limit to the Council's action, see J.A. Frowein, N. Krisch, 'Article 41', in Simma, *supra* note 43, p. 745 and M. Bennouna, 'L'embargo dans la pratique des Nations-Unies – Radioscopie d'un moyen de pression', *Bancaja*, 1997, p. 221. See also M. Bothe, *supra* note 54, pp. 76-79. According to Kirgis 'the Security Council in a Chapter VII situation should respect the principle of proportionality – or what might be better described as the principle of avoiding excessive disproportionality. Strict proportionality cannot be expected in all cases, and it might not even be appropriate in the context of enforcement action designed to halt aggressive behavior. At the same time, there is no call in the Charter for enforcement beyond what is actually necessary to thwart an actual threat to the peace or to end a breach to the peace' (*supra* note 82, p. 517). See also S. Talman, 'The Security Council as World Legislature', *American Journal of International Law*, vol. 99, 2005, pp. 175ff., *passim*.

97 See Resolution 809(1993), preambular paras. 6 and 7; Resolution 827(1993), preambular paras 3 and 4 and 955(1994), preambular paras. 4 and 5.

of whatever nature, whether specific or general – it appears that, even if possibly legal under that provision, the Council's determinations have an important effect on the exercise of its further Chapter VII powers. The ease the Council has recently shown in creatively interpreting those powers raised criticism among States and scholars (including those who believe in the Council's broadest discretion under Article 39). It seems important therefore that the Council carefully exercises its Article 39 powers as the consequent choice of the necessary Chapter VII enforcement measures is predicated upon those determinations.

Chapter 8

The Political Offence Concept in Regional and International Conventions Relating to Terrorism

MICHAEL DE FEO[1]

Introduction

The United Nations Office on Drugs and Crime was most grateful for the invitation to participate in the Conference on 'International Cooperation and Counterterrorism' held at the Faculty of Jurisprudence of the University of Trento on 29-30 April 2004. The theme of that encounter, and the analyses presented by several speakers relating to regional conventions against terrorism, were of great interest and relevance to UN anti-terrorism efforts. Indeed, the agenda was so full of valuable presentations that many of the stimulating topics that were raised could only be explored in depth outside the confines of the conference itself, including the subject of this chapter.

In its Resolution 1373 of 28 September 2001 the United Nations Security Council called upon all States to ratify and implement 12 universal anti-terrorism conventions and protocols. The two most recent and broadly applicable of those instruments are the 1997 International Convention for the Suppression of Terrorist Bombings and the 1999 International Convention for the Suppression of the Financing of Terrorism. Those two instruments, which are universal in the sense that they are open to membership by all Member States of the United Nations, contain articles which provide, in virtually identical language, that:

> None of the offences set forth in Article 2 shall be regarded, for the purposes of extradition or mutual legal assistance, as a political offence or as an offence connected with a political offence or as an offence inspired by political motives. Accordingly, a request for extradition or for mutual legal assistance based on such an offence may not be refused on the sole ground that it concerns a political offence or an offence connected with a political offence or an offence inspired by political motives.[2]

---

1 Legal Advisor, Terrorism Prevention Branch, United Nations Office on Drugs and Crime, Vienna, Austria. These remarks are made in a personal capacity and do not necessarily reflect the views of the UNODC.

2 Article 11 of the 1997 International Convention for the Suppression of Terrorist Bombings. Article 14 of the 1999 International Convention for the Suppression of the Financing

The political offence concept in regional agreements

A number of presentations at the Conference on International Cooperation and Counterterrorism analysed the provisions of anti-terrorism conventions among regional groups, a term used broadly to apply to groupings which may extend across more than one geographic area, such as the Organization of the Islamic Conference. Many regional organizations have adopted conventions defining terrorist offences and denying the applicability of the political offence exception to those offences. These conventions can be divided into two groups, those that simply abolish the political offence exception for defined terrorist offences, and those that abolish the exception but exclude from the scope of the instrument armed struggles for liberation or self-determination. For the sake of brevity, these provisions will be referred to in this discussion as 'armed struggle' exclusions.

Regional agreements that simply abolish the political offence exception are the Inter-American Convention against Terrorism of the Organization of American States, the South Asian Association for Regional Cooperation Convention on Suppression of Terrorism, and the Treaty on Cooperation among the States Members of the Commonwealth of Independent States in Combating Terrorism. The European Convention on the Suppression of Terrorism announces that it is abolishing the exception in Article 2, and then in a later article permits a State Party to make a reservation preserving its right to assert the exception. While the approach in the Council of Europe's Convention may seem ambivalent, it does not present any issue of interpretation.

The provisions of another group of regional conventions present a common question of interpretation, which could only be touched upon very briefly at the Conference on International Cooperation and Counterterrorism because of time limitations. The provisions in question are found in the Arab Convention for the Suppression of Terrorism (1998), the Convention of the Organization of the Islamic Conference on Combating International Terrorism (1999), and the Organization of African Unity Convention on the Prevention and Combating of Terrorism (1998).[3]

The operative language in the English translation of the Arab Convention used in the UN publication, is found in Article 2(a):

> All cases of struggle, by whatever means, including armed struggle, against foreign occupation and aggression for liberation and self-determination, in accordance with the principles of international law, shall not be regarded as an offence. This provision does not apply to any act prejudicing the territorial integrity of any Arab State.

---

of Terrorism is identical, except for the omission of the commas in the first sentence.

3   The language of the universal and regional instruments cited in this article are taken from the United Nations publication, *International Instruments related to the Prevention and Suppression of International Terrorism*, New York, 2001. The texts of the 1997 and 1999 UN conventions represent the official English version. The texts of the regional conventions are not necessarily in the original official language of the instrument, and represent English translations used by the UN.

In the Convention of the Islamic Conference, it is Article 2 (a), which states:

> Peoples' struggle, including armed struggle against foreign occupation, aggression, colonialism, and hegemony, aimed at liberation and self-determination in accordance with the principles of international law shall not be considered a terrorist crime.

The pertinent language in the Organization of African Unity Convention appears in Article 3, paragraph 1:

> Notwithstanding the provisions of Article 1 (which defines terrorist acts), the struggle waged by peoples in accordance with the principles of international law for their liberation or self-determination, including armed struggle against colonialism, occupation, aggression and domination by foreign forces shall not be considered as terrorist acts.

Popularization of the armed struggle exception

These convention articles echo one of the most famous political statements of the last generation; that is, the first speech made by Chairman Arafat of the Palestinian Liberation Organization to the United Nations General Assembly. In that 1974 presentation, Chairman Arafat stated that:

> The difference between the revolutionary and the terrorist lies in the reason for which each fights. For whoever stands by a just cause and fights for the freedom and liberation of his land from the invaders, the settlers and the colonialists, cannot possibly be called terrorists ...[4]

The 1974 speech goes on to cite examples of armed opposition to oppression, such as the American Revolution, the European resistance against the Nazis, and struggles against colonialism. Read in the abstract, that speech, like the 'armed struggle' provisions in the three regional conventions under consideration, can be interpreted as simply invoking the right to resort to political violence in defence of rights recognized by the United Nations Charter. Given the speech's historical context, however, those remarks can also be interpreted as an assertion that the international attacks on civilians that led to many of the anti-terrorism conventions constituted legitimate political violence, and not acts of terrorism, because they were committed in a just cause.

Criminal conventions directed at the unlawful seizure of aircraft had been concluded in 1970 and 1971 after the Popular Front for the Liberation of Palestine began hijackings in 1968, a practice which resulted in the destruction of aircraft and the killing of passengers. The highly publicized kidnapping and killing of Israeli athletes at the Munich Olympic Games by the Black September group had taken place in 1972. The Convention on the Prevention and Punishment of Crimes against

---

4 *Le Monde Diplomatique*, http://www.monde-diplomatique.fr/cahier/proche-orient/arafat74-en.

Internationally Protected Persons, including Diplomatic Agents (1973) had just been negotiated in response to attacks on State representatives and diplomats, including the killing of the Jordanian Prime Minister in Cairo and of American and Belgian diplomats in Sudan, both events attributable to sympathizers with the Palestinian cause.

International violence directed at civilians was a prominent characteristic of the particular struggle that Chairman Arafat was defending when he stated that those who fought for the freedom and liberation of their land could not possibly be called terrorists. Given the context and chronology of political violence preceding the speech, Chairman Arafat's words could be interpreted as an assertion that crimes against civilians were not terrorism because they were committed in a just cause. That position would be in conflict with the general approach of the anti-terrorism conventions and protocols developed by the United Nations and its affiliated agencies to protect civilians and non-combatants from targeted or indiscriminate violence, and with explicit provisions in the two most recent UN conventions specifically rejecting the political offence exception and any ideological or political justifications for violence against civilians and non-combatants.

That same issue of the legality of political violence aimed at civilians was still a concern when the three regional conventions were negotiated in 1998 and 1999. Increasing numbers of civilians were the victims of violent attacks committed in the name of struggles for national liberation, self-determination, or related ideological motives, including the Palestinian struggle. Thus, it is relevant to consider what those conventions provide with respect to violence directed at civilians.

'In accordance with international law'

A common question of interpretation raised by these three instruments involves the exclusion from the scope of the conventions of armed struggles 'in accordance with the principles of international law'. Phrased in classical international law terminology, is it only the *jus ad bellum*, the reasons for resorting to armed struggle, or also the *jus in bello*, the means used in the struggle, that must be in accordance with international law principles in order for the struggle to be excluded from the coverage of the three conventions?

Normally, the interpretation of treaties is exclusively the concern of the treaty partners. However, these 'armed struggle' convention articles may implicate the provisions of two UN anti-terrorism instruments, to which the States Parties of the above three conventions may also be parties, as well as of Security Council Resolution 1373 of 28 September 2001.[5]

Article 6 of the 1999 International Convention for the Suppression of the Financing of Terrorism provides that:

---

5   Available at www.un.org/Docs/sc/committees/1373.

Each State Party shall adopt such measures as may be necessary, including, where appropriate, domestic legislation, to ensure that criminal acts within the scope of this Convention are under no circumstances justifiable by considerations of a political, philosophical, ideological, racial, ethnic, religious or other similar nature.

The International Convention for the Suppression of Terrorist Bombings, 1997, contains slightly expanded language in its Article 5, including the phrase: '… in particular where they (criminal acts within the scope of the Convention) are intended or calculated to provoke a state of terror in the general public or in a group of persons or particular persons…'.

States that are parties to the 1999 and 1997 UN conventions are required to adopt such domestic measures as might be necessary to ensure that criminal acts within the scope of the Convention are under no circumstances justifiable by consideration of a political, philosophical, ideological or similar nature. The motivation for armed struggles for liberation and self-determination is indisputably a political consideration. If the same States were parties to one of the regional conventions, the question may be asked whether refusing to extradite or to furnish mutual legal assistance in reliance upon an armed struggle exclusion would constitute either a *de jure* or a *de facto* justification of an otherwise criminal act by considerations of a political or ideological nature.

Security Council Resolution 1373

In addition, the question may arise whether reliance upon the armed struggle exclusion would violate a State's duties under Security Council Resolution 1373. That resolution has both non-binding and mandatory articles. The non-binding articles include a call in Operative Paragraph 3(g) to '… ensure, in conformity with international law … that claims of political motivation are not recognized as grounds for refusing requests for the extradition of alleged terrorists'.

In addition to Paragraph 3, Operative Paragraph 2 of the resolution announces decisions expressly stated to have been adopted under Chapter 7 of the United Nations Charter. Paragraph 2 is, therefore, binding upon all Member States under Articles 25 and 39. Operative Paragraph 2 of Resolution 1373 contains the famous phraseology that the Security Council has decided that States shall 'Deny safe haven to those who finance, plan, facilitate, or commit terrorist acts or provide safe havens'. If a country relied upon the armed struggle exclusion in a regional convention to decline to extradite or prosecute persons who had committed acts defined as offences under one of the universal anti-terrorism conventions, the further question could be asked – would that country be providing a safe haven to persons who financed, planned, facilitated or committed terrorist acts, in arguable disregard of a binding provision of Resolution 1373?

Interpretation of the armed struggle provisions

The answer to these questions requires a determination of '... the ordinary meaning to be given to the terms of the treaty in their context and in the light of its object and purpose'.[6]

Such a determination is not a simple task, as demonstrated by Article 3 of the Organization of African Unity Convention. Paragraph 1 of Article 3 excludes struggles for liberation or self-determination from being considered to be terrorist acts, but is immediately followed by paragraph 2, which states that 'political, philosophical, ideological, racial, ethnic, religious or other motives shall not be a justifiable defence against a terrorist act'.

Struggling for self-determination or national liberation is the ultimate political motive. It would seem somewhat of a conceptual anomaly if the first paragraph of Article 3 means that the political motive of an armed struggle categorically excludes all acts committed in pursuit of that struggle from being characterized as terrorist offences, regardless of their nature or victims, whereas the Article's second paragraph declares those same considerations to be irrelevant. Counterpart provisions legitimizing armed struggles, but also making political motives irrelevant as a defence to international cooperation, appear in the Conventions of the Arab League and of the Organization of the Islamic Conference.

This apparent anomaly is easily resolved if the phrase 'in accordance with the principles of international law' is interpreted to require not merely *jus ad bellum*, the right to use force in a struggle for liberation and self-determination, but also *jus in bello*, that is, avoidance of the use of force against civilians as required by humanitarian law principles. Under that construction, the States Parties to the regional conventions would not be justifying a criminal offence for political or ideological considerations, because an attack on civilians, even in a just struggle, would be treated on its merits as a possible crime. Resolution 1373 would not be implicated, because a person who observes humanitarian law principles with respect to means of conflict and persons targeted would not be committing acts of terrorism within the meaning of the resolution.

If the 'in accordance with international law' requirement applies to the means of violence used, as well as to the legitimacy of the causes for the resort to an armed struggle, the regional conventions providing that political considerations are not to be recognized as a grounds for withholding international cooperation would complement and not contradict the 'armed struggle' exclusions in those instruments. Acts targeting civilians would be considered crimes for which political or ideological considerations would constitute no defence, no matter how legitimate the struggle.

The 'armed struggle' language in the three regional conventions could, therefore, be understood as simply affirming the legitimacy of a resort to political violence *in*

---

6   Section 3, Interpretation of Treaties, Article 31, General Rule of Interpretation, Vienna Convention on the Law of Treaties of 1969, United Nations, *Treaty Series*, Vol. 1155, p. 331; http: //www. un.org/ law/ilc/texts/treaties.htm.

extremis, when a people have no other means to vindicate basic human rights, and so long as the means used also conform to the principles of international law. So interpreted, the dilemmas associated with the armed struggle language are resolved.

Summary

In conclusion, there are two interpretations that can be applied to the 'armed struggle' exclusions in regional conventions. One would interpret the phrase 'in accordance with principles of international law' as applying only to the *jus ad bellum*, the legitimacy of the resort to armed struggle itself, in which case all political violence committed in that struggle would be excluded from the coverage of the conventions. That interpretation would implicate possible conflicts with the overall approach of the twelve UN anti-terrorism conventions and protocols, and with the specific language and obligations of the two most recent UN anti-terrorism conventions, the Terrorist Bombing Convention of 1997 and the Terrorist Financing Convention of 1999, and of Security Council Resolution 1373.

An alternative approach would interpret the 'in accordance with the principles of international law' phrase as applying not only to the justification for resorting to violence, but also to the means and targets of the political violence used, to the *jus in bello*, and would prohibit attacks on civilians under humanitarian law principles developed to govern the conduct of armed hostilities. This interpretation would resolve any potential conflict between UN and regional instruments.

As indicated previously, the very full and rich agenda of the Conference on International Cooperation and Counterterrorism, hosted by the School of Law of the University of Trento, did not permit exploration of all of the issues raised by the many stimulating presentations. Among those issues was the question of which interpretation of the 'armed struggle' exclusion best conforms to the previously cited interpretation criterion of the Vienna Convention on the Law of Treaties of 1969.

It would, therefore, be of great interest and utility if future attention were to be focused on this issue among practitioners, academic authorities and those familiar with the negotiation of the relevant instruments, in order to bring about a rigorous intellectual analysis of what appears to be a very fundamental question concerning the legitimacy of and limitations upon political violence.

Chapter 9

Terrorism as a Crime Against Humanity under the ICC Statute

ROBERTA ARNOLD[1]

Introduction

Following the attacks of 11 September, a major question that has arisen within the international community is the efficiency of the existing anti-terrorism legal regime. Notwithstanding the enactment, since the 1970s, of a series of conventions[2] aimed at addressing this crime, these have proven to be less effective than expected. Partly the reason has been their focus on sub-forms of terrorism, rather than the phenomenon in its complexity, thus failing to cover its more modern manifestations. At the same time, the widespread belief that terrorism is a subjective notion, dependent on an individual's political beliefs – from which the motto 'one man's terrorist is another man's freedom fighter' derives – has made it impossible to achieve universal consensus on a comprehensive anti-terrorism convention. Another reason is that the enforcement of the existing instruments very much depends on the political willingness of the State Parties to support the international cooperation in criminal matters. Often the exceptions provided under extradition law, such as the clause that a State cannot be compelled to extradite its own citizens – as occurred in the *Lockerbie* Case[3] – or the political offence exception, have allowed terrorists to find safe havens. The aim of this chapter is to study an alternative way, namely that of trying to prosecute terrorism, as understood in the common language – that is, as a violent act aimed at raising fear within the population, in order to force a government or a community to meet the political demands of the perpetrators – as a crime against humanity under Article 7 of the Rome Statute for an International Criminal Court (ICC).

---

1   Ministry of Defence, Berne. These remarks are made in a personal capacity and do not necessarily reflect the views of the Swiss Ministry of Defence.

2   For a list of the conventions, see *Extract from the Report of the Secretary General on measures to eliminate international terrorism* (Doc. A/57/183), as updated on 10 December 2002, at http://www.un.org/law/terrorism/terrorism_table_update_12-2002.pdf.

3   See R. Arnold, *The ICC as a new instrument for repressing terrorism*, Ardsley: Transnational Publisher, 2004, at p. 12.

In order to attempt this task, the chapter will be structured as follows. The next section will provide a brief definition of crimes against humanity under existing international law and the ICC Statute. The following section will discuss whether there are any precedents, according to international jurisprudence, supporting the possibility of prosecuting terrorism as a crime against humanity. The fourth part will discuss whether terrorism possesses the elements of crimes against humanity under Article 7 ICC Statute. The final part will draw some conclusions.

The definition of crimes against humanity

Pursuant to Article 5 of the ICC Statute, the International Criminal Court has jurisdiction over 'serious crimes of concern to the international community as a whole.' These include crimes against humanity as referred to in Article 7.[4] The

---

4   'For the purpose of this Statute, "crime against humanity" means any of the following acts when committed as part of a widespread or systematic attack directed against any civilian population, with knowledge of the attack:
(a) Murder;
(b) Extermination;
(c) Enslavement;
(d) Deportation or forcible transfer of population;
(e) Imprisonment or other severe deprivation of physical liberty in violation of fundamental rules of international law;
(f) Torture;
(g) Rape, sexual slavery, enforced prostitution, forced pregnancy, enforced sterilization, or any other form of sexual violence of comparable gravity;
(h) Persecution against any identifiable group or collectivity on political, racial, national, ethnic, cultural, religious, gender as defined in paragraph 3, or other grounds that are universally recognized as impermissible under international law, in connection with any act referred to in this paragraph or any crime within the jurisdiction of the Court;
(i) Enforced disappearance of persons;
(j) The crime of apartheid;
(k) Other inhumane acts of a similar character intentionally causing great suffering, or serious injury to body or to mental or physical health.
2. For the purpose of paragraph 1:
(a) "Attack directed against any civilian population" means a course of conduct involving the multiple commission of acts referred to in paragraph 1 against any civilian population, pursuant to or in furtherance of a State or organizational policy to commit such attack;
(b) "Extermination" includes the intentional infliction of conditions of life, *inter alia* the deprivation of access to food and medicine, calculated to bring about the destruction of part of a population;
(c) "Enslavement" means the exercise of any or all of the powers attaching to the right of ownership over a person and includes the exercise of such power in the course of trafficking in persons, in particular women and children;

definition contained therein recalls the one enshrined in customary international law,[5] as restated in the *Charter of the International Military Tribunal of Nuremberg* (IMT) and the Statutes of the International Criminal Tribunals for, respectively, the Former Yugoslavia (ICTY) and Rwanda (ICTR). However, this has undergone important changes since the early 20th century, when it was conceived as an auxiliary provision to war crimes, with the aim of protecting the fundamental aspects of the human being. Pursuant to the ICC Statute, for instance, it is no longer required that crimes against humanity have a nexus with an armed conflict. On the other hand, common requirements are that the crimes be committed within the framework of a widespread or systematic attack, on the basis of a policy – either state or non-state based – and against a civilian population. Moreover, Article 7 specifies that the definition provided for in this provision shall be intended for 'the purpose of this Statute'. Particular attention will thus be paid to the issue of whether it may contain new elements, specific to the ICC's needs.

(d) "Deportation or forcible transfer of population" means forced displacement of the persons concerned by expulsion or other coercive acts from the area in which they are lawfully present, without grounds permitted under international law;

(e) "Torture" means the intentional infliction of severe pain or suffering, whether physical or mental, upon a person in the custody or under the control of the accused; except that torture shall not include pain or suffering arising only from, inherent in or incidental to, lawful sanctions;

(f) "Forced pregnancy" means the unlawful confinement of a woman forcibly made pregnant, with the intent of affecting the ethnic composition of any population or carrying out other grave violations of international law. This definition shall not in any way be interpreted as affecting national laws relating to pregnancy;

(g) "Persecution" means the intentional and severe deprivation of fundamental rights contrary to international law by reason of the identity of the group or collectivity;

(h) "The crime of apartheid" means inhumane acts of a character similar to those referred to in paragraph 1, committed in the context of an institutionalized regime of systematic oppression and domination by one racial group over any other racial group or groups and committed with the intention of maintaining that regime;

(i) "Enforced disappearance of persons" means the arrest, detention or abduction of persons by, or with the authorization, support or acquiescence of, a State or a political organization, followed by a refusal to acknowledge that deprivation of freedom or to give information on the fate or whereabouts of those persons, with the intention of removing them from the protection of the law for a prolonged period of time.

3. For the purpose of this Statute, it is understood that the term "gender" refers to the two sexes, male and female, within the context of society. The term "gender" does not indicate any meaning different from the above.'

5 R. Dixon, 'Crimes Against Humanity,' in O. Triffterer (ed.), *Commentary on the Rome Statute of the International Criminal Court,* Baden-Baden: Nomos Verlagsgesellschaft, 1999, pp.117–128, at p. 123.

The actus reus

Like customary law, Article 7 of the ICC Statute omits any requirement of a nexus between these crimes and an armed conflict: they can be perpetrated independently from war crimes or crimes against the peace.[6] Thus, all types of terrorist acts, be they committed during an armed conflict or peacetime, may be prosecuted under this heading, as long as the other elements are also given.

An important aspect is whether the list of crimes contained in Article 7 of the ICC Statute is exhaustive or illustrative. As mentioned, this definition, like the one contained in the ICTY and ICTR Statutes, was drawn from customary law. Since there are several arguments supporting the thesis that the lists contained in the Statutes of the two UN ad hoc tribunals are illustrative,[7] by analogy the same may be held true for the list provided by the ICC Statute.[8]

The requirement that the crimes be 'committed as part of an attack' was introduced as a jurisdictional threshold.[9] It is not necessary that the individual acts of a single perpetrator constituted the attack itself,[10] but there must be a sufficient nexus between the two. The required degree is not defined.[11] Pursuant to the ICTY and ICTR, this nexus may be suggested by similarities between the acts occurring within the attack and those committed by the accused, the nature of the events, the circumstances and the temporal and geographical proximity of the acts with the attack.[12] 'Attack' means a 'course of conduct involving the multiple commission of acts referred to in Article 7'.[13] It is not to be understood as an 'armed conflict' in

---

6   Dixon, *supra* note 5, at pp. 125,127; S. Ratner, J. Abrams, *Accountability for Human Rights Atrocities in International Law – Beyond the Nuremberg Legacy,* Oxford: Oxford University Press, 2001, 2nd ed., at p. 56; R.S. Lee, *The International Criminal Court: The Making of the Rome Statute, Issues, Negotiations, Results,* The Hague: Kluwer, 1999, at pp. 92–93; E. Greppi, *I crimini di guerra e contro l'umanità nel diritto internazionale,* Turin: UTET, 2001, at pp. 173–174; Arnold, *supra* note 3, at p. 256.

7   On the specificities of the notion of crimes against humanity under the ICTY and the ICTR, see Arnold, *supra* note 3, at pp. 214 ff.

8   Moreover, the notion of 'inhuman acts' contained in the definition is a very broad concept, which can encompass more acts than the ones explicitly indicated in the Rome Statute. See M. Boot, 'Crimes Against Humanity', in O. Triffterer (ed.), *Commentary on the Rome Statute of the International Criminal Court,* Baden-Baden: Nomos Verlagsgesellschaft 1999, pp. 129–166, at p. 155; E. Greppi, *supra* note 6, at p. 180.

9   R. Clark, 'Crimes Against Humanity and the Rome Statute of the International Criminal Court,' in R. Clark et al. (eds), *Essays in Honor of George Ginsburgs: International and National Law in Russia and Eastern Europe,* The Hague: Kluwer, 2001, pp. 139–156, at p. 152.

10 Dixon, *supra* note 5, at p. 124; Greppi, *supra* note 5, at p. 178.

11 Dixon, *supra* note 5, at p. 125.

12 *Ibid.*

13 *Elements, UN Doc. PCNICC/2000/1/Add.2, Introduction to Article 7.* See also Dixon, *supra* note 5, at p. 124. For the notion of attack under the ICTY Statute, see *Prosecutor v. Kunarac, Kovac and Kunovic,* ICTY, Case IT-96-23 and IT-96-23/1 'Foca,' TC, Judgment of

the sense of international humanitarian law (IHL)[14] and need not be of a military character.[15] According to paragraph (2)(1) of Article 7, the attack is associated with the concept of 'widespread or systematic', [16] indicating that it has to involve multiple acts and emanate from (follow) or contribute (promote) to a state or organizational policy.[17] The policy element is:

> ... what unites otherwise unrelated inhumane acts, so that they may be accurately described as an 'attack,' considered collectively, rather than a mere crime wave or other domestic criminal behavior. This is what elevates crimes of individuals to the international sphere of concern.[18]

Both state and non-state actors with *de facto* powers can promote a policy:[19]

> It is understood that 'policy to commit such attack' requires that the State or organization actively promote or encourage such an attack against a civilian population.

The policy may be pursued actively or by omission.[20] Responsibility can be attributed to non-state actors, too.[21] Thus it can be argued that events like 11 September, orchestrated by an international criminal organisation (Al Qaeda), whose link with a governmental regime (*in casu* the Afghani) is difficult to prove, may nevertheless be prosecuted as a crime against humanity.

Several authors argue that, as in the ICTY and the ICTR Statutes, under Article 7 of the ICC Statute the word 'civilians' means persons of any nationality who have not

---

February 22, 2001, para. 415, referring to *Prosecutor v. Tadic*, Case IT-94-1-A, Decision on the Form of the Indictment, November 14, 1995, para. 11.

14 Greppi, *supra* note 6, at p. 174.

15 *Elements, UN Doc. PCNICC/2000/1/Add.2, Introduction to Article 7*. See also Dixon, *supra* note 5, at p. 124. He refers to the findings of the TC in *Prosecutor v. Akayesu*, Case ICTR-96-4-T, Judgment of September 2, 1998, para. 581, holding that also a system of apartheid, or exerting pressure on the population to act in a particular manner, may come under the purview of an attack.

16 On the debate whether these criteria had to be cumulative rather than alternative, see Greppi, *supra* note 6, at p. 175 ff.; Clark, *supra* note 9, at p. 154.

17 Boot, *supra* note 8, at 158. Concerning the notion, the drafters of the Elements decided to leave the matter to the evolving jurisprudence of the ICC.

18 D. Robinson, 'The Context of Crimes Against Humanity,' in R.S. Lee (ed.), *The International Criminal Court: Elements of Crimes and Rules of Procedure and Evidence*, Ardsley: Transnational Publishers, 2001, pp. 61–79, at p. 64.

19 *Elements, UN Doc. PCNICC/2000/1/Add.2, Introduction to Article 7*. See also Boot, *supra* note 7, at p.159; Robinson, *supra* note 18, at p. 64.

20 *UN Doc. PCNICC/2000/1/Add.2, Introduction to Article 7*, at n. 6.

21 See Lee, *supra* note 6, at p. 97. On the requirement of a state policy under Article 6(c) of the IMT Charter, see M.C. Bassiouni, *Crimes Against Humanity in International Criminal Law*, Dordrecht: Martinus Nijhoff, 1992, at p. 248. On the drafting history, see Ratner, Abrams, *supra* note 6, at p. 68.

or are no longer taking an active part in the hostilities.[22] As observed by Robinson, though, the *Elements of Crime* do not address the meaning of 'civilian population', due to the debates held in Rome on whether to include combatants and whether all persons, in peacetime, should be considered civilians. The matter was left to the jurisprudence of the ICC.[23]

The mental element

The personal reasons of the perpetrator are irrelevant. He/she must have had either constructive or actual knowledge of the overall widespread or systematic attack on the civilian population.[24] It is neither necessary that he/she knew about the inhumanity of his/her actions nor that these constituted crimes against humanity.[25] Knowledge of the policy, although required by the jurisprudence of the UN *ad hoc* tribunals,[26] it is not mentioned in the *Elements of Crime*. Paragraph 2 of the introduction thereto states that the perpetrator is not required to know all the details of the policy. Although this may suggest that the author must have been partly aware of it, this issue will also have to be clarified by the ICC.[27] Should the Court decide that the author had intended to implement a policy, this may be the qualifying element of crimes against humanity that generally encompasses acts of terrorism: the latter, in fact, are always perpetrated in furtherance of a policy.

The next step will be to examine whether international jurisprudence based on the customary notion of crimes against humanity is supportive of the thesis that terrorism may be prosecuted under this heading.

International jurisprudence supporting the prosecution of terrorism as a crime against humanity

Since the definition of Article 7 of the ICC Statute relies on customary law, like the ones contained in the Statutes of the ICTY and ICTR and the International Military Tribunal of Nuremberg (IMT), one must examine whether the jurisprudence of these international tribunals is supportive of the view that terrorism may be prosecuted as a crime against humanity.

Already in 1919, the *Commission on the Responsibility of the Authors of the War and on Enforcement of Penalties* considered 'systematic terrorism' a crime

---

22 Dixon, *supra* note 5, at 127; Greppi, *supra* note 5, at p. 179.

23 Robinson, *supra* note 18 , at p. 78.

24 See the *Elements, UN Doc. PCNICC/2000/1/Add.2, Introduction to Article 7*; Greppi, *supra* note 6, at 179; Robinson, *supra* note 18, at p. 73.

25 Dixon, *supra* note 5, at p. 128.

26 *Prosecutor v. Kayishema and Ruzindana*, TC Judgment of May 21, 1999, Case ICTR-95-1-T, para. 133; Robinson, *supra* note 18, at p. 72.

27 Robinson, *supra* note 18, at p. 73.

against humanity.[28] This position was strengthened by the IMT, which considered the terrorization of civilians both as a war crime and a crime against humanity.[29] One of the major problems faced by the IMT in holding the Nazi regime responsible of war crimes committed against the German Jewish population, had been that the latter did not fit the notion of 'protected civilians' under international humanitarian law (IHL). According to IHL, only civilians owning a nationality different from that of the perpetrators are protected persons. The others should invoke the protection of domestic law. Due to this, victims of the Nazi regime of German nationality, in particular German Jews and political opponents, could not invoke serious war crimes in relation to their persecution and extermination. Thus, the count of crimes against humanity was created as an alternative. A passage evidencing the use of this count to address the Nazis' policy of terror is provided by the indictment for the common plan or conspiracy of a crime against peace (Count One):

> In order to make their rule secure from attack and to instil fear in the hearts of the German people, the Nazi conspirators established and extended *a system of terror* against opponents and supposed or suspected opponents of the regime. They imprisoned such persons without judicial process, holding them in 'protective custody' and concentration camps, and subjected them to persecution, degradation, despoilment, enslavement, torture, and murder. These concentration camps were established early in 1933 under the direction of the Defendant Goering and expanded as a fixed part of the *terroristic policy* and method of the conspirators and *used by them for the commission of the Crimes against Humanity* hereinafter alleged. Among the principal agencies utilized in the perpetration of these crimes were the SS and the Gestapo, which, together with other favored branches or agencies of the State and Party, were permitted to operate without restraint of law.[30] [emphasis added]

The Prosecutor's argument was accepted by the IMT in its judgment:

> After the Nazi advent to power, and particularly after the elections of 5th March, 1933, the SA played an important role in establishing a *Nazi reign of terror* over Germany. The SA was involved in outbreaks of violence against the Jews and was used to arrest political opponents and to guard concentration camps, where they subjected their prisoners to brutal mistreatment . . . Isolated units of the SA were even involved in the steps leading

---

28 See Greppi, *supra* note 6, at 114; K. Kittichaisaree, *International Criminal Law*, Oxford: Oxford University Press, 2001, at p. 86.

29 The distinction between the two counts has never been too clear. For example, the IMT *Rosenberg* and the *Frank* judgments, to be found at www.yale.edu/lawweb/avalon/imt/proc/judrosen.htm and http://www.yale.edu/lawweb/avalon/imt/proc/judfrank.htm respectively, found the accused guilty for both war crimes and crimes against humanity, without specifying in detail the differences.

30 Nuremberg Trial Proceedings Vol. 1, Indictment: Count One, para. 3(a): Consolidation of control, at http://www.yale.edu/lawweb/avalon/imt/proc/count1.htm. See also the comments on the SS and the SA of Sir David Maxwell-Fyfe, Deputy Chief Prosecutor for the UK, 29 August 1946, 214th day, at http://www.yale.edu/lawweb/avalon/imt/proc/08-29-46.htm, at 232 and 234.

up to aggressive war and in the commission of war crimes and *crimes against humanity*.[31] [emphasis added]

Another very clear passage is the address of the Chief Prosecutor for the French Republic:

> Mr. President, Your Honors: We have asked you to condemn the leaders responsible for the drama which has bathed the world in blood. Today, ... we seek from your justice the moral condemnation of an entire coherent system, which has brought civilization into the gravest danger it has known since the collapse of the Roman world ... 'Humanity,' says our great Bergson, 'groans, half crushed by the weight of the progress it has made ... The increased body awaits the addition of a soul, and the machine requires a mystic faith.' We know what it is, this mystic faith. The person ... is to say ... no longer an isolated human being, ... but ... a ... social man, who finds his full development only in fraternal communion with his neighbour. ... It is this mystic faith which in the realm of politics has inspired all the written or traditional constitutions of all civilized nations ever since Great Britain, the mother of democracies, guaranteed to every free man, by virtue of Magna Carta and the Act of Habeas Corpus, that he should be 'neither arrested nor imprisoned, except by the judgment of his peers delivered by the due process of the law ...' It is this faith which inspired the American Declaration of 1776 ... It is that which inspired the French Declaration of 1791 ... Does not the idea of the high dignity of the human individuality also inspire the Constitution of the Union of Soviet Socialist Republics ... Finally ... the Charter of the United Nations.'[32]

He further held that:

> It was against this mystic faith that Hitler ... attempted a violent reaction, by opposing to it his barbarous ideology of race distinction, his primitive conception of social life regulated by biological laws alone. For he not only envisaged establishing the military domination of Germany in Europe, but his ambition was to impose on the world his 'culture,' which overthrows all the moral and intellectual foundations upon which the civilized world has rested ever since the dawn of the Christian era.[33]

It is clear that Hitler's regime was considered a violation of the fundamental ideas of civilization and human rights, and thus a crime against humanity. A similar opinion was expressed by Mr. Dodd, Executive Trial Counsel for the US:

---

31 IMT Judgment: The Accused Organizations, at http://www.yale.edu/lawweb/avalon/ imt/proc/judorg.htm#sa. However, since it could not be proven that, beyond some specific units, the members of the SA had *generally* participated in or even known of the criminal acts, the Tribunal did not declare the SA to be a criminal organization within the meaning of Article 9 IMT Charter.

32 Address of M. Auguste Champetier de Ribes, Nuremberg Trial Proceedings, Vol. 22, 215th day, Friday 30 August 1946, at http://www.yale.edu/lawweb/avalon/imt/proc/08-30-46.htm, at pp. 297–298.

33 Nuremberg Trial Proceedings, Vol. 22, 215th day, Friday 30 August 1946, at http://www.yale.edu/lawweb/avalon/imt/proc/08-30-46.htm, at p. 298.

All knew that the Gestapo was organized for the specific purpose of *persecuting the victims* of Nazi oppression – the Jews, the Communists, and the Churches. The right to use torture in interrogations had to be known to all who interrogated. There could be no secrecy as to the criminal aims of the Gestapo or the *criminal methods* by which this primary *agency of terror* carried out its work. And that it was *an instrument of terror* was known not merely to the membership – it was known throughout Germany and Europe, and in every country of the world, where the very name Gestapo became the watchword of terror and of fear … they shall not escape condemnation for the vast crimes they have committed through a false and flimsy defense of ignorance in their own circles. For long, long years after this hall is emptied and for centuries beyond present perspective, *the roll call of terror against humankind* will be led by these appellations – Nazi, Nazi Party Leadership, SA, SD, SS, and Gestapo.[34] [emphasis added]

He concluded that:

By a declaration of criminality against these organizations, this Tribunal will put on notice not only the people of Germany, but the people of the whole world. Mankind will know that no crime will go unpunished because it was committed in the name of a political party or of a state; that no crime will be passed by because it is too big; that no criminals will avoid punishment because there are too many.[35]

These considerations were recalled in the IMT's Judgment on Crimes against Humanity:

With regard to *crimes against humanity*, there is no doubt whatever that political opponents were murdered in Germany before the war, and that many of them were kept in concentration camps in circumstances of great horror and cruelty. *The policy of terror* was certainly carried out on a vast scale, and in many cases was organised and systematic. The policy of persecution, repression and murder of civilians in Germany before the war of 1939, who were likely to be hostile to the Government, was most ruthlessly carried out. … The persecution of the Jews during the same period is established beyond all doubt. To constitute crimes against humanity, the acts relied on before the outbreak of war must have been in execution of, or in connection with, any crime within the jurisdiction of the tribunal.[36]

Unfortunately, since most of these acts had been perpetrated before the outbreak of the war in 1939, they fell beyond the Court's jurisdiction. The crimes that occurred afterwards were instead deemed to be linked to Germany's war of aggression, thereby coming within its competences. Thus, the IMT's jurisprudence evidences that terrorism may be prosecuted as a crime against humanity. But there are also

---

34 Nuremberg Trial Proceedings, Vol. 22, 214th day, 29 August 1946, *supra* note 29, at pp. 264–265.

35 Nuremberg Trial Proceedings, Vol. 22, 214th day, 29 August 1946, *supra* note 29, at p. 269.

36 Judgment: The Law Relating to War Crimes and Crimes Against Humanity, at http://www.yale.edu/lawweb/avalon/imt/proc/judlawre.htm.

several passages in the ICTY's jurisprudence supporting this view.[37] Most recently, the *Second Amended Indictment against Slobodan Milosevic* charged the former President of Serbia with crimes against humanity for having planned, instigated, ordered, committed or otherwise aided and abetted in a deliberate and widespread or systematic *campaign of terror* and violence directed at Kosovo Albanian civilians living in Kosovo in the Federal Republic of Yugoslavia.[38] In *Krstic*, the accused was found guilty of persecution for the terrorizing of Bosnian Muslim civilians in the enclave of Srebrenica from 11 July 1995:

> The Trial Chamber characterises the humanitarian crisis, the *crimes of terror* and the forcible transfer of the women, children and elderly at Potocari as constituting *crimes against humanity*, that is, persecution and inhumane acts.[39] [emphasis added]

The TC concluded that:

> ... on the basis of the humanitarian crisis and *crimes of terror* at Potocari and the forcible transfer of the women, children and elderly from Potocari to Bosnian Muslim-held territory, from 11 to 13 July, General Krstic incurs responsibility under Article 7(1) for inhumane acts (forcible transfer, count 8 of the Indictment) and persecution (murder, cruel and inhumane treatment, *terrorisation,* destruction of personal property and forcible transfer, count 6 of the Indictment).[40] [emphasis added]

Another passage states the following:

> Based on the totality of the evidence, it is clear that murder, torture, rape, beatings and other forms of physical and mental violence were strategically and systematically committed against non-Serbs in Omarska. Most of these atrocities appear to have been committed with a premeditated intent to create an *atmosphere of violence and terror* and to persecute those imprisoned ... The Trial Chamber finds that the elements of persecution as a *crime against humanity* have been satisfied.[41] [emphasis added]

But also the ICTR, although more moderately, provides for some interesting passages. For example, in *Kayishema and Ruzindana* the Prosecutor observed that the use of terrorist methods may bring about such serious mental and physical harm that it may amount to genocide, provided that it was committed with the required *mens rea.*[42] It should in fact be recalled that genocide is a special type of

---

37 *Prosecutor v. Blaskic*, TC Judgment of 3 March 2000, Case IT-95-14, para. 205.

38 *Prosecutor v. Slobodan Milosevic et al.*, Second Amended Indictment, Case IT-99-37-PT, 29 October 2001, at http://www.un.org/icty/indictment/english/mil-2ai011029e.htm. For details, see Arnold, *supra* note 2, at p. 247.

39 *Prosecutor v. Krstic*, TC Judgment of 2 August 2001, Case No. IT-98-33, para. 607. See also paras 533, 537, 538, 727.

40 *Prosecutor v. Krstic*, TC, *supra* note 38 , para. 653.

41 *Prosecutor v. Kvocka*, TC Judgment of November 2, 2001, Case IT-98-30/1, para. 197.

42 *Prosecutor v. Kayishema*, TC, *supra* note 25, paras 107, 110.

crime against humanity, which distinguishes itself via the requirement of a special genocidal intent.

Thus, international jurisprudence supports the argument that terrorism may be prosecuted under the customary definition of crimes against humanity. In the next section it will be discussed whether this may hold true also under the definition provided by Article 7 of the ICC Statute, which has some specificities of its own.

The prosecution of terrorism under Article 7 of the ICC Statute

Terrorism as such was excluded from the ICC's jurisdiction, notwithstanding the opposition of countries like Algeria, India, Sri Lanka and Turkey.[43] The major arguments were that: (1) the offence was not well defined; (2) the inclusion of this crime would politicize the Court; (3) some acts of terrorism were not sufficiently serious to warrant prosecution by an international tribunal; (4) prosecution and punishment by national courts would be more efficient.[44]

However, there are two ways in which terrorism may be prosecuted under Article 7 of the ICC Statute: (1) as one of the (illustratively) listed sub-categories of crimes against humanity, such as murder or torture, or (2) as an 'inhumane act' pursuant to Article 7(1)(k).

Terrorism as one of the listed sub-conducts

The most obvious proposal is to prosecute terrorism under the sub-heading of murder (Article 7(1)(a)). According to the *Elements of Crime*, the perpetrator must have killed one or more persons. The terms 'killed' and 'caused death' are interchangeable.[45] Events like the 11 September attacks, for example, may be prosecuted under this heading: the acts were multiple and coordinated, caused the death of thousands of people, and were in furtherance of a terrorist policy by an international criminal organisation – Al Qaeda – against a government – the US,[46] thereby being 'systematic.' By being aimed at several targets (the Twin Towers, the Pentagon and the White House), they were also 'widespread.' At least the attack on the World Trade Center caused civilian victims. More complicated is the situation of the army officials involved in the attack on the Pentagon. In this case it may be argued that while the attack was being carried out, they were not involved in armed hostilities but were simply carrying out administrative functions. Thus, as

---

43 *UN Doc. A/CONF.183/C.1/L 27.*

44 A. Cassese, 'Terrorism Is Also Disrupting Some Crucial Legal Categories of International Law', *European Journal of International Law,* vol. 12, 2001, p. 993.

45 *Elements, UN Doc. PCNICC/2000/1/Add.2,* at 159; Robinson, *supra* note 18, at 64.

46 J.D. Fry, 'Terrorism as a Crime Against Humanity and Genocide: The Backdoor to Universal Jurisdiction,' *UCLA Journal of International Law and Foreign Affairs,* vol. 7, 2002, pp. 169 ff., p. 190.

non-military targets, they were civilians in the sense of Article 7 of the ICC Statute, too.[47]

A somewhat difficult issue is to establish whether 'classical' forms of terrorism often occurring as single incidents, like the *Lockerbie* Case, may be prosecuted as crimes against humanity.[48] Regarding the hijackings perpetrated by Palestinian movements in the 1970s and 1980s, the situation is simpler: these acts pursued a policy of self-determination of the Palestine Liberation Organisation (PLO) and similar movements.[49] Since the acts do not have to constitute the 'attack', a single killing perpetrated in the knowledge of a policy aimed at a widespread and systematic attack may be encompassed. Thus, the numerous suicide bombing attacks that followed the beginning of the 'second Intifada' in 2000 may form part of a widespread and systematic attack and amount to crimes against humanity.[50]

An interesting question, which will need to be addressed by the ICC, is the time that may elapse between different acts, in order to be still considered as jointly forming part of the same overall widespread and systematic attack. If time is irrelevant, it may (for example) be argued that the attacks on an Israeli-owned hotel on 28 November 2002 in Mombasa (Kenya), in which three Israelis died, and the car bomb attack in Kuta (Bali) in which about 200 people were killed, all form part of the same widespread and systematic attack in furtherance of Al Qaeda's terrorist policy.[51]

In none of these cases is it necessary to prove a 'special intent': it is enough to show that the perpetrators committed the sub-offences intentionally. Thus, since terrorist acts imply the intentional killing of the victims, the mental requirements do not pose many problems for the prosecution of terrorism under this heading.

An alternative provision is Article 7(1)(e). This outlaws the 'imprisonment or other severe deprivation of physical liberty in violation of fundamental rules of international law.' The perpetrator must have imprisoned one or more persons or severely deprived them of physical liberty. The conduct must have been so grave to constitute a violation of fundamental rules of international law.

The IMT considered a crime against humanity the unlawful internment of German political opponents in concentration camps, adopted as a tool to implement

---

47 See *Prosecutor v. Bagilishema*, Case ICTR-95-1A-T, 7 June 2001, para. 79; Fry, *supra* note 46, at p. 191, stating that what matters is the victim's role at the moment of the attack, rather than their status.

48 The details are discussed in Arnold, *supra* note 3, p. 263 ff.

49 For example, the Popular Front for the Liberation of Palestine (PFLP), Hamas, Force 17, Hamas. See HRW, 'Erased in a Moment: Suicide Bombing Attacks Against Israeli Civilians,' October 2002, Chapter V, at www.hrw.org/reports.2002/isrl-pa.

50 M. Asser, 'Who Are Hamas?,' BBC News, 6 June 2003, at http://news.bbc.co.uk/1/hi/world/middle_east/1654510.stm.

51 Information available on the website of the International Policy Institute for Counter-Terrorism (ICT), Herzliya (Israel), at http://www.ict.org.il.

the Nazis' terrorist campaign against the German civilian population.[52] It may also cover other forms of terrorism, like the hostage-taking at Moscow's Dubrovka Theater in October 2002.[53] Also the policy of enforced disappearance of political opponents supported by the Argentinean and Chilean military in the 1970s may be encompassed,[54] even though this crime is more specifically addressed in Article 7(1)(a)(i).[55]

In conclusion, it may be argued that, given the circumstances, terrorism may constitute torture as a crime against humanity under Article 7(1)(e) and (f). It may also constitute persecution, subject to Article 7(1)(h), which considers a crime against humanity as any:

> … [p]ersecution against any identifiable group or collectivity on political, racial, national, ethnic, cultural, religious, gender as defined in paragraph 3, or other grounds that are universally recognized as impermissible under international law, in connection with any act referred to in this paragraph or any crime within the jurisdiction of the Court.

Like the ICTY Statute,[56] Article 7 of the ICC Statute also requires a discriminatory ground for this (and only for this) count.[57] Article 7(2)(g) specifies that persecution is the intentional and severe deprivation of fundamental rights, by reason of the identity of the group or collectivity to which an individual belongs.[58] The discriminatory intent must be based on political, racial, national, ethnic, cultural, religious, gender or other grounds universally recognized as impermissible under international law.[59] Cultural and political groups may be protected, too. The persecutory act must have

---

52 *Nuremberg Trial Proceedings*, Vol. 1, Indictment: Count One, para. 3(a): consolidation of control, at www.yale.edu/lawweb/avalon/imt/proc.

53 BBC, 'Hostages Speak of Storming Terror,' BBC News World Edition, 26 October 2002, at http://news.bbc.co.uk/2/hi/europe/2363679.stm. BBC 'How Special Forces Ended Siege,' BBC News World Edition, 29 October 2002, at http://news.bbc.co.uk/2/hi/europe/2363601.stm.

54 Similar facts occurred under Pinochet in Chile. See E. Lutz, K. Sikkink, 'The Justice Cascade: The Evolution and Impact of Foreign Human Rights Trials in Latin America,' *Chicago Journal of International Law*, vol. 2, 2001, p. 1; Human Rights Watch (HRW), 'Cuando los tiranos tiemblan: el caso Pinochet,' 1999, at http://www.hrw.org/spanish/informes/1999/pinochet2.html.

55 With regard to the latter norm, the *Elements of Crime* require that the perpetrator arrested, detained, or abducted one or more persons and that he refused to acknowledge that deprivation of freedom or to give information on the fate or whereabouts of such person or persons. The crime, thus, is composed by the 'arrest,' and the subsequent refusal to reveal information.

56 *Prosecutor v. Tadic*, AC, Judgment of 15 July 1999, Case IT-94-1, para. 283.

57 Dixon, *supra* note 48, at p. 123; D. Robinson, 'The Context of Crimes Against Humanity' in Lee (ed.), *supra* note 18, at p. 63.

58 Articles 7(1)(h) and (2)(g) of the ICC Statute. The provision was loosely based on the approach of the 1996 ILC Draft Code and the ICTY.

59 Boot, *supra* note 8, at p. 148.

a link with another crime within the jurisdiction of the Court or an act referred to in Article 7(1).[60] With regard to the 11 September attacks, the problem is that although most victims were US citizens, they were not the primary targets of the attack, nor were they targeted because of their nationality. The real targets were the Twin Towers and their symbolic representation of Western society. The attack on the Indonesian island of Bali, in Kuta, on 12 October 2002, may instead be considered as the crime against humanity of persecution, in that the attack was discriminatingly aimed at the Australian tourists as a reprisal against the alliance of the Australian government with the US in the 'war on terror'.[61] The same holds true in relation to the aircraft and ship hijackings perpetrated by Palestinian movements in the 1970s and 1980s, such as the Entebbe incident, the 1972 Munich Olympic attacks, or the *Achille Lauro* attack, which were intentionally aimed at Israeli citizens. As long as there is no temporal limitation, it may be argued that these multiple acts constituted a widespread and systematic attack of the Palestinian movements, in furtherance of the PLO's terrorist policy.

Terrorism as an 'inhumane act'

Article 7(1)(k) bans '[o]ther inhumane acts of a similar character intentionally causing great suffering, or serious injury to body or to mental or physical health.' The relevant elements are that: (1) the perpetrator inflicted great suffering, or serious injury to body or to mental or physical health, by means of an inhumane act; (2) such act was of a character similar to any other act referred to in Article 7(1); (3) the perpetrator was aware of the factual circumstances that established the character of the act.

Article 7(1)(k) was intended to encompass all inhumane acts, which are impossible to list comprehensively,[62] thereby following the approach of the Statutes of the UN *ad hoc* tribunals.[63] In observance of the principle of legality, the condition is that the inhumane acts must have a similar nature and gravity of the other acts listed in Article 7(1)[64] and cause certain defined harm. As clarified by the *1996 International Law Commission Draft Code*, these must be acts 'which severely damage physical or mental integrity, health or human dignity, such as mutilation and severe bodily

---

60 G. Witschel, W. Rückert, 'Article 7(1)(h) – Crime against humanity of persecution,' in Lee (ed.), *supra* note 18, pp. 94–97, at p. 95; Clark, *supra* note 9, at p. 149.

61 BBC, 'Bali Attack "'Targeted Australians'"', 10 February 2003, BBC News World Edition, at http://news.bbc.co.uk/2/hi/asia-pacific/2743679.stm; Atika Shubert, 'Bali Bombing Trial Opens', 12 May 2003, CNN.com World, at http://edition.cnn.com/2003/WORLD/asiapcf/southeast/05/12/bali.bomb/index.html. The attack was apparently perpetrated by the Jemaah Islamiyah, which has close links to Al Qaeda.

62 G. Witschel, W. Rückert, 'Article 7(1)(k) – Crime Against Humanity of Other Inhumane Acts,' in Lee, *supra* note 18, pp. 106–108, at p. 106.

63 *Ibid.*, at p. 107.

64 *Ibid.*, at p. 108.

harm.'[65] The difference between this crime and torture lies in the lower gravity of the harm inflicted, which, pursuant to the general *mens rea* criteria set by Article 30 ICC Statute, must be intentional. Thus, this provision may be used as 'catch-all norm' for terrorist acts which fail to fall under other sub-headings of crimes against humanity (as long as the acts were intended to inflict the kind of damage envisaged by this provision). It may be argued that terrorism, due to its nature, always constitutes an inhumane offence. Therefore, it may be encompassed by Article 7 of the ICC Statute.

The only counter-argument may be that the primary aim of terrorists is to terrorize the population in order to compel a State or an international organization to meet their political demands. The infliction of pain on the victims is secondary. This kind of intention, however, would constitute *dolus indirectus* and be still encompassed by Article 30. Few are the conceivable cases, in fact, in which a terrorist may recklessly or even negligently cause severe damage to a victim's physical and mental integrity in order to achieve its primary goal.

Summary and observations

Article 7 of the ICC Statute recalls the customary definition of crimes against humanity. It requires that the act be committed as part of a widespread or systematic attack, against a civilian population and in furtherance of a policy, be this state or non-state based. The attack needs neither to be armed – as under the UN Charter – nor to be based on discriminatory grounds – as required by the ICTR Statute. The notion of 'civilian' is not to be understood as strictly as within the context of the laws of war and may, therefore, encompass also prisoners of war and former combatants. The ICC will have to clarify, though, whether combatants may be covered, too. Concerning perpetrators, the ICC Statute conforms to international law by encompassing both civilians and members of the armed forces, be these state or non-state representatives.

Although terrorist acts do not constitute a specific sub-heading, a detailed analysis of the elements of the crimes listed in Article 7 of the ICC Statute leads to the conclusion that these may be prosecuted; for example, as the crime against humanity of murder, torture, imprisonment or other severe deprivation of physical liberty in violation of fundamental rules of international law, persecution, enforced disappearance, and, more generally, as an inhumane act pursuant to Article 7(1)(k), as long as the specific required elements are given.

This approach finds support in the jurisprudence of the IMT and the UN *ad hoc* tribunals, in particular the ICTY. Various IMT decisions prove, for instance, that the Nazi regime, based on a policy of terror, was often implemented through methods amounting to crimes against humanity. Similarly the ICTY considered a crime

---

65 *1996 International Law Commission Report*, Chapter II, Draft Code of Crimes Against the Peace and Security of Mankind, Article 18, at http://www.un.org/law/ilc/texts/dcodefra.htm.

against humanity the mistreatment of Kosovo Albanians and Bosnian Muslims as an implementation tool of the policy of terrorization of the Serbian authorities.

Article 7 of the ICC Statute requires that the acts be multiple and in furtherance of *a policy*: this criterion is usually met by terrorist activities of international entity. An example is the number of terrorist attacks planned by Al Qaeda. Thus, for example, the Bali and 11 September attacks may be considered as part of the same widespread and systematic attack on the civilian population of the US and other Western countries, committed in furtherance of the terrorist policy of an international organization.

The argument that single and random terrorist acts cannot be encompassed may be countered with the reasoning that a single incident may be prosecuted as a crime against humanity, as long as it had a sufficient nexus with other similar acts, thereby forming part of an overall widespread or systematic attack. Acts which cannot be 'caught' by Article 7 of the ICC Statute are probably so random and low profiled that they may be better addressed by national domestic provisions like murder, for example.

There are several advantages in prosecuting terrorism as a crime against humanity under the ICC Statute. Firstly, Article 7 of the ICC Statute is based on customary law and, thus, applicable universally. At the same time, unlike the ICTR Statute, the ICC Statute requires a discriminatory intent only for the crime of persecution under Article 7(1)(h). Thus, Article 7 may also cover acts of terrorism which have been conducted within the framework of an attack lacking this specific intent. On the other hand, cases like the Bali and the 11 September attacks, or the several terrorist acts perpetrated against Israeli citizens, in which the victims have arguably been chosen because of their particular national, political, or religious affiliation, may be prosecuted under this specific count.

Secondly, the offences can be committed either by a governmental or non-governmental entity. Thus, both state and non-state terrorism is addressed.

Thirdly, as already mentioned, a wide range of victims is covered. Unlike under IHL, the notion of civilian population is extended to every person who is not performing *de facto* combating functions, independently from his or her nationality. Thus, crimes against humanity cover diplomats, government representatives, detainees, prisoners of war, members of the armed forces who are either sick, wounded or more generally *hors de combat*, as well as common civilians who have the same nationality as the perpetrators. What matters is the function exercised during the attack, rather than the status.

Fourthly, from a procedural point of view not discussed in detail in this paper, the ICC Statute provides for the concept of 'surrender' rather than 'extradition' to the international court.[66] Pursuant to Article 102 of the ICC Statute, surrender refers to 'the delivering up of a person by a State to the Court, pursuant to this Statute', whereas extradition refers to the delivering up of a person by one State to another as provided by treaty, convention or national legislation. There is a basic distinction between

---

66 See Arnold, *supra* note 3, at pp. 63 ff.

the transfer to an equal sovereign State and to an international body established by international law, with the participation and consent of the Member States. On this basis, it can be argued that the exceptions applicable to a State's own nationals and political offenders under extradition law do not apply here.

Finally, prosecution under the heading of crimes against humanity permits us to avoid lengthy discussions about the legitimacy of the goals pursued by the terrorists. As long as an act is committed in furtherance of a policy in complete disregard of the value of humanity, it is banned. The end does not justify the means. Thus, the numerous attacks organized and launched against Israel in furtherance of a policy of self-determination – like the hijacking of the *Achille Lauro* in 1985, the 1972 Munich Olympics attack, or the Entebbe incident in 1976 – by Palestinian movements, may be viewed as multiple acts forming part of an overall widespread and systematic attack and be prosecuted under this heading. Much depends on the degree of temporal proximity required. However, this will be a task for the ICC jurisprudence.

In conclusion, therefore, prosecution of terrorism as a crime against humanity under Article 7 of the ICC Statute would present several advantages and could provide for a valuable alternative to the existing international anti-terrorism instruments.

PART II
Prevention and Suppression of International Terrorism in the Regional Framework

Chapter 10

The Council of Europe

ROBERTO BELLELLI[1]

A Council of Europe perspective on the fight against terrorism

The events of 11 September 2001 prompted the Council of Europe (CoE) to deal with counter-terrorism, in the legal field, by intervening on pre-existing conventional norms and by studying some relevant issues with the aim of enhancing the legal basis of counter-terrorism measures while ensuring full respect for human rights, democratic principles and the rule of law.

Obviously, the CoE looks into the matter from its peculiar perspective of promotion and protection of human rights, in the light of the principles of the European Convention on Human Rights, as interpreted by the relevant case-law of the European Court of Human Rights. Moreover, the ongoing works in the field in various other international *fora* – in particular, in the United Nations and the OSCE – suggest avoiding duplication or interferences. On the other hand, the complexity of the matter as such, in relation to its political, social, cultural and religious implications, suggests pursuit of uncontroversial solutions between Member States. There is also the prospect of the wider contribution that the elaboration of the CoE might give, through the opening of the treaties to third States.

In such a context, the CoE has no longer tackled the fight against terrorism with a sectorial approach (which seems to have been incapable of producing rapid and effective results), but rather with a comprehensive and multidisciplinary prospective, inclusive of all the legal issues related to the terrorism.

The Guidelines on human rights and fight against terrorism

A first remarkable achievement in the CoE's activities is represented by the *Guidelines on human rights and fight against terrorism*, drafted by the group of specialists on human rights and fight against terrorism (DH-S-TER) and adopted by the Committee of Ministers on 11 July 2002.

The Guidelines are based on the principles drawn by the European Convention on Human Rights, as interpreted in the case-law of the Court, as well as on other relevant acts of the Committee of Ministers and of the Parliamentary Assembly, on

---

1   President of the Military Tribunal of Turin.

the UN International Covenant for Civil and Political Rights and on the Observations of the UN Committee of Human Rights.

With such a legal basis, the Guidelines reach an operative dimension, in particular in the light of the jurisdiction of the European Court of Human Rights. In fact, the effectiveness of the Guidelines goes well beyond the value and legal strength of the instrument through which they were adopted, as they might represent (for States, practitioners and individuals) reliable and authoritative parameters for assessing the legality of the concrete measures adopted in the counter-terrorism action.

The Guidelines are the first international legal text on human rights and the fight against terrorism. They proceed on the basis that States have an imperative duty to protect their populations against possible terrorist acts and to cooperate with one another in the fight against terrorism: however, it is precisely in situations of crisis, such as those brought about by terrorism, that respect for human rights is even more important, and that even greater vigilance is called for. The Guidelines seek to demonstrate that the need to respect human rights is in no circumstances an obstacle to the efficient fight against terrorism and that it is perfectly possible to reconcile the requirements of defending society and the preservation of fundamental rights and freedoms. The Guidelines aim to help States in finding the right balance. They are designed to serve as a realistic, practical guide for anti-terrorist policies, legislation and operations which are both effective and respectful of human rights.

Human rights standards allow States to take efficient and legitimate measures to defend democracy and the rule of law, provided that these measures are reasonable and proportionate. The Guidelines therefore recognize that the specificities of the fight against terrorism may require some adaptation of the usual procedures, while at the same time setting out basic requirements to be respected by States in such matters as:

- the prohibition of arbitrariness;
- the absolute prohibition of torture;
- legal guarantees for arrest and police custody, as well as for pre-trial detention;
- the prohibition of the retroactivity of laws;
- the right to a fair trial;
- the prohibition on extraditing a person to a country where he or she risks being sentenced to death;
- respect for peremptory norms of international law and of international humanitarian law.

The essential basis of protection and promotion of human rights and the need to avoid any misunderstanding on the focus of the specific action of the CoE obviously underlined primarily the destructive nature and disvalue of the terrorist threat with respect to human rights. Thus, in first place the Guidelines reaffirm the existence of a positive obligation on States to adopt all measures needed for the protection of fundamental rights and, primarily, the right to life. As a result of this approach,

States have a right to fight terrorism, but the limits to the exercise of such a right must be defined. The limits to be considered in the legitimate action of States against terrorism are exactly the aim of the Guidelines, which include the following:

- respect for human rights and the principle of legality;
- need for checks on the measures adopted;
- prohibition of discriminations, torture, inhuman or degrading treatment;
- respect for privacy in the collection or in the preservation of data, as well in any coercive measures and in the investigation methods;
- time limitation for police custody;
- regular supervision of pre-trial detention by a court;
- possibility of more severe restrictions on the liberty of those imprisoned for terrorist activities;
- duty to refuse the refugee status to persons seriously suspected of involvement in terrorist activities;
- prohibition of extradition to a requesting State, when the person sought is at risk of being sentenced to death, subjected to torture or to inhuman or degrading treatment or punishment, or the extradition request has been made for the purpose of prosecuting or punishing on a discriminatory ground, or when the person's position is at risk of being prejudged on these grounds;
- suspension or limitation of the property of persons or organizations suspected of terrorist activities;
- possibility of temporary derogations to certain obligations ensuing from the international instruments of protection of human rights, to the extent strictly required by a situation of war or public emergency which threatens the life of the nation and excluding any derogation from the right to life, from the prohibition against torture or inhuman or degrading treatment or punishment, from the principle of legality of sentences and of measures, as well as from the principle of non-retroactivity of criminal law;
- respect for peremptory norms of international law, and in particular of international humanitarian law;
- duty of a State to contribute to the compensation of the victims of terrorist attacks which took place in its territory, as far as their persons or health are concerned and when compensation is not fully available from other sources, in particular through the confiscation of the property of the perpetrators.

New Guidelines are currently under preparation for supplementing the 2002 Guidelines in the field of the protection of victims of terrorist acts, and may include emergency assistance (in particular medical, psychological, financial and social); continuing or long-term assistance; definition of a role for the victims in the investigation process; effective access of the victims to the law and to justice; protection of victims' privacy and family life; and the giving of information to victims.

Priorities in the CoE's action

Several priorities were identified in the CoE's counter-terrorism action through the activities performed in 2001 and 2002 by the 'Multidisciplinary Group for International Action against Terrorism' (GMT) and, since 2004 by the 'Committee of experts on terrorism' (CODEXTER), established by the Committee of Ministers. Currently, the following priorities are the subject of studies and further elaboration:

- the research on the concepts of *apologie du terrorisme* and incitement to terrorism, in the light of existing lacunae in international law as far as their treatment is concerned, and taking into account the need to keep an appropriate balance between the prevention of the *apologie* and of the incitement and the need to ensure the fundamental right to freedom of expression;
- the protection of witnesses and *pentiti* as well as relevant special investigative techniques, in a common approach for identifying measures to suppress organized crime and terrorism, in particular through the facilitation of international cooperation and, for investigative techniques, the identification and use of best practices by judicial and police authorities. Both criminal phenomena, though rooted in deeply differing cultural, social and economic causes, share apparent common characteristics, including the stability of the organization and the threat resulting thereof, as well as frequent common operative means;
- international judicial and police cooperation;
- the fight against terrorism financing;
- identity questions related to terrorism;
- compensation of victims of serious crimes, including terrorism;
- the effectiveness of national judicial systems in fighting terrorism;
- the establishment of an European register of national and international standards;
- the added value of a global European convention against terrorism.

At the current stage of preparatory works, among the mentioned priorities the initiatives for the protection of witnesses and *pentiti* might result in some conventional instrument. This would probably have positive effects also for the agreements concluded and the protection activities performed by International Tribunals and, in particular by the Victims' and Witnesses' Unit established under the Rome Statute of the International Criminal Court within the Registry. The definition of some aspects related to the notion of *apologie* of and incitement to terrorism is still more controversial.

As to a possible European comprehensive convention against terrorism, the initiative would aim at contributing to the ongoing United Nations' works for the elaboration of a comprehensive convention against terrorism (and to the strictly related elaboration of the Convention for the suppression of acts of nuclear terrorism) which has stalled before the UN Ad Hoc Committee, mainly for the controversial exclusion from its scope of the activities of Parties in conflict or of the Armed Forces.

However, opinions are divergent on the opportunity of starting such a parallel negotiation in the European regional forum, mainly on the consideration that the UN ongoing process could be jeopardized instead of facilitated, taking also into account that the main interlocutors in the Arab world would not be represented in the European negotiating forum.

This situation would still allow for a CoE activity through normative instruments or recommendations, although limited in scope, to fill some lacunae in the existing CoE instruments, due to the thematic nature of the 1977 European Convention against terrorism.

Main areas identified for possible intervention currently include principles as well as preventive and co-operation measures. In this connection, relevant items would include:

- scope;
- duty to investigate;
- criminalizing conducts such as public provocation to commit acts of terrorism;
- recruitment and training for terrorism;
- liability of entities;
- measures to prevent the abuse of the right of asylum and of the refugee status;
- awareness raising;
- freezing of assets;
- identity questions;
- exchange of information and a network of contact points.

The Amending Protocol to the 1977 European Convention

The Protocol amending the 1977 European Convention for the suppression of terrorism was drafted by the GMT in 2002, adopted on 7 November 2002 by the Committee of Ministers and open to signature in Strasbourg on 15 May 2003. To date, the Protocol has been signed by 45 (all) Member States and ratified by 43, although for its entry into force the ratification of all Parties to the Convention is required.

The European Convention for the suppression of terrorism (Strasbourg, 27 January 1977, entered into force on 4 August 1978) is limited in scope, and is aimed at facilitating the extradition procedure among Member States.

To that end, the Convention adopted the depoliticization clause for a minimum number of core crimes: none of the crimes included in the list under Article 1 could be considered as political offences or offences related to political offences or inspired by political motives. The list included offences provided for by the UN Conventions for the repression of the illicit seizure of aircraft (1970) and against the safety of civil aviation (1971), as well as offences committed against internationally protected persons, the taking of hostages and the use of explosives, and the responsibility for attempt and participation in the mentioned offences.

In addition, States might decide not to consider as political crimes other offences entailing violence against life, physical integrity or liberty of persons.

At the same time, such limitation on the lawful refusal of extradition resulting from the depoliticization clause was balanced by the non-discrimination clause (Article 5), allowing the requested State to refuse extradition when there is sufficient ground to believe that the request is presented with the aim to prosecuting or punishing a person because of his or her race, religion, nationality or political belief.

However, the provision on reservations did seriously hinder the obligation of depoliticization under Article 1. According to Article 13 of the Convention, any State could reserve the right to refuse extradition with respect to any offence included in the Article 1 list which was considered as a political offence, or an offence connected with political offences, or as an offence inspired by political motives, provided that it undertakes to take into due consideration, when evaluating the character of the offence, any particularly serious aspects of the offence, including that it created a collective danger to persons, that the victims were foreign to the motives behind the action, or that cruel or vicious means have been used in committing the offence. Setting apart the peculiarity of the approach according to which the gravity of an offence could be derived from its political or non-political nature, the possibility of reservation has been largely utilized by States, greatly hindering the effectiveness of the Convention.

The 2003 Amending Protocol was, therefore, prompted by the double need to update the 1977 Convention and to enhance its effectiveness through some revisions, which led to a new text of the Convention, consolidated with the Protocol. Minor technical adjustments include:

- the automatic inclusion of offences under the Convention as extraditable offences in any extradition convention or other treaty existing between contracting States (Article 4);
- the arbitration clause (Article 11);
- the provisions on the participation of third States (Article 14);
- the Conference of States Parties against Terrorism (Article 17).

However, main and substantial innovations introduced by the Protocol bring a wider list of offences into the scope of the Convention: the grounds for refusal of extradition; a mechanism for monitoring the implementation of the Convention; provisions for the progressive expiration of reservations; and the opening of the Convention to the participation of third States.

The list of conducts which may be considered as political offences for the purpose of refusing extradition has been updated by introducing under Article 1 the ten UN thematic Conventions which provide for criminalization obligations.

Further updating of the list of treaties under Article 1 is now possible, by means of amendments that might add to the list only UN treaties on international terrorism already entered into force (Article 13).

Moreover, the new text of Article 5 recalls that there is no obligation to extradite to countries where a person risks being subjected to death penalty, torture, or inhuman or degrading treatment, unless the requesting State gives sufficient assurance that the death penalty will not be imposed or, where imposed, will not be carried out and that the person sought will not be subject to life imprisonment without possibility of parole (if life imprisonment is not allowed by the law of the requested State).

The monitoring mechanism falls within the responsibilities of the European Committee on Crime Problems (CDPC), which shall submit a yearly report to the Committee of Ministers and is entitled, *inter alia*, to make recommendations concerning the proposals for amendments of the Convention and to express opinions on any questions concerning its application (Article 10).

The revision of the provisions on reservations is crucial to the expected enhancement of the effectiveness of the Convention. To this end, the amended text introduces a mechanism for reducing progressively the declarations made by States Parties to the Convention to reserve the right to refuse extradition in respect of any offence mentioned in Article 1 which it considers to be a political offence, an offence connected with a political offence or an offence inspired by political motives (Article 16).

Although the provision has been debated at length, consensus was not achieved for a more effective solution, based on the non-applicability of reservations. The compromise was prompted by the conflicting needs to allow to contracting States the preservation of their own fundamental legal principles and to ensure the progressive implementation of the Convention and compliance with Security Council Resolution 1373 (2001), calling upon all States to 'ensure…that claims of political motivation are not recognized as grounds for refusing requests for the extradition of alleged terrorists'.

The Convention acknowledges that the law or the constitution of a State may represent an obstacle for the full acceptance of the obligations resulting from Article 1, and accordingly allows States to make reservations on the implementation of Article 1. The adopted solution still allows for reservations from States Parties to the Convention on 15 May 2003 (time of opening to signature of the Protocol), but the State shall specifically indicate the offences to which its reservation applies and shall undertake to apply the reservation on a case-by-case basis. Furthermore, the validity of reservations expires after a three year period, though they may be renewed for the same duration. However, reservations will expire if not renewed upon reasoned notification to the Secretary General of the CoE, and through this mechanism reservations should progressively be reduced.

In conformity with the principle *aut dedere aut judicare* provided for under Article 7, where a State refuses extradition in application of a reservation, it shall submit the case to its competent authorities for the purpose of prosecution. The good faith in the refusal of the requested State may be checked through the CoE's monitoring of the judicial activity performed in the requested State, with the aim of assessing the conformity of the refusal with the Convention and of submitting an opinion to the Committee of Ministers for the purpose of issuing a declaration thereof (Article 16, 7 and 8).

Such monitoring, as well as that on the whole Convention, falls within the competence of the Conference of States Parties against Terrorism (COSTER), which is also responsible for ensuring the exchange of information on significant legal and policy developments pertaining to the fight against terrorism. The COSTER should also have general consultative status in the field and prompt measures to improve international cooperation in the area of the fight against terrorism. In the global perspective of the fight against terrorism, and consistent with the reference to all the relevant universal Conventions against terrorism, the Convention is open to participation of CoE's observer States and also, upon consent of States Parties, to third States (Article 14).

Conclusions

With respect to the 1977 Convention, the 2003 Amending Protocol represents a step forward in facilitating extradition. However, the non-harmonized characteristics of the legal systems of the CoE's Member States did not allow for overcoming the wide States' discretion in granting international counter-terrorism assistance and cooperation. In particular, the resulting consolidated instrument does not substantially improve assistance and cooperation between Member States of the European Union which enjoy a more advanced legal framework, as also noted in some interpretative declarations on the occasion of the signature of the Protocol. However, the effectiveness of the amended European Convention will depend on the increased awareness of CoE's Member States and of the whole international community, as the participation itself to the Convention and the practice of States will show.

Chapter 11

The Organization of American States

RENAN VILLACIS[1]

The countries in the Western Hemisphere have unfortunately not been spared from the scourge of terrorist acts which have afflicted all regions of the world, the worst mass attack taking place on 11 September 2001. Yet the region had been ravaged by other terrorist attacks before that date. Though most of the terrorist attacks in the region were the result of domestic terrorist groups, there had been cases of international terrorism as well. In this connection, most of the focus within the region has been on the need to cut off the financing of terrorist groups and to prevent such groups from seeking a haven in the region.

In its pursuit of combating the terrorist threat, the countries of the Americas have sought to establish appropriate legal regimes that would nonetheless maintain the respect for the rule of law.

The main forum for taking counter-terrorism action at the regional level has been the Organization of American States (OAS), which has had a long history of elaborating a series of international instruments on a wide range of topics since its inception in 1948, building upon the prior tradition of hemispheric conventions.

As background, it can be noted that terrorism was on the agenda of the OAS back in 1960s. The issue of terrorism and human rights had been discussed in the Inter-American Human Rights Commission, as far back as 1970. In drafting a counter-terrorism convention in the 1970s, another OAS body, the Inter-American Juridical Committee, recommended analysing the social, economic, educational and cultural causes which have an impact on violence.

At the level of a legal regime, in 1971 the OAS adopted the Convention to Prevent and Punish the Acts of Terrorism (hereinafter the 1971 OAS Convention), which focused on individuals with a political or diplomatic status which made them more likely to be terrorist targets.

More recently, in the 1990s terrorism was high on the list of the OAS priorities. Two high-level conferences were held in Lima and Montevideo in 1996 and 1999.

The 2002 OAS Convention, whose full name is the Inter-American Convention on Terrorism, is a direct result of the 11 September attacks against the US. The OAS countries embarked upon the elaboration of an international instrument that would

---

1   United Nations Secretariat, Office of Legal Affairs, Codification Division, New York. These remarks are made in a personal capacity and do not necessarily reflect the views of the UN Secretariat.

strengthen their anti-terrorism efforts in October 2001. The main proposals of the provisions in the Convention originated from the US, with important contributions from other OAS members, in particular Argentina, Chile, Mexico and Peru. After three meetings of the Working Group, chaired by Mexico, the final outcome of these efforts was adopted at the OAS General Assembly in Bridgetown, Barbados on 3 June 2002.

The Convention was immediately signed by 30 out of the 34 States members of the OAS. Although four States which had to address certain internal legal issues did not immediately sign the Convention, three of them did so *a posteriori*. The Convention currently has 33 signatures and 8 ratifications. It entered into force on 10 July 2003 after receiving its sixth ratification.

The main points dealt with by the 2002 OAS Convention include its scope, the strengthening of international cooperation, the issues of asylum and refugee status, extradition, the suppression of the financing of terrorism and the human rights dimension of the fight against terrorism.

The Convention has 6 preambular paragraphs and 23 operative paragraphs. The object and purpose of the Convention is to 'prevent, punish and eliminate terrorism'. The negotiations on the OAS Convention sought to give it an added-value with regard to the global efforts and, accordingly, it is an instrument that is consistent with, and builds upon, previous United Nations conventions and protocols related to terrorism and United Nations Security Council Resolution 1373. The OAS Convention seeks to improve regional cooperation in counter-terrorism efforts through exchanges of information, experience and training, technical cooperation and mutual legal assistance.

The central provision is of course the definition of the offence. There was some discussion on the issue of defining terrorism. Some States had a definition in their national legislation, but others did not. Specific proposals to define terrorism were made by Argentina, Chile, Peru and the US. Nonetheless, in the end it was agreed to forgo defining terrorism *strictu senso* in order to avoid having the same discussions and the lack of results in other fora.

Therefore, the OAS Convention follows the sectoral approach contained in the United Nations conventions and protocols and does not contain a specific definition of terrorism, but instead determines as offences falling under its scope, those offences established in the international instruments listed in Article 2. This method of establishing offences by referring to other instruments was already resorted to in the 1999 UN Convention for the suppression of the financing of terrorism and has been used in other recent counter-terrorism instruments, since it greatly simplifies the need to restate the numerous and sometimes extremely detailed offences contained in those instruments.

States which are not parties to one or more of the 10 international instruments listed in Article 2, can make a statement declaring which specific instrument shall not be deemed as included in Article 2. A State which ceases to be a party to one of the Conventions can also make a similar declaration.

One characteristic contained in the Convention, which differs from other regional instruments, is Article 3 whereby State parties commit themselves to becoming parties to the international instruments previously referred to and to adopt the necessary measures to implement such instruments. In the case of other conventions, there is usually exhortatory language contained in the preamble.[2]

Following in the steps of the UN Bombings Convention, the OAS Convention contains, in Article 11, a depoliticization provision whereby, for the purposes of extradition and mutual legal assistance, none of the offences under the Convention's scope may be regarded as a political offence or an offence connected with a political offence or an offence inspired by political motives. Extradition or mutual legal assistance may not be denied solely on the ground that it concerns a political offence. In this connection, there is also another provision, Article 13, whereby States commit themselves to ensuring that neither asylum nor refugee status is granted to persons who might have committed an offence falling under the purview of the Convention.

These particular provisions are noteworthy because they go to the root of what most States in the Western Hemisphere have long considered a vital regional institution, the institution of political asylum.

Given our rather tumultuous history in the region, the institution of political asylum developed over the course of many decades and it was codified in several regional conventions dealing with diplomatic and territorial asylum. The Inter-American Conventions dating from 1928, 1933, 1939 and 1954 resolved the problem of determining whether an alleged crime was political or not by allowing the State granting asylum to make that determination, since to allow the accusing State to do so would always result to the detriment of the accused. The OAS Convention thus, for the first time on the hemispheric level, severely restricts the definition of political offences or their predicate offences and it clearly excludes the possibility of granting asylum or even refugee status for persons suspected, with reasonable grounds, of having committed an offence falling under its scope. During the negotiations, some States were wary about denying or limiting the institution of asylum with regard to persons suspected of taking part in terrorist activities. The respective provision on this matter was ultimately incorporated in the Convention. One must know that, for example, Mexico has submitted an interpretation indicating the asylum is part of international human rights law, which is safeguarded by Article 15 of the Convention. In any event, the inclusion of the pertinent articles in the Convention constitutes a fundamental departure from principles and institutions which most countries in the region considered almost sacrosanct.

The OAS Convention also replicates the Bombings Convention in having a non-discrimination provision which allows a requested State party not to provide legal assistance if it has substantial grounds for believing that the request has been made

---

2   This undertaking, however, is qualified by the need for States to proceed in accordance with their respective constitutions.

for the purpose of prosecuting an individual because of his/her particular beliefs, nationality or ethnic origin.

Another noteworthy feature of the OAS Convention is the importance given to human rights. One can understand how vital such provisions are bearing in mind the massive violations of human rights which the countries of the region have faced in past decades. The inclusion of an article dealing with human rights was controversial during the negotiations. Some States held the view that it was unnecessary, since any action by the OAS was guided by the Charter of the Organization, as well as by the American Declaration on the Rights and Duties of Man. A majority of other States however were convinced of the need to include an article on human rights. This latter view prevailed and therefore Article 15 of the Convention calls for States to fully respect the rule of law, human rights and fundamental freedoms. It is also somewhat more specific than the similar provision in the UN Bombings Convention by making particular mention of, *inter alia*, international human rights law and international refugee law when referring to the rights and obligations of States and individuals under international law that are not affected. In addition, any person taken into custody must be guaranteed fair treatment in accordance with the applicable domestic law and international law. It should also be noted that in 2002 the Inter-American Human Rights Commission submitted a report on Terrorism and Human Rights, which serves as a guideline to interpret the OAS Convention.

Borrowing from recent UN conventions, in particular the Bombings Convention, the OAS Convention contains provisions which facilitate the exchange of cooperation and information.

One of these measures includes the transfer of persons in custody to another State party so as to facilitate obtaining evidence for an investigation or for prosecuting offences this text follows the respective UN Bombings Convention provision.

Other provisions in the OAS Convention call upon States to implement strict border controls and to confiscate money and other assets belonging to groups identified as being affiliated with terrorists. It is particularly noteworthy that the State parties assume the obligation of instituting a legal and regulatory regime for combating the financing of terrorism, which should include, *inter alia*, a comprehensive domestic regulatory and supervisory regime for banks and other financial institutions; measures for the detection and monitoring movement of cash and other valuables; and the establishment of financial intelligence units in each State party to serve as a collection centre of data on terrorist financing and money laundering. The OAS Convention also contains provisions for the seizure and confiscation of funds or other assets related to the offences falling within its scope.

Among the other cooperation measures established by the OAS Convention is the obligation to afford expeditious mutual legal assistance; improve the border and customs control including the improvement of controls on travel and identity documents; as well as promoting technical cooperation and training programs.

One of the main operational features of the OAS Convention is the mechanism it establishes in order to carry out its purposes. The cornerstone of this effort is the Inter-American Committee against Terrorism (known by its Spanish acronym as

CICTE). The CICTE is a specialized counter-terrorism body which was established in 1998 with the mandate of sharing experiences and information about terrorism and related individuals and groups, as well as cooperating in investigating terrorism operations and their sources of financing. With the enhanced role assigned to it by the OAS Convention, CICTE has become the primary counter-terrorism tool at the hemispheric level. CICTE works to provide States with the tools that allow them to implement the OAS Convention. This process includes, *inter alia*, the exchange of model legislation, use of an online reference database, etc. It also coordinates closely with regional Financial Action Task Force type bodies. CICTE was reinforced in 2002 with the establishment of an Executive Secretariat, composed of individuals seconded from Governments.

In order to enhance the counter-terrorism efforts, the OAS Convention calls for holding periodic meetings of the States parties.

One of the grave shortcomings that countries in the region face is the upgrading of capacity to address the terrorist threats. Although political will may be present, counter-terrorism capabilities are lacking in many countries. Some domestic legal systems do not have terrorism as a criminal offence and therefore resort must be made to laws of a secondary criminal nature in order to deal with terrorist acts. Though some countries have sought to adopt counter-terrorism bills, there have been internal debates about the scope of broader powers that would be granted to governments under those laws.

Summary

The OAS Convention has reinforced the institutional framework and the legal regime for counter-terrorism efforts in the Americas and it has become the main coordination mechanism in the region in the post 9/11 era.

Another notable feature is that the Convention establishes a broad jurisdiction by covering offences committed not just within a State but also beyond the territory of a State party. Nonetheless, it also contains an article which excludes the extra-territorial exercise of jurisdiction, an issue which has led to some difficulties in different cases, some not necessarily related to terrorism.

Chapter 12

The League of Arab States

MAHMOUD SAMY[1]

I hope within the coming few minutes I will be able to shed some light on a vital convention that paved the way for coordinated Arab efforts to fight terrorism, joining forces with the international community – the Arab Convention on Suppression of Terrorism.

In a changing world and after the horrific events of 11 September, the growing menace of international terrorism became an increasing threat to our human civilization, societies, and set of values: this required a global response from each and every member of the international community. Solidarity and unity against this threat are instrumental factors to guarantee the success of worldwide efforts capable of defeating this dangerous threat: the Arab Convention is without doubt to be considered a building block in this global effort, along with other regional conventions and the United Nations' endeavours to serve this cause.

On 22 April 1998 at the seat of the Arab League in Cairo a joint meeting of the Ministers of Interior and Justice of the League of Arab States (LAS) adopted the Arab Convention on the Suppression of Terrorism.

The Convention is an elaborate outcome of the Arab League and its members' endeavour to maximize the level of cooperation among them in the field of combating international terrorism. To understand and analyse this Convention we need to view it as a part of a long process within the League's efforts to enhance cooperation in this field.

This process included the adoption of an Arab strategy to combat terrorism which was approved in 1994 and gave rise to a preliminary three-year phased plan adopted by the council in 1998; this was followed by another three-year plan in early 2001.

The Arab strategy to combat terrorism sought the following goals:

- to combat terrorism and eliminate its causes;
- to maintain the security and stability of the Arab world and protect it from terrorism;
- to further the principles of legality and the rule of law;
- to promote the maintenance of the security of the individual in the Arab world

---

1   Legal Counsel, Permanent Mission of Egypt to the United Nations in New York. These remarks are made in a personal capacity and do not necessarily reflect the views of the Ministry of Foreign Affairs of Egypt.

and to enhance respect of human rights;
- to promote the maintenance of the security and safety of public institutions and facilities in the Arab States;
- to convey the true image of Islam and Arab civilization;
- to enhance and develop cooperation among the Arab States;
- to improve cooperation with other countries and international organizations.

In 1996, in a parallel effort the Council of Arab Interior Ministers adopted a code of conduct by which the Member States took upon themselves to pursue terrorists, and prevent them from crossing the borders and residing on their territories. The Arab countries agreed on the necessity of exchanging information in the fields of investigations and judicial procedures, which highlighted the importance of transparency and swift flow of information between law enforcement authorities in Member States. There was also a recognition of the importance of ports and border control, in order to avoid the transportation or use of weapons, ammunitions and explosives for illegal activities.

In an effort to reach a comprehensive outcome built upon the aforementioned efforts, and to provide the appropriate framework of the Arab cooperation in the field of combating terrorism, the need for a structured legal instrument emphasizing all related aspects became imperative. Henceforth, in 1998, a draft regional convention was adopted and signed by 16 Member States: Bahrain, United Arab Emirates, Egypt, Algeria, Saudi Arabia, Jordan, Palestine, Tunisia, Sudan, Libya, Yemen, Oman, Syria, Lebanon, Morocco, and Djibouti. The convention entered into force in 7 May 1999, and then Qatar joined in 2004.

The text of the Convention was deposited with the Secretariat of the United Nations, and it was issued as General Assembly Documents A/54/301, A/55/179 and A/56/160.

In principal, the Convention defines the acts of terrorism, distinguishing them from other acts, criminalizing them, and furthermore it associates the Convention with other international conventions on terrorism. It also specifies the commitments of Member States to refrain from any involvement, connection with or support to terrorism: it commits the members to coordinate and cooperate in bringing terrorists to justice, providing them with a thorough illustration of *modus operandi* guaranteeing an efficient execution of the terms of the Convention. To further support this execution, Member States can rely on the implementing procedures which come in an exhaustive 65-page document which explains the practical mechanism of implementation and provides the necessary executive forms.

The Convention is composed of 42 articles divided into three parts as follows:

- Part 1 deals with definition and general rules;
- Part 2 focuses on bases of Arab cooperation and comprises two chapters, the first chapter covering the security field, and the second chapter covering the judicial field;
- Part 3 deals with the mechanism of law enforcement and includes a detailed

description of extradition procedure, judicial deputization, and witness and expert protection procedures.

The obligations stated by the convention can be categorized in two categories:

- The first is political, by which the parties obligate themselves not to organize, finance or commit terrorist acts, or to take part in such acts in any way, and to cooperate among themselves in combating terrorists' crimes, and to provide and exchange information to that aim.
- The second is on the judicial level by which the contracting states commit themselves to coordinate, cooperate and to provide assistance to each other within their existing judicial and legal regimes.

At this point, I would like to stress the fact that the effective implementation of this convention is greatly attributed to the comprehensive and elaborative articles of the judicial cooperation that easily provide Member States with a precise and detailed course of legal action to encounter terrorism in a regional framework.

It is well known that a major obstacle to the international dialogue regarding combating terrorism is the definition of terrorism and the distinction between this crime and other acts which are not illegal, thus becoming a delaying factor in the General Assembly deliberation and slowing down the effort to reach agreement on legal instruments that could enhance the international framework. But unlike the situation in the UN the Arab States share a clear view regarding the acts which constitute terrorism and which are not. They clearly differentiate between criminal acts of terrorism and other acts that fall within legitimate rights of people to struggle against foreign occupation and aggression: let me quote here Article 1.2 that defines acts of terrorism as follows:

> Terrorism: Any act of violence or threat of it regardless of its motives or objectives, in the execution of [a] criminal project, individual or collective, aiming at terrorizing people, or harming them or jeopardizing their lives, freedom or security, or harming the environment, or any facility, public or private properties, or occupying it, capturing it, or endangering any national resource.

Let me here put emphasis on the fact that the definition focuses on the description of the material act constituting the crime, irrespective of motives or objectives of the criminal.

While Article 1.2 clearly defined terrorism, Article 1.3 defines the terrorist crime and links it to the international instruments in that field, as it states:

> [a] terrorist crime is any crime or attempt of it, committed in execution of a terrorist purpose in any of the contracting States, or on any of its citizens, properties or interests, punished by its internal law. Also considered terrorist crimes prescribed in the following conventions, except what has been excluded by the legislation of the contracting States or which they are not signatories to:

A. The Tokyo Convention concerning crimes and acts committed on board aircraft signed on 14/09/1963.
B. The Hague Convention on combating illegal seizure of aircraft signed on 19/12/1970.
C. The Montreal Convention for the suppression of illegal acts against the safety of civil aviation, signed on 23/09/1972, and the appendix protocol signed in Montreal on 10/05/1984.
D. The New York Convention on preventing and prosecuting crimes against persons covered by the international protections, including diplomatic representatives, signed on 14/12/1973.
E. The Convention on kidnapping and hostage taking, signed on 17/12/1979.
F. The United Nations Convention on marine law of 1983, especially what concerns marine piracy.

Another aspect of the Convention is dealing with issues of finance of terrorism and trans-border control of hazardous and lethal materials. Article 3, which deals with preventive procedures, prohibits the finance of terrorist acts in all its forms and covers the issue of banning the transportation of lethal materials, demanding Member States:

> ... to develop and foster the systems of detecting any transport, import, export and use of arms, ammunition and explosives and/or any other means of aggression, killing and destruction. Whilst reviewing their monitoring procedures across borders and customs to prevent the transport of these materials whether between contracting States or to others, except for legal purposes in a specified manner.

Obviously this Article does not only cover conventional weapons and materials, but it also extends the scope to monitor and control any transportation of unconventional materials (which includes weapons of mass destruction), and it is not only limited to transportation between Member States but also transport to non-member States.

Following the entry into force of the Convention the Councils of Arab Ministers of Justice and of Interior decided to establish a joint committee aiming to produce a document comprising the Implementation Measures of the Convention in the judicial and security fields. This document included a thorough list of procedures and 52 executive forms that would facilitate the implementation of the convention and allow the transformation of the legal instrument into a practical mechanism of a daily cooperation and practice between different legal and security regimes of the Member States. The document came into effect on 1 January 2001.

The Criminal Police Bureau, a subsidiary body of the Council of Arab Ministers of Interior, was assigned to follow up the Member States' implementation of the Convention. It was requested to prepare an annual report to be submitted to meetings of Justice and Interior Ministers of the Arab League: three reports have already been presented – for the years 2001, 2002 and 2003. To maintain an efficient and satisfactory implementation of the convention and its executing measures, the Bureau was assigned (in collaboration with Member States) the duty to review and assess these measures and the executive forms after five years of practice.

In March 2002, in an additional effort to further the effectiveness of the convention the Arab League Council decided to include the following acts within the scope of the Convention:

- incitement and applauding terrorism;
- printing and distribution of documents supporting terrorism;
- collecting charity contributions for the benefit of terrorism;
- the acquisition and usage of property for terrorism.

Consequently, a drafting committee formulated an amendment to the Convention that corresponds with the Council's decision and that was finally adopted early this year; accordingly the Secretariat of the Arab League requested the Member States to take the necessary constitutional measures ratifying the introduced amendment.

The Convention also focused on many details that facilitate judicial cooperation between different and sometimes diverse legal systems. A good example is the procedure for judicial deputization, in which the obligation of each party is specifically detailed. Another good example of its precision and elaboration is dealing with issues such as items and revenues generated from the crime to avoid any possible controversy between the parties. It also paid due attention to the mechanism of law enforcement covering issues such as extradition mechanisms and defining the competent authorities and procedures.

In the final analysis we would find that the Convention sustains certain characteristics making it highly practical. First, despite the fact that it did not create or establish new institutional structures, it benefited from the already existing bodies of the Arab League, namely the Council of the Arab Ministers of Interior, and the Council of Ministers of Justice which have actively participated in crafting the Convention. It also benefited from other subsidiary bodies such as the Criminal Police Bureau. The relation between the Convention and these bodies is not only limited to the execution of its terms, but also to the revision and the assessment of its application and also the monitoring of the parties' compliance.

Second, the adoption of the Convention in 1998 presented an outstanding example for regional legal cooperation in combating terrorism, paving the way for other regional organizations to realize the possibility of achieving such levels of cooperation and thus being encouraged to follow. The OAU and the OIC came up with their own legal instruments on the subject. A comparative analysis will reveal a great deal of similarity in the structure, the philosophy and even the language of the three conventions. But unfortunately, due to the limitation of time I will not be able to thoroughly go into this.

Allow me here to briefly talk about the international cooperation aspects of the Convention and its relation with other intentional legal instruments, in addition to the United Nations efforts in this field.

Like other regional agreements, the Convention is designed to improve the cooperation between the Member States; nevertheless it did not overlook the importance of reaching out, participating and consolidating forces in the international efforts to combat terrorism. This was obvious since it aligned itself with six international conventions. It also concurrently committed the parties (in some aspects) to extend the provisions to non-parties, as I illustrated earlier in the case of border control.

Pursuant to Security Council Resolution 1373 (2001) and comprehending the necessity to amalgamate the Arab efforts with the global response against terrorism, a meeting of a group of experts convened in the seat of the Arab League to study the essential measures to correspond with the resolution on both the regional and national levels. The expert group adopted a number of recommendations guiding the Member States through the implementation procedures of the resolution; it was politically endorsed by the League on both the ministerial and summit levels.

In its recommendations, the group affirmed the support of the Arab States for the United Nations' efforts to eradicate international terrorism, especially those being made to convene an international conference under the auspices of the United Nations, and to elaborate a comprehensive international counter-terrorism convention. Such a convention would need to incorporate a precise definition of terrorism, differentiating between it and the legitimate right of people to resist occupation and aggression. It would also need to embrace the concept of state terrorism, condemning terrorism in all its forms and manifestations regardless of its motives and rationale (thus conforming to the definition incorporated in the Arab Convention on the Suppression of Terrorism) and stressing the need to eliminate its possible causes, especially the occupation of territory and the denial of the right of people to self-determination and to sovereignty over their territory, so as to maintain the territorial integrity of the State.

The Arab League also provided the Secretariat of the United Nations with a report detailing the League's effort in the field of combating terrorism and this was issued as Document A/57/183; meanwhile the League's Secretariat continues to update the status of signature and ratification of Member States of the related international conventions.

The Arab League was always keen to participate in all meetings with the CTC (Counter-Terrorism Committee) held with international and regional organizations, which took place in New York in March 2003, Washington in October 2003, and finally in Vienna in May 2004.

To conclude, I find it important to stress the fact that terrorism is a multidimensional phenomenon that needs a matching approach. I hope I have presented you with a perspective of the legal aspect of the efforts exerted in our region in combating terrorism. Nevertheless, we believe these goals will not be achieved unless there is a wider integrated coordination, not only in the law enforcement and legal fields but more importantly in all related dimensions of terrorism, politically, socially and economically. In order to succeed we must deeply and thoroughly deal with all its aspects.

Chapter 13

The Organization of the Islamic Conference

MAHMOUD HMOUD[1]

Introduction

Before discussing the Convention of the Organization of the Islamic Conference on Combating International Terrorism, I would like to provide a brief background on the efforts and measures taken by the Organization in relation to terrorism and the context in which action has been taken.

Members of the OIC come from different regions of the world. However, the organizations are mostly composed of African and Asian States, including Middle Eastern ones. The events that took place in such regions, together with the political background which shaped the creation of most of those States, are important factors in understanding the action or the reaction of the OIC to international terrorism.

One key factor in the conflict is the Middle East with its various layers, complexities and repercussions. Other regional and international territorial disputes play a role, yet to a lesser extent.

Another key factor is the composition of OIC from States which mainly earned their independence between the 1940s and the 1970s from major colonialist powers which had used harsh methods to quell any resistance or opposition during their years of occupation.

Also, national liberation movements were often described by the colonial powers as terrorist organizations. As occupied nations became sovereign and independent, the leaders and governments of those nations viewed the notion of terrorism from an alternative angle. The background of occupation and colonialism gave a different perspective on the approach and means to fighting terrorism and to the framework in which such fight should take place.

A third factor is the role of Islam, the common denominator of the members of the organization. After 11 September, the focus on Islam as a religion, culture and a civilization intensified. The terrorist attack by Al Qaeda in the US has brought the battle against terrorism to the forefront. It also gave rise to alternative approaches in

---

1   Legal Counsel, Permanent Mission of Jordan to the United Nations in New York. These remarks are made in a personal capacity and do not necessarily reflect the views of the Ministry of Foreign Affairs of Jordan.

international law and international relations which infringe on the traditional rules which existed before the 11 September attacks. These ranged from pre-emption to resolutions under Chapter VII ordering States to take certain measures which are essentially reserved to the States themselves as sovereign nations, and this variation created uncertainty and unease about what to expect. This, together with the implicit and sometimes explicit statements associating Islam with terrorism, has led to various forms of response by Islamic States. Some acted in a defensive manner, sensing that they are being targeted in the fight against terrorism for different reasons. Others took a proactive approach, trying to cooperate with the international efforts and adopting effective measures to prevent terrorist acts, enforce the relevant laws and bring the perpetrators to justice.

However, the Islam factor and the false and sometimes malicious association with terrorism preceded 11 September. Thus, such an association has been a key factor in framing OIC efforts in dealing with terrorism.

Action by the OIC in relation to terrorism has taken three forms:

- political statements such as the declarations and resolutions of OIC summits and conferences;
- the Code of Conduct for the fight against terrorism endorsed by the 1994 Islamic Summit held in Casablanca;
- the 1999 Convention of the Organization of the Islamic Conference on Combating Terrorism which entered into force on 7 October 2002.

Declarations and resolutions

Although non-binding in nature, such declarations and resolutions reflect the political stand OIC members take in relation to terrorism and the measures which should be taken by OIC members on OIC and international levels. However, the language used serves to accommodate the various points of view, thus providing limited indication of the common principles guiding the organization's actions against terrorism.

Yet, there was emphasis on three principles in the various declarations and resolutions:

- The condemnation of terrorism in all its forms and manifestations and the need for cooperation on all levels to fight the phenomenon. In this regard, the resolutions, such as Resolution 65/9 of the Ninth Islamic Summit, adopted a language similar to and along the lines of the Declaration on Measures to Eliminate International Terrorism (UN GA Resolution 49/60).
- The need to distinguish between the armed struggle (in the exercise of the right of peoples to self-determination and fighting foreign occupation) from acts of terrorism. However, it should be noted that, although this statement has been constantly used in OIC declarations and resolution, the legal means by which such distinction can be realized was never clarified in such documents. One exception, though, was the declaration of the Tenth Islamic Summit held

in Malaysia in 2003. Paragraph 50 of the declaration provides that cases of alien occupation are governed by international humanitarian law.
•   The assertion that Islam is a religion of peace and tolerance and condemnation of acts of terrorism perpetrated by religious extremists.

It should be noted that the issue of state terrorism has been a focus in the various resolutions and declarations. However, they do not provide guidance on the common understanding of the term, its elements and conditions and its scope. Some resolutions referred to aggression and foreign occupation as acts of state terrorism, without clarifying legal and political links between such terms.

Following 11 September, the OIC followed a more proactive approach on the political level by adopting a plan of action to combat international terrorism during a ministerial meeting held in Malaysia in 2002. The plan established an open-ended Ministerial-level Committee with a mandate to formulate and recommend to Member States practical measures to combat international terrorism. The plan also provides that OIC members would work towards the early conclusion of the draft comprehensive convention on international terrorism which is being negotiated in the Sixth Committee of the General Assembly. It also states that OIC members would continue working with other countries and supporting the international community, including implementing Security Council Resolution 1373 and becoming parties to the relevant international conventions.

The Code of Conduct

The Code *per se* is a political declaration of a non-binding nature. It was adopted in Resolution 4317-P of the Seventh Islamic Summit in Morocco (1994) and has been quoted in the various declarations and resolutions of the OIC. Further, the preamble of the OIC Convention stipulates that the code rules guided the adoption of the Convention. No Member State has ever expressed reservations on its content or objected to its application. This general and consistent acceptance, together with the specific actions that the code mandates on OIC Member States, lead to the conclusion that the document developed a legally binding character.

The Code has three main principles to guide OIC members in their measures to combat terrorism:

•   A declaration that terrorism cannot be justified and must be condemned regardless of its origins, causes and purposes. However, the Code provides that this principle is without prejudice to the legitimate rights of people under occupation to struggle for independence and self-determination.
•   A commitment by OIC members to combat terrorism and to take firm and effective bilateral and collective steps to prevent such acts. Under this principle, members' undertakings were set in the Code:
   – refraining from committing, attempting or participating, in any way, in financing, instigating or supporting directly or indirectly acts of terrorism;

– taking measures to ensure that their territories are not used in any terrorist activity and to deny terrorists any safe harbour;
– enhancing cooperation among OIC members, in accordance with their national laws and international obligations, in combating terrorist acts. This includes prosecuting the perpetrators or extraditing them to a State which has jurisdiction, and exchanging information on the terrorists and their activities.

• A commitment to ensure the protection, security and safety of diplomatic and consular missions in accordance with the relevant conventions.

The OIC Convention (1999)

The Convention was adopted by the Islamic Conference of Foreign Ministers which was held in Burkina Faso in 1999.

The Convention entered into force in 2002 after the deposit of the seventh instrument of ratification in accordance with article 40 of the Convention. It has two main aspects:

• it defines terrorism and terrorist crimes; and
• it sets out areas of cooperation between OIC members in combating terrorism and the procedure for implementation in the different areas of cooperation.

The definition of 'terrorism' and 'terrorist crimes'

The OIC Convention provides two separate yet overlapping definitions for the terms 'terrorism' and 'terrorist crimes'. Such a distinction is problematic and creates difficulty in the application of an instrument dedicated primarily to law enforcement.

In addition, the definition of the term 'terrorism' is wide and encompasses certain ambiguous and sometimes political concepts, thus adding to the difficulty in applying and enforcing the convention. According to Article 1.1 which defines the term, terrorism has the following elements:

• It is any act of violence, or threat thereof, notwithstanding its motives or intentions;
• it has to be perpetrated to carry out an individual or collective criminal plan; and
• it aims at:
    – terrorizing people or threatening to harm them or imperilling their lives, honour, freedom, security or rights;
    – exposing the environment or facility or public or private property to hazards or occupying or seizing them;
    – endangering a national resource or international facilities; or

- threatening the stability, territorial integrity, political unity or sovereignty of independent States.

As for the definition of 'terrorist crime' in Article 1.3, the crime has the following elements:

- It is any crime executed, started or participated in;
- to realize a terrorist objective;
- in any contracting State or against its nationals, assets or interests or foreign facilities and nationals residing in its territory;
- which is punishable by its domestic law.

Further, Article 2(d) includes in the scope of terrorist crimes 'all forms of international crimes, including illegal trafficking in narcotics and human beings and money laundering, aimed at financing terrorist objectives.' However, the Article does not define international crimes nor does it set out its elements and conditions. The only qualification is the financial dimension which should associate with the 'terrorist objective'.

Under Article 2.4, terrorist crimes also include those which are mentioned in the 12 major international sectoral conventions, to the extent that a contracting State is a party to those conventions.

The two definitions provide for more questions than answers, creating uncertainty in applying and enforcing the convention:

- How can the two terms be distinguished when they relate to the same content and describe 'acts'?
- How can the difference in intentions of the perpetrators under the two definitions be reconciled?
- Is *any* act of violence or threat thereof qualified as terrorism even if the aim was not realized?
- Is exposing the environment or any facility to hazards or threatening the sovereignty of independent States actually an *aim* of the perpetrator or a *result*?
- What is the meaning of the word 'terrorist objective' used in the definition of terrorist crime?
- Is determining a certain act as 'terrorism' or 'terrorist crime' an objective or subjective test? This is particularly important when the act aims at threatening the stability, territorial integrity or sovereignty of a State.
- Why does the definition of 'terrorist act' not consider a crime committed by a national of a State party a crime?

Those are some of the legal concerns about the definitions of the two terms which need to be addressed in order to make the convention an effective law enforcement instrument. The two definitions should be:

- unified and streamlined;
- specific and clear in their legal content;
- conform with definitions under other international instruments;
- reflect the seriousness of the acts committed.

It should be noted that the Convention excludes peoples' struggles against foreign occupation aiming at liberation and self-determination from the scope of the definition of terrorist crimes as long as such struggles are in accordance with international law (Article 2(a)). Therefore, the convention recognizes that an act exercising self-determination has to conform to international law, including international humanitarian law; otherwise it is illegal and should be criminalized. Yet the Convention does not clarify which act may be a legitimate exercise and which is not; a matter which may create difficulty in the application, especially when the act is not clearly against a military target or does not serve a military objective during the time of war.

Areas of cooperation

Cooperation under the provisions of the convention has two main aspects, which we now consider.

Cooperation in taking measures to prevent and combat terrorism in the State parties' territories and to refrain from sponsoring terrorist activities

Under Article 3.1, a contracting State is committed not to execute, initiate or participate, in any form, in organizing, financing, committing, instigating or supporting terrorist acts. This is a specific obligation on the State entailing its international responsibility if it fails to respect such an obligation. However, what undermines this commitment is the shortcoming of the definitions of 'terrorism' and 'terrorist acts' and its vulnerability for political interpretations.

Article 2 provides for positive obligations in the field of prevention and combat. Among such obligations is the obligation to cooperate and coordinate with other contracting States, without specifying the means and conditions of such coordination and cooperation. Contracting States also have to strengthen trans-border and customs controls and enhance internal security measures, including those related to public transportation.

States have to promote security intelligence activities and coordinate in this respect with each other. They have to establish relevant data bases on terrorist groups and exchange the relevant information. A contracting State which receives specific information on a terrorist act to be perpetrated against the interests of another State should communicate such information expeditiously. Contracting States should also assist each other in investigation, exchange expertise and cooperate in the educational field.

Thus, the Convention is very ambitious in the extent of obligations of prevention and combating to be fulfilled. However, it is left to the discretion of each contracting State to decide how to fulfil the obligations to cooperate. Unless it was the common interest of the relevant States to cooperate in certain aspects of a certain case, such cooperation may not be achieved solely on the basis of the legal nature of the obligation.

Extradition

The Convention contains provisions on judicial cooperation in relation to extradition. It also provides for a *general* obligation on the State party to prosecute or extradite (the *aut dedere aut judicare* principle outlined in Article 3(b)(i)) without requiring it to establish the terrorist act as a crime under its national law or subject to its criminal jurisdiction. This undoubtedly undermines the *aut dedere aut judicare* principle. Further, the Convention does not provide for the compulsory and optional forms of criminal jurisdiction, and matters of conflict in jurisdiction are dealt with ambiguously and selectively, including under Article 6, as explained below. It can also be said that the Convention is a combination of provisions containing elements of a law enforcement instrument and an extradition treaty, with more emphasis on extradition procedure.

The lack of a provision on requiring the establishing of terrorist acts as crimes under national jurisdiction has significant legal implications on the implementation of judicial cooperation, including on the extradition process. This becomes more pertinent when viewed in light of the definitions of terrorism and terrorist crimes in Article 1 which may be subject to State parties' different interpretations. When the national authorities of a State requested to extradite do not conclude that the act committed was in fact a terrorist one, there is no dispute settlement mechanism under the convention to resolve the matter.

The lack of a specific obligation on the establishment of criminal jurisdiction also proves to be problematic due to certain flaws in the provisions of the convention related to the conditions of extradition and its procedure. Here are some examples:

- There is inconsistency between Articles 5 and 7. The former compels the State to extradite those indicted or convicted of a terrorist crime. Yet the latter imposes the obligation to extradite even if the case is still under investigation in the requesting States; that is, when no indictment has been reached in that case.
- The Convention deals with the controversial issue of political crimes without success. Article 2(b) makes it clear that terrorist crimes shall not be considered political crimes. This article is totally contradicted by Article 6(1) which does not permit extradition when the crime committed is deemed by the requested State as one of a political nature. Article 6(1) then provides that the application is subject to Article 2(b) which is in fact a redundant disclaimer clause.
- Article 6 provides for cases in which extradition is not permissible. However,

as mentioned earlier, it deals selectively and ambiguously with matters related to competent jurisdictions. It also allows the perpetrators of terrorist acts in certain cases to escape punishment and prevents a State from exercising national jurisdiction on a terrorist crime it may consider within its competence. It interferes in matters which are essentially left to the requesting State to decide under its national laws. Among the situations which allow denial of the extradition request are the following:

– Paragraph 3 of the Article reads: 'If the crime for which extradition is requested was committed in the territory of the requested Contracting State, unless this crime has undermined the interest of the requesting Contracting State and its laws stipulate that the perpetrators of those crimes shall be prosecuted and punished providing that the requesting country has not commenced investigation or trial … '. The question arises: what options does the requesting State have when the requested State has ended investigation but decided not to prosecute or try?

– Paragraph 4: 'If the crime has been the subject of a final sentence which has the force of law in the requested Contracting State … '. Accordingly, even if the perpetrator of a terrorist act in the requesting State was convicted for another unrelated crime in the requested State, or the sentence was trivial, this would be enough to stop the requesting State from exercising jurisdiction, no matter how grave the terrorist act was.

– Paragraph 5: 'If the action at the time of the extradition request elapsed or the penalty prescribed in accordance with the law in the Contracting State Requesting extradition … '. Thus, the requested State has the right to make its own judgment on a criminal law matter of the requesting State.

– Paragraph 6: 'Crimes committed outside the territory of the requesting Contracting State by a person who was not its national and the law of the requested Contracting State does not prosecute such a crime if perpetrated outside *its* territory by such a person …'. It is not clear which situation this paragraph is contemplating. It confuses matters of jurisdiction and does not decide which State in fact has jurisdiction. It also allows the perpetrators of terrorism to escape punishment and makes it clear that the State party is not under obligation to criminalize the terrorist act.

– Paragraph 7: 'If pardon was granted and included the perpetrators of these crimes in the requesting Contracting State …'. This interferes with the national jurisdiction of the requesting State. Further, it does not take into consideration factual developments in the case which would reverse the pardon of the requesting State.

– Paragraph 8: 'If the legal system of the requested State does not permit extradition of its national, then it shall be obliged to prosecute whosoever commits a terrorist crime if the act is punishable in both States by a freedom-restraining sentence for a minimum period of one year or more. The nationality of the person requested for extradition shall be determined according to the date of the crime taking into account the investigation undertaken in this respect by the requesting State.' Accordingly, if the crime was not punishable under the law of the requested State, the perpetrator would then enjoy impunity.

The only situation which can be contemplated under Article 6 to legally compel the requesting State to extradite is when the crime has been committed in the requesting State's territory by a person who is not a national of the requested State.

Other forms of judicial cooperation

A contracting State which has jurisdiction over a case may request another contracting State to undertake, on its behalf, certain judicial procedures in the requested State's territory. Article 9 provides examples of such procedures which include hearing witnesses, communicating legal documents, collecting evidence and detaining the suspects. However, the requested State has the option to reject such a request or to postpone it if it overlaps with ongoing investigation in that State or if it considers the request contrary to its national interests and public order.

Conclusion

The Convention needs to be reviewed by the OIC in order to make it an effective law enforcement instrument for combating terrorism. Such a review should include redefining terrorism and terrorist acts and unifying the two terms; revisiting the issue of political crimes; establishing terrorist acts as crimes under national laws and providing for the situations where jurisdiction must be established; and refining the language of the Convention to overcome ambiguities and legal uncertainties.

Chapter 14

The African Union

ALLIEU IBRAHIM KANU[1]

Long before the terrorist acts of 11 September 2001, Africa has had to grapple with international terrorism. On 7 August 1998, more than 250 innocent civilians were killed in the twin bombings of the African embassies in Kenya and Tanzania. In my view, at the time, the international community demonstrated little empathy for those who died and were injured in those attacks. The attacks in Kenya and Tanzania were so horrendous that war had to be declared against the perpetrators of those heinous acts. Even the ensuing investigations and trial of those arrested for those crimes received very little attention in the world press.

However, the attacks of 11 September in New York and Washington propelled the world into action. The United Nations immediately went into action and war was declared on terrorism. The United Nations has since 11 September passed a number of resolutions proscribing terrorism and calling on States to put in place in their domestic legal systems, measures aiming to combat international terrorism in all its forms and manifestations.

For Africa, the fight against terrorism had long begun prior to the attacks in the US. After the attacks in Kenya and Tanzania, African countries realized that action had to be taken against the scourge of international terrorism. On 14 July 1999 at Algiers, Algeria, the Organization of African Unity, now the African Union, adopted the Convention on the Prevention and Combating of Terrorism. The Convention has been signed by 46 States with 32 ratifications and depositaries: the number of signatories and ratifications to this convention is a practical and concrete expression of Africa's commitment to fight the scourge of terrorism.

Before examining some of the provisions of the Convention, it should be noted that Africa has also subscribed to all the measures adopted by the United Nations to combat terrorism and in particular, Resolution 49/60 of the General Assembly of 9 December 1994, together with the annexed Declaration on Measures to Eliminate International Terrorism. Also, many African countries have become parties to the 12 sectoral Conventions on Terrorism and actively participate in current efforts to put in place a comprehensive Convention against Terrorism. I will come back to these efforts in the Ad Hoc Committee established by Resolution 51/210.

---

1   Ambassador and Deputy Permanent Representative of Sierra Leone to the UN in New York. These remarks are made in a personal capacity and do not necessarily reflect the views of the Ministry of Foreign Affairs of Sierra Leone.

Now let us examine some of the core provisions of the Algiers Convention. It has 12 preambular paragraphs which by and large reaffirm Africa's commitment to the fight against terrorism and 23 Articles, together with the 12 sectoral conventions annexed to it.

Article 1 of the Convention defines the Convention, States Parties and Terrorist Acts. Article 2 declares what African States will be undertaking in becoming States Parties. These are stated in Article 2(a-d) of the Convention.

Article 3 states in clear terms what is outside the scope of the Convention. I shall come back to this article when considering the suggestions contained in the Report of the High-level Panel and the Report of the Secretary-General.

The African Convention defines a 'Terrorist Act' as any act which violates the criminal laws of a State Party and which may endanger the life, physical integrity or freedom of, or cause serious injury or death to, any person, any number of persons or group of persons or causes or may cause damage to public or private property, natural resources, environmental or cultural heritage and is calculated or intended to:

1. Intimidate, put in fear, force, coerce or induce any government, body, institution, the general public or any segment thereof, to do or abstain from doing any act or to adopt or abandon a particular standpoint or to act according to certain principles; or
2. Disrupt any public service, the delivery of any essential service to the public or to create a public emergency; or
3. Any promotion, sponsoring, contribution to, command, aid, incitement, encouragement, attempt, threat, conspiracy, organizing or procurement of any person, with the intent to commit any act referred to in paragraph (a)(i)-(iii).

Article 1 is all-encompassing and picks out all the elements that constitute terrorism as a crime against humanity. The article sharply brings into focus the activities of individuals who are in positions of authority and command and who influence the activities of combatants engaged in internal conflicts. These individuals, in as much as they have influence over rebel movements, are criminally responsible for the actions of these rebel movements. If the rebels are deemed to bear the greatest responsibility for atrocities committed against an innocent population, those who aid and assist them in carrying out their heinous crimes should equally be held responsible for these crimes. In my view, there is no distinction between those who carry out acts enshrined in Article 1 of the African Convention and those who carry out acts proscribed in all international instruments, including, in particular, resolutions of the United Nations. Those who engage in activities proscribed by Article 1 of the African Convention, albeit they carry out these crimes in internal armed conflicts, are all terrorists. I cannot see any difference between those who attacked the twin towers in New York, the Pentagon in Washington, the US embassies in Kenya and Tanzania and those who burned houses and cut off the limbs of innocent civilians in Sierra Leone, Liberia or the Democratic Republic of the Congo. They are all terrorists who should be held responsible for their actions.

In Article 2 of the African Convention, African States undertake to initiate action and put in place mechanisms to combat terrorism. The Convention also has provisions inviting States to cooperate with each other in the fight against terrorism. It also has provisions on the extradition of any person charged with or convicted of any terrorist act carried out on the territory of another State Party and whose extradition is requested by one of the States Parties, in conformity with the rules provided for in the Convention. The Convention in Part 5 calls for extra-territorial investigations and mutual legal assistance among States Parties in conformity with their sovereign rights.

In Article 3, the African Convention excludes from its scope of application the right of national liberation movements fighting against colonial domination and alien occupation in accordance with the principles of international law. The Convention also states in Article 3(2) that political, philosophical, ideological, racial, ethnic, religious or other motives shall not be a justifiable defence against a terrorist act. What the African Union is re-emphasizing is that terrorism, in line with the African Convention, cannot be justified under any circumstances, not even for situations or circumstances mentioned in Article 3(2).

Some academics and even some so-called terrorism experts who have argued that poverty, underdevelopment and terrorism are not related, should examine what happened in my country, Sierra Leone, and in places like Liberia, Rwanda and Angola, countries that represent the poorest and most underdeveloped in the world. In these countries, many more people have died from terrorism than have been killed in Europe and North America. If atrocities committed by the Revolutionary United Front in Sierra Leone do not constitute terrorism, then we will abysmally fail to understand how poverty, lack of development, bad governance and dictatorship help to create terrorists.

Discussing Africa's fight against terrorism will not be complete without taking into account recent realities within the United Nations and these are considerations of the propositions contained in the Report of the High-level Panel in Document A/59/565 on Threats, Challenges and Change and the Secretary-General's Report in Document A/59/2005 on progress in the larger freedoms: towards development, security and human rights for all.

The African Union welcomed the call by the High-level Panel and by the Secretary-General, H.E. Kofi Annan, on the international community, to re-energise its efforts to combat the scourge of terrorism. The African Union cannot accept and will not accept the attempts being made to equate terrorism with the legitimate struggle waged by peoples for their liberation as long as the struggle is in accordance with the principles of international law.

The African Union is of the view that the propositions for a definition of terrorism proffered in the two reports could be helpful in the international community's efforts to galvanize a unified and concerted response to terrorism in all its forms and manifestations. It is the view of the African Union that the definitions suggested in the two reports do not address the issue of the right of self-determination enshrined in the Charter of the United Nations and ignore the right of national liberation movements fighting against colonial domination and alien occupation.

Other issues which the High-level Panel Report paid scant attention to in paragraph 160 of its Report are the issues of state terrorism and the right to resist foreign occupation. In my view, I believe the issue of state terrorism, at this stage of our attempt to craft a comprehensive international convention against terrorism, should be set aside. The illegitimate use of force by States is already thoroughly regulated under international law. However, I strongly support the right of peoples to resist occupation but this right cannot include the killing and maiming of civilians.

We in Africa know what terrorism is and the devastating effect of terrorism on the morale of the people and development. Aside from the African Convention, the African Union took further measures to strengthen its application. In July 2003, the Assembly of the African Union, in its second ordinary session in Maputo, Mozambique, adopted a decision on the elaboration of a code of conduct on terrorism in general and terrorism in Africa in particular. At its third ordinary session of the Executive Council, the African Union adopted a decision on the draft protocol to the African Union Convention on the Prevention and Combating of Terrorism.

Apart from Africa's regional response to terrorism, the seriousness of this phenomenon has also led to sub-regional responses. In West Africa, in 2002, Senegal hosted a conference of 30 African countries to discuss how to respond to international terrorism. The Conference came out with the Dakar Declaration Against Terrorism in which the African Heads of State solemnly registered their abhorrence of acts of terrorism and committed themselves to work with others in the global effort to suppress such acts in all their forms and manifestations. In Dakar, during the African Summit Against Terrorism, the President of my country, Sierra Leone, Alhaji Dr. Ahmad Tejan Kabbah, registered our country's commitment to the fight against terrorism. At the moment, the Republic of Sierra Leone has no specific legislation on the combating of terrorism. However a number of offences under its criminal code and Criminal Procedure Act 1965, such as murder, extortion, the illegal possession of fire arms and ammunition, may generally apply to acts of terrorism.

There is now in West Africa greater cooperation among the States to combat organized crime and terrorism. The West African States have also put in place, at a domestic level, actions required by the various United Nations Security Council resolutions, including in particular, Resolutions 1373 and 1267. The various measures put in place by African States to meet their obligations under these resolutions are described in their respective reports to the Council. As already stated in this chapter, many African States are parties to the 12 sectoral conventions on terrorism and have to meet certain obligations under those conventions. On the other hand, we have Security Council resolutions which also put obligations on African States. The 12 sectoral conventions are multilateral treaties, unlike Security Council resolutions. What is the efficacy of these resolutions vis-à-vis the multilateral conventions? Even though this is an interesting point, I will resist the temptation of discussing it in this chapter.

Now let me turn to East Africa, where there has also been sub-regional cooperation among the countries in the region, all directed to combating terrorism. In the struggle against terrorism in that part of Africa, one needs to commend the involvement of the developed countries, particularly the US which has forged a partnership with countries like Kenya in a combined task force that seeks to check terrorism. Also as part of the international campaign against terrorism a special anti-terrorism squad, composed of the German Naval Air Wing, was established in Mombasa to monitor ships plying the Gulf of Aden and the Somali Coast.

I will be remiss if I fail to discuss one essential African approach to combating terrorism and this is the issue of tackling its root causes such as poverty, underdevelopment, inequality and the ensuing despair leading to frustration, anger and alienation, especially of the youths who rightly or wrongly believe that they have no stake in society and thus are exploited by terrorists.

In the Report of a Conference jointly organized by the government of Norway and the New York-based International Peace Academy, *Fighting Terrorism for Humanity*, it was pointed out by one of the discussants that:

> … perceptions of marginalization and exclusion require long-term initiatives in which the United Nations should have a key role. Eradicating terrorism requires new policies towards non-traditional security threats, including finding solutions to economic, environmental and social problems that extremists manipulate and exploit. We in Africa believe that for the fight against terrorism to be successful, the international community must address the root causes and conditions that impel people towards terrorist acts.[2]

In this regard, the United Nations must play a crucial role. A number of working groups, commissions and high-level panels have in the past been set up by the UN. These bodies have all come up with brilliant and erudite reports, the recommendations of which are yet to be practicalized and implemented. However, I dare say that I am on this occasion very optimistic with regard to the implementation of the recommendations of the High-level Panel Report. This is why the African Union supports the recommendation pertaining to the establishment of 'A special capacity Building Trust Fund'. This fund will enhance the capacity of the United Nations to provide technical assistance to Member States in their national efforts to prevent and combat terrorism. The rules governing the fund should be democratic enough to help strengthen the regional counter-terrorism mechanisms, especially the operationalization of the African Union Convention on Terrorism and the Algiers based African Study and Research Centre on Terrorism. The United Nations must act and should be perceived to be acting in a fair and impartial manner in combating terrorism, notwithstanding the role of geopolitics. Africa notwithstanding its limited capacity has been in the forefront in the fight against terrorism and will always cooperate with the international community in providing a unified response to this phenomenon.

---

2 Conference report, p. 5.

Chapter 15

NATO

MARCO PERTILE[1]

Introduction

After the end of the Cold War, the North Atlantic Treaty Organization (NATO) acknowledged that its activities had to focus less on classical interstate conflicts and concentrate more on new, partly unpredictable, threats arising from the changing nature of the security environment. At the time, NATO's legal and political discourse mentioned terrorism as one of the possible challenges in the re-definition of the Alliance's tasks, but the issue was not considered the main one.

It is therefore quite telling that the North Atlantic Council (NAC) qualified the terrorist acts of 9/11 as an attack against all Member States under Article 5 of the North Atlantic Treaty.[2] The key-norm of the Treaty was invoked for the first time since the establishment of the Alliance in quite a different scenario than the one envisaged in 1949.

Since then NATO has rapidly begun to adapt its structure, its activities, and its capabilities to the fight against terrorism. Today one may affirm that the Alliance is (at least formally) amongst the most active international organisations operating in the field. Indeed the adoption of the fight against terrorism as one of chief objectives of NATO fits in a process of transformation that was already under way. That process was re-oriented but did not need to be radically re-directed: it involved the material activities carried out by the Alliance, the norms regulating them and the general functioning of the Alliance.

In the next paragraphs, with reference to those specific aspects, we will describe NATO's role in the fight against terrorism. The analysis will take into account the transformation of NATO and the relevant normative framework.

The normative framework

The legal basis of NATO's involvement in the fight against terrorism is quite a tricky issue. As is probably known, the founding treaty is a short text composed of 12 articles, which mirrors the original objective of the Alliance: defending Member States from threats originating in classical interstate disputes. NATO was established

---

1   PhD, Research Fellow, Department of Legal Sciences, University of Trento.
2   On the point, see subsection on the invocation of Article 5 below.

as a defensive military pact and was conceived to act within the legal bounds related to the primacy of the UN Security Council.[3]

The legal obligations arising from the North Atlantic Treaty are limited. The cornerstone is Article 5 according to which 'The Parties agree that an armed attack against one or more of them in Europe or North America shall be considered an attack against them all (...)'. In such a case, Member States pledge themselves to take such action as they deem necessary. As further demonstrated *inter alia* by Article 7, those actions must comply with the collective security system and, in particular, with Article 51 of the United Nations Charter. Simply put, the core of the originary legal system of the Alliance may be summarized as follows: once a relevant armed attack occurs, the Parties are under a legal obligation of *opinio juris* as concerns the scope of the attack coupled with a half-hearted obligation to subsequently reach an agreement on positive actions.[4]

Obviously, no explicit reference to terrorism is made in the founding treaty, which was framed to address the necessities of the bipolar world order. However, the Treaty is quite flexible and has been largely supplemented by subsequent integrations, possibly of a customary nature.[5] Fundamental aspects ranging from the internal organic structure of the Alliance, to the voting procedure, and the objective, as well as the material activities carried out, have largely developed irrespectively of the existence of any relevant treaty provision.[6] A cardinal role has been played by the unanimous decisions of the North Atlantic Council, as concerns policy documents or single issues.

As to terrorism, the adoption of the two Strategic Concepts of the Alliance (the Rome Strategic Concept of 1991 and the Washington one of 1999) is particularly relevant. Those documents, the legal nature of which is doubtful, directed the transformation of NATO and introduced the issue of terrorism in its legal discourse. The Rome Strategic Concept acknowledged that, after the end of the West/East confrontation, armed attacks might originate not only from the Eastern bloc.[7] Yet the possibility of equating terrorist acts and armed attacks against Member States

---

3   See J.S. Ignarski, 'North Atlantic Treaty Organisation', in R. Bernhardt (ed.), *Encyclopaedia of Public International Law*, Amsterdam: North Holland, 2000, pp. 646 ff., pp. 646-647; E. Cannizzaro, 'N.A.T.O.', in *Digesto delle Discipline pubblicistiche*, Turin: UTET, 1995, pp. 52 ff., pp. 53-55.

4   Cf. B. Conforti, *Le Nazioni Unite*, Padua: CEDAM, 2005, p. 242; Cannizzaro, *supra* note 3, pp. 61-62.

5   In view of its flexible nature, the North Atlantic Treaty has been defined as a 'treaty on wheels'. See B. Simma, 'NATO, the UN, and the Use of Force', *European Journal of International Law*, vol. 10, 1999, pp. 1 ff., p. 18.

6   Cannizzaro, *supra* note 3, p. 58.

7   The Alliance's New Strategic Concept agreed by the Heads of State and Government participating in the meeting of the North Atlantic Council, para. 40, at: http://www.nato.int/docu/basictxt/b911108a.htm (accessed: 20/02/2005).

was not yet envisaged, not even by the Washington Strategic Concept.[8] Terrorism (as well as the proliferation of weapons of mass destruction and the disruption of the flow of vital resources) was placed amongst the new multi-faceted risks that could affect the Alliance's security.[9] On the level of substantial security strategies, the Rome Concept did not go much beyond stating that a 'broad approach' – combining dialogue, cooperation and the maintenance of a defence capability – was needed.[10] By contrast, the Washington Concept, sharing a similar threat assessment, made explicit reference to possible new activities of the Alliance in the context of crisis management. That marks a departure from the North Atlantic Treaty under which the only operative activities are collective self-defence actions under Article 5. The Washington Concept consciously underlines the point qualifying the new activities as 'non-Article 5' operations.[11]

Two other points should be made in this respect. The Concept, while paying lip service to respect for the collective security system, seems to allow for the possibility of carrying out peacekeeping missions or even coercive operations without a mandate from the Security Council.[12] Furthermore, the geographical limits of the Alliance's operations are extended. While the North Atlantic Treaty explicitly makes clear that the area of action of NATO is the North Atlantic region (Europe and North America), the new instrument refers also to security challenges arising 'in and around the Euro-Atlantic area'.[13] It is not clear though whether only crises at the periphery of the Alliance are to be considered. The language of the document might lead one to think that any crisis functionally related to the Alliance's security interests is relevant, no matter where it occurs.[14]

To sum up, the Washington Strategic Concept seems to provide legitimacy to new kinds of NATO's operations: 'non-Article 5' operations and 'out of area' operations. As will be seen, the two categories that are not mutually exclusive, are relevant to classify some of the recent anti-terrorism activities of the Alliance.

---

8   The Washington Strategic Concept made a distinction between 'Any armed attack on the territory of the Allies, from whatever direction (...) covered by Articles 5 and 6 of the Washington Treaty' and 'risks of a wider nature, including acts of terrorism'. See Press Release, NAC-S(99)65, 24 April 1999, para. 24, at: www.nato.int/docu/pr/1999/p99-065e.htm (accessed: 20/02/2000).

9   The Alliance's New Strategic Concept, *supra* note 7, para. 12.

10 *Ibid.*, para. 14.

11 The Washington Strategic Concept, *supra* note 8, para. 31.

12 E. Cannizzaro, 'La nuova dottrina strategica della NATO e l'evoluzione della disciplina internazionale dell'uso della forza', in N. Ronzitti (ed.), *NATO, conflitto in Kosovo e Costituzione italiana*, Milan: Giuffré, 2000, pp. 43 ff, pp. 48-49.

13 The Washington Strategic Concept, *supra* note 8, para. 20.

14 Cannizzaro, *supra* note 12, p. 51.

The relationship between the North Atlantic Treaty and the Strategic Concepts: the intricacies of identifying ultra vires *activities of the Organization*

A substantial part of the Washington Strategic Concept seems incompatible with the North Atlantic Treaty. As has been seen, respect for the UN Charter is mandatory under Article 7 of NATO's founding treaty and the Concept provides for new activities of the Alliance (non-Article 5 and out of area), which may possibly be carried out without the necessary authorization of the UN Security Council.

However, leaving aside the legality of the actions of the Alliance in light of the UN Charter, one may think that the issue of the compatibility of the strategic concepts and the NAC's decisions in general with the founding treaty should not be overemphasized.

In this respect the decision-making process that has developed in the Alliance has to be taken into account: all decisions are taken according to the unanimity rule. Moreover, the approval of any material operation is subordinated to a double-step procedure that involves the consensus of Member States at all stages. First, the North Atlantic Council agrees by consensus that a specific operation can be undertaken by the Alliance. Then consent is required again for each Member State to participate in the activity. The first step binds Member States to consider a given activity as legally carried out by the Alliance, but only the second gives rise to the obligation to materially participate in it.[15]

From a conceptual point of view, it has been maintained that the international personality of NATO is not beyond doubt.[16] One could think that the Alliance is to be considered as a 'highly developed institutional union of states' and that its organs act as common organs of Member States.[17] According to this approach, considering the peculiarity of NATO's decision-making process, the legal basis of activities that are 'outside' the treaty but not prohibited by it does not need to be sought in the founding treaty.[18]

Be that as it may, the practice of the organization and its voting system demonstrate that the internal legal order of NATO is not to be interpreted in light of the principle of delegated powers or of the rule *expressio unius est exclusio alterius*.[19] The founding treaty is open to *praeter legem* integrations. Admittedly, a

---

15 T. Gazzini, 'NATO's Role in the Collective Security System', *Journal of Conflict & Security Law*, Vol. 8, 2003, pp. 231 ff., pp. 243-244.

16 A. Barbera, *Le vicende del Trattato del Nord-Atlantico: revisione de facto o interpretazione evolutiva?*, *Rassegna Parlamentare,* Vol. 49, 1999, pp. 815 ff., pp. 831-832; *contra* A. Pellet, 'L'imputabilité d'éventuels actes illicites – Responsabilité de l'OTAN ou des Ètats membres', in C.Tomuschat (ed.), *Kosovo and the International Community – A Legal Assessment*, The Hague: Kluwer, 2002, pp. 193 ff, p. 198.

17 Gazzini, *supra* note 15, pp. 242-246. *Contra* A. Pellet, *supra* note 16, p. 198.

18 Gazzini, *supra* note 15, pp, 245-246.

19 On the principle of delegated powers, see M. Rama Montaldo, 'International Legal Personality and Implied Powers of International Organisations', *British Yearbook of International Law*, Vol. 44, 1970, pp. 111 ff., p. 114. For the application of the rule *expressio*

general limit of compatibility is the need to respect the primacy of the UN Charter as concerns the international regulation of recourse to armed force.[20] In any case, from a strictly internal point of view, the finding of a breach would be of little significance, all decisions being based on the unanimous consent of Member States. From this perspective, Member States are barred from protesting against a breach of the treaty to which they consented.[21] On the other hand, the fact remains that all pacts contrary to *jus cogens* are null and void.[22] Therefore any decision (be it interpretative, integrative or emendatory) should be so considered when at odds with the prohibition of the use of force in international relations.

It should also be underlined that, as was anticipated before, the binding nature of the strategic concepts is debatable.[23] In the present writer's opinion it is quite unlikely that they entail legal obligations. One should consider the *opinio juris* clearly expressed by some members of the Alliance that qualified the obligations arising from the documents as political.[24] The absence of any reference to additional sources in the North Atlantic Treaty, the vague content and the non-technical language of the provisions should be also taken into account. It seems plausible that the strategic concepts would bring about general political commitments that might be legally implemented on a case by case basis. They may seem not compatible with the North Atlantic Treaty, but it is only by carefully analysing the activities of the Alliance that one may understand whether new internal customary rules emerge.

On the whole, it is therefore with respect to the obligations arising from the UN Charter and from general international law, rather than the unclear constraints deriving from the North Atlantic Treaty, that the recent activities of NATO in the field of counter-terrorism should be assessed. The situation is further complicated by the fact that, while the internal legal order of NATO is undergoing transformation,

---

unius est exclusio alterius (or 'the negative pregnant') to the Statutes of the International Organisations, see E. Lauterpacht, 'The Development of the Law of International Organizations by the Decisions of International Tribunals', *Recueil des Cours de l'Academie de Droit international de la Haye*, Vol. 4, 1976, pp. 379 ff, pp. 436-437.

20 Simma, *supra* note 5, p. 3.

21 Arguing that, in view of the double-step voting procedure adopted by the NAC in case material activities are at issue, it is very unlikely that a member State might invoke the invalidity of the Strategic Concept, see Cannizzaro, *supra* note 12, p. 62, note 27.

22 Article 53, Vienna Convention on the Law of Treaties. See, Simma, *supra* note 5, p. 19.

23 Three options can be put forward as concerns their legal qualification. In light of their adoption by unanimous decision of the NAC in the composition of the Heads of State and Government, they have been considered as simplified form agreements. By contrast, the view has been taken that their vague content and non-legal language qualify them as soft law instruments. The strategic concepts – being adopted by the NAC (formally an organ of NATO) – could also be regarded as an informal internal source, hierarchically subordinated to the founding Treaty. Cf. Gazzini, *supra* note 15, pp. 243-247; Cannizzaro, *supra* note 12, p. 61; A. Carlevaris, 'Accordi in forma semplificata e impegni derivanti dal Trattato NATO', in Ronzitti (ed.), *supra* note 12, p. 108.

24 Cf. Gazzini, *supra* note 15, p. 245.

the international regulation of the use of force also seems to be involved in a process of change.[25] Yet the pace of change (and perhaps its nature) may not be synchronized in the two systems.

The Alliance's activities in the struggle against terrorism

The Atlantic Alliance's involvement in the fight against terrorism is concerned both with a number of strictly defensive measures and with peace-keeping or peace-implementing missions aimed at the stabilization of post-conflict areas.

As will be seen in detail later, the first category mainly concerns a number of specific measures that the Allies were requested to adopt by the United States in the aftermath of 9/11 attacks. With regard to the second, reference can be made to the UN-mandated international force deployed in Afghanistan (ISAF) and to the re-orientation of NATO's presence in Bosnia (SFOR) and Kosovo (KFOR).

The invocation of Article 5 and the operations thereby performed

On 12 September 2001, the NAC declared itself to be prepared to consider the attacks on the WTC and the Pentagon as carried out against all members of the Alliance, provided that they were 'directed from abroad'.[26] On 2 October, after having been briefed by the US, the Council took the view that the attacks had been carried out by individuals who were 'part of the world-wide terrorist network of Al-Qaeda, headed by Osama bin Laden and his key lieutenants and protected by the Taliban'.[27] On the basis of the invocation of Article 5, the United States required the other 18 Allies to adopt eight measures aiming 'to expand the options available in the campaign against terrorism'.[28]

The measures implementing the invocation of Article 5 are:

1. the enhancement of intelligence-sharing amongst the Allies;
2. the provision of assistance to States threatened by terrorism because of their support for the Alliance;
3. the improvement of security for US and other allies' facilities;
4. the granting to the US of blanket overflight rights

---

25 A. Cassese, 'Terrorism is also Disrupting some Crucial Legal Categories of International Law', *European Journal of International Law*, Vol. 12, 2001, pp. 993-1001.

26 Press Release (2001)124, 12 September 2001, at: http://www.nato.int/docu/pr/2001/p01-124e.htm (accessed: 6/7/2005).

27 Statement by NATO Secretary General, Lord Robertson, 2 October, at: www.nato.int/docu/speech/2001/s011002a.htm (accessed: 6/7/2005).

28 Statement to the Press by NATO Secretary General, Lord Robertson, on the North Atlantic Council Decision On Implementation of Article 5 of the Washington Treaty following the 11 September Attacks against the United States, at: www.nato.int/docu/speech/2001/s011004b.htm (accessed: 6/7/2005).

5. and of access to ports and airfields;
6. the deployment of Naval Forces to the Mediterranean;
7. the deployment of AWACS aircraft to patrol US airspace.

As demonstrated also by the language employed in justifying them, the key feature of the agreed actions is their accessory character with respect to the operations conducted by the US. Far from being directly involved in the attack against Afghanistan and in operation Enduring Freedom, the role of the Alliance consisted of supporting and facilitating the coercive action led by the US.[29] Although NATO members individually participated in the latter, any involvement of the Alliance and the NAC in the direction and planning of the action was ruled out from the beginning. That can be interpreted in light of the difficulties that had arisen in the functioning of the chain of command during Operation Allied Force in Kosovo.[30] The decision of the US to keep a free hand in the exercise of what was perceived as their right to self-defence seems to be the result of a strategic choice.

As to the content of the measures adopted, the deployment of naval and air forces is probably the most significant development. Both the resulting operations, Active Endeavour and Eagle Assist respectively, entail some elements of novelty.

Eagle Assist Operation Eagle Assist started on 9 October 2001 and was terminated less than one year after. For the first time NATO forces (AWACS aircrafts) were deployed to the US.[31] The aim of the operation was to monitor the American airspace in order to avoid further attacks. The deployment replaced the American aircrafts that were engaged in the campaign against Afghanistan. It is of some interest for our purposes to note that the Alliance was devoted to an exclusively defensive role while combat operations were being carried out in Afghanistan by the US and a coalition of States.

Active Endeavour Active Endeavour is a naval operation carried out in the Mediterranean Sea since October 2001.[32] Its mandate, which has been periodically revised and extended, includes providing escorts to non-military ships requesting it and, most of all, monitoring commercial ships in order to detect terrorist activities. Ships navigating throughout the Mediterranean Sea are systematically requested to identify themselves and, in case suspicion arises, NATO Forces proceed to 'compliant boardings' in order to check the documents and inspect the cargo.[33] According to the

---

29 E. Myjer, N.D. White, 'The Twin Towers Attack: An Unlimited Right to Self-Defence?', *Journal of Conflict and Security Law*, Vol. 7, 2000, pp. 5-17, p. 15.

30 J. Miranda-Calha, *NATO's out of area operations*, Draft General Report, 056 DSC 05 E, 30 March 2005, p. 11 para. 46, at: www.nato-pa.int (accessed: 5/07/2005).

31 Statement of the Secretary General on the Conclusion of the Operation Eagle Assist, 30 April 2002, at: www.nato.int/docu/update/2002/04-april/e0430a.htm (accessed: 06/07/2005).

32 See Operation Active Endeavour at: www.afsouth.nato.int/operations/Endeavour/Endeavour.htm (accessed: 25/06/05).

33 *Ibid.*

Alliance, boarding is 'conducted in accordance with the rules of international law'; that is, with the master's and the flag State's compliance.[34]

As is known, treaty law and customary international law permit non-compliant boarding only in a limited number of cases, which, at present, do not include anti-terrorism operations.[35] Thus, in the present case, the consensual nature of the boarding is a necessary element of the legality of the operation. It should also be pointed out that the monitoring of the Mediterranean Sea should be implemented in a manner compatible with the principle of freedom of navigation on the High Seas. From this point of view, under the law of the sea the request of identification must not involve the stopping and the challenging of the ship.

A crucial issue in order to assess the scope of the operation is to understand what exactly the aim of the monitoring is. In other words one may fail to understand which ships may be regarded as suspect. The point is strictly connected to the absence of a shared definition of terrorism in the legal framework regulating the activities of the Alliance.[36] Should the shipping of arms to the Palestinian National Authority be considered a terrorist activity? And what about the delivery of technical components, which might be employed in the preparation of weapons of mass destruction, to one of the so-called 'rogue' States?

At present it seems that Active Endeavour has met with the substantial acquiescence of the international community.[37] As a matter of speculation, one may wonder what will happen (or what has happened in cases which might have not reached the public) when the approached ship refuses its consent. Will the Alliance's units desist from boarding in case there are reasonable grounds for suspecting that the approached ship is involved in terrorist activities? At the least, it is plausible to think that some measure of coercion will be employed in order to 'obtain' the consent of the master or of the flag's State. Moreover, it would be interesting to know whether the Alliance, in such cases, is ready to share the view of some of its members and make reference to a very relaxed interpretation of the requirements of self-defence.[38] Would the assumption that a certain ship can be considered as a (indirect) threat to the security of Member States be enough to justify non-compliant boarding? It being quite clear that the law of the sea does not permit forcible boarding on grounds of counterterrorism, one may expect the Alliance to be tempted to make reference to self-defence as a possible justification in those very cases.[39]

---

34 *Ibid.*

35 Article 110, United Nations Convention on the Law of the Sea. Cf. I. Brownlie, *Principles of Public International Law*, Oxford: Oxford University Press, 2003, pp. 227-230.

36 See subsection headed 'Article 5 and the fight against terrorism' below.

37 Gazzini, *supra* note 15, p. 261.

38 See the 'National Security Strategy' at: http://www.state.gov/documents/organization/15538.pdf (05/06/2005).

39 For similar considerations, with reference to the Proliferation Security Initiative, see M. Byers, 'Policing the High Seas: The Proliferation Security Inititiative', *American Journal of International Law*, vol. 98, 2004, pp. 526 ff., pp. 540-542.

Operation Active Endeavour can be compared to a similar initiative concerning the fight against proliferation of weapons of mass destruction (that is, the Proliferation Security Initiative), which is being carried out at the global level by the US and a group of 'like-minded' States.[40] Unlike the latter, Active Endeavour takes place in a defined area and is being implemented by the Atlantic Alliance together with Naval Forces from Russia and Ukraine. It is also to be noted that many of the coastal States of the Mediterranean are partners of NATO in the context of the 'Mediterranean Dialogue' and that they did not object to the operation. On the whole, considering the systematic nature of the monitoring, the extent of the patrolled area, and the amount of forces involved, the view may be taken that contentious cases will probably arise. On those occasions, the Alliance might be tempted to neglect the necessary consensual nature of boarding in case suspects of involvement in terrorist activities arise. On the whole, one might be led to think that the pre-conditions of a customary modification of the law of boarding are given and perhaps that may happen in the form of a regional custom. Yet this point obviously requires a thorough examination of the practice and a very careful assessment of the possible emergence of *opinio juris*.

Article 5 and the fight against terrorism – some remarks

The invocation of Article 5 to justify NATO's involvement in the fight against terrorism raises a number of questions.

Considering the original scope of the provision, one might take the view that the requirements of Article 5 were extensively interpreted in the present occasion. As has been said before, the Alliance's scope of action was tied to the UN Collective Security System. The concept of armed attack under the North Atlantic Treaty was meant to be analogous to the relevant provision of the UN Charter, Article 51. As has been recently reasserted by the International Court of Justice, in that context the concept of armed attack was exclusively related to an armed confrontation between States.[41] Now it seems that, as long as the NAC is satisfied that an armed attack is *directed from abroad*, that could trigger the invocation of Article 5. Could one think that terrorist actions carried out by a group of individuals may also amount to an armed attack against a Member State? In cases in which the intensity of the terrorist acts is such that the effects are the same as those of a traditional interstate armed attack, that interpretation seems consistent with the object of the North Atlantic Treaty.

40 Proliferation Security Initiative: Statement of Interdiction Principles, Fact Sheet, September 4 2003, at: www.state.gov/t/np/rls/fs/23764.htm (accessed 5/07/05). See, Byers, *ibid.*, pp. 526 ff.; A.C. Winner, 'The Proliferation Security Initiative: The New Face of Interdiction', *The Washington Quarterly*, Vol. 28, 2005, pp. 129-143.
41 Legal Consequence of the Construction of a Wall in the Occupied Palestinian Territory, ICJ Advisory Opinion, para. 139, at: http://www.icj-cij.org/icjwww/idocket/imwp/imwpframe.htm (accessed: 06/07/2005).

However, one may speculate on what exactly qualifies as an armed attack *directed from abroad* under the present interpretation of Article 5. As is known, the 9/11 attacks were partly prepared in Afghanistan, but were organized in Hamburg and were carried out by individuals who were legally residents in the US. The crux lies in understanding whether a substantial involvement of some kind by a State is needed.[42] That may happen not only in case the State exerts control over a group of terrorists but also when it provides support or merely tolerates the carrying out of the preparations for terrorist acts on its territory.[43] Leaving aside the first case, which is uncontested, are the other two options covered by Article 5?

Indeed, the NAC's invocation of Article 5 does not seem to consider State involvement as a necessary element. One might argue that an armed attack is *directed from abroad* when imputable to individuals who are part of a global terrorist network with a global strategy, irrespective of any State involvement. The nationality and the place of residence of the perpetrators, as well as the place where the training and the preparations are carried out, would seem to be irrelevant. On the contrary, terrorist attacks with a specific objective of an internal nature, such as the ones that affected some European countries in the last decades, may seem to be excluded from the present scope of the Atlantic solidarity.

Another crucial question lies in ascertaining what the meaning of terrorism is in the legal system of the Alliance. Leaving aside the threadbare debate concerning a generally accepted definition, once it is determined that NATO is also charged with the fight against terrorism, the need for an internal definition arises. In other words, the Alliance needs to know what it is fighting against. Unlike the European Union, NATO's members never agreed to a shared concept of terrorism and one must turn to the practice of the Organization to find some elements of a definition.[44] The uncertainties related to the concept of terrorism reverberate on the extent of the commitments undertaken by the members as a consequence of the invocation of Article 5. One could fail to understand, for instance, what the time limit of the obligations thereby arising is. Again, the scope of the issue must not be overestimated. It has been mentioned already that the decision-making process of the Alliance

---

42 R. Grote, 'Between Crime Prevention and the Laws of War: Are the Traditional Categories of International Law Adequate for Assessing the Use of Force against International Terrorism', in C. Walter, S. Vöneky, V. Röben, F. Schorkopf (eds), *Terrorism as a Challenge for National and International Law, Security versus Liberty?*, Berlin-Heidelberg: Springer, 2004, pp. 951 ff, p. 965; C. Stahn, ' 'Nicaragua is dead, long live Nicaragua' – the Right to Self-defence Under Art. 51 UN Charter and International Terrorism', in Walter, Vöneky, Röben, Schorkopf (eds), *ibid.*, pp. 848-852.

43 Cf. A. Randelzhofer, 'On Article 51', in B. Simma (ed.), *The Charter of the United Nations – A Commentary*, Oxford: Oxford University Press, 2002, pp. 788 ff., p. 802, who argues that terrorist acts carried out by individuals are attributable to a State also when the latter merely tolerates them.

44 The Council of the European Union adopted a precise definition of terrorism. See Framework Decision 2002/475, in OJEC L164, 22 June 2002. On this point, see *infra* P. De Cesari, 'The European Union and the Fight against Terrorism', p. 216.

subordinates participation in material operations to an *ad hoc* manifestation of will. Along the same lines, it can be further argued that the invocation of Article 5 only creates a mild obligation to adopt measures deemed necessary. Yet the point is not devoid of any practical effect.

To put it roughly, two conceptions are possible. On the one hand NATO's efforts against terrorism can be seen as part of a global war that may last for years. On the other, the invocation of Article 5 may be restricted to the measures that are necessary to react and repel attacks of the 9/11 type. The existence of different approaches amongst the Allies emerged clearly during the last Gulf War. Up to now, that has been the most important test to understand how Member States interpret their commitments in the context of the fight against terrorism.

When the US forces were re-deployed in the Middle East, at the time of the attack against Iraq, the Italian Government made reference to the first approach. Relying mainly on the authorization to overfly granted in 2001 under Article 5 of the North Atlantic Treaty, the Minister for Defence maintained in 2003 that the overflight of the Italian territory was not the object of a new decision and did not need to be approved by the Parliament.[45]

As for the second conception, one may point out that a group of Member States constantly refused to approve the involvement of the Alliance in the Iraqi conflict. That emerged clearly when, in January 2003, the US asked NATO to deploy Patriot missiles, AWACS aircrafts, and military units to defend Turkey in view of possible Iraqi attacks.[46] Although Turkey had formally requested consultations under Article 4 of the North Atlantic Treaty, the NAC was unable to reach a decision.[47] The stalemate was resolved through a decision of the Defence Alliance Committee that was conditioned on NATO's involvement being exclusively defensive.[48] At the end of the conflict, a substantial NATO's role in the stabilization of Iraq was firmly refused by some Member States.[49] At present the Alliance's presence in Iraq is very limited and only concerns the training of the new Iraqi army.

At least, one has to note that Member States are prepared to discuss on a case by case basis the extent of the Alliance's involvement in operations of an allegedly counter-terrorist character.[50] It is also to be noted that the official documents of the

---

45 Audizione del Ministro della Difesa presso le Commissioni Difesa della Camera e del Senato, 21 January 2003, at: www.difesa.it (accessed: 6/07/2005).

46 *Keesing's Record of World Events*, February 2003, Iraq.

47 *Ibid.*

48 Press release, 16 February 2003, at: www.nato.in/docu/pr/2003/p030216e.htm. On the point see also the speech of the German Chancellor, Gerhard Schröder at the Bundestag: *Bullettin der Bundesregierung* of 19 March 2003, No. 24-2.

49 P. Jarreau, 'Le président américain vient sur le Vieux Continent à la recherche d'appuis pour la reconstruction de l'Irak', *Le Monde*, 2 juin 2004, p. 2; J.P. Stroobants, 'L'OTAN débat de l'ampleur de son engagement dans la formation de la nouvelle armée irakienne', *Le Monde*, 11 September 2004, p. 4.

50 It is of some interest that in October 2004, when US officials proposed a merger between Enduring Freedom (the US-led combat mission in Afghanistan) and ISAF (the

Alliance seem to be carefully drafted in order to avoid references to the indeterminate concept of 'war on terrorism'. 'Campaign against terrorism' or 'fight against terrorism' are the more frequently recurring phrases.[51]

Leaving terminological debates aside, it is however clear that one of the reasons justifying the critical attitude towards the Iraqi war was the scepticism regarding the existence of a substantial link between Al Qaeda and the Iraqi régime. Indeed, the view might be taken that in light of its characteristics, particularly the relaxed interpretation of the requirements of immediacy and necessity, the operation against Afghanistan itself (Enduring Freedom) can hardly qualify as conducted in self-defence.[52] The unconditional support to that operation by Member States might thus demonstrate NATO's readiness to become involved in counter-terrorism coercive activities at the global level, even beyond the scope of self-defence action.[53] However, the difficulties that the Secretary-General of the Alliance encountered in obtaining troop contributions for the contextual UN-mandated mission in the region (ISAF) may cast some doubts on NATO's willingness to assume the command of costly out of area operations.[54]

Only future events might clarify what the 'drift of the current' is, yet it seems plausible that terrorist attacks, when supported by convincing evidence and attributable to a global terrorist network, will activate the mechanisms of the Alliance. The influence that terrorism exerted on NATO seems considerable and durable.[55]

NATO-led reconstruction mission in the same Country), the proposal met with substantial opposition by France and Germany on the grounds that it could have rendered the difference between combat and reconstruction irrelevant. See Miranda-Calha, *supra* note 30, 4 para. 21. Fear of a US disengagement may have also been at the basis of the refusal, see: J. P. Stroobants, 'Le commandant de l'ISAF demande à l'OTAN des renforts pour l'Afghanistan', *Le Monde,* 29 October 2004, p. 3.

51 See, *inter alia,* Statement by NATO Secretary General, 2 October 2001, at www.nato. int/docu/speech/2001/s011002a.htm; Press Release M-NAC-2(2001)159, 6 December 2001, at: www.nato.int/docu/pr/2001/p01-159e.htm; Tackling Terror: NATO's New Mission, Speech by NATO Secretary General, 20 June 2002, at: www.nato.int/docu/speech/2002/s020620a. htm (all documents accessed: 6/07/2005).

52 Cf. E. Myjer, N.D. White, *supra* note 29, pp. 5 ff.

53 See Press Release (2003)152, 4 December 2003, Final Communiqué, Ministerial Meeting of the North Atlantic Council held at NATO Hedaquarters, Brussels, para. 4, at: www.nato.int/docu/pr/2003/p03-152e.htm (accessed: 3/07/2005).

54 B. Koenders, *NATO and the Use of Force, General Report*, 165 PC 04 E rev. 2, p. 1, at: www.nato-pa.int (accessed 5/07/2004).

55 See the *Prague Summit Declaration*, Press Release (2002)127, 21 November 2002, para. 4, at: www.nato.int/docu/pr/2002/p02-127e.htm (accessed: 16/03/2005). The Heads of State and Government of the Alliance declared that the process of transformation of the Alliance should be perceived as aiming to 'protect our populations, territory and forces from *any armed attack, including terrorist attack,* directed from abroad' (emphasis added).

NATO and post-conflict management – an indirect contribution to the fight against terrorism

Apart from defensive measures adopted under Article 5, NATO implemented terrorism-related operations also at the level of post-conflict management and stabilization.

In general terms, NATO's involvement in crisis management was already sanctioned by the Washington Strategic Concept and constituted the core of the much debated 'out of treaty' development. Indeed the facts had partially anticipated such a legal/political rationalization, since NATO had already played a dominant role in the Yugoslav crisis, both within the framework of UN Security Council control and unilaterally.[56]

After the end of the conflict in Former Yugoslavia, NATO assumed command of peace-implementing operations in Bosnia (SFOR) and Kosovo (KFOR).[57] The legal basis of such operations is twofold. Both the peace agreements concluded at the end of the military conflicts and the relevant UNSC Resolutions are to be relied on in this respect.[58] Their mission revolves around providing security and ensuring the implementation of the peace accords, but no specific reference is made to the issue of international terrorism.

After 2001, NATO partially re-oriented its activities in the Balkans in order to take into account the threat of international terrorism. However, with the exception of sporadic action against groups allegedly having links with Al Qaeda, the activities that the Alliance labelled as 'against terrorism' are quite in line with the usual role of peace-implementing forces engaged in reconstructing state institutions and providing security. They focus on combating the smuggling of arms and drugs as well as the illegal movement of people. In cooperation with the European Union, the OSCE, and the Stability Pact, the Alliance is also implementing an ambitious programme concerning border security issues.[59]

NATO's role in the context of ISAF, the multinational UN-mandated operation in Afghanistan, is similar. ISAF was created in 2001, after the Bonn Conference, to

---

56 For a comprehensive survey, see T. Gazzini, 'NATO Coercive Military Activities in the Yugoslav Crisis (1992-1999)', *European Journal of International Law*, vol. 12, 2001, pp. 391-435.

57 In December 2004, SFOR was terminated and substituted by an EU mission (Operation Althea). NATO, however, established headquarters in Sarajevo that will undertake counter-terrorist activities. It is be noted that, in the context of the Berlin Plus arrangements, Operation Althea will draw heavily on NATO's resources and support. See Press Release (2005)076, 9 June 2005, para. 5, at: www.nato.int/docu/pr/2005/05-076e.htm.

58 See SC Resolution 1031/1995 for the operation in Bosnia Herzegovina, and SC Resolution 1244/1999, for the Kosovo one. Cf. M. Guillame, 'Le cadre juridique de l'action de la KFOR au Kosovo', in Tomuschat (ed.), *supra* note 15, pp. 243 ff.

59 See Common Platform of the Ohrid Regional Conference on Border Security and Management, 22-23 May 2003, at: http://www.un.org/Docs/sc/committees/1373/regional_action.html (accessed: 5/7/2005).

assist the Afghan Transitional Authority in providing security in the Kabul area and in the reconstruction of Afghanistan. NATO's Member States participated individually in the operation from the beginning and constituted the bulk of it. In 2003 NATO directly assumed the leadership of ISAF in order to provide stability to the mission (since then command had shifted amongst troop-contributing countries every six months). The mandate of the operation was periodically renewed and extended, but apart from the mentioning of ISAF's role in securing the conduct of national elections, its nature did not change.[60] The geographical extent of the operation has been limited and covers at present about 50 per cent of the Afghan territory. That reflects a sharp separation of tasks between Enduring Freedom, the US-led operation carrying out coercive counter terrorism actions in the non-pacified areas, and ISAF, the NATO-led mission endowed with a traditional peace-implementing mandate. One may think that a choice lies at the basis of the concomitant presence of the two operations. At least in the initial phase, the US, being the only member of the Alliance able to perform worldwide enforcement operations autonomously, preferred unilateral action in order to avoid the constraints that multilateralism imposes, even in the NATO context.[61]

On the whole, the Alliance in these cases seems to contribute to the fight against terrorism only in an indirect way.[62] Providing security to a region and reconstructing the institutions of a State certainly creates a hostile environment for terrorists, but, to a certain extent, that seems to be a mere by-product of the presence of a peace force.[63]

Terrorism and the process of change in the Atlantic Alliance

In addition to providing a legal/political justification for performing the above-mentioned material activities, it is to be pointed out that terrorism exerted substantial influence in the process of transformation of the Alliance. Its military capabilities, as well as its internal structure, and the relationships with partners were re-assessed in light of the exigencies of counter-terrorism.

---

60 Cf. SC Resolution 1563 (2004). See Shimkus, Muñoz-Alonso, *Progress in the War against Terrorism, Special Report*, 148 DSC 03 E rev 1, November 2003, p. 5, para. 27, at: www.nato-pa.int (accessed: 5/07/2004).

61 Cf. I. Johnstone, 'US-UN Relations after Iraq: The End of the World (Order) As We Know It?', *European Journal of International Law*, Vol. 15, 2004, pp. 829-830.

62 On the indirect nature of ISAF's contribution to the fight against terrorism, cf. V. Santori, *Le misure del Consiglio di Sicurezza contro il terrorismo internazionale*, unpublished PhD thesis, University of Teramo, pp. 123-127.

63 Cf. Press Release (2004)096, 28 June 2004, Istanbul Summit Communiqué, para. 4: 'NATO's aim is to assist in the emergence of a secure and stable Afghanistan, with a broad-based, gender sensitive, multi-ethnic and fully representative government, integrated into the international community and cooperating with its neighbours. *Establishing and sustaining peace in Afghanistan is essential to the well-being of the Afghan people and to our shared struggle against terrorism*' (emphasis added).

The enhancement of military capabilities

From an operational point of view, the underlying assumption of the transformation process is that the Alliance is to be rendered capable of a quick and effective reaction to terrorism. Under this perspective the most significant developments are:

- the establishment of NATO's Response Force, a rapidly deployable force which serves as a model for the general transformation of NATO's forces;[64]
- the progressive improvement of intelligence sharing and the creation of a permanent Terrorist Threat Intelligence Unit;[65]
- the approval of a military concept for defence against terrorism in the context of a comprehensive effort to improve and transform the Alliance's military capabilities.[66]

The adoption of those measures points towards further enhancement of NATO's involvement in 'out of treaty' and 'out of area' operations. As concerns the latter operations, the Response Force, for instance, is conceived to be rapidly deployed 'wherever needed, as decided by the Council'.[67] With reference to new 'out of treaty' missions, it has been reported that the permanent intelligence unit 'will analyse *general terrorist threats*, as well as those that are more specifically aimed at NATO'.[68] That obviously once again raises concerns about the potential indeterminacy of the concept of terrorism.

Similarly, NATO's Military Concept for Defence against Terrorism introduces a classification of the activities that the Alliance can perform to face terrorism: Consequence Management, Military Cooperation, Anti-Terrorism, and Counter-Terrorism.[69] The legality of the first two categories is in principle self-evident, while the third is said to deal with defensive measures such as air and maritime protection, sharing of intelligence, standardized warning conditions and defensive procedures.[70] The legality of Counter-Terrorism, as defined by the military concept, is much more problematic as it consists of 'offensive military action designed to reduce terrorists' capabilities'.[71] Counter-terrorist actions can be carried out according to two different models: NATO in the lead and NATO in support (of other international

---

64 Press Release (2005)076, *supra* note 56, para. 12.

65 NATO Update, 29 June 2004, Heads of State and Government Strengthen NATO's Anti-Terrorism Efforts, at: www.nato.int/docu/update/2004/06-june/e0629e.htm (accessed: 25/06/05) (emphasis added).

66 NATO's Military Concept for Defence Against Terrorism, at: www.nato.int/ims/docu/terrorism.htm (accessed: 01/07/05).

67 Press Release (2002)127, 21 November 2002, Prague Summit Declaration, para. 4 a, at: www.nato.int/docu/pr/p02-127e.htm (accessed: 25/06/05).

68 NATO Update, *supra* note 64, (emphasis added).

69 NATO's Military Concept for Defence Against Terrorism, *supra* note 66.

70 *Ibid.*

71 *Ibid.*

organisations), but neither of the two models seem to take into account the primacy of the Security Council in the international regulation of the use of force. Despite an opening *caveat* according to which NATO's actions should 'have a sound legal basis and fully comply to the relevant provisions of the UN Charter and of relevant international norms', no explicit reference is made to the need for a Security Council mandate when performing coercive counter-terrorism operations. Indeed some passages of the Concept seem to be inspired by an extensive interpretation of pre-emptive self-defence.[72]

NATO's cooperation with other international actors

Considering that the primacy of the United Nations in the field of maintenance of international peace and security is explicitly recognized by the North Atlantic Treaty, one might expect the relationship between NATO and the UN to be particularly intense. From this point of view, NATO Heads of State and Government undertook to implement the obligations arising from SC Resolution 1373/2001.[73] On its part NATO participated in the special meeting of the UN Counter-terrorism Committee (CTC) devoted to the role of international organisations operating in the field and regularly communicated the main features of its relevant activities.[74]

Yet, as a matter of fact, material cooperation between the two organizations is limited to the field of information sharing and to the (quite formal) control that the Security Council exercises over the NATO-led missions authorized under Chapter VII.[75]

It is noteworthy that NATO has developed an extensive net of relationships with other international actors independently of any coordinating role of the United Nations. The decision to establish permanent links with other organizations and States preceded the 9/11 attacks, but was comprehensively re-oriented and strengthened in view of the specific needs of counter-terrorism. NATO enhanced its strategy of progressive involvement of non-member States in the establishment of partnerships and political *fora* aimed at reaching consensus for the political goals of the Alliance. The Mediterranean Dialogue, the NATO-Russia Council, the South East Europe

---

72 'Allied nations agree that terrorists should not be allowed to base, train, plan, stage and execute terrorist actions and that the threat may be severe enough to justify acting against these terrorists and those who harbour them, as and where required, as decided by the North Atlantic Council' (emphasis added), *ibid.*

73 See Press Release (2004)057, 2 April 2004, Declaration on Terrorism, issued at the Meeting of the North Atlantic Council in Foreign Ministers Session held in Brussels on 2 April 2004, at: http://www.nato.int/docu/pr/2004/p04-057e.htm (accessed: 04/07/2005).

74 See, for instance, Letter dated 6 December 2002 from the Secretary General of the North Atlantic Treaty Organisation addressed to the Secretary General of the United Nations, S/AC.40/2003/SM.1/2; Special Meeting with International, Regional and Subregional Organisations, Provisional Summary Record of the Second Part of the 57th Meeting, S/AC.40/SR.57/Add.1, p. 9.

75 Cf. S/1386(2001), para. 9; S/Res/1563(2004), para. 4.

Initiative, the Euro-Atlantic Partnership, and the NATO-Ukraine Partnership are all frameworks for political negotiations with different levels of institutionalization. After 2001, terrorism became a key aspect in the political dialogue and the various *fora* revolving around the Alliance conveyed the support of dozens of non-member countries to NATO's policies in the fight against terrorism.

In general terms, NATO's persistent influence on such a large number of partners may have a deep impact on the formation of international law and on the functioning of the organs of the United Nations. From this point of view, one may think that in some instances NATO plays a leading role in the adoption of decisions that subsequently are formally sanctioned by the United Nations.

Concluding remarks

From a theoretical point of view, one may note that the internal legal system of the Alliance is undergoing transformation to address the issue of terrorism. Out of area and out of treaty operations are increasingly legitimized in relation to terrorism by the legal/political discourse of Member States. An extensive interpretation of the notion of armed attack under Article 5 of the North Atlantic Treaty has emerged. However, if one considers the material activities carried out in the fight against terrorism, the view may be taken that the Alliance, despite the rhetoric of Article 5 and of the Atlantic solidarity, has been marginalized. NATO's role has been confined to strictly defensive measures assisting the US and *ad hoc* coalitions, and to post-conflict missions that contribute to the fight against terrorism in an indirect way. Quite often NATO has also acted as a multilateral forum through which Member States have reached consensus at a regional level.

Rather than having a strong influence on substantive activities, counter-terrorism seems to be employed as a legal/political basis to justify the engagement of the Alliance in certain contexts, the extension of its competencies, and a continuous process of transformation. In any case, lacking a shared definition of the concept of terrorism amongst Member States, the Alliance's new tasks are to a certain extent indefinite. Terrorist attacks attributable to a global terrorist network seem to be perceived as within the scope of NATO competencies, but there are borderline cases for which an assessment will only be possible by analysing future practice. The voting system allows for Member States to discuss on a case by case basis their engagement on material activities and recent practice demonstrates that positions may be varied.

At present, the issue of compatibility between NATO's terrorist-related activities and the Charter of the United Nations is mainly theoretical. Whereas declarations and documents of debatable legal value envisage the possibility of performing counter-terrorist functions beyond the Collective Security System, the material activities carried out by NATO in the field seem to fall within the existing UN framework. Recent events lead one to think that NATO may not be considered an alternative to the United Nations, at least as concerns providing multilateral control over the use of force. When coercive activities are at issue, both organizations risk irrelevance.

Chapter 16

The Organization for Security and Cooperation in Europe (OSCE)

PIETRO GARGIULO[1]

The issue of terrorism within the CSCE framework

In the wake of the 9/11 attacks against the US, the fight against terrorism has become a priority also among the activities of the Organization for Security and Cooperation in Europe (OSCE).

The problem of terrorism, however, was already a concern for the States participating in the kick-off phase of the pan-European cooperation process – we are referring here to the diplomatic exercise known as the Conference on Security and Cooperation in Europe (CSCE) that subsequently gave rise to the OSCE.[2] In fact,

---

1   University of Teramo.

2   It is well-known that the events occurring in Europe at the end of the 1980s (the fall of the Berlin Wall and the collapse of the Soviet Union) have substantially changed the European political order, causing significant consequences even within the CSCE, which in that period started to radically modify both its functional and institutional characteristics. The key initiative in these changes was the Paris Summit of 19-21 November 1990 and the adoption of the *Charter of Paris for a New Europe*. This document redesigned the principles, the contents and the organization of cooperation within the CSCE. Based on these changes, in the 1990s the CSCE not only considerably developed its activities, including the operational ones, but it also improved its decision-making procedures, the mechanisms for verifying the compliance of participating States with the undertaken obligations and the entire institutional apparatus. The Budapest Summit of 5-6 December 1994 ratified the change of the denomination into *Organization* for Security and Cooperation in Europe. On the Charter of Paris, see, in literature, S.J. Roth, 'The CSCE 'Charter of Paris for a New Europe' a New Charter in the Helsinki Process', *Human Rights Law Journal*, vol. 11, 1990, pp. 373 ff.; V.Y. Ghebali, 'La Charte de Paris pour une nouvelle Europe', *Défense Naionale*, 1991, p. 73 ff.; Sacerdoti, 'Il nuovo ordine pubblico europeo dalla Carta di Parigi alla Unione europea', in Sacerdoti (ed.), *Diritto e istituzioni della nuova Europa: i testi normativi del nuovo assetto europeo con saggi introduttivi e note*, Milan: Giuffré, 1995, pp. 225 ff. As regards the transformation of CSCE into OSCE and, in particular, the institutional developments, see G. Nesi, 'Dalla CSCE all'OSCE: la Conferenza di riesame di Budapest', *La Comunità internazionale*, vol. 49, 1994, p. 736 ff.; B. Tarasyuk, 'The Transformation of the C.S.C.E. into an International Organization', *Studia Diplomatica*, vol. XLVII, 1994, pp. 109 ff.; W. Hoynck, 'From CSCE to the OSCE: The Challenge of Building New Stability', *Helsinki Monitor*, vol. 4, 1995, pp. 11 ff.; K. Möttöla,

the Helsinki Final Act of 1975, while defining the principles governing the relations among CSCE States, indicated – within the context of the Sixth Principle relating to non-intervention in internal affairs – that participating States would have to refrain, among other things, from providing 'direct or indirect assistance to terrorist activities, or to subversive or other activities directed towards the violent overthrow of the regime of another participating State'.[3]

In the Follow-up Meetings[4] of Madrid (1983) and Vienna (1989), the features of cooperation against terrorism were specified in greater detail within the context of the initiatives regarding the security 'basket' in Europe.

The condemnation of terrorism – both within the States and in international relations – as a form of violence that 'endangers or takes innocent human lives or otherwise jeopardizes human rights and fundamental freedoms',[5] is the assumption

---

'The OSCE: Institutional and Functional Development in an Evolving European Security Order', in M. Bothe, N. Ronzitti, A. Rosas (eds), *The OSCE in the Maintenance of Peace and Security: Conflict Prevention, Crisis Management and Peaceful Settlement of Disputes*, The Hague: Kluwer, 1997, pp. 1 ff.

3   The Helsinki Final Act of 1 August 1975 closed the negotiations started on 3 July 1973 with the specific intent of establishing a permanent discussion forum between Western States and those of Eastern Europe. It contained the principles and recommendations that for a long time had represented the three main issues (the so-called 'baskets') for pan-European cooperation: security; science and technology, environment; human rights and others (information, culture, education, etc.). The first of the three above mentioned baskets – the one concerning security – included, among other things, a Declaration on the principles governing relations among the States participating in the CSCE (the so-called Helsinki Decalogue). This Declaration mostly reproduced pre-existing international rules that however, within the context of the CSCE, took on special importance, being an expression of the will to find an agreement on several fundamental values with which States were called to comply, regardless of their politico-ideological system. As regards negotiations within the CSCE, see V. Ferraris, *Testimonianze di un negoziato: Helsinki-Ginevra-Helsinki 1972-75*, Padua: CEDAM, 1977, p. 660. As regards the Helsinki Final Act, see J.-F.Prevost, 'Observation sur la nature juridique de l'Acte final de la Conférence sur la Sécurité et la Coopération en Europe', *Annuaire français de droit international*, vol. 21, 1975, pp. 129 ff.; H.S. Russel, 'The Helsinki Declaration: Brobdingnag or Lilliput?', *American Journal of International Law*, vol. 70, 1976, pp. 242 ff.; M. Coccia, 'Helsinki Conference and Final Act on Security and Cooperation in Europe', in R. Bernhardt (ed.), *Encyclopaedia of Public International Law*, Vol. X, Amsterdam: New Holland, 1987, pp. 216 ff.

4   The Helsinki Final Act did not envisage the creation of a permanent institutional body for the implementation of the cooperation in the 'baskets' indicated in the previous note, but it rather limited itself to stating the participating States' intention to pursue the multilateral negotiation process started by the Conference through the so-called *Follow-up Meetings,* the role of which essentially was to verify the implementation of the provisions established by the Final Act.

5   Cf. the Concluding Document of the Madrid Summit of 6 September 1983. For a collection of the abstracts of the main CSCE/OSCE documents concerning terrorism, see OSCE, *OSCE Commitments and International Legal Instruments Relating to Terrorism. A Reference Guide*, 2003. The other CSCE/OSCE documents mentioned in this paper and not

on which the encouragement of the States to adopt 'resolute' measures in countering the phenomenon is founded.

Prevention is the approach that has enjoyed the greatest attention. Indeed, participating States are encouraged to take 'all appropriate measures in preventing their respective territories from being used for the preparation, organization or commission of terrorist activities, including those directed against other participating States and their citizens'.[6] In detail, the adoption of measures aimed at forbidding the illegal activities of individuals, groups and organizations that instigate, organize or perpetrate acts of terrorism is suggested. Moreover, participating States confirmed what had already been established in Helsinki at 1975, undertaking to refrain from assisting, either directly or indirectly, terrorist or subversive activities or other activities of any kind aimed at overthrowing the regime of another participating State.[7]

The main tool for eradicating the phenomenon of terrorism is the reinforcement of bilateral and multilateral cooperation, and especially the latter through the international organizations most actively committed to combating terrorism (United Nations, ICAO and IMO). In practical terms, on the one hand these organizations are invited to promote the exchange of information and, on the other, to implement international instruments for the prevention and suppression of acts of terrorism.[8]

Other two aspects of the initiatives examined thus far are worthy of special attention: the first is the focus on acts of terrorism directed at diplomatic or consular representatives and the request to participating States to adopt effective measures to prevent and eliminate them;[9] the second concerns the call on States to guarantee the extradition or prosecution of persons implicated in terrorist acts and to reinforce cooperation at judicial level in order to settle any cases of conflict of jurisdiction as well.[10]

The launch of the institutionalization process for cooperation throughout Europe involved specific changes in the approach to the problem of terrorism. Indeed, in the *Charter of Paris for a New Europe*, while defining the problems relating to security, the participating States identify the dangers that threat the stability of their societies – basically, all activities that violate their independence, sovereignty and national integrity – and 'unequivocally condemn all acts, methods and practices of terrorism as criminal', expressing their firm intent to fight the phenomenon through reinforced bilateral and multilateral cooperation.

---

contained in the above mentioned collection can be consulted on the OSCE website www. osce.org.

6   *Ibid.*

7   *Ibid.*

8   Cf. the Concluding Document of the Vienna meeting (CSCE, Follow-up Meeting 1986-1989, Vienna, 4 November to 19 January 1989, *Concluding Document*), and in particular points 9, 10, 10 (2) and 10 (6).

9   *Ibid.* point 10 (4).

10 *Ibid.* point 10 (5).

At the Helsinki Summit of July 1992, the approach to the problem of terrorism remains essentially the same. In the summit's final document, in fact, not only terrorism is once again condemned as a phenomenon that threatens security, democracy and human rights, but the need is reiterated for participating States to adopt measures aimed at preventing activities sustaining acts of terrorism and to encourage the exchange of information.[11]

As already indicated above,[12] the 'model' for cooperation defined within the CSCE was transformed during the Budapest Summit of 1994. Despite the importance of the historical moment, further emphasized by the title of the meeting's concluding document – *Towards a Genuine Partnership in a New Era* – the problem of terrorism is addressed using the same approach previously indicated.

The Declaration adopted by the Budapest Summit acknowledges that societies within the OSCE area are being increasingly threatened by terrorism, once again condemns the phenomenon and reiterates the intent to combat it through the commitment to enhance cooperation between participating States.[13]

Moreover, in the *Code of Conduct on Politico-Military Aspects of Security* – which is part of the document adopted by the Summit – participating States undertake, on the one hand, not to support in any way acts of terrorism and, on the other, to take the appropriate measures for preventing and combating terrorism in all of its forms. However, as regards this second profile, the Code refers exclusively to the need to implement the commitments undertaken in the relevant international agreements and, in particular, the obligation to prosecute or extradite perpetrators of acts of terrorism.[14]

The OSCE's concept of security and the fight against terrorism

In the initiatives following those examined above, the problem of cooperation in combating terrorism in the OSCE area is defined more clearly within the security strategy promoted by the Organization.

Since the very beginning of the pan-European cooperation process the participating States had acknowledged that security in the area did not coincide with the mere absence of conflicts and that the maintenance of a secure and stable region was not an exclusively politico-military affair. Indeed, the concept of security inspiring the Organization includes, as an essential component, not only politico-military issues but also those relating to human rights and democracy, to economics and to the environment.

---

11 Cf. CSCE, 1992 Summit, Helsinki, 9-10 July 1992, *The Challenges of Change*, para. 26.

12 Cf. *supra* note 2.

13 Cf. CSCE, 1994 Summit, Budapest, 5-6 December 1994, *Towards a Genuine Partnership in a New Era*, para. 6 of the Declaration.

14 *Ibid.* para. 26 of the Code.

The adoption of such an approach makes the cooperation within OSCE specially suitable for tackling the numerous threats and challenges against the security of the European continent in the post Cold War's geopolitical area.

The model for a security policy for OSCE suitable with the new state of affairs was adopted during the Lisbon Summit of 1996. The approach on which the model is based consists of cooperative security founded on democracy, the respect for human rights and fundamental freedoms, the rule of law, market economy and social justice. The key elements of this concept are globality and indivisibility of security and the loyalty of the States in adhering to common values and commitments as well as the sharing of common rules and behaviours.

Within this context, the *Lisbon Declaration on a Common and Comprehensive Security Model for Europe for the 21st Century* indicates that terrorism, together with other criminal phenomena, is an increasing concern for the entire OSCE community and, consequently, it invites the States to ensure full cooperation in combating this phenomenon in all its forms and practices.[15]

During the subsequent Istanbul Summit, held in November 1999, the participating States once again confirmed the Organization's security concept through the key elements indicated above. The *Charter for Security in Europe*, in particular, specifies several phenomena – international terrorism, violent extremism, organized crime and drug trafficking – as growing challenges to the security of the continent and specifically states that 'terrorism in all its forms and manifestations is unacceptable'. Consequently, the OSCE States undertake to intensify their efforts in preventing the preparation and financing of any act of terrorism on their territories and in denying terrorists safe havens.[16]

Among the OSCE initiatives we are examining in this context, the conclusions reached by the Vienna Ministerial Council of 2000 are also noteworthy. This document clearly shows the evolution of the Organization's security concept from security of the States and Governments to security of individuals. In fact, when discussing the new challenges the Organization is called to meet, the Ministers expressed their intention to improve 'human security' – the safety of the individual from violence through armed conflicts, gross violations of human rights, terrorism – so as to improve the quality of life of all individuals within the OSCE region.

As regards terrorism more specifically, the document essentially reaffirms the condemnation of the phenomenon and the participating States' commitments as defined in the documents previously examined. It is important, however, the statement that both international cooperation and individual actions by the States aimed at combating terrorism should be conducted in compliance with the principles of the Charter of the United Nations, of international humanitarian law and human rights, as well as of relevant international conventions.[17]

---

15 Lisbon Summit Declaration, 1996, para. 2.

16 Cf. Istanbul Summit, 1999.

17 Cf. Vienna Ministerial Council, 2000.

The OSCE's initiatives for combating terrorism following 9/11: the Bucharest Plan of Action

As already mentioned in the foreword, after the 9/11 attacks, the issue of terrorism became a priority item on the OSCE's agenda.[18]

Just one month after the attacks, the Organization's Permanent Council expressed its support for the military actions against Afghanistan and, therefore, for the right of legitimate defence, both individual and collective, of the US and of the Coalition States in accordance with the Charter of the United Nations. In the same declaration the Permanent Council stated the States' obligation to prevent and repress terrorism.

Moreover, during the course of its ninth meeting held in Bucharest in December 2001, OSCE's Ministerial Council approved a decision[19] on the fight against terrorism in which the Organization's participating States pledged '[to] defend freedom and protect their citizens against acts of terrorism, fully respecting international law and human rights'.

On the same occasion the Ministerial Council adopted an Action Plan for combating terrorism that represents the first organic and exhaustive plan of measures the Organization and the participating States undertook to adopt in the fight against terrorism.[20] In general, the Plan underlines the added value of the role played by OSCE in combating terrorism and deriving from its specifics strong and comparative advantages, including its broad *membership* and its comprehensive concept of security capable of bringing together the politico-military, human and economic dimensions.[21]

As regards the international obligations relevant to the fight against terrorism, the document commits participating States to become parties, by 31 December 2002, to the 12 Conventions and Protocols on anti-terrorism issues promoted by the United Nations[22] that, together with the resolutions of the UN Security Council

---

18   As regards the consequences that the 9/11 attacks had on the Organization's activities see A. Bloed, 'The OSCE and the War Against Terror', *Helsinki Monitor*, vol. 12,, 2001, pp. 313-317.

19   Cf. *Decision on combating terrorism*, doc. MC(9).DEC/1, in OSCE, Ninth Meeting of the Ministerial Council, Bucharest, 3 and 4 December 2001.

20   The *Bucharest Plan of Action for Combating Terrorism* is attached to the decision indicated in note 19 above.

21   Cf. point 2 of the Plan of Action.

22   Reference is made to the 12 international conventions promoted by the United Nations and by several specialized Institutes of the UN system that, as we all know, have originated from the need to contrast specific types of terrorism. The instruments in question are collected in United Nations, *International Instruments Related to the Prevention and Suppression of International Terrorism*, New York, 2001.

pertaining to terrorism,[23] are considered the 'global legal framework for the fight against terrorism'.

The political commitments determined by the document concern instead the utilization of the Forum for Security Cooperation[24] for the application of the politico-military measures defined by the Organization, and more specifically the Code of Conduct on Politico-Military Aspects of Security[25] and the Document on Small Arms and Light Weapons.[26]

The Plan of Action then goes on to define a broad range of sectors and measures for combating terrorism coherent with the final aims and activities of the Organization.[27] All this is based on the recognition of the fact that, although no circumstance or cause can justify it, terrorism finds fertile grounds of individual consensus in the existence of social, political and economic problems, as well as other conditions that need to be addressed.[28]

---

23 The Plan of Action expressly mentions, at point 4, resolutions 1269 (1999), 1368 (2001), 1373 (2001) and 1377 (2001).

24 The Forum for Security Cooperation was established on the occasion of the 1992 Helsinki Summit (See Chap. V of the document mentioned *supra* at note 11). In the Document participating States agreed to launch new negotiations on arms control, disarmament and confidence-building measures, as well as on the enhancement of regular meetings and the intensification of cooperation on security problems and to reduce the risks of conflict. The Forum was charged with the task of leading the work on the topics indicated.

25 The *Code of Conduct on Politico-Military Aspects of Security* (DOC.FSC/1/95 dated 3 December 1994) governs the politico-military relations among participating States. It reconfirms the guiding principles for international relations among States contained in the Helsinki Final Act, but also introduces new rules concerning the role of armed forces in democratic societies. Finally, the Code also establishes a control mechanism consisting in the States' drawing up of a questionnaire about the application of the foreseen measures.

26 The *Document on Small Arms and Light Weapons* (FSC.JOUR/314 dated 24 November 2000) establishes rules, principles and measures aimed at reducing the stockpiling and development of these arms. The Document addresses numerous aspects: the control and exchange of information relating to the production, import, export and transit of arms, the commitments regarding surplus stocks, the specific measures for post-conflict rehabilitation scenarios.

27 Each of the institutions involved by the Action Plan has prepared a 'road map' on terrorism. See, in particular: *OSCE Secretariat's Road Map on Terrorism*, SEC.GAL/35/02/ Draft 1 (19 March 2002); *ODIHR 'Road Map' for Implementation of the Bucharest Plan of Action for Combating Terrorism*, ODIHR:GAL/72/01 (27 December 2001); *OSCE Parliamentary Assembly Road Map for the Implementation of the Bucharest Plan of Action for Combating Terrorism*, PA.GA/1/02 (18 March 2002); *OSCE High Commissioner on National Minorities on the OSCE 'Road Map' for Combating Terrorism*, HCNM.GAL/4/02 (14 March 2002); *Road Map of the Forum for Security Co-operation for Implementation of the Bucharest Plan of Action for Combating Terrorism*, FSC.DEC/5/02 (20 March 2002); *'Road Map' of the OSCE Representative on Freedom of the Media for the Implementation of the Bucharest Plan of Action for Combating Terrorism*, FOM.GAL/2/02 (8 March 2002).

28 Cf. point 9 of the Plan of Action.

Essentially, these are (first of all) measures that belong to the traditional fields of action of the Organization: political (the promotion of democratic institutions, of the rule of law, of human rights, of tolerance and of multi-culturalism);[29] security (prevention of conflicts and the promotion of the peaceful settlement of disputes);[30] economic (fight against corruption, illegal economic activity, unemployment, poverty and disparities).[31]

As regards more directly the sectors and measures for combating terrorism, the Plan of Action mentions the strengthening of national legislation, underlining the importance of implementing the international obligations deriving from anti-terrorism conventions,[32] the suppression of the funding of terrorism through preventive measures, the criminalization of the phenomenon and the freezing of terrorist assets,[33] the prevention of movement of terrorists by adopting effective border controls and controls on the issuance of identity papers and travel documents also in order to prevent their counterfeiting and fraudulent use.[34]

Special attention is then paid to the fight against organized crime, considered closely linked to the phenomenon of terrorism. Within this framework, the participating States are invited to take all necessary steps to prevent on their territories the illegal activity of individuals, groups or organizations that instigate, finance, organize or engage in the perpetration of acts of terrorism or other illegal activities directed at the violent overthrow of the political regime of another participating State.[35]

Finally, although it considers the United Nations the framework for the global fight against terrorism, the Action Plan underlines the need for close cooperation and coordination among all international and regional organizations and the importance of initiatives aimed at establishing close contact with non-governmental organizations and the structures representing civil society to create a *network* for the international coalition against terrorism.[36]

The Programme of Action of the Bishkek International Conference on Enhancing Security and Stability in Central Asia

The first occasion for assessing the application of the Bucharest Plan of Action was the 'International Conference on Enhancing Security and Stability in Central Asia: Strengthening Comprehensive Efforts to Counter Terrorism', held in Bishkek on 13 and 14 December 2001, co-organized by OSCE and the United Nations Office for Drug Control and Crime Prevention (UN/ODCCP).

---

29 Cf. points 10 and 11 of the Plan of Action.
30 Cf. point 14 of the Plan of Action.
31 Cf. point 13 of the Plan of Action.
32 Cf. point 16 of the Plan of Action.
33 Cf. point 24 of the Plan of Action.
34 Cf. point 26 of the Plan of Action.
35 Cf. point 19 of the Plan of Action.
36 Cf. point 27 of the Plan of Action.

The involvement of the latter largely explains the attention paid by the international conference to the link between the measures for combating terrorism and those relating to organized crime.[37]

The Programme of Action[38] adopted at the end of the Conference can be divided substantially into two parts: the frame of reference for cooperation in combating terrorism, and the measures for preventing and countering the phenomenon.[39]

As regards the first aspect, the Bishkek Programme of Action confirms the commitments already made in the Bucharest Plan of Action, namely support of the key role played by the United Nations and the call on inter-governmental – international and regional – organizations to reinforce their cooperation and coordination in order to develop synergies in their activity, thus enhancing the effectiveness of their assistance to the States.[40]

More complex is the part of the Programme of Action dedicated to terrorism prevention and combating measures developed on the basis of the documents previously adopted by both OSCE and UN/ODCCP.[41] Three aspects of this part are worthy of mention, in particular.

The first concerns the bonds between terrorism and organized crime. The Programme suggests the strengthening of cooperation between agencies operating in the two separate sectors both at national and at regional and international levels, in the first case through the exchange of operational information, in the second case by creating communication channels.[42]

The problem of terrorist financing is the second aspect focused on by the Programme of Action. The Programme recommends that States adopt three types of measures: the adoption of anti-money laundering legislation and the creation of structures capable of preventing and suppressing the phenomenon; the ratification of the relevant international instruments, most significantly the 1999 UN International Convention,[43] if necessary the application of the standards of financial accountability and transparency contained in the recommendations on money laundering and on

---

37 In fact, the debate that developed within the context of the Bishkek International Conference is also based on the 'UN Action Plan for the Implementation of the UN Declaration on Crime and Justice: Meeting the challenges of the 21st Century', adopted in April 2000.

38 Cf. *Bishkek International Conference on Enhancing Security and Stability in Central Asia: Strengthening Comprehensive Efforts to Counter Terrorism*, 13-14 December 2001, 'Programme of Action', on the already mentioned OSCE website.

39 The Programme of Action actually contains a third part dedicated to the specific needs of combating terrorism deriving from the geographical contiguity of Central Asia with Afghanistan.

40 Cf. paras 3 and 4 of part I of the Programme of Action.

41 As regards the Plan of Action for the implementation of the Vienna Declaration, specific reference is made to the measures contained in Section VII of that document.

42 Cf. paras 2 and 3 of part II of the Programme of Action.

43 The International Convention for the Suppression of the Financing of Terrorism was adopted by the UN General Assembly on 9 December 1999 by means of UN resolution 54/169. It came into force on 10 April 2002.

terrorist financing of the *Financial Action Task Force*,[44] as well as the freezing of the assets of individuals and bodies linked to terrorist financing, as established in Resolution 1373 (2001) of the Security Council; the strengthening of the gathering and updating of information, including analysis methods, regarding the criminal activities carried out for the purposes of furthering terrorism.[45]

Finally, the third aspect regards the economic, social and cultural measures indicated in the document. In general, States are encouraged to address the economic and social problems exploited by terrorists in order to gain support and financing, mostly by focusing their attention on sustainable development policies.[46] More specifically, the Programme then suggests that States address inter-ethnical frictions by fostering dialogue and tolerance between majorities and minorities, that they promote active civil society engagement, underlining the importance of tolerance in all aspects of social relations and the significant role played by dialogue between civilizations as a means of reaching mutual comprehension and the removal of threats to peace.[47]

The OSCE's Charter on Preventing and Combating Terrorism

One year after the Bucharest meeting, the Ministerial Council met in Porto, in deciding that the participating States and the Organization's institutions had to intensify their joint efforts in the fight against terrorism,[48] also adopted the *OSCE Charter on Preventing and Combating Terrorism*.[49]

This document too mainly reiterates the considerations, commitments and recommendations provided in the Bucharest Plan of Action and therefore confirms the intention to use the three (politico-military, economic and humanitarian) dimensions of OSCE's activity to assist participating States, at their request, in the fight against terrorism in all its forms.

Several aspects of this document, however, are worthy of mention as they represent a further or totally new stage of development with respect to the Bucharest Plan of Action.

---

44 FAFT is an inter-governmental body founded at the 1989 Paris G7 Summit with the purpose of developing and promoting policies, both at national and international level, to combat money laundering. Only in 2001 was its mandate expanded to include the processing of measures for combating terrorist financing. These measures are contained in the *Eight Special Recommendations* adopted in October 2001 with the specific purpose of denying terrorists access to the international financial system. The text containing the recommendations can be viewed at www.faft-gafi.org.

45 Cf. paras 4, 5 and 6 of part II of the Programme of Action.

46 Cf. para. 16 of part II of the Programme of Action.

47 Cf. paras 11, 12 and 13 of part II of the Programme of Action.

48 Cf. *Decision n.1 Implementing the OSCE Commitments and Activities on Combating Terrorism*, doc. MC(10).DEC/1 dated 7 December 2002.

49 Cf. *OSCE Charter on Preventing and Combating Terrorism*, doc. MC(10).JOUR/2 dated 7 December 2002.

The first aspect consists, on the one side, in the recognition – in accordance with the provisions of Resolution 1373 (2001) of the Security Council – that acts of international terrorism are a threat to peace and to regional and international security[50] and, on the other, in the consequential reaffirmation, from this perspective, of OSCE's obligations – OSCE being a regional arrangement under Chapter VIII of the UN Charter – of contributing in the global fight against terrorism.

A second aspect regards the rather numerous references to the respect for human rights within the context of the anti-terrorism 'campaign'. In fact, in the Charter, the Organization's Member States confirm the importance of complementing the commitment to combating terrorism with the reaffirmation of OSCE's fundamental principles.[51] Consequently, participating States undertake to carry out all anti-terrorism measures in accordance with the rule of law, the UN Charter and the relevant provisions of international law, international standards of human rights and, where applicable, international humanitarian law.[52] Moreover, Member States underline that terrorism cannot be identified with 'any nationality or religion' and that action against terrorism is not directed 'against any religion, nation or people'.[53] Within this context, it seems right to stress that the Charter encourages the States to adopt the appropriate initiatives to make sure that asylum is not granted to any persons who have planned, facilitated or participated in terrorist acts, pursuant to national and international law, and through the correct application of the exclusion clauses contained in the 1951 Convention relating to the *status* of refugee and its 1967 Protocol.[54]

The third and last aspect regards the special emphasis placed on arms control, disarmament and non-proliferation as critical elements not only as regards the cooperative security among Member States but also in reducing the risks of terrorist access to weapons and materials of mass destruction and to conventional weapons. In this context, the Charter reiterates the participating States' commitment to minimizing these risks through national efforts and by reinforcing existing international instruments, particularly the OSCE principles governing non-proliferation, by supporting their implementation and, where applicable, universalization.[55]

Conclusions

The initiatives dedicated to combating terrorism promoted within the CSCE/OSCE framework that we have previously examined deserve several conclusive remarks.

A first aspect worthy of being highlighted is the evolution of the approach to the phenomenon of terrorism and, consequently, of the measures deemed suitable

---

50 Cf. para. 3 of the Charter.
51 Cf. para. 5 of the Charter.
52 Cf. para. 7 of the Charter.
53 Cf. para. 2 of the Charter.
54 Cf. para. 10 of the Charter.
55 Cf. para. 28 of the Charter.

for fighting it. In fact, initially – that is, in the CSCE period – the accent was placed essentially on the issue of States supporting terrorism. The measures encouraged by CSCE were aimed essentially at reiterating the need for States to respect principles and obligations well anchored in international legal order (abstention from organizing, encouraging, aiding or participating in acts of terrorism and vigilance aimed at making sure their territories were not used for activity aimed at carrying out acts of terrorism against other States, cooperation in preventing acts of terrorism and in prosecuting terrorists, etc.). The approach changes radically with the transformation of CSCE into OSCE and with the progressive growth within the Organization of the importance of the 'human security' concept founded more on the needs of individuals than on those of States and Governments. Consequently, the cooperation among the Organization's participating States against terrorism extends to all of the Organization's activities, including the economic, social and cultural ones. This a considerably new development, in that it indicates the recognition on the part of the Organization's Member States of the need to address and find adequate solutions also to the deep-set causes of terrorism that are also of an economic, social and cultural nature.

The second aspect regards the recent acknowledgement, in compliance with the developments seen within the United Nations, of international terrorism as a threat to international peace and security. From this viewpoint, it is possible to discern the special emphasis with which the Organization reaffirms its role in combating terrorism as a regional arrangement under Chapter VIII of the United Nations Charter.

The third and last aspect is the persistent calling of the Organization to the respect of human rights and of international humanitarian law. This is specially significant if one considers that it is precisely under this profile that the most recent national and international initiatives for combating terrorism[56] have attracted the greatest criticism. The recommendations for compliance with internal and international law are undoubtedly interesting since it is the only way to guarantee the correct balance between security requirements and the need to safeguard the rights of individuals, of democracy and of the rule of law that terrorist violence makes particularly difficult on a daily basis.

---

56 Regarding these aspects, we invite our readers to consult our works *Diritto internazionale e lotta al terrorismo*, I, *Le norme internazionali convenzionali, Le altre attività di cooperazione tra Stati, I diritti nazionali*, Naples: Editoriale Scientifica, 2003 and 'Le Nazioni Unite e la lotta al terrorismo: realizzazioni, difficoltà, prospettive', in *Biblioteca della Libertà*, n. 178, Anno XL, 2005, pp. 55 ff.

Chapter 17

The European Union

PATRIZIA DE CESARI[1]

Initial forms of cooperation among Member States in the fight against terrorism

In the fight against terrorism Community institutions initially concentrated their efforts above all on activities at intergovernmental level. Their action became more effective when Member States realised that they needed to achieve judicial cooperation in criminal matters to combat terrorism more decisively.[2]

Until the beginning of the 1990s terrorism was dealt with at two levels. The first was at the level of cooperation between Ministers of the Interior and, more specifically, between the police forces and intelligence services of the various Member States. The second level took place in the area of political cooperation at the meetings of the European Council, which initially started as an informal body of political cooperation bringing together Heads of State and Government of Member States. In this latter context, which is regulated by the intergovernmental method and based on unanimous decisions, the results achieved have been through policy instruments such as declarations, common positions and joint actions.

Member States have reiterated their intention to combat all acts of terrorism for some time now. Following terrorist attacks by the IRA, and upon the initiative of the UK, the European Council decided on 26 June 1976 to establish an intergovernmental cooperation programme between Member States in the area of European internal security and police affairs.[3]

---

1   University of Trento.

2   On EU action against terrorism see N. Venneman, 'Country Report on the European Union' in C. Walter, S. Voneky, V. Roben, F. Schorkopf (eds), *Terrorism as a Challenge for National and International Security versus Liberty?* Berlin-Heidelberg: Springer, 2004; C. Fijnaut, J. Wouters, F. Naert, *Legal Instruments in the Fight against International Terrorism. A Transatlantic Dialogue*, Leiden/Boston: Martinus Nijhoff, 2004; L. Benoit, 'La lutte contre le terrorisme dans le cadre du deuxième pilier: un nouveau volet des relations extérieures de l'Union européenne', *Revue Droit Union européenne,* 2002, pp. 283-313; J. Wouters, F. Naert, 'Of Arrest Warrants, Terrorist Offences and Extradition Deals: an Appraisal of the EU's Main Criminal Law Measures against Terrorism after 11 September ', *Common Market Law Review*, vol. 41, 2004, pp. 909–932.

3   See J. Charpentier, 'Vers un espace judiciaire europeén', *Annuaire français de droit international*, vol. 24, 1978, pp. 927 ff. for the first attempts at cooperation.

Within this context the TREVI Group,[4] which was set up in 1976, played an important role as a regular but informal cooperation unit outside the EC Treaty framework. The group was made up of senior officials from Ministries of the Interior and heads of police. It had the task of strengthening and improving intra-community cooperation on intelligence and police services; it developed techniques to prevent terrorist acts and adopted measures to control arms trafficking and measures related to the protection of security and police affairs.

Other groups and committees have played a significant role on extradition and cooperation in criminal matters. These include the Political Committee of Foreign Ministers.[5] This Committee did not have specific tasks related to terrorism, but dealt with this issue when various events led Member States to adopt a Community position on external policy particularly towards third countries which were thought to be supporting international terrorism.

In 1985 the Political Committee set up an ad hoc working group on terrorism, which met to coordinate activities devised by the Committee in the fight against terrorism.

At its meeting on 27 January 1986, following terrorist attacks in December of 1985, the European Council of the Ministers of Foreign Affairs adopted a major political declaration on international terrorism and announced important general principles on which Member States had expressed agreement. These principles amount to a total condemnation of terrorism in all its forms, as well as a condemnation of its perpetrators, accomplices, instigators and any governments sponsoring terrorism. It also established a new permanent body called the Working Group to combat international terrorism, which was to deal with all counter-terrorism activities that until then had been performed by various other bodies.

It is following the Single European Act, which was adopted on 14-27 February 1986 and which came into force on 1 July 1987[6] that Community Member States began to seriously take into consideration the need for coordinated action to tackle terrorism. This need was also felt with a view to establishing a common market requiring a single borderless space in which goods, persons, services and capital could move freely. On this point, reference must be made to the General Declaration on Articles 13 and 19 of the Act, adopted by the Conference of representatives of Member States at the time it was signed, as well as the political declaration by Member States on the free movement of persons. This declaration affirmed that nothing in the provisions of Articles 13 and 19 affected the right of Member States to

---

4   TREVI stands for Terrorism, Radicalism, Extremism and International Violence. Specific working groups were set up called TREVI 1 (terrorism); TREVI 2 (public order); TREVI 3 (drug trafficking and organized crime). For a detailed analysis of TREVI see R. Wehner, *Europäische Zusammenarbeit bei der polizeilichen Terrorismusbekämpfung aus rechtlicher Sicht,* Baden-Baden : Nomos-Verl.-Ges., 1993, pp. 229 ff.

5   On the work of the Political Committee see P. LeJeune, *La cooperation policière européenne contre le terrorisme,* Brussels: Bruylant, 1992, pp. 67 ff.

6   In *Official Journal of the European Communities* (hereinafter *OJEC*), L 169, 29 June 1987.

take such measures as they considered necessary to control immigration from third countries as well as combat terrorism, crime, drug trafficking and the trafficking of works of art and antiques. Member States also announced that they would cooperate in this area without prejudice to the powers of the European Community. To this end the TREVI 1992 working group was set up in December 1988 with the task of improving police cooperation.

The fight against terrorism between the Second and Third Pillars of the European Union

Following the Maastricht Treaty, which was signed on 7 February 1992[7] and which entered into force on 1 November 1993, the three European Communities (which changed their name from the EEC to the EC) were supported by two new forms of cooperation called the Second and Third Pillars of the Union. These were a Common Foreign and Security Policy (CFSP) and Cooperation in the field of Justice and Home Affairs (CJHA), two areas which were previously the exclusive domain of national jurisdiction. The First Pillar, instead, dealt with the mechanisms and policies forming part of the activities of the three Communities established in the 1950s.

The fight against terrorism comes under the Third Pillar of the Union and is specifically mentioned by Article K.1 of the Maastricht Treaty, but it also touches aspects linked with a common foreign and security policy, whose fundamental objectives are to preserve peace, strengthen security as well as consolidate democracy and the rule of law. It is worth recalling that the Second Pillar is based on the intergovernmental method and the instruments available to the EU in this area are joint actions, common positions and systematic cooperation. Indeed, a number of common positions have been adopted in the fight against terrorism and are of importance due to their close relationship with the Community Regulations issued in the same period. They are the common positions on a CFSP, under Article 15 of the Treaty, which define the EU's approach on a particular geographical or thematic question. The purpose of adopting a common position is to set limits on the national policies of individual Member States.

However, it is under the Third Pillar on Cooperation on Justice and Home Affairs, which was previously regulated solely by international conventions, that the majority of important measures have been adopted. The intergovernmental method continues to be used to adopt acts in this Pillar too.

It is in this context that Member States signed the Europol Convention in Cannes on 26 July 1995, which came into force on 1 October 1998.[8] This Convention led to the establishment of the European Police Office (Europol). The Convention seeks to improve police cooperation through a permanent exchange of information between Europol and the competent national authorities of Member States. Following the

---

7   In *OJEC* C 191, 29 July 1992.

8   In *OJEC* C 316, 27 November 1995, pp. 2 ff.

Council's decision of 3 December 1998[9] Europol was instructed to deal with crimes committed or likely to be committed in the course of terrorist activities against life, limb, personal freedom and property.

Further impetus in the fight against terrorism came from the European Parliament's Resolution of 1997[10] which contains the first European definition of terrorism. It focuses in particular on international terrorism and more modern forms such as computer-related terrorism. The Resolution advocates the adoption of long-term strategies to combat terrorism at its roots and underlines the need for its prevention and repression while respecting fundamental human rights.

This was followed by Council joint action 98/428/JHA of 29 June 1998 on the establishment of a European judicial network with responsibility also for terrorist acts[11] and joint action 98/733/JHA of 21 December 1998 which made participation in a criminal organization in Member States of the European Union[12] punishable, and which requires Member States to establish proportionate and dissuasive penalties and obliges them to provide assistance in pursuing terrorism-related crimes.

The Amsterdam Treaty, which was signed on 2 October 1997[13] and which came in force on 1 May 1999, introduced major changes in the field of Justice and Home Affairs (CJHA). Some Third Pillar subjects, such as visas, asylum, immigration and judicial cooperation in civil matters, were transferred to the First Pillar and therefore to the Treaty that established the European Community (new Title IV), to be dealt with by the integration method, or Community method, which possesses legislative instruments and procedures adopted through the founding treaties of the Community. As a result the Third Pillar changed its name from 'Cooperation in the field of Justice and Home Affairs' (CJHA) to 'Police and Judicial Cooperation in Criminal Matters' (Title VI of the Treaty on European Union). The area remained regulated by intergovernmental procedures and was not communitized. It should, however, be noted that preventing and combating terrorism were explicitly mentioned as necessary to achieve an area of freedom, security and justice (Article 29, para. 2 Treaty on European Union).

As a result of the Nice Treaty, which was signed on 26 February 2001[14] and entered into force on 1 February 2003, the Eurojust cooperation unit received formal investiture as a body of the EU. It consisted of a team of prosecutors from all Member States delegated with strengthening efforts to combat serious crime and facilitating judicial cooperation in trans-national investigations.[15]

---

9   In *OJEC* C 26, 30 January 1999, pp. 22 ff.

10   The resolution was published in *OJEC* C 55 of 24 February 1997, p. 27 ff.

11   In *OJEC* L 191, 7 July 1998, pp. 4 ff. The purpose of this organ is to enable judicial authorities to exchange information. It is made up of central authorities responsible for international judicial cooperation.

12   In *OJEC* L 351, 29 December 1998, pp. 1 ff.

13   In *OJEC* C 340, 10 November 1997.

14   In *OJEC* C 80, 10 March 2001.

15   This cooperation unit was proposed at the Tampere European Council of 15-16 October 1999.

Nevertheless, the EU Commission's proposal to set up a European Public Prosecutor's office was not approved in Nice, and was submitted once again in January 2002. It was later re-proposed in Article III-274 of the Treaty adopting the Constitution for Europe, which provides that the European Council (or Council of Ministers) may decide unanimously to create a European Public Prosecutor's Office. This Office will initially be responsible for combating crimes affecting the financial interests of the Union.

However, it was following the terrible terrorist attack of 11 September 2001 that the Community strategy became more incisive. At the European Council of 21 September 2001 the Member States adopted the Plan of action on terrorism[16] which contains some important policy guidelines to combat terrorism. The plan envisaged enhanced judicial and police cooperation, as well as the setting up of a team of specialists in the fight against terrorism that would cooperate with their US counterparts, together with the development of international legal instruments. Furthermore, the European Council called on Member States to ratify, without delay, all existing international conventions on terrorism; to adopt the measures necessary to combat all forms of financing of terrorism. It also assigned the 'Transport Council' the task of adopting the measures necessary to make air security more effective. Coordination of global EU action was also strengthened through greater commitment in the area of a common foreign and security policy.

The plan was later bolstered by various important initiatives. The majority are measures that fall under judicial cooperation in criminal matters within the Third Pillar of the EU. The initiatives in this area include the European arrest warrant,[17] the Framework Decision on combating terrorism,[18] the Framework Decision on joint investigation teams,[19] the Commission's proposal on a third Money-Laundering Directive,[20] as well as agreements with the US on extradition and mutual legal assistance.[21]

The Madrid bombings once again brought the fight against terrorism to the forefront of the European agenda and led to the Council adopting a new Declaration on combating terrorism and a Declaration on solidarity against terrorism[22] on 25 March 2004. On this occasion the 2001 action plan was revised and new strategic objectives set, while those that had already been implemented were enhanced. At

16 See the conclusions at http:/ue.eu.int.
17 See section headed 'Measures to promote judicial cooperation' below.
18 See section headed 'The harmonization of criminal provisions' below.
19 In *OJEC* L 162, 20 June 2002, pp. 1 ff.
20 The proposal was adopted by the Commission on 30 June 2004. It enlarges the scope of directives 1991/308/EEC and 2001/97/EC to trust and company service providers and extends the anti-money laundering preventive mechanism to transactions suspected to be associated with terrorist financing.
21 See section headed 'Conclusions' below.
22 See both at http://ue.eu.int.

its meeting of 17-18 June 2004 the European Council endorsed the revised plan and identified a number of priority issues.[23]

In its Communication of 20 October 2004 on Prevention, Preparedness and Response to Terrorist Attacks[24], the EU Commission sought to reach out to all EU citizens and explain to them the nature of the fight against terrorism, the EU's strategy for prevailing over it as well as the legal and policy instruments at its disposal. The EU Commission underlined that all social actors must participate in the fight against terrorism, and that national Parliaments, economic agents and civil society organizations must be involved. It also emphasized the need to ensure that the fight against terrorism be fully integrated into EU external relations policy; it emphasized that it was working to allocate, as a matter of urgency, funds for supporting the victims of terrorism and their families, and communicated that 11 March of every year would be a day to honour the memories of the victims of terrorism and an occasion for civic and democratic debate.

As we have seen, the Community has adopted many initiatives. However, on closer examination there appear to be some clear problems and these include the difficulty, on the part of Member States, to implement the decisions taken at Community level as well as the need to ensure that any initiatives respect democratic principles and fundamental rights.

On the European continent, and outside the European Community, an important role in the fight against terrorism has been performed by the Council of Europe, the organization created in 1949 to protect and promote the common heritage of ideals as well as the economic and social development of European countries. On 27 January 1977 the Council of Europe adopted the European Convention on the Suppression of Terrorism.[25] This instrument falls outside the Community framework but was ratified by all Community Member States. The Convention lists crimes related to terrorism, partly referring to conventions in force worldwide and partly including other criminal acts. The list of terrorist crimes was recently revised by an amendment Protocol adopted on 15 May 2003, but is not as yet in force.[26]

The Council of Europe's Convention proposes facilitating the extradition of terrorists. Unfortunately the strength of this Convention is compromised by the reservation laid down by Article 13, which permits contracting States to refuse extradition in cases where they consider the offence to be a political offence.

Within the framework of the fight against terrorism the Council of Europe adopted 'Guidelines on Human Rights and the Fight against Terrorism'[27] on 11 July 2002. These guidelines reaffirm a State's obligation to protect everyone against terrorism.

---

23 Brussels European Council of 17-18 June 2004 - Presidency conclusions, 10679/2/04 REV 2, at http://ue.eu.int.

24 See the Communication from the Commission to the Council and the European Parliament of 20 October 2004, doc. COM (2004) 698 final at http://europa.eu.int.

25 The Convention came into force on 4 August 1978. It can be found at http://www.coe. int.

26 See the text on the Protocol at http://www: coe.int.

27 The Guidelines are published at http://www.coe.int.

They also stress that all measures taken by States to combat terrorism must be lawful and respect fundamental human rights and that torture must be prohibited.

The European Union's area of freedom, security and justice

The more recent measures mentioned in the EU's fight against terrorism were adopted in the area of freedom, security and justice, introduced by the Amsterdam Treaty and confirmed by the Nice Treaty (recital 11 of the preamble and Article 2, fourth sentence, of the Treaty on European Union). The Treaty adopting a Constitution for Europe (Article I-3) defines this area as one of the fundamental objectives of the EU. It is founded on mutual trust among national authorities, on the automatic recognition of the judicial decisions and extra-judicial documents issued in Member States,[28] and on operational cooperation of national competent authorities, including police services, customs and other specialised crime prevention services.

The area of freedom, security and justice is an advanced form of intergovernmental cooperation also covering extradition and judicial assistance. It provides nationals and residents ample freedom of movement, which is achieved when conditions of security and a fair access to justice are guaranteed.

This form of judicial cooperation was the result of the conclusions of the Tampere European Council on 15-16 October 1999 and was better defined in the Council's Programme on the recognition and execution of decisions, adopted on 30 November 2000.

At the end of the first five-year phase towards the creation of an area of freedom, security and justice, the Commission provided new guidelines for the subsequent phase and identified some priorities. These include promoting a consistent criminal policy in order to combat serious crime and terrorism more effectively, as well as placing Eurojust at the centre of this policy, also with a view to the possible establishment of a European Public Prosecutor's office.[29]

The Hague Programme on strengthening freedom, security and justice in the European Union, endorsed by the European Council of 4-5 November 2004,[30] emphasizes the fight against terrorism and introduces *inter alia* the principle of availability of information which may help the fight against terrorism. The new Programme is designed in particular to improve the guarantee of fundamental rights, to reinforce the protection of victims, but also to improve the training of those working in the field of justice.

---

28 This principle, stated in the Programme of measures to implement the principle of mutual recognition of criminal judgments, adopted by the Community, is considered a cornerstone of EU judicial cooperation both in civil and criminal justice. See *OJEC* 15 January 2001.

29 See Doc. COM (2004) 401 of 2 June 2004 of the Commission at http://europa.eu.int.

30 See the Hague Programme, Annex I to the conclusions of the Brussels European Council of 4-5 November 2004, Doc. 14292/4 at http://europa.eu.int.

The more recent measures adopted in the fight against terrorism, to which we shall return in the following sections, come under the framework of this integrated judicial area.

It should be noted that the provisions regarding the area of freedom, security and justice in the existing Treaties are subdivided between the First and Third Pillar and are contained respectively in Title IV of the Treaty establishing the European Community on 'Visas, asylum, immigration and other policies related to the free movement of persons', as well as Title VI 'Provisions on police and judicial cooperation in criminal matters'. These Pillars are merged in the Treaty adopting the Constitution for Europe. Hence, if this Treaty enters into force the merging of the Pillars will lead to the communitization of judicial cooperation in criminal matters thereby reducing the difficulties linked to the legal basis of some measures. Under Article I-42 of the Constitution's Treaty the area of freedom, security and justice will be achieved through laws and framework laws designed to approximate national legislations. This will mean abandoning the instruments of the Third Pillar in favour of more general binding legislation.

The notion of terrorism in European Union law

It is not easy to say what exactly the term terrorism is, and providing a definition means distinguishing it with reference not only to ordinary crimes, but also with respect to acts considered lawful or governed by international law. The relationship between terrorism and freedom fighting, but also between terrorism and fundamentalism is controversial. The need to establish a common definition of terrorism was also felt by the Community since the majority of EU Member States does not have a definition of terrorist offences and only a few Member States possess legislation specifically dealing with the subject.

The abovementioned Resolution on combating terrorism in the European Union of 1997 contains the first definition of terrorism.[31] It was revised to some extent by the Recommendation of the European Parliament on the role of the European Union in combating terrorism of 5 September 2001.[32] This notion of terrorism is based on the presence of three aspects, one objective and two subjective, which must characterize the act for it to be considered a terrorist act. Firstly, the act must have an objective element that is made up of the use of violence against a country, its institutions, its population in general or specific individuals; it must be an act committed with specific reasons for the use of violence such as separatist aspirations, extremist ideological beliefs, religious fanaticism or desire for profit; finally the act must be committed with the intention to create a climate of terror among official authorities or specified groups and persons.

This definition of terrorism excludes freedom fighters. In this regard, the European Parliament emphasized in its Recommendation that the right of self-

---

31 See *supra* note 10.
32 See at http://www2.europarl.eu.int.

determination may be considered a criterion to distinguish freedom fighters from terrorists specifying that: 'acts of resistance in third countries against State structures which themselves employ terrorist measures' cannot be considered terrorist acts as opposed to similar acts in European States governed by the rule of law.

After 11 September 2001, we find a definition of terrorism in the Council's Framework Decision 2002/475/JHA of 13 June 2002 on Combating Terrorism.[33]

This is a precise definition which combines a list with an abstract definition. It is a kind of definition that was already used by the international Convention on the prevention and suppression of terrorism, which was signed in Geneva on 16 November 1937.[34]

Article 1 of the Framework Decision starts with a general definition qualifying an act as a terrorist act and then lists the crimes specifying them. The list includes: attacks upon a person's life, attacks upon a person's physical integrity, kidnapping or hostage taking, hijacking of ships and aircraft, the manufacture of arms, the release of dangerous substances, interfering with or disrupting the water supply, power supply and other fundamental natural resources the effect of which is to endanger human life, and also includes among the offences threatening to commit any of the acts listed. A terrorist act also comprises participation in the activities of a terrorist organization including supplying information or material resources, or funding its activity in any way, in the knowledge of the fact that such participation will contribute to the criminal activities of the group.

The acts listed, which are in any case defined as 'offences under national law' can be considered acts of terrorism and be distinguished from ordinary crimes solely in the presence of the conditions envisaged in the abstract definition. It should be noted that the acts listed differ in part from the ones that are currently envisaged by the international conventions dealing with terrorism.

According to this general definition the offences listed are to be considered terrorist crimes when these are intentional acts, which, 'given their nature or context, may seriously damage a country or an international organization'. These are acts accompanied by the specific aim that the perpetrator seeks to achieve and it must consist of the aim of seriously intimidating a population, compelling a government to perform or abstain from performing any acts to destabilize or destroy the fundamental political, economic, social or constitutional structures of a country or of an international organization.

The framework decision therefore appears to require a specific intention unlike international conventions on terrorism which require that such acts be pursued regardless of the objectives that the perpetrators seek to achieve.

---

33 Framework decision 2002/475/JHA, in *OJEC* L 164 of 22 June 2002, pp. 3 ff. The definition in this framework decision had been adopted by the Common Position of the Council of European Union of 27 December 2001 on the application of specific measures to combat terrorism in *OJEC*. L 344 of 28 December 2001, pp. 93 ff.

34 The Convention never came into force. The text was published in LN Doc. C. 546 M 383. 1937.

Paragraph 11 of the Preamble of the Framework Decision on Combating Terrorism excludes from its scope actions by armed forces during periods of armed conflict. These are actions which are governed by international humanitarian law.[35] Armed forces, according to the Geneva Conventions are also considered people 'fighting against colonial domination and alien occupation and against racist regimes in the exercise of their right of self determination'. Freedom fighters and parties to an international conflict or a civil war are thus excluded from the field of application of terrorist crimes. A similar clause was included in the International Convention for the Suppression of Terrorist Bombings, adopted in 1998, Article 19, para. 2, of which provides that: 'The activities of armed forces during an armed conflict, as those terms are understood under international humanitarian law, which are governed by that law, are not governed by this Convention...'. The drafters of the global convention on the suppression of terrorism would like to include a similar clause, but at present there is no general consensus on the tenor that this provision should have.

We must also remember that within the Framework Decision on Combating Terrorism, the definition of terrorism cannot be interpreted too widely. It is worth pointing out that Article 1, para. 2, provides that the framework decision must not have the effect of altering the duty to respect the fundamental rights and the fundamental legal principles that are enshrined in Article 6 of the Treaty on European Union. With regard to this, recital 10 lays emphasis on the need to respect the rights safeguarded by the European Convention to protect human rights and fundamental freedoms and which form part of the common constitutional traditions of Member States, as principles of Community law, which are reflected in the European Union's Charter of Fundamental Rights, notably Chapter VI thereof.[36] The recital states that nothing in the framework decision may be interpreted as a measure intended to reduce or restrict the right to strike, freedom of assembly, of association or of expression, including the right to form a trade union with other persons or to join a trade union to protect their interests and the related right to demonstrate.

The harmonization of criminal provisions in the legislations of Member States through the Framework Decision of 13 June 2002 on combating terrorism

The Council's Framework Decision 2002/475/JHA of 13 June 2002[37] seeks to harmonize the laws and regulations of Member States establishing the minimum rules relating to the constituent elements of criminal acts and their penalties. The decision falls within the context of judicial cooperation in criminal matters. One of the spheres making up the area of freedom, security and justice, and its legal grounding lies in Article 34 of the Treaty on European Union, which defines the

---

35 The Common Position on the application of specific measures to combat terrorism of 27 December 2001 does not contain such a limitation of its scope. The Common Position is published in *OJEC* L 344 of 28 December 2001, pp. 93 ff.

36 See recital 10 of the declaration.

37 See *supra* note 33.

procedure adopting the framework decision, its purpose and its legal value. A framework decision is adopted by the Council acting unanimously, following a proposal of a Member State or the European Commission and after receiving the consent of the European Parliament.

As regards its legal value, a framework decision is binding on Member States in terms of the result to be achieved, while national authorities are free to decide on the form and methods to achieve this result. The framework decision establishes a duty to implement by a certain date: Member States are required to adopt the national provisions necessary to achieve the objective set out in the framework decision.

The Framework Decision of 13 June 2002 can be seen as a stimulus to reach a uniform definition of terrorism among different Member States, in that, as we have already said in the preceding section, it obliges them to criminalize any act that could damage an organization or a State, committed with the intention to intimidate a population and to seriously destabilize or destroy the political, economic or social structures of a State.

These may be acts committed by one or more individuals and against one or more Member States. Those directing or participating in the activities of a group or inciting, aiding and abetting an offence must also be punished.

The framework decision defines a terrorist organization as a structured group of more than two persons, established over a period of time, and acting in concert to commit terrorist offences. Member States are required to ensure that even legal persons are considered liable for the abovementioned offences (Article 7).

The decision establishes standards as regards the sentences and penalties that Member States are to adopt. These must be effective, proportionate and dissuasive penalties which may entail extradition. Furthermore it establishes rules to reduce the sentences of terrorists who have turned informants.

To ensure that such offences may be pursued effectively, the declaration requires Member States to adopt measures on jurisdiction. Article 9 in particular provides that every State shall take the necessary measures to establish its jurisdiction over the terrorist offences. In addition each Member State can extend its jurisdiction if the crime is committed in the territory of another Member State. This last clause is new insofar as it envisages a sort of universal regional jurisdiction. Every Member State establishes its own jurisdiction over terrorist acts committed abroad not only by its nationals but also by its residents. This is an exorbitant jurisdiction that does not appear in international conventions on criminal matters. One final change is the provision by which each State must also establish its jurisdiction over offences committed against an institution or a body of the European Union.

The extent of each State's jurisdiction can lead to conflicts between two or more Member States that consider themselves competent to judge the offence. This is why Article 9 lays down a procedure whereby each State must coordinate its action and establish its jurisdiction so that judicial proceedings are centralised in just one Member State. To this end account must be taken of the territory in which the offence was committed, the nationality or the residence of the perpetrator, the State of origin of the victims and the territory in which the perpetrator was found.

Finally, each Community Member State must establish its jurisdiction for the abovementioned offences in cases where extradition or surrender of its suspected or convicted nationals is not granted either to another Member State or a third country. This provision is based on the principle *aut dedere aut judicare*, which has been adopted by many international conventions on terrorism.

The framework decision also underlines that Member States must provide appropriate assistance to the victims of the crime and to their families.[38]

The deadline by which to implement the framework decision was set for 31 December 2002. A number of Member States had not done so on this date and other States had only done so partially.[39]

The EU Plan of Action on Combating Terrorism adopted by the European Council of 17-18 June 2004 and later developments

Following the tenor of its Declaration on Combating Terrorism of the 25 March 2004,[40] the European Council adopted the detailed revised EU Plan of Action on Combating Terrorism on 18 June 2004[41] clearly setting out the future tasks, fixing the guidelines and naming the responsible bodies and urging the institutions and Member States to fulfil the commitments within the established deadlines.

In the above declaration of 25 March 2004 the European Council underlined that terrorist acts constitute an attack against the values on which the EU is founded, and invited Member States to do everything within their power to combat them in accordance with the principles of the EU, the provisions of the United Nations Charter and the duties enshrined in United Nations Security Council Resolution 1373 of 2001. The European Council called on the Union to take a more active part in efforts by the international community to prevent and stabilize regional conflicts and to promote the rule of law. In order to develop existing cooperation, it also called on Member States to take any steps that remain necessary to implement fully and without delay all legislative measures taken by the EU. More specifically the European Council called on Member States to implement the framework decision on the European arrest warrant, the decision on joint investigation teams, the decision concerning money laundering; to implement the decision regarding the execution of provisions freezing assets or evidence, the decision establishing Eurojust, the decision on the confiscation of assets, instrumentalities and proceeds of crime and the decision on attacks against information systems; to ratify the convention on judicial assistance in criminal matters, as well as its protocol, and the three protocols of the Europol convention. The European Council also urged that the work concerning the framework decision on mutual recognition of confiscation orders be concluded as early as possible, and invited the EU Commission to submit a proposal to establish a

---

38 This measure was already included in framework decision 2001/220/JHA.
39 See Doc. SEC(2004)348, 18 March 2004 of the Commission at http://europa.eu.int.
40 See *supra* note 22.
41 See *supra* note 23.

European programme for the protection of witnesses in terrorist cases. The European Council also called on Member States to improve the efficiency of their information systems and to strengthen border controls and document security.

The European Council of 17-18 June 2004 reaffirmed the Union's guidelines regarding joint cooperation in the fight against terrorism, and welcomed the EU's revised action plan and the strategic objectives already set out in annex I of its declaration of 25 March 2004. They can be summarized as follows:

1. Improve international consensus and enhance international efforts to combat terrorism, and support the fundamental role of the United Nations. The Union will work to ensure adherence to the United Nations conventions on terrorism to agree on the adoption of a comprehensive United Nations convention to suppress acts of terrorism.
2. Limit terrorists' access to financial resources and to other economic resources.
3. Maximize the capacity of European Union bodies and of Member States to detect, investigate and prosecute terrorists and prevent terrorist attacks; in particular through Europol, Eurojust and the Police Chiefs task force, and through the promotion of effective cooperation between Member States in exchanging intelligence.
4. Protect the security of international transport and ensure effective systems of border control.
5. Increase the capacity of the European Union and Member States to deal with the consequences of a terrorist attack by cooperating more closely with other international organizations, including NATO.
6. Identify and address the factors that favour support for terrorism and recruitment into terrorism, by also developing strategies to promote inter-religious and cross-cultural understanding.
7. Reinforce counter-terrorism capacity building also in third countries by developing technical assistance strategies and including counter-terrorism clauses in all agreements.

On the occasion of the adoption of the Action Plan of 18 June 2004 the European Council also stated that it would review the Plan twice a year. The first such review was adopted at the meeting of 14 December 2004. An important document was drafted by the Presidency in close cooperation with the Counter-Terrorism Coordinator and the Commission. This document contains a statement of the actions adopted according to the strategic objectives of the EU's Action Plan and an annex showing an overview of the implementation by Member States of EU legislation in the fight against terrorism as well as ratification of the relevant UN Conventions.[42] After June 2004 considerable progress was achieved.

---

42 See doc. 1609004 of 14 December 2004 at http://ue.eu.int.

As for border and document security the Council reached an agreement on biometric indicators in passports and on the institution of the European Border Agency.

As regards the latter the Council adopted Regulation 2007/2004 on 26 October 2004 establishing a European Agency for the Management of Operational Cooperation at the External Borders of the Member States of the European Union.[43] The Agency became operational in May 2005 and will facilitate the application of existing and future Community measures relating to the control of external borders by ensuring the coordination of Member States' actions in the implementation of those measures. The Council has also reached an agreement to exchange information on lost and stolen passports with Interpol.

In line with this effective multilateralism, the EU gave high priority to supporting the key role of the United Nations in the fight against terrorism ratifying and/or implementing the counter-terrorism resolutions and UN conventions.

The EU has intensified cooperation with the US in accordance with the EU-US Declaration on combating terrorism of 26 June 2004[44] particularly in the field of countering terrorist financing.

The EU Solidarity Programme on the consequences of terrorist threats and attacks

On 25 March 2004 the Heads of State and Government of the Member States also declared[45] that it was their firm intention to act jointly against terrorist acts, based on the solidarity clause enshrined in article I-43 of the Treaty adopting a Constitution for Europe.

Member States undertook to cooperate in solidarity with each other to prevent the terrorist threat in the territory of a Member State, to protect democratic institutions and the civilian population in the event of a terrorist attack and to provide mutual assistance.

The declaration, like Article I-43, expressly mentions making available military resources to Member States among the instruments that the Union is willing to mobilize. These military resources are also supposed to prevent the terrorist threat in the territory of Member States as well as protect the democratic structures and the civilian population from a possible terrorist attack. It would therefore appear that the possibility of preventive military action to repress terrorist groups is not excluded. On the other hand, this would appear to be in conflict with the principle of the prohibition to use force expressed in Article 2.4 of the United Nations Charter. Hence Article I-43 appears to support what until now has been the minority opinion

---

43 The regulation is published in the *Official Journal of the European Union* (hereinafter *OJEU*) L 349 of 25 November 2004.

44 See the Dromoland Castle declaration of 26 June 2004 on external relations at http://europa.eu.int.

45 See *supra* note 22.

among legal scholars, which considers preventive military attacks against terrorist organisations to be legitimate. The right to reply with force not only to a terrorist attack but also to acts deemed as threats to the peace is thus recognized, thereby going beyond the cautious nature of UN Security Council Resolutions 1368 and 1373.

Following its declaration of 25 March 2004, the Council, together with the Commission, adopted a draft Solidarity Programme on 1 December 2004 on the consequences of terrorist threats and attacks.[46] The Programme specifies the competences of the Union organs and of Member States, thereby helping the national parliaments to understand the Union's objectives and to facilitate their plans at a legislative level.

The recently nominated counter-terrorism coordinator[47] will have the task of assisting the Council in implementing the action plan.

At its meeting of 16-17 December 2004[48] the European Council urged by June 2005 further assessment of the capabilities that Member States could make available in relation to the coordination mechanism on civilian protection, including joint exercises and coordination of public information and improved medical resources.

Specific restrictive measures on the financing of terrorism

Resolution 1373/2001, which was adopted by the UN Security Council on 28 September 2001, approved various measures to foster cooperation between States to prevent and suppress the financing and preparation of terrorist acts. The Resolution calls on States to criminalize the wilful provision or collection, by any means, of funds and to freeze funds and other financial assets or economic resources of persons or entities who commit or attempt to commit or participate in terrorist acts. The Resolution furthermore calls on States to do whatever they can to prevent terrorist acts by denying asylum and support to those persons involved in terrorist acts. They must prevent the recruitment of members of terrorist groups; establish serious penalties against those who help commit acts of terrorism; provide mutual assistance and exchange information; establish effective border controls; adopt provisions designed to prevent counterfeiting and falsification of documents; and intensify investigation activities.

In compliance with this Resolution, the European Union adopted a series of measures to strengthen the fight against terrorism in Europe. In particular, the EU Council adopted Common Position 2001/931/CFSP on the application of specific measures to combat terrorism.[49] This common position was adopted in the area of a common foreign and security policy and, hence, in the Second Pillar which, under

---

46 See doc. 15480 of 1 December 2004.

47 On the occasion of the Council of 25 March 2004, Mr. Gijs de Vries was appointed as Counter-Terrorism Coordinator.

48 See Presidency conclusions Doc. 16238/1/04 REV1 at http://ue.eu.int.

49 *OJEC*, L 344, 28 December 2001, pp. 93 ff.

Article 15 of the Treaty on the European Union, defines the EU's position on this issue. Member States must then ensure that their domestic policies comply with the EU's position. They are free to choose the methods to achieve this result. It should be noted that common position 2001/931/CFSP takes as its legal basis not only Article 15, but also Article 34 of the Treaty on European Union, which is the provision that sets out the instruments that the EU uses in the area of judicial and police cooperation; that is, within the Second Pillar. The specific character of the fight against terrorism, which is linked to the fight against crime and linked to aspects falling within the CFSP area, led the EU to adopt a flexible attitude in using the Treaty's instruments and to found the common position on legal bases belonging to different Pillars.

Common position 2001/931/CFSP establishes a list of persons, groups and organizations involved in terrorist acts against which States should freeze funds and other financial assets. The list was drawn up on the basis of investigations conducted by competent judicial or police authorities of Member States and is updated and revised every six months. Article 2 of the EC Treaty, within the limits of the powers that are conferred upon it, orders the freezing of funds and of other financial or economic resources of persons on the list and ensures that funds and resources are not made available to them. For their part, Member States must provide mutual assistance for the purposes of preventing and combating terrorist acts (Article 4) as part of judicial and police cooperation in criminal matters.

Common position 2001/931/CFSP is the basic common position. Other common positions have been adopted since this one, each repealing and incorporating the preceding one. The last two to be adopted were 2004 /500/CFSP of 17 May 2004 and 2005/220/CFSP of 14 March 2005.[50]

Likewise, in compliance with UN Security Council Resolution 1373 it adopted common position 2001/930/CFSP[51] on the fight against terrorism. This envisages the freezing of funds and of other financial or economic resources of persons or entities that facilitate, attempt to commit or commit terrorist acts in the territory of Member States.

Council Regulation 2580/2001[52] on the specific restrictive measures against certain persons and entities to combat terrorism is intended to implement UN Security Council Resolution 1373 in the European Union. The measures adopted were economic, such as the freezing of assets or economic resources.

This Community Regulation is compulsory in all its elements and is directly applicable in each of the Member States, unlike common positions which require positive action from Member States establishing the instruments necessary so that their domestic policies comply with the goal of the common position.

---

50 Common position 2004/500/CFSP of 17 May 2004 in *OJEU* L 196 of 3 June 2004. This position was later updated by Council decision of 14 March 2005 and is published in *OJEU* L 69 of 16 March 2005, p. 59.

51 *OJEC*, L 344, 28 December 2001, pp. 90 ff.

52 *OJEC*, L 344, 28 December 2001, pp. 70 ff.

The Regulation is complementary to administrative and judicial procedures applied to terrorist organizations in the European Union and in third countries and envisages the freezing of funds and of other economic and financial resources held by individuals, persons groups or entities. These are identified in a periodically revised list by the EU Council through specific decisions taken unanimously. According to Article 2, para. 3, of the Regulation, the list is drawn up by the Council in compliance with provisions under Article 1, paragraphs 4, 5 and 6, of common position 2001/931/ CFSP. The most recently updated list was adopted by Council decision 2005/221/ CFSP of 14 March 2005,[53] which repealed 2004/306/EC of 2 April 2004.[54] This is a consolidated list that replaces and incorporates preceding ones.

The Regulation 2580/2001 adopts some autonomous concepts such as 'funds and other financial activities', 'freezing of funds and other financial activities and economic resources', 'banking and other financial services' and 'controlling a legal person'. As regards the definition of terrorist acts reference is made to common position 2001/931/CFSP. The Regulation also establishes some derogations which, in specific cases, allow competent authorities to grant authorizations to unfreeze funds or other financial activities.

The list contained in Regulation was drawn up by the Council of the European Union independently and without reference to decisions adopted by UN Security Council bodies and includes terrorists and terrorist groups of various origins including European ones.

In the fight against terrorism the European Union also adopted specific measures against the Islamic terrorist network Al Qaeda in compliance with UN Security Council resolutions 1267/1999, 1333/2000 and 1390/2002. In this case regulation 881/2002 was adopted by the Council on 27 May 2002 and imposed specific restrictive measures against certain persons and entities associated with Osama bin Laden, the Al Qaeda network and the Taliban.[55] Unlike the list found in regulation 2580/2001, the list referred to in this last instrument exclusively concerns the Islamic network Al Qaeda and was drawn up on the basis of the list drafted by the Security Council's Sanctions Committee.

Regulation 881/2002 was adopted on the basis of the Council's common position of 27 May 2002[56] directly against Osama bin Laden, members of the Al Qaeda organization and the Taliban and repealed preceding common positions adopted from 1996 onwards.

The legal basis of Regulation 881/2002, like Regulation 2580/2001, is grounded in articles 60, 301 and 308 of the Treaty founding the European Community, since both fall under the First Pillar. To understand the reference to these three provisions it must be recalled that Article 60 refers to the adoption of urgent measures by

---

53 *OJEU* L 69, 16 March 2005.

54 *OJEU* L 99, 3 April 2004.

55 *OJEC* L 139, 29 May 2002, pp. 9 ff. Regulation 881/2002 replaces the preceding regulation 467/2001.

56 *OJEC* L 139/4, 29 May 2002, pp. 4 ff.

the Council on the movement of capital and payments; Article 301 provides that, whenever a common position or a joint action on foreign policy and common security envisage action by the Community to interrupt or reduce partially or totally economic relations with one or more third countries, the Council may adopt the necessary urgent measures acting on a qualified majority. Regulations 2580/2001 and 881/2002 were not intended to break off relations with Member States, but to adopt restrictive measures against certain persons or groups. As a result it turned out necessary to adopt Article 308 on the implicit powers of the Community as the legal basis. This solution enabled the Community to adopt legislative acts that could be directly applied in Member States in the fight against terrorism, an issue that straddles the Second and Third Pillars; that is, in areas where there are no legislative acts characteristic of the First Pillar, but only instruments aimed at furthering intergovernmental cooperation.

Following the adoption of the revised Action Plan on Combating Terrorism of June 2004, the Commission proposed further measures to the European Council against the financing of terrorism particularly the regulation on controls of cash entering and leaving the Community and the third money laundering directive.[57] At the same time the Commission also submitted proposals to the Council without delay to prevent charity organizations being used as channels for funding terrorism.

Measures to promote judicial cooperation: the creation of Eurojust and the framework decision on the European arrest warrant

Alongside the abovementioned measures, which specifically deal with terrorism, the EU adopted some instruments on judicial cooperation to make the fight against terrorism more effective.

The conclusions of the Tampere European Council on 15-16 October 1999 led to a European judicial cooperation unit being set up. Council decision 2002/187/ JHA of 28 February 2002[58] led to the establishment of Eurojust. This legal body is made up of a national member seconded by each Member State who is a judge, prosecutor or police officer of equivalent competence. The purpose of Eurojust is to promote coordination and cooperation on serious cross-border crime related to criminal investigation and proceedings involving at least two Member States, as well as cooperation on the execution of extradition requests. Besides offences committed by organized crime Eurojust's competence covers all crimes for which Europol is competent, and therefore includes terrorism. Through the intermediation of Eurojust, regular contacts have been created between terrorism magistrates, prosecutors and judges. Under Article III-274 of the Treaty which adopts the Constitution for Europe, Eurojust was transformed from just a judicial cooperation unit into an organ with

---

57 Communication from the Commission to the Council and the European Parliament on the Prevention of and the Fight against Terrorist Financing COM (2004) 700 Final of 20/10/2004 at http://europa.eu.int.

58 In *OJEC* 63, 6 March 2002, pp. 1 ff.

wider powers which could be attributed, through a European law, the power to initiate criminal proceedings, while at present it is limited to asking national authorities to do so. Furthermore the Council of Ministers, following a unanimous vote may, from Eurojust (Article III-275), establish a European Public Prosecutor's Office, which will be responsible for investigating, prosecuting and bringing to justice, in liaison with Europol, the perpetrators of serious crimes with repercussions in different Member States and offences which harm the Union's financial interests. It will be able to exercise the functions of Prosecutor in the national courts of Member States in relation to such offences.

Of particular importance in the fight against terrorism is the Council's Framework Decision 2002/584/JHA of 13 June 2002 on the European arrest warrant and on surrender procedures between Member States.[59] It was adopted as part of judicial cooperation in criminal matters which, as we have already seen, is one of the spheres falling within the area of freedom, security and justice.

Its legal basis is to be found in Articles 31 and 34 of the Treaty on European Union. Article 31 provides that cooperation between judicial authorities regarding proceedings and enforcement of decisions should be accelerated. Paragraph b of Article 31 only refers to procedures to facilitate extradition, while extradition would be abolished in a single judicial area.

As I have already stated with regard to the Council's Framework Decision of 13 June 2002 on combating terrorism, examined above, under Article 34, this act is binding on Member States as to the results to be achieved 'but leave to the national authorities the choice of form and methods'. The Framework Decision on the European arrest warrant therefore established a duty to implement by 31 December 2003. Member States have transposed it into national law, but after the original deadline.

In this regard, it should be noted that a framework decision does not have direct effect on relations between Member States. To some extent it is similar to a directive. This similarity, however, is limited to the definition of its general typical features. Instead it differs from it as regards the consequences ensuing from Member States' failure to implement it. Failure to implement a directive can lead to an action by the Commission or by another Member State before the European Court of Justice, or to the possibility of a directive being applied since it is directly applicable, if detailed.

In contrast a framework decision does not entail direct effect and, under the Third Pillar, the Commission does not have the power to promote an action against a State that has not transposed a framework decision into national law. However, it should be noted that under Article 35, para. 7, of the Treaty of European Union the Court of Justice has jurisdiction to rule a dispute between Member States concerning the interpretation or application of acts adopted under Article 34, para. 2. Such disputes may include the failure to apply or incorrect application of a framework decision.

---

59 Published in *OJEC* L 190, 18 July 2002 and as modified in *OJEU* L 43, 8 February 2003.

Under Article 34, para. 3, of Framework Decision 584/2002/JHA the Council performed a review of its practical application by Member States one year after the deadline of implementation.

It must also be added that under Article 31 of the same Framework Decision the provisions contained in it replaces the corresponding provisions of the international conventions on extradition from 1 January 2004.[60]

Turning now to consider the content of the Framework Decision, it should be pointed out that the European arrest warrant amounts to a judicial decision issued prior to the arrest and surrender of a wanted person in another Member State.

The Framework Decision does not set out the conditions under which a European arrest warrant may be issued, which are left to national legislation. It does, however, include detailed provisions on the form that the warrant should take and the information that it should contain. To this end a form is included in the annex to the Framework Decision.

The provisions introduced by the Framework Decision are based on the principle of the automatic recognition of the decision to arrest a person taken by other Member States. This principle is founded on mutual trust among Member States (recital 10 of the preamble).

It has been said that the European arrest warrant might lead to lower standards of justice and less protection of fundamental rights.

To begin with the fact that the offences listed are not defined has been criticized. This decision is in conflict with the principle of legality of criminal offences, enshrined in international instruments on the protection of human rights. This seems particularly true in the case of the crime of terrorism.[61] With regard to this last point it must be said that the definition of the above crime can in any case be found, as we have seen, in other Community legislative acts.

The decision to remove the principle of double jeopardy for the offences listed in Article 2 also aroused concerns since if the criminal behaviour is considered a crime in both legal systems it could lead to greater protection of human rights. However, it must be remembered that the framework decision operates between legal systems that have a certain degree of homogeneity. It considers the crime of terrorism[62] particularly

---

60 Extradition was regulated by the European Convention on Extradition of 13 December 1957 and by the European Convention of 27 January 1977 on the suppression of terrorism. The Convention implementing the Schengen Agreement set up the SIS – a mechanism to improve information systems between Member States on wanted persons and facilitating contacts between the national authorities at the time of arrest. The Convention on extradition between Member States of the European Union, adopted on 27 September 1996, and the Convention on the simplified extradition procedure between Member States of the European Union of 10 March 1995 did not enter into force.

61 See G. Knoops, 'International Terrorism: The Changing Face of International Extradition and European Criminal Law', *Maastricht Journal of European and Comparative Law*, vol. 10, 2003, p. 1163.

62 In addition to other offences such as trafficking in human beings, illicit trafficking in drugs and other serious crimes listed in Article 2.

serious and requires that effective proportionate and dissuasive criminal penalties be adopted on the part of all Member States.[63] Hence the removal of the principle of double jeopardy does not appear to have any major practical importance.

Nor is a refusal to extradite envisaged when the crime is defined by the executing State as political. But it must be observed that the solutions adopted by the Council have been accepted by international conventions starting with the European Convention on Extradition of 15 October 1957.[64]

The principle of non-discrimination, found in all extradition treaties, only appears in the preamble.[65] This decision caused some surprise, above all due to the consequences that applying it could have on the execution of the European arrest warrant.

In any case the Framework Decision introduces some measures to protect the individual rights of the wanted person, which the surrender procedure must respect.

Indeed the Framework Decision provides two sets of safeguards: those regarding the procedure leading to the arrest and surrender of the wanted person when executing a European arrest warrant issued in another Member State and those related to a possible violation of the wanted person's rights in the issuing State.

In relation to the first aspect, the executing State is required to provide appropriate safeguards of a 'fair trial' in the proceedings leading to the final decision on the execution of a European arrest warrant. Firstly the principle of *ne bis in idem* applies. It is a ground for mandatory non-execution of the European arrest warrant if the wanted person 'has been finally judged by a Member State in respect of the same acts provided that where there has been sentence, the sentence has been served or is currently being served or may longer be served under the law of the sentencing Member State' (Article 3.2). The safeguards also include the protection of minors. Furthermore a judicial authority may refuse to execute the European arrest warrant if the wanted person may not, owing to his age, be held criminally responsible for the acts on which the arrest warrant is based (Article 3.3). A specific safeguard is envisaged in cases in which the decision was rendered *in absentia*, if the person concerned is not summoned in person or informed of the date and place of the hearing (Article 5.1).

As regards the second set of safeguards, there are a number of specific safeguards regarding the wanted person that must be provided in the issuing State.

The Framework Decision once again establishes a minimum threshold also with this second set of safeguards. The guarantees are minimal. These are the right to be informed of the reasons for the arrest, the right to legal counsel (Article 11), the right to be heard by the executing judicial authorities (Article 14) and the right to proceedings within a reasonable time (Article 17).

---

63 See Article 5 of framework decision 2002/475/JHA.

64 Article 5 of the Convention on extradition between Member States of the European Union of 27 September 1996 envisages the removal of this traditional limit on extradition for crimes listed in para. 2 of Article 5.

65 Recital 12.

Finally, it must be noted that the failure to respect fundamental rights in the issuing State is not one of the substantial reasons for refusal to execute a European arrest warrant.

The set of safeguards envisaged by the framework decision are therefore rather limited.

The Council's solution can be explained by virtue of a number of considerations. Firstly it must be recalled, as already envisaged in recital 12 of the Preamble and in Article 1, para. 3, of the decision, that all Member States must respect the fundamental rights and the fundamental legal principles enshrined in Article 6 of the Treaty on European Union and contained in the Charter of Fundamental Rights of the European Union.

It is worth recalling that Article 6 of the Treaty on European Union states that EU Member States are bound by the provisions, including a fair trial, that are contained in the European Convention for the protection of human rights and fundamental freedoms, signed in Rome on 4 November 1950, and form part of the common constitutional traditions of Member States as general principles of Community law.

It is true that these are consolidated rights and that the decision is founded on the high level of trust between Member States; however, in my opinion, to eliminate all uncertainty, it would be advisable to have more guarantees both in procedural and substantial terms.

These observations apply all the more to the crime of terrorism, in relation to which Member States often neglect the respect for established rights and guarantees. In this respect the Commission's decision to publish a green paper entitled 'Procedural safeguards for suspects and defendants in criminal proceedings throughout the European Union' with the purpose of establishing minimum standards for procedural safeguards is to be welcomed.

Conclusion

The European Union, as we have seen, has responded to recent brutal terrorist attacks by adopting a number of measures, above all in the area of judicial cooperation in criminal matters. Unfortunately, however, Member States have been too slow to implement these measures.

To facilitate the task of developing counter-terrorist policies the European Council adopted an action plan which will also help national parliaments understand the objectives of the EU and facilitate their plans at a legislative level.

The numerous instruments adopted in the field of Justice and Home Affairs, concerning not just terrorist crimes but also other crimes, have reinforced Community action in the fight against terrorism. Of particular importance in this respect are the European arrest warrant and the future instrument on the free movement of judicial decisions, whereby judicial decisions, such as the arrest, confiscation and freezing of assets would be mutually recognized. Of equal importance will be future measures to protect and assist the victims of terrorism and witnesses in terrorism-related cases. In this regard, the Commission was asked by the European Council to submit, without delay, a European protection programme.

A decisive role will also be played by the strategy to dismantle the financial systems supporting terrorism that can only be successful if there is effective cooperation with financial and banking institutions.

The European security and defence policy will also play a role. However, military action alone will not be sufficient to defeat terrorism. It is necessary to further enhance cooperation between judicial bodies, police forces and intelligence services. It is also necessary to combat the causes that give rise to terrorist phenomena.

International cooperation is also a fundamental element in the fight against terrorism. The Action Plan approved by the European Council clearly specifies the need to foster cooperation with the US and with other countries to counter the terrorist threat.

In the past, cooperation with the US on criminal justice was based on bilateral agreements signed with individual Member States, while today agreements have been reached between the European Union and the US. More specifically two agreements were signed in Washington on 25 June 2003 – the Extradition Agreement[66] and the Mutual Legal Assistance Agreement.[67] Both these instruments, however, were the result of secret negotiations, a system for which there appears to be no justification, given the importance of these agreements and their implications in the protection of fundamental rights.

Finally, further agreements have been signed with the US, namely the agreements of 30 September 2004[68] on container security and on the processing and transfer of PNR data.[69]

66 *OJEU* 2003, L 181/27.
67 *OJEU* 2003, L 181/34.
68 *OJEU* 2004, L 304/34.
69 *OJEU* 2004, L 183/84.

Chapter 18

The European Union and Human Rights

EGERIA NALIN[1]

European measures against terrorism before and after 11 September 2001

For the last ten years the European Union (hereinafter EU) has considered terrorism as a threat to democracy, to the free exercise of human rights and to economic and social development.[2] It has therefore adopted numerous specific measures having an impact on terrorism and played its full part in the global coalition against terrorism, under the aegis of the United Nations. After the attack on the Twins Towers in 2001, the European Council declared that terrorism is a real challenge to the world and to Europe and that the struggle against terrorism has become a priority for the EU. In addition, the Council of the EU reaffirmed the determination of the EU to increase actions for the prevention and suppression of terrorism under the aegis of the United Nations Security Council.[3]

In the meantime, the Security Council, considering terrorism as a threat to international peace and security and acting under Chapter VII of the UN Charter, had already adopted Resolutions 1267, of 15 October 1999, and 1333, of 19 December 2000, that strongly condemn the continuing use of Afghan territory, especially areas controlled by the Taliban, for the sheltering and training of terrorists and planning of terrorist acts, and require that the Taliban turn over Osama Bin Laden to appropriate authorities of a country where he has been indicted or where he will be arrested and effectively brought to justice. Those resolutions, in order to enforce that demand, put in place the ban on flights and the freeze on funds of the Taliban of Afghanistan; the former also established the Taliban Sanctions Committee (para. 6) for ensuring that States implement the measures decided in that context, and the latter (para. 8 (c)) instructed such a Committee to maintain an updated list, based on information provided by States and regional organizations, of the individuals and entities designated as associated with bin Laden. After 11 September 2001, the Security Council adopted, on 28 September, Resolution 1373, providing that States shall:

---

1   University of Bari.

2   See La Gomera Declaration, adopted at the informal Council meeting on 14 October 1995.

3   See the extraordinary meeting of the European Council, on 21 September 2001, and the meeting of the Council of the EU, on 8 October 2001.

- complement international cooperation in criminal and judicial fields to prevent and suppress terrorism;
- become parties to and implement as soon as possible the relevant international conventions and protocols relating to terrorism;
- establish as serious criminal offences in domestic law acts of terrorism, or participation in financing, planning, preparation or perpetration of terrorist acts, or in supporting terrorist acts; and
- ensure that any person who participates in these activities is brought to justice.

In that very resolution, the Security Council decided that each State should prevent and suppress the financing of terrorist acts, by freezing funds and other financial assets or economic resources of persons or entities who commit, or attempt to commit terrorist acts, or participate in, or facilitate the commission of terrorist acts; furthermore, such prevention and suppression of the financing of terrorist acts should be achieved by prohibiting the making available (directly or indirectly) of any funds, financial assets or economic resources or financial or other related services for the benefit of these persons and entities.

All the Security Council resolutions decide binding measures for UN Member States – including EU Member States – for the maintenance of international peace and security (Article 25, Charter), but not for the EU itself; anyway the above mentioned resolutions concern matters of competence of the EU, so that the Council of the EU, acting pursuant to Title V of the Treaty of European Union (TEU), decided to adopt common positions and regulations implementing those UN resolutions and continuing its efforts for the suppression and prevention of the financing and preparation of acts of terrorism. Consequently, the Council:

- adopted Common Position 1999/727/CFSP, concerning restrictive measures against the Taliban;
- adopted Regulation 337/2000, concerning a flight ban and a freeze of funds and other financial resources in respect of the Taliban of Afghanistan;
- implemented Resolution 1267/1999;[4]
- adopted Common Position 2001/154/CFSP, concerning additional restrictive measures against the Taliban;
- adopted Regulation 467/2001 (that repealed Regulation 337/2000), prohibiting the export of certain goods and service to Afghanistan, strengthening the flight ban and extending the freeze of funds and other financial resources in respect

---

4 Common Position 1999/727/CFSP, of 15 November 1999 (not now in force), is published in *OJEC* L 294, 16 November 1999, p. 1 ff.; Regulation 337/2000, of 14 February 2000 (not now in force either), is published in *OJEC* L 43, 16 February 2000, pp. 1 ff. Although Common Positions define the approach of the EU on a particular matter and oblige Member States to cooperate to achieve their aims and to conform to their directives and objectives, in accordance with Article 15 of the TEU, they do not entail direct effect.

of the Taliban of Afghanistan, in order to implement Resolution 1333/2000.[5]

It should be recalled that Regulation 467/2001 contains, in Annex I, the list of persons, entities and bodies to whom the freeze of funds imposed by the regulation applies; such a list shall be amended or supplemented by the Commission on the basis of determinations by the Security Council or the Taliban Sanctions Committee. Finally, Common Positions 2001/930/CFSP (on combating terrorism) and 2001/931/ CFSP (on the application of specific measures to combat terrorism[6]), and Regulation 2580/2001 (on specific restrictive measures directed against certain persons and entities with a view to combat terrorism[7]) implement UN Resolution 1373.

Common Position 2001/930/CFSP provides quite a complete list of means and methods to suppress and prevent terrorism. It demands that EU Member States shall:

- either freeze funds and other financial assets or economic resources of any person or entity who commits, or attempts to commit, or participates in, or facilitates the commission of terrorist acts, and prohibit their access to funds, financial assets or economic resources, directly or indirectly (Articles 1-3);
- adopt laws and regulations to establish as serious criminal offences terrorist acts or participation in financing, planning, preparation or perpetration of terrorist acts (Articles 4-8);
- exchange operational information and increase assistance in connection with criminal investigations and proceedings (Articles 9, 11 and 12);
- increase effective border controls and establish measures to prevent counterfeiting or fraudulent use of identity papers and travel documents (Article 10);
- become parties to the relevant international conventions and protocols relating to terrorism;
- increase cooperation and full implementation of the relevant international conventions, protocols and UN Security Council resolutions related to terrorism (Articles 14-15);
- adopt appropriate measures to ensure that asylum-seekers have not planned, facilitated or participated in the commission of terrorist acts;
- ensure that refugee status is not abused by the perpetrators, organizers or facilitators of terrorist acts and that extradition of alleged terrorists is not refused for the claim of political motivation (Articles 16-17).

---

5   Common Position 2001/154/CFSP, of 26 February 2001 (not now in force), is published in *OJEC* L 57, 27 February 2001, p. 1 ff.; Regulation 467/2001, of 6 March 2001 (not now in force either), is published in *OJEC* L 67, 9 March 2001, pp. 1 ff.

6   Common Positions 2001/930/CFSP and 2001/931/ CFSP, adopted on 27 December 2001, are published in *OJEC* L 344, 28 December 2001, pp. 90 ff. and 93 ff.

7   Regulation 2580/2001, of 27 December 2001, is published in *OJEC* L 344, 28 December 2001, pp. 70 ff.

Common Position 2001/931/CFSP provides that Member States shall ensure, as much as possible, police and judicial cooperation in criminal matters related to terrorism within the framework of Title VI TEU (Article 4), and that the European Communities (hereinafter EC) shall establish the freezing of funds, financial assets and economic resources of persons or entities involved in terrorist acts, within the limits of powers conferred by the TEC (Article 2). Persons and entities involved in terrorist acts in accordance with articles of this common position are listed in an Annex, reviewed at least once every six months. The list is drawn up on the basis of information furnished by the UN Security Council about persons and entities related to terrorism and against whom it orders sanctions, or by 'competent authority' of the EU Member States, in respect of persons, groups and entities concerned by investigation or prosecution for terrorist acts, or for an attempt to perpetrate, participate in, or facilitate such an act, based on serious and credible evidence, or clues, or condemned for such deeds (Article 1, para. 4).

In accordance with Article 1, para. 2, of this Common Position, persons, groups and entities involved in terrorist acts included in the list are the ones who commit or attempt to commit, facilitate or participate in the commission of terrorist acts; groups and entities owned or controlled directly or indirectly by such persons and associated persons, groups or entities. Terrorist acts (Article 1, para. 3) are specifically listed (crimes against a person's life or psycho-physical integrity of a person; crimes causing extensive destruction of public and private property; the manufacture, possession, acquisition, transport, supply or use of weapons; the release of dangerous substances or causing fires, explosions or floods to endanger human life). Such acts must be:

- intentional;
- committed with the aim of seriously intimidating a population;
- or committed with the aim of unduly compelling a government or an international organization to perform or abstain from performing any act;
- or committed with the aim of seriously destabilizing or destroying the fundamental political, constitutional, social, or economic structures of a country or an international organization;
- or, given their context or nature, seriously damaging a country or an international organization.

For the purposes of Article 1 of this Common Position, terrorist acts shall also include the threat of commission of the listed terrorist acts, the direction of a terrorist group or the participation in the activities of a terrorist group in any way, with knowledge of the fact that such participation will contribute to the criminal activities of the group.

Regulation 2580/2001 applies to persons, groups and entities listed in the Annex to Common Position 2001/931/CFSP but the Council, by unanimity, shall review and emend such a list (Article 2, para. 3). The Regulation establishes exceptions to the freezing of funds, the conditions and procedures to grant authorization to use frozen funds for essential human needs or to unfreeze funds (Articles 5-6) and lists in the Annex the competent authority of each Member State.

EU action against terrorism has been strengthened further on adopting, in the framework of Pillar III, numerous measures having an impact on terrorism and organized crime (such as the establishment of the European Police Office – EUROPOL)[8] and on the mutual recognition of judicial decisions and the abolishment or simplification of procedures of extradition to remove delay inherent to extradition procedures (such as the framework decision on the European arrest warrant and the surrender procedures between Member States).[9]

In the same context, the Council also adopted framework decisions 2002/475/ JHA on combating terrorism.[10]

The Framework Decision on combating terrorism defines terrorist offences, including the offences relating to terrorist groups, and establishes common jurisdictional rules to ensure that such offences may be effectively prosecuted. Definition of terrorist offences is quite identical to that of terrorist acts provided by Common Position 2001/931/CFSP as regards aims, context and intentional commission of the acts specifically listed. Member States shall take the necessary measures to ensure punishment, as criminal offences under national law, of listed terrorist acts, of the direction of a terrorist group and of participation in the activities of a terrorist group, including by supplying information or material resources, or by funding its activities in any way, with knowledge of the fact that such participation will contribute to the criminal activities of the terrorist group. In the framework of Article 2, terrorist group means a structured group of more than two persons, established over a period of time and acting in concert to commit terrorist offences. States shall take measures to punish, in accordance with national law, inciting or

---

8   Convention based on Article K.3, TEU, on the establishment of a European Police Office (EUROPOL Convention), of 26 July 1995 (in *OJEC* C 316, 27 November 1995, pp. 2 ff.). EUROPOL aims to ensure cooperation within the competent authority of Member States dealing with prevention and suppression of terrorism, through exchange of information about serious forms of organized crime, collection and analysis of information, assistance in national investigations. The Council decision of 3 December 1998 (in *OJEC* C 26, 30 January 1999, pp. 22 ff.) instructs EUROPOL to deal with crimes committed or likely to be committed in the course of terrorist activities against life, limb, personal freedom and property.

9   The Framework Decision 2002/584/JHA, of 13 June 2002, is published in *OJEC* L 190, 18 July 2002, pp. 1 ff. The European arrest warrant is a judicial decision issued by a Member State and addressed to another Member State in order to ask the surrender or arrest of a requested person for the purposes of conducting a criminal prosecution or executing a custodial sentence or a judicial order. The Member State of execution may refuse to execute the European arrest warrant only in exceptional cases specifically listed in the framework decision (Articles 3-4). Anyway, it should be recalled that, although Framework Decisions are binding upon Member States as to the result to be achieved, they leave to each State the choice about forms and methods of implementation and do not entail direct effect (Article 34, TUE). Italy did not implement such a decision until now.

10   The Framework Decision 2002/475/JHA, of 13 June 2002, is published in *OJEC* L 164, 22 June 2002, pp. 3 ff.

aiding or abetting or attempting to commit one of the listed offences (Article 4); shall establish effective, proportionate and dissuasive criminal penalties, which may entail extradition (Article 5, para. 1); and shall exercise their jurisdiction if the terrorist offences are committed in their territory, or the offender is one of their nationals or residents, or the offence is committed for the benefit of a legal person established in their territory, or against people and institutions of the Member State in question or based in that Member State. The Framework Decision does not exclude the exercise of criminal jurisdiction by Member States in accordance to national law (*universal jurisdiction*) but States shall extradite or exercise jurisdiction (*aut dedere aut judicare*).

The question of presumed violation of fundamental human rights in fighting terrorism

The analysis of the above mentioned European measures against terrorism underlines the existence of the risk of sacrificing some fundamental human rights and freedoms guaranteed by both the international and national (constitutional) law of human rights, such as the right of property and the freedoms of association, expression and the exercise of economic activities by alleged financiers of terrorists. In particular the enlistment of alleged terrorists or supporters of terrorists may become a concrete violation of presumption of innocence and to the right of *due process*, a kind of verdict of guilty without admitting the alleged terrorists to be heard and to defend themselves.[11] Moreover, as Article 4 of Common Position 2001/931/CFSP refers to activities of active or passive supporters of terrorism, it could refer to each person who expresses opinions in favour of the reasons of terrorists, or who is part of an association or who demonstrates in favour of the reasons of terrorists, if he/she acknowledges that in those contexts terrorists are planning their attacks.

At present, two applications are submitted to the Court of First Instance of the EC (case *Aden and others* and case *Sison*)[12] and another one to the European Court

---

11 See E. Bribosia, A. Weyembergh (eds), *Lutte contre le terrorisme et droits fondamentaux*, Brussels: Bruylant, 2002; C. Warbrick, 'The Principles of the European Convention on Human Rights and the Response of States to Terrorism, *European Human Rights Law Reports*, 2002, pp. 287 ff.; J. Fitzpatrick, 'Speaking Law to Power: The War Against Terrorism and Human Rights', *European Journal of International Law*, vol. 14, 2003, pp. 264 ff.; S. Peers, 'EU Responses to Terrorism', *International and Comparative Law Quarterly*, vol. 52, 2003, pp. 227 ff.; S. Von Schorlemer, 'Human Rights: Substantive and Institutional Implications of the War Against Terrorism', *European Journal of International Law*, vol. 14, 2003, pp. 265 ff., especially pp. 274 ff.; P. De Sena, 'Esigenze di sicurezza nazionale e tutela dei diritti dell'uomo nella recente prassi europea', in SIDI, *Ordine internazionale e valori etici. VIII Convegno, Verona, 26-27 giugno 2003*, Naples: Editoriale Scientifica, 2004, pp. 195 ff.

12 Court of First Instance, *Aden and others v. Council and Commission*, case T-306/01 R, order of the President of 7 May 2002, in *European Court Reports*, 2002, p. II-2387 ff.; *Sison v. Council*, case T-47/03 R, order of the President of 15 May 2003, in *European Court Reports*, 2003, p. II-02047 ff.

of Human Rights (*Segi and others and Gestoras Pro Amnistia and others v. Austria, Belgium, Denmark, Finland, France, Germany, Greece, Ireland, Italy, Luxembourg, Portugal, Spain, Sweden, The Netherlands and United Kingdom*).[13]

In the *Aden* case, applicants (who are Swedish citizens of Somali origin and a non-profit-making association governed by Swedish law) claim the repealing of the Commission Regulation 2199 of 12 November 2001, amending the above mentioned Regulation 467/2001 with the introduction, in the annexed list of persons, groups and entities to whom regulation applies, of their names, the declaration that the Council Regulation 467/2001 is inapplicable pursuant to Article 241 of the TEC, and the suspension of the operation of Regulations 467/2001 and 2199/2001, in so far as they refer to the applicants and until judgement is given in the main proceedings.

In particular, the applicants state (order, paras 61-64) that the defendant institutions infringed their right to a fair hearing, because their names had been put on the list annexed to the regulation for the suggestions of a political organ, such as the UN Taliban Sanctions Committee; neither the Council nor the Commission examined the grounds on which the Committee had put them on the list; moreover they had not first been heard or given the opportunity to defend themselves. In addition, they consider that, because of the enlistment, they are suffering economic loss, since their financial resources are frozen and it is also impossible for them to be taken on by an employer or to engage in any occupation, and that they are suffering a non-material harm, because sanctions exclude them from normal life in society and the accusation of being a terrorist relegates them to the margins of society. Harm is also due to the infringements of their fundamental rights and freedoms because no judge can check the very basis of the sanctions that are not the consequence of a specific accusation.

Until now, the President of the Court of First Instance has just adopted an order dismissing the application for the interim relief. In fact, as regards the urgency, contrary to what the applicants contended considering that infringement of their rights and fundamental freedom is continuing and cannot be compensated retrospectively, the President of the Court of First Instance found that the material damage alleged is in principle always reparable and that, in the present case, the Swedish Government paid benefits to the applicants which should have enabled them to satisfy their own basic needs and those of their families. As regards non-material damage, although the President of the Court of First Instance agreed that it comprises the harm to their honour, reputation and dignity that caused to their families, he considered that the suspension of application of Regulation 2199/2001 could do no more than the annulment of that regulation, when the main action is decided.

In the *Sison* case, the applicant, born in the Philippines but resident in The Netherlands, claims for both the annulment of Decision 2002/974/EC, of 12 December 2002 (which implemented Article 2, para. 3, of Regulation 2580/2001)

---

13 European Court of Human Rights, case *Segi (and others) and Gestoras Pro Amnistia (and others) v. Austria, Belgium, Denmark, Finland, France, Germany, Greece, Italy, Luxembourg, Portugal, Spain, Sweden, The Netherlands, United Kingdom*, decision of 23 May 2002, available on the website: http://www.echr.coe.int.

and the repeal of Decision 2002/848/EC, of 28 October 2002 (which put the name of the applicant on the list provided by the mentioned regulation), also the suspension of the operation of such a decision, in so far as it mentions his name. In fact, Mr Sison recalls that such a mention caused the freezing of all his funds and financial resources and the loss of social benefits and health insurance so that he can satisfy neither his basic needs, nor those of his family.

In addition, the applicant considers that the financial restriction, the increased personal surveillance to which he is subject, the restriction of his freedom of movement and the fact of being stigmatized as a terrorist in the public opinion amount to inhuman and degrading treatment, as defined in Article 3 of the European Convention of Human Rights and Fundamental Freedoms, of 4 November 1950. These infringements of his fundamental rights cause moral damage and a risk to the personal security and physical integrity of the applicant. Finally, the enlisting of his name jeopardizes the applicant's role as chief political consultant of the National Democratic Front of the Philippines, which was particularly important in the signatory of all the major bilateral agreements between the National Democratic Front of the Philippines and the Philippine Government.

In the interlocutory proceedings, in spite of Mr Sison's submission, the President of the Court of First Instance (order, paras 34-41) dismissed the application for interim relief for the absence of the condition relating to urgency. In fact, as regards economic damage, he considered that it is not irreversible and irreparable since Articles 5 and 6 of the regulation allow national authority to grant the partial use of the frozen funds or the total unfreezing of the funds for humanitarian needs: the procedures pursuant to Articles 5 and 6, combined with the domestic remedies available to the applicant under Dutch law in respect of decisions taken by the competent authority pursuant to those provisions, would enable him to avoid serious and irreparable economic damage (order, para. 39).[14] As regards the non-material damage alleged by Mr Sison, the President found that it would be remedied by the annulment of the regulation in the judgement in the main action.

Finally, in the case before the European Court of Human Rights, *Segi and Gestoras Pro Amnistia* submitted that Common Positions 2001/930/CFSP and 2001/931/CFSP infringed their rights under the European Convention of Human Rights and its Protocol n. 1, of 20 March 1952. The applicants, labelled as an integral part of the Basque terrorist organization ETA and put on the list annexed to Common Position 2001/931/CFSP, were ordered to suspend their activities. The enlistment and its consequences caused the applicants irreparable damage to their fundamental rights to presumption of innocence, freedom of expression and action

---

14 On that subject, it should be noted that, contrary to the above mentioned conclusion, any material damage suffered by the applicant would not be a direct result of the adoption of the contested decision. In the *Aden* case, the President of the Court of First Instance considered that the economic damage is not irreparable just because of the *actual* economic benefit paid by the Swedish Government and decided to review his decision if, in the future, the Swedish Government ceases to pay the benefits!

as an association, to the use of their assets, to a hearing by a tribunal and to a fair trial (Articles 34, 6 (paras 2, 10, 11 and 13) and 6 (para. 1) of the European Convention of Human Rights, and Article 1 of the Protocol n. 1), because they were unable, as individual applicants, to challenge in the Court of Justice of the EC the decisions and measures taken by EU Member States by these common positions.[15]

The Court declared the applications inadmissible, because the enlistment in the Annex to the Common Position 2001/931/CFSP causes no infringement of the fundamental rights under the Convention, neither do the Common Positions entail direct effects or produce a direct and actual infringement of the rights secured to them by the Convention. In addition, according to the list, the applicants are subject only to Article 4 of the Common Position, aimed at improving police and judicial cooperation between the EU Member States in the fight against terrorism. The Court acknowledged that Article 4 might be used as the legal basis for national or conventional concrete measures, which could affect the applicants, but these future concrete measures would be subject to the form of national or international judicial review before the competent authority.

In conclusion, it should be recalled that the decision of the European Court of Human Rights dismissed the application just for procedural reasons and that, even if the Court usually admits that States, in fighting terrorism, might derogate to certain rights and freedoms they shall always respect principles of proportionality[16] and can never derogate from the fundamental rights to life, from the prohibition against torture and slavery and from the principle *nulla poena sine lege* (Article 15 of the European Convention of Human Rights).

As regards the *Aden* case, the *Sison* case and the *Segi and Gestoras Pro Amnistia* case, in my opinion, enlistment causes a violation of the fundamental right of the applicants to defend themselves, to *due process* and to presumption of innocence, which is contrary to proportionality. In fact, financing of terrorism could be suppressed although enlistment is the result of a brief judicial procedure, in which the suspect can be heard and the final decision could be challenged before another and superior

---

15 On that subject, see the next section of this chapter.

16 On 13 December 2001, the UK adopted the *Anti-Terrorism, Crime and Security Act*, which derogates to Article 5, para. 1, of the European Convention of Human Rights, providing for potentially indefinite detention of foreign nationals who are suspected of involvement in terrorism and cannot be extradited. The UK law has been submitted to the opinion of the Commissioner for Human Rights of Council of Europe (opinion 1/2002, of 28 August 2002, Doc. CommDH (2002) 8, available on the website http://www.coe.int) under Article 15 of the European Convention of Human Rights, and the Commissioner found that the derogation was in contrast with the principles of necessity – because it could be most useful monitoring the activities of the suspect – and of proportionality – because potentially indefinite detention is permitted irrespective of a direct threat for public security in the UK. See O. De Schutter, 'La Convention européenne des droits de l'homme à l'épreuve de la lutte contre le terrorisme', in Bribosia, Weyembergh (eds), *supra* note 11, pp. 85 ff., especially pp. 126 ff.; E. Katselli, S. Shah, 'September 11 and the UK Response', *International and Comparative Law Quarterly*, vol. 52, 2003, pp. 245 ff., especially pp. 252 ff.

judicial authority. Moreover, the alleged non-material damage, which involves the social relations of the suspected terrorist, is real, serious, often irreparable and the application for interim relief could even be dismissed when the conditions of *prima facie case* and urgency are fulfilled, under the balance between the rights of the applicants and the superior interest of States to protect their own population and to cooperate with the UN in fighting terrorism.[17]

Means and methods to protect suspected terrorists against violations of fundamental human rights

The risk of serious infringement of fundamental human rights and freedoms of suspected terrorists is strengthened by the judicial means at the disposal of any person, group or entity, whose fundamental rights are violated by anti-terrorism measures.

In fact, on the one hand, the European Court of Human Rights admits that it has jurisdiction on violations of the European Convention by States Parties in implementing the EU law; on the other, according to the mentioned decision in *Segi and Gestoras Pro Amnistia* case, since the anti-terrorism measures adopted by the EU as common positions are general and cannot entail direct effects, thus they cause no infringement of the fundamental rights under Convention.

The EC Court of Justice could play a more important role in protecting human rights infringed by law measures against terrorism: article 46, TEU, provides that the Court shall exercise its powers with regard to the actions of institutions under Article 6, para. 2, TEU, in so far as the Court has jurisdiction under TEU and TEC; moreover fundamental human rights and freedoms violated by anti-terrorism measures are the ones traditionally recognized by the Court of Justice as fundamental principles of the EC.

Anyway, the Court of Justice has no jurisdiction regarding acts and actions within CFSP, while, under Pillar III, it shall review the legality of framework decisions and decisions on grounds of lack of competence, infringement of an essential procedural requirement, infringement of the Treaty or of any other rule of law relating to its application or misuse of powers, but only in actions brought by States and the Commission (Article 35, para. 6, TEU). Finally, neither European institutions, nor States can ever challenge Common Positions before the Court, as they are considered political acts and the result of intergovernmental cooperation.

On the basis of the foregoing, individuals addressed under European anti-terrorism measures may challenge before the Court of First Instance only the legality of Regulations implementing Common Positions, as, in accordance with Article 230, para. 4 of the TEC, a natural or legal person may institute proceedings against a decision addressed to that person or against a decision which, although in the form

---

17 In the *Aden* case (order, paras 86-87), both the Commission and the Council supported such an opinion.

of a regulation or a decision addressed to another person, is of *direct* and *individual* concern of the former.

The Court considers that an applicant is regarded directly by a measure if this affects his legal position by itself, leaving no choice to Member States in implementing the measure, since such implementation is automatic and results from Community rules without the application of other intermediate national rules.[18] Thus, both in the *Aden* and in the *Sison* cases, that very condition is fulfilled, as the challenged regulations and decision do not need any national act of implementation and, in addition, the enlistment itself causes a direct moral harm in respect of the dignity and social relations of the alleged terrorists. Moreover, according to the Court, applicants will be regarded as individually concerned by a regulation only if it affects their legal position by reason of certain attributes peculiar to them, or by reason of a factual situation which differentiates them from all the other persons and distinguishes them in the same way as the addressee.[19] In spite of such a strict interpretation of the condition to be individually concerned,[20] there is no doubt that the European measures against terrorism, challenged in the *Aden* and *Sison* cases, concern the applicants individually, since they put their names on the list of persons and entities to whom those measures apply![21]

It should be recalled that natural or legal persons, whose rights are violated by European measures against terrorism, may also bring a case before the European Court, in order to obtain the review of legality of a Community measure, through a proceeding before a national court, giving rise to a reference to the Court of Justice for a preliminary ruling under Article 234, TEC.

---

18 CJEC, *CAM*, case 100/74, judgement of 18 November 1975, in *European Court Reports*, 1975, p. 1393 ff., especially para. 19; *Dreyfus v. Commission*, case C-386/96, judgement of 5 May 1998, in *European Court Reports*, 1998, p. I-2309 ff., especially paras 40-44.

19 CJEC, *Plaumann v. Commission*, case 25/62, judgement of 15 July 1963, in *European Court Reports*, 1963, p. 195 ff., especially point 1; *Codorniu v. Council*, case C-309/89, judgement of 18 May 1994, in *European Court Reports*, 1994, p. I-1853 ff., especially paras 18 ff.

20 Commentators, Advocates General and members of the Court often criticized the notion of individual concern, as strictly interpreted by the Court, since it could sometimes create cases of denial of justice. In the light of the above remarks, the Court of First Instance, in the Jégo-Quéré case, suggested a new interpretation of the notion of individual concern (case T-177/01, judgement of 3 May 2002, in *European Court Reports*, 2002, p. II-2365 ff., para. 51), but, immediately later, the Court of Justice, in the *Unión de Pequeños Agricultores* case, upheld the traditional interpretation (case C-50/00 P, judgement of 25 July 2002, in *European Court Reports*, 2002, p. I-6677 ff.).

21 In such a case, the Court (*Roquette Frères v. Council*, case 138/79, judgement of 29 October 1980, in *European Court Reports*, 1980, p. 3333 ff., especially paras 13 and 16; *Maizena v. Council*, case 139/79, judgement of 29 October 1980, in *European Court Reports*, 1980, p. 3393 ff., especially paras 13 and 16) found that the regulation could be considered a set of individual decisions, one of which is taken in respect of the applicant and is of direct and individual concern to him/her.

However, as Advocate General Jacobs suggested in his opinion relating to the *Unión de Pequeños Agricultores* case, national courts might decline to refer the question to the Court of Justice and, in addition, national courts might formulate the questions to be answered by the Court of Justice limiting or modifying the questions referred by individuals.[22] Moreover, since Community regulations do not require acts of implementation by national authorities, there may be no measure to challenge before national courts, as far as the individual deliberately violates the rules laid down by the measures, and relies on the invalidity of those rules as a defence in criminal or civil proceedings directed against him!

In the case of measures against terrorism adopted pursuant to Titles V and VI of the TEU, it should also be considered that the Court of Justice has no jurisdiction with regard to acts adopted in the area of CFSP, whereas, within Pillar III (Article 35, para. 2, TEU), Member States may accept the jurisdiction of the Court to give preliminary rulings on the validity and interpretation of framework decisions, decisions and conventions established under Title VI, and on the validity and interpretation of the measures implementing them, but they might limit this competence of the Court to the request made by any court or tribunal against whose decision there is no judicial remedy.

In any event, action under Article 234, TEC, even if the Court of Justice finds that the act is illegal, does not annul it but obliges the institution that adopted such an act to emend it or to suppress it, in order to eliminate its illegality aspects.[23]

Recently, the Court of First Instance expressly underlined the serious lack of adequate jurisdictional protection with regard to anti-terrorism measures under Pillars II and III, whereas it considered unfounded a compensation claim for damage suffered on account of the enlistment of the names of the applicants in the Annex to Common Position 2001/931/CFSP (as emended by common positions 2002/340/CFSP, of 2 May 2003, and 2002/462/CFSP, of 17 June 2002).[24] In the very order, the Court noted that, in accordance with Article 288, para. 2, TEC, it has no jurisdiction if the prejudice is caused by acts adopted pursuant to Title VI TUE,[25] and that, in such a case, the applicants can not claim compensation before national jurisdictions!

---

22 Opinion of the General Advocate Jacobs, delivered on 21 March 2002, in *European Court Reports*, p. I-6677 ff., paras 42 ff.

23 CJEC, *Schwarze*, case 16/65, judgement of 1 December 1965, in *European Court Report*, 1965, p. 1082 ff.; *Ireqs Arkady v. Council and Commission*, case 238/78, judgement of 4 October 1969, in *European Court Report*, 1969, p. 2955 ff.

24 Court of First Instance, *Segi and others v. Council and United Kingdom*, case T-338/02, order of the President of 7 June 2004, unpublished.

25 The Court noted that, according to the list annexed to common position 2001/931/CFSP, the applicants are subject only to its Article 4, aimed at improving police and judicial cooperation between the Member States of the EU in the fight against terrorism (see *supra*, note 2); thus it considered necessary to rule only on the very question whether it has jurisdiction on compensation for damage suffered on account of common positions under Title VI TUE. Anyway, that is true even with regard to acts and activities under Title V TUE, since, according to TUE, the Court has no power within CFSP.

In conclusion, we must note that access to the courts is one of the essential elements of a community based on the rule of law, such as the European Union. We must also note, as the Court of Justice always underlines, that the right to an effective remedy for everyone, when his/her rights and freedoms guaranteed by European law are violated, is based on the constitutional traditions common to Member States, and on Articles 6 and 13 of the European Convention of Human Rights, and has been reaffirmed by Article 47 of the Charter of Fundamental Rights of the European Union (proclaimed in Nice on 7 December 2000). However, the system of judicial remedies described above appears neither adequate nor satisfactory for the purpose of protecting fundamental rights and freedoms of the suspected terrorists.

The Treaty establishing a Constitution for Europe[26] (hereinafter European Constitution) will probably improve the situation for individuals affected by legal measures against terrorism. In fact, the European Constitution provides that the Court of Justice shall exercise all its powers (with a few exceptions) with regard to the actions and acts both under the present EC and Third Pillars.[27] In addition, it states that if the Council adopts *European decisions* within CFSP, providing for restrictive measures against natural or legal persons (such as, for example, the freezing of funds and economic resources of suspected terrorists or the other measures limiting their fundamental rights and freedoms), the legal or natural persons may institute proceedings to review the legality of such measures before the Court of Justice (Article III-376). This review could take place if the addressees of those decisions are individually and directly concerned by the very decisions, or if such acts are a regulation of direct concern to the applicant and do not entail the implementation of specific measures (Article III-365, para. 4).

---

26 The Treaty establishing a Constitution for Europe, signed in Rome on 29 October 2004, is published in *OJEU* C 310, 16 December 2004, p. 1 ff.

27 Consequently, in accordance with Article III-370, the Court shall finally have jurisdiction in disputes regarding compensation for damages, even when the serious prejudice is suffered on account of acts and activities related to the area of freedom, security and justice.

PART III
Terrorism, International Security and the Use of Force

Chapter 19

Panel Discussion

Giuseppe Nesi

Did the so-called 'war' against terrorism that started after 9/11 affect the concept of international security and the principles governing the use of force in international relations? More specifically, is the inherent right of self-defence as perceived in international law subject to different interpretations after 9/11? Could anticipatory self-defence be considered 'less unlawful' or 'more acceptable' or even legitimate in international law if foreseeable terrorist attacks against national and international security are at stake? Does the fight against terrorism justify the resort to the use of force in any circumstance where a State evaluates that the use of armed force is the only instrument enabling the very State to defeat terrorism? Are there other means short of the use of force that can be usefully exploited to defeat this scourge?

These are only some of the questions this panel discussion is going to address, after the role of the UN and of regional organizations in counter-terrorism has been examined in previous sessions. 'Terrorism, International Security and the Use of Force' is the title of this last session in which eminent panellists will give their views on a topic that has been highly debated in recent times.

The participants in this panel discussion are: Professor Georges Abi-Saab who taught for some decades at the Graduate Institute of International Studies in Geneva and is today a Member of the Appellate Body of the WTO and a member of the Institut de Droit International; Professor Jordan Paust of the Law Centre of the University of Houston, in Texas; Professor Ugo Villani, University of Rome, 'La Sapienza'; and last but not least, Ms. Elizabeth Wilmshurst, an eminent expert in international law. Ms. Wilmshurst worked for a long period at the Legal Service of the Foreign Office in London and is now at the Royal Institute of International Affairs, Chatham House, one of the most prestigious institutions of international relations all over the world.

I am a little intimidated by the presence of such an eminent panel, but I will do my best to 'lead the traffic'. May I invite Elizabeth Wilmshurst to take the floor.

Elizabeth Wilmshurst

I am introducing what is a fairly new topic for us: 'Terrorism and the Use of Force'. It was mentioned in the first session of this meeting that the 'war against terrorism' is just a rhetorical flourish; every lawyer I know has difficulties with this term. I was still working in the Foreign Office when it first began to be used; a question was asked in Parliament in October 2002: 'Is the United Kingdom legally at war and, if so, with whom?' The answer the Government gave is a useful one; I often quote it. It reads in part: 'The term "the war against terrorism" has been used to describe the whole campaign against terrorism, including military, political, financial, legislative and law enforcement measures.'

Terrorists are criminals and they must be dealt with by means of criminal justice. That has to be the general rule, as we have been discussing. A State deals with its domestic terrorism, if it can, through its own domestic criminal justice system. Or mechanisms of international cooperation can be used to ensure that evidence and the suspect are handed over to a State able and willing to bring the terrorist to justice, whether under one of the network of multilateral anti-terrorism conventions dealing with specific aspects of terrorism, or perhaps in the future under a new global terrorism convention. If these fail, it is open to the Security Council to require, under Chapter VII of the Charter, that a State hand over to justice suspects who are sheltering in its territory, as was done in respect of Libya after the Lockerbie disaster. The Council has more than once declared terrorism to be a threat to international peace and security. There are those who hope that in the future the Statute of the International Criminal Court will deal with terrorism under that name; at present it has jurisdiction over terrorism only in the context of other crimes such as crimes against humanity or targeting civilians in armed conflict.

But any assertion that terrorism may legitimately be dealt with *only* by methods of criminal justice takes too restrictive a view of international law and flies in the face of reality. If all other means fail, military force may have to be used; if the State in which the terrorists are situated cannot or will not deal with the problem, it may be that international force will be necessary.

I want to look very quickly at the case of Afghanistan, that is, the conflict which began in Afghanistan in October 2001, and to raise some questions. In the case of this conflict it is important to remember that there had been several attempts to solve the terrorist problem without resorting to force. Security Council Resolutions 1267(1999) and 1333(2000) demanded that Afghanistan hand over to justice Usama bin Laden and close terrorist training camps. Those attempts had failed. The attacks in the US on 11 September 2001 followed. If it had been possible to use peaceful methods to deal with the threats of further attacks of the kind perpetrated on 11 September, that should have been done. But the Security Council resolutions had failed to make the Taliban deal with the Al Qaeda terrorists. The view was taken that all means possible had been used short of force. So one of the criteria for the use of force in self-defence had been met. Force was necessary because every other means had been used. Further attacks could take place at any time; there was unlikely to be any warning. The military action was forward-looking to prevent imminent future attacks, rather than a backward-looking act of retaliation for what had gone before. This was made clear in the letters to the Security Council reporting action against Afghanistan, which relied on the justification for the military action as the need to take action in anticipatory self-defence. The UK letter for example explained that troops were being used '...in exercise of the inherent right of individual and collective self-defence, recognised in Article 51 following the terrorist outrage of 11 September, to avert the continuing threat of attacks from the same source.'[1]

Are there legal difficulties in categorizing the military action that took place as self-defence? The questions raised in this context include the following. First, may a State use force in self-defence against terrorist non-state actors? Secondly, may force be used in relation to a State which is not itself responsible for the attacks? Thirdly, what are the rules of international humanitarian law that apply if the actor on one side is a State or States, and on the other a group of terrorists?

There is considerable support for the argument that a State is entitled to use force in self-defence against a non-state actor which has used or is threatening imminent force against that State, where the threat cannot be averted in any other way. In the case of Afghanistan, Security Council resolutions 1368(2001) and 1373(2001) explicitly referred to the right of self-defence, references that would be difficult to understand if they did not have some relevance to the terrorist group which had carried out the atrocities. And NATO States members made a declaration on 12 September in relation to Article 5 of the North Atlantic Treaty,[2] which recognized that this was an armed attack against the US. Furthermore – why not? The *Caroline* case itself concerned non-state actors. Finally, there is nothing in the Charter or in common sense to say that if a terrorist group can use as much force as a State itself can use, the threatened State may not be able to act to avert further attacks.

In any event, the conflict in Afghanistan did involve the authorities of the State, not merely non-state actors. Military action was taken against the Taliban as well as against Al Qaeda. Was that justifiable? If the threat posed by Al Qaeda was attributable directly to the Taliban regime under the international law rules on State responsibility[3] the use of force in self-defence was clearly justifiable. That would

---

1   The Government explained in the House of Lords through Baroness Amos: 'The military coalition is engaged in an armed conflict in self-defence against those who perpetrated the terrorist attack of 11 September and those who harbour and sustain them.'

2   'The parties agree that an armed attack against one or more of them in Europe or North America shall be considered an attack against them all, and consequently they agree that, if such an armed attack occurs, each of them, in exercise of the right of individual or collective self-defence recognised by Article 51 of the Charter of the United Nations, will assist the party or parties so attacked by taking forthwith, individually, and in concert with the other parties, such action as it deems necessary, including the use of armed force, to restore and maintain the security of the North Atlantic area.' On this point see also Marco Pertile's chapter in this volume on NATO.

3   Article VIII of the International Law Commission articles on State responsibility provides as follows: 'The conduct of a person or group of persons shall be considered an act of a State under international law if the person or group of persons is in fact acting on the instructions of, or under the direction or control of, that State in carrying out the conduct.' The ILC in its commentary on the Article draws on the Nicaragua case (Military and Paramilitary Activities in and against Nicaragua (Nicaragua v United States of America 1986)) in the International Court of Justice; the Court analysed the notion of control in relation to the US

have been so if the Al Qaeda network acted on the instructions of or under the control of the Taliban regime, or if the Taliban assets were integrated with those of the Al Qaeda network or, probably, if the Taliban assets directly supported Al Qaeda and it was therefore necessary to neutralize them to avert the threat from Al Qaeda. There was also a question whether it was necessary to weaken the military power on which the Taliban regime depended so as to end the threat from Al Qaeda and to allow the threat to be dealt with. In this last case the acts of the terrorists may not have been attributed to the Taliban administration under international law, but without such action the threat from Al Qaeda could not have been averted. The argument was that the threat came from Al Qaeda but that without the regime itself being neutralised, the threatened attack could not be effectively dealt with.

So, in Afghanistan the conflict concerned not only the non-state actors but also the administration of the State. Certainly, in the UK at least, we categorized this as an interstate conflict, and the Geneva Conventions in relation to an international conflict were quite clearly applicable. That was also the view of the US at that time.

The more difficult question relates to a terrorist group operating from a State which bears no responsibility for the group's actions. We need to suppose the example of a failed or failing State with no effectively functioning administration. The administration may be willing to deal with terrorists in its country by criminal justice means, but may be simply unable to; it may be willing to hand them over to another State for prosecution or trial but be unable to find them. But for political reasons it may be unwilling to allow the military forces of a large military power into its territory to deal with those terrorists. International law does not attribute responsibility for those terrorists to that State. But supposing there is the threat of an imminent attack from the terrorists concerned: is the threatened State entitled to take action in self-defence to avert it, if there is no alternative way of dealing with the attack?

It may of course be possible for the threatened State to resort to the Security Council in these kinds of circumstances. But in the hypothetical example given here, suppose that there is an obstacle in going to the Council, suppose that there is a Council member who is going to veto any authorization, or suppose that there is not enough time because the threatened attack is so imminent. This is a difficult situation and different views have been taken. On one view, the traditional rules of international law require that there be no intervention in a sovereign State (even

---

and the *contras*, and stated: 'Despite the heavy subsidies and other support provided to them by the United States, there is no clear evidence of the United States having actually exercised such a degree of control in all fields as to justify treating the contras as acting on its behalf... All the forms of the United States participation mentioned above, and even the general control by the respondent State over a force with a high degree of dependency on it, would not in themselves mean, without further evidence, that the United States directed or enforced the perpetration of the acts contrary to human rights and humanitarian law alleged by the applicant State.' Thus while the US was held responsible for its own support for the *contras*, only in certain individual instances were the acts of the *contras* themselves held attributable to it, based upon actual participation of an direction given by that State.

a so-called failed State) unless that State itself is responsible for the attack. The ordinary rules of State responsibility apply. On this view, international law would not allow the use of force against non-state actors within the territory of a State not itself responsible for a threatened attack. On another view, force may be used against the terrorist group whatever the conduct of the State concerned, provided that the criteria for the use of force in self-defence are strictly adhered to and in good faith: in accordance with those criteria force may be used only if there is an armed attack (or the threat of an imminent armed attack), the force must be proportionate to the need to avert the attack and the use of force must be necessary as being the only means possible to avert the attack. A further view would allow action in self-defence but only if the State in which the terrorist group was found was regarded as harbouring the terrorists, either actively or by implicitly giving approval.

If self-defence is permissible against the terrorist group in those circumstances, the question is raised as to the appropriate rules of international humanitarian law (*jus in bello*) that are applicable. If there is a conflict between a State and a terrorist group in another State but the latter State is not involved in the conflict, what kind of armed conflict is it? Is this a non-international armed conflict within Article 3 of Geneva Conventions?

It may be that the case of Afghanistan was so unusual as not to require further discussion. I am not sure however that the circumstances will never happen again. It may be that the proper course to take in circumstances such as these is always to seek authorization from the Security Council. In the case of Afghanistan, for example, why did not the US and allied forces go to the Council for authorization under Chapter VII, even though they may have been entitled to act in self-defence? There was time to do so. There was nothing then to indicate that the Council would not have given the authorisation needed. In the days immediately following the atrocities of 11 September, other Council members, with the whole world, were in entire sympathy with the US, and would very likely have given whatever was asked.

But it is unrealistic, and not required by the Charter, to demand that in circumstances where a State is threatened by a terrorist group it will always be necessary to resort to the Security Council; in this world that is not always going to be possible. The possibility of recourse to self-defence is always likely to be necessary. We can hope that the International Court of Justice may address some of these questions when and if it gives its advisory opinion on the Legal Consequences of the Construction of a Wall in the Occupied Palestinian Territory.[4] In Jordan's written submissions, for example, the question was addressed as to whether the construction of the wall can be classified as a measure of self-defence against what are considered to be armed attacks against Israel. It certainly could be an interesting Opinion if it does deal with that kind of question.

I have raised the questions. I have not answered all of them.

---

4   The Advisory Opinion was given by the International Court of Justice on 9 July 2004 [note by the Editor].

Giuseppe Nesi

Thank you very much, Elizabeth. You have raised a mountain of questions. I am sure that the other panellists will provide some answers. Now I give the floor to Jordan Paust.

Jordan J. Paust

Actually Elizabeth has raised some of the points that I would like to raise. I would like to provide you with an approach, not necessarily the 'Answer', but one possible answer. Some of you might disagree with what I am about to say, but that's partly why it is an interesting conference.

Starting by assessing that the *Caroline* incident was a recognition of supposed customary international law, what was the *Caroline* case about? It involved really something like an armed insurgency, partly from within Canada and from within the US. In a nutshell, this oppressor from the north, the UK, beat up on this weak developing State, the US, and entered our territory without our consent to attack the ship *Caroline* when it was docked in US waters in a US port. We decried the illegal use of force in our territory. The *Caroline* incident is recognized as a situation involving what we call non-state actor attackers. So the *Caroline* incident is in fact relevant under customary international law and there was a recognition by the United Kingdom and the US that non-state actor attacks can 'trigger claims of self-defence' (whether anticipatory self-defence or not is quite debatable) and I agree that this is so.

I also agree that the Security Council and NATO recognized the right of self-defence with respect to Al Qaeda non-state actor attacks. Certainly Al Qaeda is a non-state actor. Again, from earlier discussion, Al Qaeda did not attempt to represent a State as far as I know. They do not simplistically represent a 'nation,' another actor in the international legal process. Al Qaeda is not a belligerent without recognition as a belligerent, as in the Confederate States of America in the case of the US civil war in the 1860s, when Great Britain and other countries preferred to recognize the Confederate States of America as belligerent, thus triggering application of all of the laws of war to that armed conflict. Also, Al Qaeda does not control a territory. They do not have something like a government. They might have something like a military force because there are certain cells that operate apparently under what used to be a command structure, but they do not seem to meet the minimal criteria for an insurgency – which would trigger according to Article 3 in Protocol II of the Geneva Conventions. And I would say that the laws of war then cannot apply to a conflict with Al Qaeda. There cannot be a 'war' with Al Qaeda as such. And I think it is important that the international community has refused to recognize applicability of the 1949 Geneva Conventions to a circumstance of armed violence below the level of an insurgency. Common Article 3 of the 1949 Conventions was radical at that time and even with adoption of the 1977 Protocols the international community has refused to apply the laws of war below the level of insurgency. There is a certain danger that might follow if you do. For example, Al Qaeda might claim war victories, combatant status, that the laws of war do apply and that they can engage in a lawful targeting of military targets. Some of this might or might not be preferable in terms of limiting social violence, but it would be radically new in the application of humanitarian law.

With respect to the intervention in Afghanistan, I am one who believes that because of *Caroline* especially and because, as Elizabeth said, there is nothing in Article 51 that limits the process of armed attack which triggers the right to self-defence to state actor attacks and because of the history of tolerance of self-defence in the past against non-state actor attacks, that it is a preferable and policy-serving interpretation of the Charter, although some refer to this as the 'textualist' approach. The framers of the UN Charter knew how to use the word 'State' in Article 2 paragraph 4, in terms of limiting three types of use of force, and from the face of the instrument they choose not to use the term 'State' in Article 51 – so I think that Article 51 can be triggered by non-state actor attacks. And here there is where Elizabeth and I disagree a bit: I believe that the US, for example (because I am an American?, but I do not think so), would have had a right to attack Al Qaeda in Afghanistan with limited use of weaponry and if there had been an avoidance of attacking Taliban military forces. Of course when we were there on 7 October 2001, we immediately hit all the Taliban positions that we could as well, but I think we were involved in an international war at that time, as soon as we went in, because we were fighting the *de facto* government of Afghanistan (and for some countries, the *de jure* government), the Taliban.

If you can go in and target those who are engaged in ongoing processes of armed attack against you, your nationals, your embassies abroad, this is permissible under Article 51 in terms of self-defence. Are you at war with Al Qaeda? No. You cannot be. But was the US use of force against the Taliban permissible under Article 51? I think that that was highly problematic and it might have even been illegal. Why? Because what were the Taliban doing? They did not finance Al Qaeda; it seems just the reverse. Was the Taliban regime the government of a harbouring State? A failed State? I do not think so. They were belligerents under the laws of war, engaged in a belligerency with the Northern Alliance before the US intervention. They were controlling most of the territory of Afghanistan. They had a government. They could field an army. They had a recognizable group of people within their sway. They met all the criteria for belligerent status, with outside recognition as a belligerent and they even had three or four States that recognized the Taliban government as the legitimate government of Afghanistan.

With respect to Al Qaeda attacks on the US, its embassies and nationals, direct responsibility of the Taliban has not been publicly proven. Additionally, you need a direct involvement of the Taliban in the process of armed attack by Al Qaeda to create a circumstance when it would be permissible to use force against the State that is otherwise indirectly involved. In other words, merely because the State is harbouring non-state actors who engage in an armed attack or is financing the terrorist activities, the use of armed force against the State is not permissible under Article 51.

This point was recognized by the ICJ in *Nicaragua v. United States of America* in 1986. I do not think that the interpretation of Article 51 made in that case has been changed, and I think that that interpretation is still preferable from a policy-oriented point of view. I am not just a literalist in terms of Article 51. I think that it is preferable to read the article restrictively. The article expressly requires the existence of an initiation of an 'armed attack'. If we adopt a 'process' approach to determine when an actual attack has begun, we can recognize that self-defence can be permissible at the start of the process of armed attack, not merely near the end of a process of attack.

In Texas, as I understand, if you know someone is gunning for you, you can go after them, you do not have to wait until they come to your home and aim a weapon at your head. In Boston, I understand, you have to wait until they are ready to pull the trigger before you can engage in lawful self-defence. I am open to use of a conceptualization of a process of 'attack'. Thus, if you know that the attack has started, or especially if the process is ongoing, you can engage in responsive force in self-defence once the process starts and during the process you are not engaged in reprisal actions when you respond, which are illegal under the Charter, but you are engaged in self-defence against ongoing processes of armed attack.

I am opposed to claims to permissibility of anticipatory self-defence, when armed force is used prior to a supposedly imminent use of armed force against you. I am opposed to the 'Bush doctrine', which, on a continuum concerning supposedly triggering events such as armed attacks, anticipatory self-defence, and pre-emptive self-defence, is far beyond the triggering circumstance of pre-emptive self-defence.

The Bush doctrine is contained in a US national security strategy and it claims a broad unilateral authority (that is really unsupportable under international law) to use military force against 'rogue States and their terrorist clients before they are able to threaten or use weapons of mass destruction' or 'to pre-empt emerging threats' or 'to counter a sufficient threat to national security'. The US administration is claiming something that is somewhat moronic: the right to target States that are posing an 'imminent threat'. Logically, an 'imminent threat' is not even a threat. 'They might threaten us someday.' On the continuum, that sort of claim is, let us call it, way over on the right. 'They could threaten us' is different even from 'they do threaten us.' This is not a circumstance involving an imminent threat of action, which would be closer to an anticipatory self-defence theory; for example, 'they are just about ready to fire the weapons'. After World War I, Germany was found to have violated international law at least twice. Germany stated that they had violated the Treaty of Neutrality with Belgium because they knew the French were about to go in. That was denounced by the international community. In World War II, Germans said 'We had to go into Norway because we knew they were about to go in'. I think pre-emptive self-defence was denounced, although there was a little ambiguity in the opinions and judgments concerning that. I think that the international community has denounced pre-emptive self-defence. In any event, the claim is too dangerous and perhaps the Bush doctrine evidences how dangerous this can become: you threaten our national security and we can use military forces against you. It is a rather far-reaching doctrine.

I think that some people have been confused about the *Caroline* case and I would like to go back to that, just to exemplify why I think the use of force by the Canadians, by the UK, would have been justifiable against those who were involved in an insurgent attack against Canada at that time, but not against the US as such. *Caroline* really did not involve anticipatory self-defence. There had been ongoing attacks by insurgent groups, both within and outside Canada. The *Caroline* had been carrying troops, supplies and weaponry especially to carry out the continuous process of the attack against the government in Canada. In context, that direct involvement of the ship and crew in processes of armed attack triggers the right of responsive self-defence. I would say that there was an ongoing armed attack. Article 51 would be triggered because of the ongoing attack. It was not a measure of anticipatory self-defence. The technical terms used in communications by UK and US elites were not 'anticipatory self-defence', but simply 'self-defence'. If you look at the US claim, it was rather more restrictive than Article 51 of the Charter. According to US Secretary Daniel Webster, you cannot even use self-defence when you are under attack unless your particular method of response is necessary and proportionate, leaving no other choice. That is what he was saying. He was not saying that you can engage in an anticipatory self-defence when the first attack is imminent. We were complaining that the UK could have waited until the particular ship, the *Caroline*, went into Canadian waters as opposed to attacking the ship when it was in US waters. You did not have to come into our territory to hit that ship. Maybe today you have to hit that ship in the foreign territory: for example, if the ship is in foreign waters but the ship has nuclear weapons and you cannot wait until the nuclear weapons are fired, but that would be anticipatory self-defence that some might accept today although the US clearly would not have accepted anticipatory self-defence in the nineteenth century. Where there is an ongoing process of armed attack, that is where I draw the line, Article 51 is triggered and you can engage in responsive self-defence.

Today, anticipatory self-defence is too dangerous, especially when you have people that want to extend it to a pre-emptive self-defence. You could disagree and consider that some forms of anticipatory self-defence should be tolerated, but military force must be imminent. There is then another problem: who decides whether it is imminent? I think that the drafters of the United Nations Charter knew about this problem of unilateral determination. They did two things. First, they limited self-defence to the circumstance 'if an armed attack occurs'. This phrase is unavoidable and no matter what you think customary international law tolerated in the past, Article 51 expressly limits 'the inherent right' of self-defence by using the phrase 'if an armed attack occurs'. The trigger of 'armed attack' presents an objectively determinable circumstance, one not left to a unilateralist interpretation of events by the State seeking to use armed force in alleged self-defence. Second, they turned the power to address threats to the peace over to the Security Council, partly so that one State would not unilaterally determine that someone poses a threat and then use military force against that State. So clearly, I am not speaking as a person from the Bush administration, nor do I agree with the so-called Bush doctrine.

Giuseppe Nesi

Your description of all these matters led me to feel myself on the border between self-defence and the violation of Article 2 paragraph 4 of the Charter. You really gave the idea of what is the heart of the matter. I think that Professor Abi-Saab will add something to this interpretation.

Georges Abi-Saab

I do not know whether I shall add something, but I want to exercise self-defence, because in a meeting about a month ago I gave Elizabeth a short article I wrote about terrorism[5] and she told me that she is going to 'attack me'.

I want first of all to present the general lines of my thoughts on this subject of terrorism that has been suddenly thrust on us and into the limelight.

The title of this panel discussion: 'Terrorism, international security and the use of force' contains three elements. What is the triangular relation between them? To answer this question I would slightly reformulate the title as 'Terrorism: collective security or individual use of force?'. How can we best face terrorism? By collective security or by individual use of force, self-defence if you want? I think the systemic preference of international law goes in the direction of the first alternative. Terrorism is not a new phenomenon. The first World War was triggered by an act of terrorism. So what is new about it today? You all probably know the book by Joseph Stiglitz (the recent winner of the Nobel Prize for economics) entitled 'Globalisation and its discontents'. Indeed, one of the discontents of globalization is that terrorism has been globalized. The question is then how to react to this globalized phenomenon through international law. In the US, they speak of 'war against terrorism'. For me, this is a rhetorical formula, like 'war against poverty'. It is a call for exceptional mobilization against a threatening scourge. But can we take it literally, calling on the law of war? Michael Howard wrote a very elegant piece in *Foreign Affairs* entitled 'What's in a name?', showing all the perversions of using the rhetoric of war in this context; the same as one of my former students, Frederic Mégret, in an article in the *European Journal of International Law* of 2002, with the title '"War"? Legal semantics and the move to violence'. Why do I consider that there is a problem here? That we are perverting the legal order by speaking of war in this respect?

War, in the technical sense, is an armed conflict necessarily involving internationally recognizable entities which are capable of being territorially defined. Let us answer the question of the *jus in bello* raised by Elizabeth: [does this extend

---

5 Reference is here to G. Abi-Saab, *The Proper Role of International Law in Combating Terrorism*, in *Chinese Journal of International Law*, 2002, pp. 304-312 [note by the Editor].

to] the conflict between two States or a State and a liberation movement struggling for self-determination over a particular territory – even if the confines of the territory of the State or of the liberation movement are not precisely defined? If the answer is in the negative, we do not have an international armed conflict. Even a non-international armed conflict is also territorially defined. Common Article 3 refers to an 'armed conflict ... occurring in the territory of a High Contracting Party', between belligerents belonging to the same party. Once there is a belligerent party from another State or if the conflict spills over beyond the boundaries of the State, it is no longer a non-international armed conflict. So technically, we cannot situate terrorism in either of these two exclusively recognizable categories in international humanitarian law. What then is the *jus in bello* applicable in the case Elizabeth spoke of?

Moreover, once you say you are applying the *jus in bello*, you are bound by its fundamental principle, the principle of the equality of the parties; you have to give the terrorist groups exactly the same standing as the US or any other country that is using force against them. You give them immunity for any act that qualifies as a mere act of war, so they can blow up all your military installations, oil reservoirs, etc. If they are taken, you have to treat them as prisoners of war. Is this the model that has been followed? And is it on the policy level the best model for dealing with terrorism? So much for the *jus in bello*.

As for the *jus ad bellum*, and particularly the question of self-defence, I am sorry to disagree with both Elizabeth and Jordan about the continued significance of the *Caroline* case. Until the Briand-Kellog Pact, we were living under the so-called 'theory of indifference'. The dominant opinion among States and international lawyers was that international law does not limit the right to use force, to resort to war. The Briand-Kellog Pact tried to change this situation but was full of holes. The Charter of the UN operated a radical shift with Article 2, para. 4. We moved from a system of general liberty or licence to a system of comprehensive prohibition. Force can be used individually only in self-defence. The use of social force in the name of the international community under Chapter VII is another matter. What was then the role of self-defence in the old system? It belonged to what used to be called 'measures short of war', a sub-category of a general liberty. But with the Charter, it became an exception to a comprehensive prohibition. Contrary pre-existing custom has been abrogated by this prohibition. This introduced a great change in the nature of self-defence. It is true that in practice the Charter has not always been respected, but that is another matter. I am speaking about the structure and the logic of the system. Can self-defence be used against non-state actors? Of course, a State can defend itself. The question arises, however, once it crosses into the territory of another State. Article 2 para. 4 prohibits the use of force against the territorial integrity of any State. To say that to attack just a bunch of individuals on the territory of a State, or bombarding its suspected nuclear installations, does not undermine the territorial integrity of that State, is legal nonsense. So, how can it be done, if at all, in the case of terrorism? And if so in which circumstances? In my view, this is only possible if the territorial State is complicit in the terrorist acts. In the Taliban case there was an active implication one way or another. I think that if international law has to develop a little in order to face the actual situation, this would be by firming up the obligation of due diligence of the territorial State. That is one area where discussion is possible; but not beyond. Otherwise, strong States, the US for example, will feel free to bombard a pharmaceutical factory or anything they may suspect to be related to terrorism, or to weapons of mass destruction, on the basis of flimsy evidence, as experience has shown, thereby spreading greater terror themselves. We really drive a very big hole in the guarantee of the Charter, in Article 2, para. 4, reducing it to naught.

Does this mean that there is nothing to be done? Of course not. Self-defence is a circumstantial and conjectural right according to the Charter. It is against an 'armed attack', which means that it has to be reactive to something that has started to move. The last decision of the International Court of Justice in the *Platform* case is very clear on that point. The Court said that use of force in self-defence can only be against an armed attack, thereby excluding any anticipatory action in the name of self-defence. If you tell me that the opinion of the Court does not count, there is no need to discuss international law any longer.

How can we then confront terrorism? The first alternative is to consider the struggle against terrorism as a question of collective security. Here I for once agree with someone with whom I rarely agree, Michael Reisman, who wrote just after 11 September a piece in the *American Journal of International Law* entitled 'In defense of world public order'. Reisman said that one of the results of the attack was 'the sheer perception of a common danger, not simply to an individual State, but to the system of world public order'. Indeed, the real danger of globalized terrorism became very apparent. There was a feeling of a real threat to the structure of world order, calling for a collective response at the same level of that threat. I would interpret the two resolutions of the Security Council adopted in September 2001 in this sense. The international community has greater powers than an individual State exercising self-defence, as it can use collective measures preventively. Collective measures have a lower threshold because they can be used against a threat while individual self-defence cannot.

Are we taking this route? I return to what Elizabeth has said: suppose that you have a failing or a failed State and it does not accept that another State attacked by terrorists pursues them on its territory. I do not see how self-defence can be invoked here, unless the territorial State, whether failed or not, has played a role in the attack. However, if this is the collective will, if the Security Council orders it, then it becomes a different matter.

This is why I believe that we have to keep in mind all the systemic implications of the actions and justifications we use. Let us not sink the ship by making big holes in it in the name of pragmatism. Let us not justify blatant perversions of well entrenched legal concepts by saying that we can do nothing about such extensive use of force by the high and the mighty in violation of Article 2, para. 4 in the guise of self-defence against terrorism. Indeed, we can do something about such abuse. We can insist on saying that it is illegal, we can even insist on the illegality of action even if it emanates from the Security Council if it goes beyond its constitutional powers. The fact that there is no pre-established system of control of legality of actions whether of individual States or even the Security Council, does not render action in violation of the basic rules of international law legal. Such action may by chance fall before an international tribunal which can pass on its legality. The *Lockerbie* case provided such an opportunity. But the International Court of Justice shied away. The International Criminal Tribunal for the former Yugoslavia (ICTY), however, did not baulk in the *Tadic* case from passing on the legality of Security Council action, although it is itself a creation of the Council. There are even some internal tribunals which have come out against the legality of the sanctions decreed by the Security Council because of their violation of some basic human rights. This is my answer to the interrogations put to us and my plea at the same time.

Giuseppe Nesi

I am sure that Elizabeth is preparing some answers to the questions she made after your comments on that. I think some of the arguments that have been used by Georges Abi-Saab are similar to those that are going to be used by Ugo Villani who I invite to take the microphone.

Ugo Villani

I would like to talk exactly on the problem on the legality of the unilateral use of force by single States (or groups of States) against other States or on their territory in order to fight international terrorism. Considering that the customary rule (deriving from Article 2, para. 4, of the UN Charter and the corresponding provision of customary international law) is that States shall refrain in their international relations from the use and even from the threat of force, we must ask whether, in the fight against terrorism, an exception to the rule may be recognized.

The first possibility is whether an exception can be justified on the basis of the right to individual or collective self-defence; also whether this exception, even if it is expressly provided for by the Charter, corresponds to a norm of customary law, as the International Court of Justice has reaffirmed on several occasions. In practice the States which use force against other States as a reaction against terrorist attacks frequently justify their behaviour as exercising their right to self-defence.[6] The reference to the right to legitimate self-defence is clear and has been repeated from several quarters also as regards Operation Enduring Freedom, carried out as

---

6   Such was the case, for example, of Israel when, in 1985, it bombarded the PLO headquarters in Tunis, or of the US which, in a letter to the Security Council of 20 August 1998, declared that it had attacked Afghanistan and Sudan 'pursuant to the right to self-defence confirmed by Article 51 of the Charter of the United Nations' as a reaction to the bloody attacks carried out on 7 August against the US Embassies of Kenya and Tanzania.

a reaction to the terrorist attacks of 11 September 2001.[7] The right to legitimate self-defence was also invoked by international organizations such as NATO and the European Union, as well as by various States, including Italy, in order to justify their participation in the military operation or the legitimacy of the operation.

The framing of the use of force against terrorist attacks in self-defence, however, poses a series of problems. The first is whether an act of terrorism can constitute an 'armed attack' ('*aggression armée*') which, as has been said, is a necessary requisite for exercising such a right.

In general terms the answer would appear to be in the negative. Despite its ferocity, it is unlikely that a terrorist attack can represent an armed attack against a State as such.[8] At the same time, an act cannot be defined as 'armed attack' in order to justify the use of force in self-defence in the case of an attack against the bodies of a State, except in extreme cases where it is directed against the supreme organs of the State with the aim of 'beheading' it in terms of its institutional apparatus. In this latter case, indeed, it may be recognized that the armed attack has as its objective the sovereignty of the State, which is expressed as a whole by its supreme bodies of government.

Also the Security Council, in its numerous resolutions adopted in countering terrorism, has always and repeatedly defined acts of international terrorism as 'a threat to international peace and security', not as a 'breach of the peace', and even less as an aggression. We may remember in particular Resolution 1368 of 12 September 2001, immediately after the attack on the Twin Towers and on the Pentagon, and Resolution 1373 of 28 September 2001, which adopted a wide-ranging and complex series of measures against terrorism. In the former the Security Council declared it was determined to combat by all means 'threats to international peace and security caused by terrorist acts'; in the latter it reaffirmed that the attacks on the US, 'like any act of international terrorism, constitute a threat to international peace and security'. The Security Council has used similar terms in its more recent resolutions, in which

---

7   It was in these terms that already by 14 September the US Senate had expressed itself by stating that such attacks 'render it both necessary and appropriate that the United States exercise its right to self-defence'; and on 20 September President Bush spoke of an act of war against the US. Once Operation Enduring Freedom had begun, the US officially notified the President of the Security Council that it had undertaken, together with other States, an action of legitimate individual and collective self-defence following the terrorist attacks of 11 September 2001.

8   The latter – justifying a reaction of self-defence – is one aimed against the sovereignty, the political independence, the territory of a State, but not one which, for example, only involves the killing of civilians, even if this occurs in the territory of the State of which the victims are citizens; neither was the attack against American citizens at a Berlin nightclub in 1986 which led to the bombardment by the US of Libya, which was held to be an accomplice in the attack; nor, of course, can an alleged plot against a former head of State such as the one denounced by the US against ex-President Bush Sr. in April 1993 by Iraq to which the US reacted by bombing secret service headquarters in Baghdad on 26 June 1993 (with the deaths of civilians as 'collateral damage').

it adopts a general strategy for combating terrorism, such as Resolution 1456 of 20 January 2003 containing a declaration on the issue of combating terrorism, and in Resolution 1566 of 8 October 2004 ('terrorism in all its forms and manifestations constitutes one of the most serious threats to peace and security').

The qualification of acts of international terrorism as threats to peace and security has two important legal consequences: it in fact authorizes the Security Council to adopt measures (also involving the use of armed force) in accordance with Chapter VII of the Charter, which establishes the competence of the Security Council in undertaking an action with respect to threats to the peace (as well as in the presence of breaches of the peace or acts of aggression). This qualification excludes, on the contrary, the possibility that the State hit by an act of terrorism may use force in self-defence, since the threat to peace and security evidently does not represent an armed attack *being carried out*, as is required by Article 51 of the Charter.

Nevertheless, albeit in exceptional cases, an act of terrorism may reach a threshold of violence such that it may be assessed as an aggression against the territory of the State (or its sovereignty or political independence). This occurs when the act of terrorism produces huge effects and hits targets of particular strategic importance belonging to a State. For example, it would seem to be undeniable that the attacks of 11 September 2001, given the breadth of their destructiveness and the shockingly high number of deaths, and given the objectives that were hit, in particular the Pentagon, constitute an 'armed attack' in accordance with Article 51 of the Charter. Indeed, these attacks may be considered as the equivalent, at least according to one hypothesis, of acts of aggression as defined in the Definition of aggression adopted by the General Assembly of the United Nations with Resolution 3314 (XXIX) of 14 December 1974; that is, bombardment against the territory of a State (Article 3, *b*).

The possibility that acts of terrorism can be qualified as armed attacks would seem to emerge also from the above-mentioned resolutions 1368 and 1373 of the Security Council. In the preamble these resolutions recognize and reaffirm 'the inherent right of individual or collective self-defence' in accordance with the Charter. This reference to self-defence, in its generic formulation, cannot mean that, in the specific case of the attack of 11 September, the US had the right to resort to force against Afghanistan in exercising its right of self-defence. As has been pointed out, in these resolutions themselves such acts of international terrorism are qualified as a 'threat', not as a breach of international peace and security. Secondly, the Security Council did not carry out any ascertainment as to the responsibility of the attacks on the US. Indeed, Afghanistan (and Bin Laden) is not even mentioned. The reference to the right to self-defence, in my opinion, only means that, in the context of international terrorism, conditions may arise for resorting to self-defence, conditions which, however, must be verified in accordance with Article 51. The exceptional vastness of the destruction caused by the act of terrorism, such that it may be configured as an armed attack, constitutes the first condition necessary for resorting to self-defence.

A further difficulty in applying the right of self-defence derives from the need to attribute acts of terrorism to a State. In fact, the right of self-defence (like the general rule on the prohibition of the use of force) concerns international relationships between States, whereas acts of terrorism are usually criminal acts carried out by private individuals. In order for a State to use force against another State (or in its territory) in self-defence it is therefore necessary to attribute those acts to a State; in other words it is necessary for an act of terrorism to be 'considered an act of that State under international law' (Article VIII of the ILC draft articles on State Responsibility).

There would seem to be no doubt that acts of terrorism are attributable to a State if the latter organizes or actively supports them, or directly carries them out through its own agents. On this question it is worth remembering the Declaration on principles of international law concerning friendly relations and cooperation among States, in accordance with the Charter of the United Nations, passed by the General Assembly with Resolution 2625 (XXV) of 24 October 1970, which states that 'every State has the duty to refrain from organizing, instigating, assisting or participating in [...] terrorist acts in another State [...], when the acts referred to in the present paragraph involve a threat or use of force'. Acts of terrorism are attributed to the State even if they are carried out by a person or group of persons who do not have an official position in a State body but who are 'in fact acting on the instructions of, or under the direction or control of, that State in carrying out the conduct'.

In the case of private individuals, however, the level of involvement of the State must be clarified in order that the acts of terrorism may be attributable to that State.

In this regard the Tribunal for the Former Yugoslavia (Chamber of Appeals) assumed a fairly broad position in its judgment of 15 July 1999 on the Tadić case. According to this judgment, in order to attribute to a State the activities carried out by a group of individuals, in particular by an organized and hierarchically structured group such as a military unit or an armed band of irregular or rebel troops, it is sufficient that the group as a whole be under the 'overall control' of a State, while it is not required that any of the activities of the group be 'specifically imposed, requested or directed by the State' (para. 122). According to this interpretation it would be possible, for example, to hold Afghanistan responsible for the acts of terrorism carried out by Al Qaeda, given the relationship of close solidarity between that group and the Taliban government.

But a more restrictive interpretation was expressed by the International Court of Justice in its famous judgment of 27 June 1986 (*Nicaragua v. United States of America*). Here the Court declared that the US could not be considered responsible for acts contrary to international humanitarian law and to human rights committed by the *contras* in Nicaragua because, however wide the control, support and financing of such forces by the US might have been, *general* control was not sufficient to attribute to the US the acts in question. To this end it would have been necessary to show that the US had ordered or imposed the commission of such acts, whereas it was quite possible that they had been carried out by members of the anti-Sandinista forces outside the control of the US. In conclusion, according to the Court, 'for this conduct to give rise to legal responsibility of the United States, it would in principle have to be proved that that State had effective control of the military or paramilitary operations in the course of which the alleged violations were committed' (para. 115).

The necessity of control by the State not simply of a general character but with reference to specific acts by groups of individuals is fully in line with the solution provided in the above-mentioned Article 8 of the ILC draft articles on State Responsibility. As has been outlined already, this establishes the attribution of the conduct of private individuals to the State if they act under the control (or instructions or direction) of the State 'in carrying out the conduct'. Thus, there can be no doubt that the condition required cannot be met by a general (or generic) control of the State over individuals; this entails a specific control over the way they behave in carrying out specific acts of terrorism.

The recognition of the right of self-defence against acts of terrorism could be framed from a different perspective. In other words, it could be hypothesized that, in cases where, because of their gravity, acts of terrorism can be qualified as an armed attack, they may come within the notion of 'indirect aggression', in accordance with Article 3, *g*, of the above-mentioned Definition of aggression of 14 December 1974, held by the International Court of Justice as an expression of international customary law in its judgment of 27 June 1986 (para. 195). As is well known, this provision configures as an aggression both 'the sending by or on behalf of a State of armed bands, groups, irregulars or mercenaries, which carry out acts of armed force against another State of such gravity as to amount to the acts listed above', and 'its substantial involvement therein' ('*le fait de s'engager d'une manière substantielle dans une telle action*'). Here the expression 'its substantial involvement therein' can be interpreted not as referring to the sending of bands or other groups, but to the commission of acts of armed force; so the State could be considered as being responsible for an indirect aggression when it is substantially implicated in acts of terrorism against another State. Consequently, the latter State might react in exercising its right of individual self-defence (and third party States in the exercising of their right of collective self-defence).

This interpretation corresponds to the one expressed by the US in the letter of 7 October 2001 to the President of the Security Council in which the permanent representative of the US, in accordance with Article 51, informed the Security Council that its State, together with other States, had initiated actions in the exercise of its inherent right of individual and collective self-defence following the armed attacks that were carried out against the US on 11 September 2001. In this letter the US government declared that the massive and brutal attacks, of which the US had been the victim at the hands of the Al Qaeda organization, 'have been made possible by the decision of the Taliban regime to allow the parts of Afghanistan that it controls to be used by this organization as a base of operation'. The presupposition for resorting to the use of force in self-defence seems to consist in an aggression carried out by the Taliban regime by allowing part of the territory of Afghanistan to be used by Al Qaeda in carrying out the attack of 11 September.

The main problem here concerns the 'substantial' involvement of the territorial State in acts of terrorism. In my opinion this type of involvement requires ascertainment with reference to the specific case, by verifying whether the conduct of the State had a decisive effect on the commission of the acts of terrorism in question. This possibility seems to be more likely in the case of positive conduct, in support of terrorist groups, but it cannot be excluded, in principle, even in the case in which the State merely tolerates the presence on its territory of terrorist organizations.

However, it must be underlined that a restrictive position, which would seem to exclude the possibility of configuring an indirect aggression in the case of support for terrorist groups, was assumed by the International Court of Justice in the judgment of 27 June 1986. The Court affirmed that 'it may be considered to be agreed that an armed attack must be understood as including not merely action by regular armed forces across an international border', but also 'the sending by or on behalf of a State of armed bands, groups, irregulars or mercenaries, which carry out acts of armed force against another State of such gravity as to amount to' (*inter alia*) an actual armed attack conducted by regular forces, 'or its substantial involvement therein'. This description, contained in Article 3, paragraph (g) of the Definition of Aggression annexed to General Assembly Resolution 3314 (XXIX), may be taken to reflect customary international law. The Court sees no reason to deny that, in customary law, the prohibition of armed attack may apply to the sending by the State of armed bands to the territory of another State, if such an operation, because of its scale and effects, would have been classified as an armed attack rather than as a mere frontier incident had it been carried out by regular armed forces.

Nevertheless, the Court declared that the concept of 'armed attack' does not include 'also assistance to rebels in the form of the provision of weapons or logistical or other support'. This form of assistance, according to the Court, may constitute a breach of the prohibition of the threat or use of force, or even an intervention in the internal or external affairs of another State (para. 195); in other words, it may entail illicit acts, but of lesser gravity than those of armed aggression (para. 247) and thus unsuited in terms of justifying the resort to the use of force in self-defence. The Court mentioned in particular, among the less serious ways (with respect to aggression) of using force, the violation of the principle contained in the Declaration on Friendly Relations according to which every State has the duty to refrain from organizing, instigating, assisting or participating in terrorist acts in another State or acquiescing in organized activities within its territory directed towards the commission of such acts, when they involve a threat or use of force (para. 191).

In the light of this judgment the mere acquiescence of the State towards terrorist activities organized on its territory could never be defined as (indirect) aggression and thus the State that is the victim of an act of terrorism could not resort to the use of armed force against the first State in exercising its right of self-defence. And even in the case of active support of the territorial State for terrorist groups, the recognition of aggression, and the consequent right of self-defence, would be extremely problematic.

Also in the case where an act of terrorism, because of its gravity and the degree of violence used, can be qualified as an armed attack and is legally attributable to a

State, self-defence is subordinate to the conditions established by Article 51 of the Charter and by customary international law, such as necessity and proportionality.

The latter in particular should be interpreted in the sense that the use of force in self-defence must be committed with the aim of fending off the armed attack. In the case where such an attack is carried out by means of acts of terrorism, therefore, the limit of proportionality implies in principle that the victim State may use force in order to target terrorist bases, training grounds, logistic and military instruments used in order to ward off terrorist attacks; but self-defence cannot consist in the massive and generalized use of armed force, aimed at 'defeating' the State accused of being responsible for the acts of terrorism, as occurred in the reaction of the US against Afghanistan after the terrorist attacks of 11 September. In this case the reaction of the US consisted in outright 'war', as can be seen both from the breadth and intensity of the military violence used, and from the element of *animus bellandi*; that is, the will to defeat Afghanistan by overthrowing the Taliban government, an objective reached with the fall of Kabul on 13 November 2001. It would seem hard to deny, then, that the reaction of the US went well beyond the limit of proportionality.

However, Operation Enduring Freedom failed to eliminate the Al Qaeda terrorist organization (or even to neutralize its leader Bin Laden). From this point of view, then, it is legitimate to wonder whether it was really 'necessary' with respect to the objective of defending itself from such an organization and, in more general terms, if 'war' is a 'necessary' instrument for combating international terrorism or, rather, whether it did not turn out to be not only exaggerated and disproportionate but also inefficacious as a response.

It should also be underlined that, in order for a State to be able to exercise its right of self-defence, it is necessary for the act of terrorism to be occurring (as is declared in Article 51); that is, it must actually be taking place. It is not enough, for example, for there simply to be the fear of an act of terrorism; in the presence of such a fear a State is required to ask the Security Council to adopt measures necessary for eliminating the threat to the peace. This must be reaffirmed also in the light of the doctrine of pre-emptive defence, as outlined by US President Bush on 1 June 2002 at the West Point Military Academy and included in the document on 'The National Security Strategy of the United States of America' of 17 September 2002. As is well known, this doctrine establishes that, faced with new threats deriving from 'rogue States' and from terrorist groups and the high likelihood that they may use weapons of mass destruction against the US, the latter can act using armed force pre-emptively to eliminate such a threat before the rogue State and their terrorist clients are able to threaten or use such weapons against the US or its allies or friends. According to this doctrine the possibility of resorting to force is not subordinate to an armed attack, and not even to the certain prediction of such an attack: an anticipatory action is necessary 'even if uncertainty remains as to the time and place of the enemy's attack'.

As the Secretary-General of the United Nations Kofi Annan pointed out in a speech of 23 September 2003 on opening the 58th General Assembly, this doctrine clashes with the Charter. The latter allows for the use of force in self-defence only if *an armed attack occurs* against a State (and until the Security Council has taken measures necessary to maintain international peace and security) (Article 51). The condition of an armed attack implies that the use of force in self-defence is lawful only in the case where the attack is still actually in progress and with the sole aim of warding off such an attack. In the hypothesis of the danger of an attack, the State involved is required to take the question before the Security Council which has the duty of ascertaining the real existence of a threat to the peace and of adopting possible measures for removing that threat.

In international case law and in the practice of the United Nations there is no reference whatsoever to any right to pre-emptive self-defence. On the contrary, in the past the Security Council, with Resolution 487 of 19 June 1981 (adopted with the favourable vote of the US), severely condemned the bombing carried out by Israel against a nuclear plant being built in Iraq (Osirak), with the aim of eliminating a threat against its own territory. Analogous condemnations were expressed by the General Assembly of the International Agency for Atomic Energy and by the General Assembly of the United Nations. As has already been observed, moreover, in the light of general international law, the use of force in self-defence must respect the limit of necessity. Faced with the fear of a possible terrorist attack it is doubtful that no alternatives exist to armed force; thus it cannot be deemed as a necessity.

In the light of the rules on self-defence, in the end, the use of force against acts of terrorism would seem to be admissible only in exceptional cases, and under the conditions and with the limits that have been outlined above. But one may wonder whether the use of armed force may be considered lawful on the basis of a new exception to the prohibition of force, which allows for such use as a form of fighting against international terrorism, in particular when it is sponsored by a State. A hypothesis of this sort could be taken into consideration on the basis of the frequent references to the need to combat terrorism, made by some States in recent years to justify their own military interventions. This emerges also from the new Strategic Concept approved by the Heads of State and Government participating in the meeting of NATO on 23 and 24 April 1999; here terrorism is included among the 'other risks' (other than an armed attack) which might entail a reaction by the Alliance not based on Article 5 of the NATO Treaty (on self-defence).

If one examines actual practice, however, such an exception cannot be held as existing. In fact, the attitude of the United Nations and, more in general, of the international community with regard to military intervention as a reaction to terrorist attacks has usually been one of condemnation (except in the case of the intervention in Afghanistan after 11 September).[9]

---

9   It is worth remembering, for example, Security Council Resolution 262 of 31 December 1968 which strongly condemned Israel's attack on Beirut airport; Resolutions 508 and 509, respectively of 5 and 6 June 1982, condemning the Israeli 'Peace in Galilee' operation against Lebanon; Resolution 573 of 4 October 1985 which qualified the Israeli attack on Tunis of 1 October as an act of armed aggression. Analogously, the bombing of Tripoli and Benghasi carried out by the US on 14 April 1986, justified as a reaction to the alleged complicity of

A less clear-cut international reaction – but certainly not one of approval – was the one concerning the attacks carried out by the US against objectives considered to be linked to terrorism, in Afghanistan and Sudan on 20 August 1998. Neither the UN Security Council nor the General Assembly passed judgment on those attacks; and some Western countries such as Australia, France, Germany, Japan, Spain and the UK showed support, or at least sympathetic understanding, for the operation. Nevertheless, there was no lack of strong protest. Besides, of course, the protests of Afghanistan and Sudan – which declared that the US missile attack represented an 'iniquitous act of aggression' – there were those of Iran, Iraq, Libya, Pakistan, Russia, and Yemen, as well as the explicit condemnation (at least as regards the attack on Sudan) by the League of Arab States.

There was a different reaction from the international community towards Operation Enduring Freedom following the terrorist attacks of 11 September 2001. This operation received the approval and support not only of Western countries, beginning with NATO; but military support and access to their own airspace was given also by other States such as Georgia, Pakistan, Qatar, Saudi Arabia, and Uzbekistan, and support even came from China, Egypt and Russia. Even the States of the Organization of the Islamic Conference asked the US not to extend the military operation beyond Afghanistan, but without actually condemning the action being taken.

This attitude of acquiescence, if not of open approval, towards the Anglo-American intervention could lead us to think that, after 11 September 2001, there has been a profound transformation in international law which, by loosening the prohibition of the use of force, has introduced a new exception to the prohibition, justified by the fight against terrorism (at least in the case of terrorism 'sponsored' by a State).

However, this line of interpretation is not convincing. There are various reasons that may have induced the States to approve American action: these are of an essentially political nature, such as solidarity with the US, the fear of appearing to the US as 'conniving' with terrorist groups, and the intent of being free to carry out 'internal' repression against terrorist groups (or defined as such) etc. But from this attitude it would not seem possible to conclude that there exists a juridical conviction (*opinio juris*) which, also according to the consistent case law of the International Court of Justice, is indispensable for the birth of a new general norm that derogates

---

Libya in their attack on a Berlin nightclub, was vigorously condemned by the UN General Assembly; Resolution 41/38 of 20 November 1986 (passed with 79 votes in favour, 28 against and 33 abstentions) 'condemns the military attack perpetrated against the Socialist People's Libyan Arab Jamahiriya on 15 April 1986, which constitutes a violation of the Charter of the United Nations and of international law, [...] calls upon all States to refrain from extending any assistance or facilities for perpetrating acts of aggression against the Libyan Arab Jamahiriya' and 'affirms the right of the Libyan Arab Jamahiriya to receive appropriate compensation for the material and human losses inflicted upon it'. The Organization of the Islamic Conference also condemned the attack with Resolution 21 of 26-29 January 1987, explicitly defining the US attack as 'aggression'.

from the prohibition of the use of force. On the other hand, the single episode of Enduring Freedom certainly cannot provide the element of the practice, which indeed – as has been pointed out – is not favourable to recognizing the use of force as a reaction to acts of terrorism. And it is worth underlining that, given the primary interest of the international community to which the rule prohibiting the use of force corresponds, any hasty reconstruction of exceptions to such a prohibition must be decidedly excluded.

Lastly, it should also be pointed out that Operation Enduring Freedom was justified mainly as the exercising of the right of individual or collective self-defence. Besides the US and NATO, other international organizations such as the European Union, as well as various States including Italy, have also expressed themselves in the same way. More in general it can be observed that the States which resort to force as a reaction to terrorist attacks usually justify themselves on the basis of the right of self-defence. We need merely recall – out of countless examples – the bombing of the PLO headquarters in Tunis by Israel in 1985, and the attacks against Afghanistan and Sudan by the US in 1998.

The constant reference – rightly or wrongly – to the right of self-defence shows that States at least doubt whether the fight against terrorism is a sufficient reason that could legitimize the use of armed force, and that they prefer to fall back on the safer and more consolidated cause of justification recognized by Article 51 of the Charter and by general international law.

The considerations that have been made so far induce us to uphold that, except in exceptional circumstances, because of the gravity of the acts of terrorism and because a State may be deemed as responsible for them, in principle it is not lawful to resort to the unilateral use of armed force in the fight against international terrorism.

The difficulty (other than in such exceptional cases) of applying the norms on self-defence highlights the fact that, perhaps, the use of force is not the most suitable means for combating terrorism, either from a juridical, or from a moral or practical viewpoint. It is not suitable from a juridical viewpoint because the norms on self-defence are created and framed in terms of the relationships between States (as is the rule on the prohibition of the use of force), and it requires a considerable degree of adaptation to apply them to a phenomenon, namely terrorism, which is usually to be seen as a crime carried out by individuals or groups of individuals. It is not the most suitable means from a moral viewpoint because the use of force in the territory of a State where there are terrorist bases entails violence and destruction and the loss of innocent lives, whose number will never be known but which, as presumably was the case in Operation Enduring Freedom, may be even higher than the victims of terrorism. Lastly, it is not suitable from a practical viewpoint because, as the activism of Al Qaeda shows, the true leaders of the organization usually manage to escape from indiscriminate bombings.

The most efficacious means of combating international terrorism remains, in my opinion, that of international cooperation through judicial means, through intelligence and police operations, through blocking the financing of terrorism, without forgetting the need for political measures aimed at removing situations of oppression, of wide-scale violations of human rights, of poverty and underdevelopment, which is where terrorism often takes root.

Giuseppe Nesi

Thank you very much. You have offered us some possible exit strategies with regard to the struggle against terrorism. I think that this last point of your intervention in reference to international cooperation and the root causes of terrorism is extremely helpful in order to provide some guidelines for the future.

I think that the debate has been so far so interesting that I feel obliged to have another round of short interventions before closing our meeting. We will follow the same order as before.

Elizabeth Wilmshurst

Of course the use of force is not the best way to fight terrorism. I began with that and I will stress it again. Force can be used only as a last resort and only if all of the other means don't work.

On an anticipatory self-defence, I would like to say just a word. I am beginning to think that it is just a question of semantics and the only difference between me and Jordan is just the use of language. In Britain I think I am right in saying that almost every international lawyer (and there are many) is happy to use the term 'anticipatory self-defence' in the same way that Jordan is using 'self-defence' without 'anticipatory'. If you have an attack, as a matter of caution you try to stop politicians from saying we must respond; we must retaliate; we must have reprisals. What you try to put their attention on is, 'Is there another imminent attack in the wings?' Only if there is can you use self-defence. So you are anticipating the next attack and therefore we are using that term. We are a million miles away from the US.

We could argue all day about Afghanistan; what I think is important, in discussing what is lawful, is that we agree on the criteria and I think there is very much [in common] between us on the criteria. International law has to depend on other people for the facts. And perhaps that is what is in dispute. But the most interesting thing is the question that, if you admit self-defence against a non state actor, and I think even George said, 'Yes you can defend yourself', then the question is, 'What about Article 2, para. 4? What happens about the fact that the non-state actor has to be in some State?' It is by the concept of due diligence on the State and I do not know whether you were saying, 'If a State does not apply due diligence in trying to get rid of the terrorists, then you bomb the State.' I would be glad if you would elaborate on that or, if not, what do you mean by due diligence there? And whether this is also the same as other people are saying, 'Now we have talked about States harbouring non-state actors, and harbouring is enough to justify the use against the state'. I think it is in this area that you have to consider whether international law needs to develop or whether we are really quite happy with it as it is. Thank you.

Jordan J. Paust

In terms of semantics, I would like to focus on process: you have one attack, you predict other attacks. I handle it with the word 'process' instead of the word 'anticipatory' with respect to the second attack, since the process of armed attack has already started.

I would like to stress another point: 'State responsibility' for various types of violations of international law is quite different than the type of responsibility that can trigger the permissibility of militarily targeting a State. For example a State can have state responsibility, be subject to juridical, economic, political, and diplomatic sanctions for 'having links' with non-state actor terrorists, not exercising due diligence in controlling its territory, harbouring terrorists, financing terrorists, tolerating terrorists – and the norm of non intervention could be triggered if the State is involved in some of these acts or omissions – but that is quite different than a circumstance where the State is directly participating in the armed attack by non-state terrorists. That is where I draw the line – the need for direct involvement in the armed attack. With respect to permissible self-defence against the State, I do not think the Taliban was directly involved in the Al Qaeda attacks on the US. British Intelligence may have the evidence of such direct involvement, but this raises the intellectual point that there is a need for objective evidence.

With respect to another issue: if the Security Council is addressing the matter under Article 39, do you lose your right of self-defence? Under Article 51, not unless the Security Council 'has taken measures necessary to maintain international peace and security'. Also, can the Security Council deny the right of self-defence? As part of the legal team for Bosnia-Herzegovina before the ICJ, we made the claim that the Security Council arms embargo against our client was illegal under the Charter because it tied two hands behind the back of our client where the border with Yugoslavia was fluid and the Bosnian Serbs were getting arms but the embargo only precluded our client from obtaining arms to defend itself. This is a violation of the right, of the inherent right, of self-defence.

You may disagree, but the issue raises another point: are there limits on the power of the Security Council under the Charter? I think that Article 24, para. 2, and Article 25 show us that there are limits, in terms of the language of the Charter. These limits involve the purposes and the principles of the Charter, evidenced, for example in the purposes and principles set forth in Article 1, 55.c (human rights). I do not think that the Security Council can violate human rights or self-determination of peoples and we are considering whether it can deny the inherent right of a State to engage in self-defence. People disagree.

In terms of Article 2, para. 4, Georges [Abi-Saab], I think Article 51 is more complex, because, if you have a right of self-defence, it overrides the prohibitions in Article 2, para. 4, whatever those are in Article 2.4. Similarly if the Security Council authorizes the use of force, as you agree, under Articles 39-42, with the duties under Articles 25 and 48, you have obviated any prior inhibitions in Article 2, para. 4. Similarly if the Security Council is veto-deadlocked, a regional organization could authorize the use of force under Article 52 and it is not inhibited from regional action authorized under Article 52 because of specified limits in Article 53 because the Security Council is veto-deadlocked from taking 'enforcement action'.

That is a collective form of action that I believe could be permissible under the Charter, as in the case of NATO's authorization concerning use of force in Kosovo, and, if it is permissible, it would obviate any limits in Article 2, para. 4.

Georges Abi-Saab

A very quick answer to this last point. My proposition is that with the Charter, we have a rule and an exception. Self-defence has become an exception to the comprehensive and mandatory rule. Thus, we cannot refer to more permissive rules which existed before the Charter on the basis of customary law to enlarge the scope of the exception, because the system has changed and self-defence became an exception to a prohibiting general rule, rather than a special application of a general permissive rule, as was the case before the Charter. But of course, if the conditions of exercising the exception are obtained, force can be used, but only within the limits of that exception. The other type is social or community force, even if it is by delegation from the Security Council to a State. It is a different type of use of force, a police type of action.

As to due diligence, if one looks at the definition of aggression, the same as at the *Nicaragua* case, the resulting norm is the same: the mere fact that a State harbours on its territory groups that are accused of attacking another State does not make it complicit in their action, nor does it permit the exercise of self-defence by using force against that State. For this the law requires something more, more implication by the territorial State.

What I am saying is that if in the instruments we are negotiating there is something to be tightened up, perhaps it would be in that direction – to increase the duty of due diligence as far as preventing illegal action originating from the State's territory. This does not apply to groups struggling for self-determination and recognized by the General Assembly. South Africa and Israel have been condemned numerous times by the Security Council and the General Assembly for their incursions in neighbouring countries, under the pretence of exercising what they claimed to be their right of self-defence.

My approach is that terrorists are criminals and should be treated as criminals under criminal law. The role of international law is to create the structure of police and judicial international cooperation in prosecuting such criminal activities. If terrorists are too powerful to be handled by simple criminal prosecution, thus posing a threat to international peace, the system of collective security in Chapter VII provides the adequate framework for responding to such a threat. On the other hand, the route of self-defence runs into many legal obstacles and is destructive of the system. It just does not square with the rules of international law which are based on territoriality. It is as simple as that, and there is no way out of it.

As for the example given of Entebbe, Israel never spoke of war against terrorists. It claimed the right of self-defence to protect its citizens abroad, a right which is not generally accepted in international law. This was a very different situation and was diversely received by the international community.

Finally, I want to comment on a point made by Professor Villani about contrary practice. I do not want to be excessively legalistic, but there is general consensus that Article 2 para. 4 is *jus cogens*. Moreover, there is a widespread but completely false idea of what is practice. I think Mr. Rosand spoke of practice in a sense that reminds me of a famous word by Abraham Chayes 'other States violate international law, the US create precedents'. The practice that is legally significant is not merely what a State does, it is the reaction of the international community to it. The fact that a State consistently violates international law does not create a practice if the international community every time reacts by saying 'we do not agree; this is a violation of the law'; even if no one can do anything about it, because it is the action of a strong aggressor or violator of international law.

The practice needed to undo a rule or to introduce an exception to a rule of *jus cogens*, according to Article 53 of the Vienna Convention on the Law of Treaties, has to take the shape of another rule of *jus cogens* which is accepted by the international community of States as a whole. I just want to recall, in the context of the prohibition of the use of force, that after Kosovo, on three successive occasions, 134 States, those of the Non-Aligned Movement, declared that there can be no legal use of force outside self-defence or authorization by the Security Council under Chapter VII, in the name of humanitarian intervention or otherwise, and that such use of force is illegal and contrary to the UN Charter. Thus, at least 134 States in addition to China and Russia refute all allegation to introduce a new exception to Article 2, para. 4, or enlarge the existing exception. For this you need to go very far beyond where we are now in trying to muster consensus in favour of such modifications.

Ugo Villani

Besides the practice relating to the cases mentioned in my previous intervention, one should bear in mind the attitude of the international community that emerges from the most recent international conventions aimed at fighting terrorism. I am referring in particular to the International Convention for the Suppression of the Financing of Terrorism, adopted by the General Assembly of the United Nations with Resolution 54/109 of 9 December 1999 (in force since 10 April 2002).

From this Convention, which is particularly advanced in providing for the means to fight against terrorism and for close cooperation among States, not only does no trend emerge which is favourable to the use of force, but indeed there is a clear-cut position by the States against such use. Articles 20 and 22 are eloquent in this respect: the former states that 'the States Parties shall carry out their obligations under this Convention in a manner consistent with the principles of sovereignty and territorial integrity of States and that of non-intervention in the domestic affairs of other States'; the latter states that 'nothing in this Convention entitles a State Party to undertake in the territory of another State Party the exercise of jurisdiction or performance of functions which are exclusively reserved for the authorities of that other State Party by its domestic law'. These provisions have a precedent in Articles 17 and 18 of the International Convention for the Suppression of Terrorist Bombings adopted by the General Assembly with Resolution 52/164 of 15 December 1997 (in force since 23 May 2001) showing that States, far from legitimizing the use of force against terrorism, are more preoccupied with making sure that the fight against terrorism may not be used by a State as a justification (or pretext) to carry out coercive acts against other States or also just to intervene in their internal questions. A similar worry emerges from Conventions adopted at regional level. The recent Inter-American Convention against Terrorism (Bridgeton, Barbados, 3 June 2002), adopted within the framework of the Organization of American States, in fact, states that 'nothing in this Convention entitles a State party to undertake in the territory of another State party the exercise of jurisdiction or performance of functions that are exclusively reserved to the authorities of that other State party by its domestic law' (Article 19).

Even more clear-cut and vigorous, against any possibility of resorting to force in the fight against international terrorism, is the position expressed by the Movement of Non-Aligned Countries at the 30th Conference of Heads of State or Government, held in Kuala Lumpur on 25 February 2003 (a position of which the UN General Assembly has taken note in Resolution 58/81 of 9 December 2003, containing measures to eliminate international terrorism). These States emphasize that international cooperation to combat terrorism should be conducted in conformity with the principles of the United Nations Charter, international law and relevant conventions, and they express the Movement's opposition to selective and unilateral actions in violation of such principles (para. 117); moreover, they reject 'the use, or the threat of the use of the armed forces against any NAM country under the pretext of combating terrorism', and 'all attempts by certain countries to use the issue of combating terrorism as a pretext to pursue their political aims against non-aligned and other developing countries', as well as the expression 'axis of evil' 'voiced by a certain State to target other countries under the pretext of combating terrorism' (para. 119). Thus the condemnation of the use of force as a means of fighting terrorism is clear and is expressed by the vast majority of the international community; that is, by the over 110 States which are part of the Movement of Non-Aligned States.

The recognition of a norm allowing the use of armed force to fight terrorism comes up against a further obstacle in the absence of a notion of terrorism that is genuinely shared by the international community. It is true that numerous resolutions of the General Assembly, from the Declaration on measures to eliminate international terrorism approved with Resolution 49/60 of 9 December 1994 to the more recent Resolution 58/81 of 9 December 2003 containing measures to eliminate international terrorism, seem to offer a definition of terrorism. In fact, they condemn 'criminal acts intended or calculated to provoke a state of terror in the general public, a group of persons or particular persons for political purposes', and they add that such acts 'are in any circumstances unjustifiable, whatever the considerations of a political, philosophical, ideological, racial, ethnic, religious or other nature that may be invoked to justify them'. Nevertheless, behind this apparently unanimous consensus, there are still distinctions and differences between States as to the qualification of terrorism and the identification of terrorist groups. First of all, according to one's stance, often those who are considered to be terrorists by some are considered as 'heroes' by others. Moreover, even those States which today are strongly determined to fight terrorism have, even in the recent past, been prepared to make use of terrorist groups, by arming and financing them.

But dissent among the States concerns the scope of the juridical concept of terrorism itself: in fact, according to a number of States, it should not include the action of those who fight for the independence of its own people. Expressions of this attitude can be found, first of all, in the regional conventions for the fight against terrorism drafted within the framework of the League of Arab States, the Organization of the Islamic Conference, and the Organization of African Unity (now the African Union). The Arab Convention on the suppression of terrorism, signed in Cairo on 22 April 1998, declares: 'All cases of struggle by whatever means, including armed struggle, against foreign occupation and aggression for liberation and self-determination, in accordance with the principles of international law, shall not be regarded as an offence [of a terrorist nature] (Article 2, *a*). The Convention of the Organization of the Islamic Conference, adopted at Ouagadougou on 1 July 1999, after defining terrorism in broad terms, asserts, in an extremely explicit manner: 'Peoples' struggle including armed struggle against foreign occupation, aggression, colonialism, and hegemony, aimed at liberation and self-determination in accordance with the principles of international law shall not be considered a terrorist crime' (Article 2, *a*). The OAU Convention on the prevention and combating of terrorism, adopted in Algiers on 14 July 1999 (Article 3, para. 1) also expresses itself in analogous terms.

As can be seen, the notion of terrorism does not cover a wide range of forms of behaviour implying an armed struggle, justified in the name of peoples' self-determination, sometimes meant in a fairly broad sense, as emerges from the reference not only to foreign occupation, to aggression and to colonialism, but also to hegemony; on the contrary, this type of behaviour, according to other – especially Western – countries, would come under the definition of terrorism.

Dissent over the question of international terrorism erupted in the UN General Assembly debate from 1–5 October 2001, shortly after the terrorist attack of 11 September. On 2 October, for example, the representative for Malaysia declared that 'acts of pure terrorism, involving attacks against innocent civilian populations – which cannot be justified under any circumstances – should be differentiated from the legitimate struggles of people under colonial or alien domination and foreign occupation for self-determination and national liberation'; and the Libyan representative, speaking on behalf of the Arab Group, asked for the calling of an international conference to arrive at a definition of terrorism, adding that the Group would oppose any attempt to classify resistance to occupation as a terrorist act.

The strong opposition to including under the definition of terrorism those acts carried out against foreign occupations was reaffirmed by the Movement of Non-Aligned Countries in the above-mentioned declaration of Kuala Lumpur of 25 February 2003. The Heads of State or Government rejected 'recent attempts to equate the legitimate struggle of peoples under colonial or alien domination and foreign occupation, for self-determination and national liberation with terrorism' (para. 106); and while supporting the convocation of an international Conference under the auspices of the United Nations to define terrorism, they declared that it was necessary to differentiate it from the struggle for national liberation, and they denounced the brutalization of people kept under foreign occupation 'as the gravest form of terrorism'.

Eloquent proof of the considerable differences existing among States as regards the definition of terrorism can be seen from the difficulty in achieving a project for an international convention on terrorism; the matter has been discussed by the General Assembly, but there are no signs of progress, precisely because of the incapacity of States to arrive at a definition. It would therefore be extremely problematic (and, in some respects, runs the risk of being abused) to justify the use of force against a phenomenon – terrorism – which has not been univocally defined in clear and shared terms.

The impossibility of justifying the use of force as a means for combating international terrorism is confirmed, albeit implicitly, by the Bruges Declaration on the use of force, adopted by the Institute of International Law on 2 September 2003. In the declaration the Institute, while repeating that acts of terrorism are prohibited by international law and constitute international crimes, vigorously affirms that force may be used only in exercising the right of self-defence or on the basis of an authorization by the Security Council.

Giuseppe Nesi

Any attempt to summarize the conclusions of the panel discussion risks over-simplifying what has been a very stimulating discussion. The rich variety of the contributions and the complexity of the topics debated make it difficult to identify any single point or cluster of convergence. Going back to the questions that were raised at the beginning of the discussion, we might say that the manner in which the fight against terrorism is being conducted has forced scholars and diplomats alike to reflect on the nature and the implementation of fundamental principles of international law that are at stake in the struggle against international terrorism.

One conclusion that can be drawn from the debate is that, while the state of emergency that now characterizes the international security environment might invite a new reading of general principles of international law – particularly the argument that armed force can be used in cases other than those currently provided for by general international law and the UN Charter – scholars and diplomats have rejected any such reading, and rightly so. International law with its traditional rules still constitutes the only framework through which States can and must operate, even in these difficult times.

At the same time, all the panellists seem to agree in their assessment of how, from a legal point of view, it is incorrect to talk about a 'war against terrorism.' While this expression might make sense as a rhetorical figure, it can be dangerous or counter-productive to use the term 'war' to describe a phenomenon that is fundamentally a matter of criminal justice. It also seems clear, however, that States cannot renounce *a priori* all the means at their disposal to counter the scourge of terrorism, especially when terrorists do not hesitate to perpetrate heinous criminal attacks on civilians. In such instances States have not only the right but also the responsibility to protect their populations.

If States should decide to use armed force in specific circumstances and in response to terrorist activities, however, they must remember that this can only be done within the limits and under the conditions provided for by international law. The use of force should always be considered a last resort to be deployed exclusively in the framework of a collective action decided on in accordance with international law.

I share the view that States should consider the main instrument for their struggle against international terrorism to be international cooperation through judicial and other means, such as intelligence, police operations, and the implementation of international conventions and the pertinent Security Council resolutions.

Relevant International Documents[1]

Anti-terrorist Conventions

When not otherwise stated, links to the texts of the following conventions are available at: http://untreaty.un.org/English/Terrorism.asp, last accessed 27/10/2005.

1. Universal Conventions

International Convention for the Suppression of Acts of Nuclear Terrorism, adopted on 13 April 2005 during the 91st plenary meeting of the General Assembly by Resolution A/RES/59/290; open for signature from 14 September 2005 until 31 December 2006 at United Nations Headquarters in New York; Signatories: 90.

International Convention for the Suppression of the Financing of Terrorism, adopted by Resolution 54/109 of 9 December 1999 at the fourth session of the General Assembly of the United Nations; Parties: 145, in *UNTS*, Vol. 2178, p. 229.

International Convention for the Suppression of Terrorist Bombings, adopted by the General Assembly of the United Nations on 15 December 1997, entered into force on 23 May 2001, Parties: 145, in *ILM*, Vol. 37, 1998, p. 251.

Convention on the Marking of Plastic Explosives for the Purpose of Detection, signed at Montreal, 1 March 1991, entered into force on 21 June 1998; Parties: 120, in *UNTS*, Vol. 2122, p. 359.

Convention for the Suppression of Unlawful Acts Against the Safety of Maritime Navigation, signed at Rome, 10 March 1988, entered into force on 1 March 1992, Parties: 126, in *UNTS*, Vol. 1678, p. 201.

Protocol for the Suppression of Unlawful Acts Against the Safety of Fixed Platforms Located on the Continental Shelf, signed at Rome on 10 March 1988, entered into force on 1 March 1992, Parties: 115, in *UNTS*, Vol. 1678, p. 294.

2005 Protocol to Convention for the Suppression of Unlawful Acts Against the Safety of Maritime Navigation, adopted on 14 October 2005, requires ratification from three States which are also party to the Convention for the Suppression of Unlawful

---

1 By Marco Pertile.

Acts but cannot come into force unless the 2005 amended Convention is already in force.

Convention on the Physical Protection of Nuclear Material, signed at New York and Vienna on 3 March 1980, came into force on 8 February 1987, Parties: 115, in *UNTS,* Vol. 1456, p. 124.

International Convention Against the Taking of Hostages, signed at New York on 18 December 1979, came into force on 3 June 1983, Parties: 153, in *UNTS,* Vol. 1316, p. 205.

Convention on the Prevention and Punishment of Crimes against Internationally Protected Persons, including Diplomatic Agents, adopted by the General Assembly of the United Nations on 14 December 1973, entered into force on 20 January 1977, Parties: 159, in *UNTS,* Vol. 1035, p. 167.

Convention for the Suppression of Unlawful Acts against the Safety of Civil Aviation, signed at Montreal on 23 September 1971, entered into force on 26 January 1973, in *UNTS,* Vol. 974, p. 177.

Protocol on the Suppression of Unlawful Acts of Violence at Airports Serving International Civil Aviation, supplementary to the Convention for the Suppression of Unlawful Acts against the Safety of Civil Aviation, signed at Montreal on 24 February 1988, in *UNTS,* Vol. 1589, p. 474.

Convention for the Suppression of Unlawful Seizure of Aircraft, signed at The Hague on 16 December 1970, entered into force on 14 October 1971, in *UNTS,* Vol. 860, p. 105.

Convention on Offences and Certain Other Acts Committed on Board Aircraft, signed at Tokyo on 14 September 1963, entered into force on 4 December 1969, in *UNTS,* Vol. 704, p. 219.

Draft Comprehensive Convention against International Terrorism, Ad Hoc Committee established by General Assembly Resolution 51/210 of 17 December 1996, A/59/894, Appendix II, available at: http://daccessdds.un.org/doc/UNDOC/ GEN/N05/460/57/PDF/N0546057.pdf?OpenElement, last accessed 28/10/2005).

2. Regional Conventions

Council of Europe Convention on the Prevention of Terrorism, opened for signature at Warsaw, 16 May 2005, CETS No. 196; 18 Signatures, 0 Ratifications, Conditions for entry into force: 6 Ratifications including 4 Member States of the Council of

Europe) (available at: http://conventions.coe.int/Treaty/EN/Treaties/Html/196.htm, last accessed 27/10/2005).

Council of Europe Convention on Laundering, Search, Seizure and Confiscation of the Proceeds from Crime and on the Financing of Terrorism, opened for signature at Warsaw, 16 May 2005, CETS No. 198; 18 Signatures, 0 Ratifications, Conditions for entry into force: 6 Ratifications including 4 Member States of the Council of Europe (available at: http://conventions.coe.int/Treaty/EN/Treaties/Html/198.htm, last accessed 27/10/2005).

Inter-American Convention against Terrorism, adopted at the second plenary session held on 3 June 2002, in *ILM* 42 (2003), p. 19 (available at http://www.cicte.oas.org/ Docs/Treaty%20as%20approved.doc, last accessed 27/10/2005).

OAS Convention to Prevent and Punish Acts of Terrorism Taking the Form of Crimes against Persons and Related Extortion that are of International Significance, concluded at Washington, D.C. on 2 February 1971, Parties: 17 (available at http:// www.oas.org/juridico/english/Treaties/a-49.html, last accessed 27/10/2005).

European Convention on the Suppression of Terrorism, opened for signature at Strasbourg on 27 January 1977, CETS No. 90; Parties: 44, in *UNTS*, Vol. 1137, p. 93 (available at http://conventions.coe.int/Treaty/EN/CadreListeTraites.htm, last accessed 27/10/2005).

SAARC Regional Convention on Suppression of Terrorism, signed at Kathmandu on 4 November 1987; Parties: 7.

Additional Protocol to the SAARC Regional Convention on Suppression of Terrorism, done in Islamabad on 6 January 2004 (available at: http://www.infopak.gov.pk/saarc/ terrorism_protocol.htm, last accessed 27/10/2005).

OAU Convention on the Prevention and Combating of Terrorism, adopted at Algiers on 14 July 1999; Parties: 36, (available at http://www.africa-union.org/Official_ documents/Treaties_%20Conventions_%20Protocols/Algiers_convention%20on% 20Terrorism.pdf, last accessed 28/10/2005).

Protocol to the OAU Convention on the Prevention and Combating of Terrorism, adopted by the Assembly of the African Union in Addis Ababa on 2 July 2004 (shall enter into force 30 days after the deposit of the 15th instrument of ratification) (available at: http://www.africa-union.org/Official_documents/Treaties_%20Conventions_ %20Protocols/The%20Protocol%20on%20Terrorism%2026July2004.pdf, last accessed 28/10/2005).

Arab Convention on the Suppression of Terrorism, signed at a meeting held at the General Secretariat of the League of Arab States on 22 April 1998, deposited with the Secretary-General of the League of Arab States (unofficial translation from the Arabic available at: http://www.al-bab.com/arab/docs/league/terrorism98, last accessed 23/10/2005).

Convention of the Organization of The Islamic Conference on Combating International Terrorism, adopted at Ouagadougou on 1 July 1999, deposited with the Secretary-General of the Organization of the Islamic Conference.

Treaty on Cooperation among States Members of the Commonwealth of Independent States in Combating Terrorism, done at Minsk on 4 June 1999, deposited with the Secretariat of the Commonwealth of Independent States.

United Nations Action

1. United Nations Security Council Resolutions

The following resolutions are available at: http://www.un.org/terrorism/sc.htm, last accessed 23/10/2005.

S/RES/1625 (2005), 14 September 2005 (Threats to international peace and security caused by terrorist acts – situation in Africa).

S/RES/1624 (2005), 14 September 2005 (Threats to international peace and security caused by terrorist acts – incitement to commit a terrorist act).

S/RES/1618 (2005), 4 August 2005 (Threats to international peace and security caused by terrorist acts – terrorist attacks in Iraq).

S/RES/1617 (2005), 29 July 2005 (Threats to international peace and security caused by terrorist acts – measures with respect to Al-Qaeda, Usama bin Laden, and the Taliban and other individuals, groups, undertakings and entities associated with them).

S/RES/1611 (2005), 7 July 2005 (Threats to international peace and security caused by terrorist acts – condemnation of terrorist attacks in London on 7 July).

S/RES/1566 (2004), 8 October 2004 (Threats to international peace and security – definition of terrorist acts).

S/RES/1540 (2004), 28 April 2004 (Threats to international peace and security – non-state actors and weapons of mass destruction).

S/RES/1535 (2004), 26 March 2004 (Threats to international peace and security caused by terrorist acts – on the revitalization of the CTC Committee).

S/RES/1530 (2004), 11 March 2004 (Threats to international peace and security caused by terrorist acts – condemnation of terrorist attacks in Madrid on 11 March 2004).

S/RES/1526 (2004), 30 January 2004 (Threats to international peace and security caused by terrorist acts – measures with respect to Al-Qaeda, Usama bin Laden, and the Taliban and other individuals, groups, undertakings and entities associated with them).

S/RES/1516 (2003), 20 November 2003 (Condemnation of the bomb attacks in Istanbul, Turkey, on 15 November 2003 and 20 November 2003).

S/RES/1465 (2003), 13 February 2003 (Condemnation of the bomb attack in Bogota, Colombia, on 7 February 2003).

S/RES/1456 (2003), 20 January 2003 (High-Level Meeting of the Security Council on combating terrorism).

S/RES/1455 (2003), 17 January 2003 (Improvement of the measures imposed by paragraph 4 (b) of Resolution 1267 (1999), paragraph 8 (c) of Resolution 1333 (2000) and paragraphs 1 and 2 of Resolution 1390 (2002)).

S/RES/1452 (2002), 20 December 2002 (Implementation of paragraph 4 (b) of Resolution 1267 (1999), and paragraphs 1 and 2 (a) of Resolution 1390 (2002)).

S/RES/1450 (2002), 13 December 2002 (Condemnation of the terrorist bomb attack at the Paradise Hotel, in Kikambala, Kenya, and the attempted missile attack on Arkia Israeli Airlines flight 582 departing Mombasa, Kenya, on 28 November 2002).

S/RES/1440 (2002), 24 October 2002 (Condemnation of the act of taking hostages in Moscow, the Russian Federation, on 23 October 2002).

S/RES/1438 (2002), 14 October 2002 (Condemnation of the bomb attacks in Bali, Indonesia, on 12 October 2002).

S/RES/1377 (2001), 12 November 2001 (Declaration on the global effort to combat terrorism).

S/RES/1373 (2001), 28 September 2001 (International co-operation to combat terrorist acts – establishment of the Security Council Counter-terrorism Committee).

S/RES/1368 (2001), 12 September 2001 (Condemnation of the terrorist attacks which took place on 11 September 2001 in New York, Washington DC and Pennsylvania).

S/RES/1363 (2001), 30 July 2001 (Establishment of a mechanism to monitor the implementation of measures imposed by resolutions 1267 (1999) and 1333 (2000)).

S/RES/1333 (2000), 19 December 2000 (Measures against the Taliban).

S/RES/1269 (1999), 19 October 1999 (International co-operation against terrorism).

S/RES/1267 (1999), 15 October 1999 (Measures against the Taliban).

S/RES/1214 (1998), 8 December 1998 (On the situation in Afghanistan).

S/RES/1189 (1998), 13 August 1998 (On the terrorist bomb attacks in Nairobi, Kenya and Dar-es-Salaam, Tanzania, on 7 August 1998).

S/RES/1054 (1996), 26 April 1996 (Sanctions against the Sudan – non-compliance with Resolution 1044 (1996)).

S/RES/1044 (1996), 31 January 1996 (Sudan – Extradition of three suspects in connection with the assassination attempt on President Mubarak of Egypt).

S/RES/731 (1992), 21 January 1992 (Condemnation of the destruction of the Pan-Am flight 103 and Union de transports aérien flight 772).

S/RES/748 (1992), 31 March 1992 (Sanctions against the Libyan Arab Jamahiriya).

S/RES/687 (1991), 3 April 1991 (Restoration of the sovereignty, independence and territorial integrity of Kuwait).

S/RES/635 (1989), 14 June 1989 (Marking of plastic or sheet explosives).

2. United Nations General Assembly Resolutions

The following resolutions are available at: http://www.un.org/terrorism/res.htm, last accessed: 23/10/2005.

A/RES/59/290, 13 April 2005 (International Convention for the Suppression of Acts of Nuclear Terrorism).

A/RES/59/195, 20 December 2004 (Human rights and terrorism).

A/RES/59/191, 10 December 2004 (Protection of human rights and fundamental freedoms while countering terrorism).

A/RES/59/80, 3 December 2004 (Measures to prevent terrorists from acquiring weapons of mass destruction).

A/RES/59/46, 2 December 2004 (Measures to eliminate international terrorism).

A/RES/58/187, 22 December 2003 (Protection of human rights and fundamental freedoms while countering terrorism).

A/RES/58/174, 22 December 2003 (Human rights and terrorism).

A/RES/58/81, 9 December 2003 (Measures to eliminate international terrorism).

A/RES/58/48, 8 December 2003 (Measures to prevent terrorists from acquiring weapons of mass destruction).

A/RES/57/220, 18 December 2002 (Hostage-taking).

A/RES/57/219, 18 December 2002 (Protecting human rights and fundamental freedoms while countering terrorism).

A/RES/57/83, 22 November 2002 (Measures to prevent terrorists from acquiring weapons of mass destruction).

A/RES/57/27, 19 November 2002 (Measures to eliminate international terrorism).

A/RES/56/160, 19 December 2001 (Human rights and terrorism).

A/RES/56/88, 12 December 2001 (Measures to eliminate international terrorism).

A/RES/56/1, 12 September 2001 (Condemnation of terrorist attacks in the United States of America).

A/RES/55/158, 12 December 2000 (Measures to eliminate international terrorism).

A/RES/54/164, 17 December 1999 (Human rights and terrorism).

A/RES/54/110, 9 December 1999 (Measures to eliminate international terrorism).

A/RES/54/109, 9 December 1999 (International Convention for the Suppression of the Financing of Terrorism).

A/RES/53/108, 8 December 1998 (Measures to eliminate international terrorism).

A/RES/52/165, 15 December 1997 (Measures to eliminate international terrorism).
A/RES/52/133, 12 December 1997 (Human rights and terrorism).

A/RES/51/210, 17 December 1996 (Measures to eliminate international terrorism).

A/RES/50/186, 22 December 1995 (Human rights and terrorism).

A/RES/50/53, 11 December 1995 (Measures to eliminate international terrorism).

A/RES/49/185, 23 December 1994 (Human rights and terrorism).

A/RES/49/60, 9 December 1994 (Measures to eliminate international terrorism).

A/RES/48/122, 20 December 1993 (Human rights and terrorism).

A/RES/46/51, 9 December 1991 (Measures to eliminate international terrorism).

A/RES/44/29, 4 December 1989 (Measures to prevent international terrorism).

A/RES/42/159, 7 December 1987 (Measures to prevent international terrorism).

A/RES/40/61, 9 December 1985 (Measures to prevent international terrorism).

A/RES/39/159, 17 December 1984 (Inadmissibility of the policy of State terrorism and any actions by States aimed at undermining the socio-political system in other sovereign States).

A/RES/38/130, 19 December 1983 (Measures to prevent international terrorism).

A/RES/36/109, 10 December 1981 (Measures to prevent international terrorism).

A/RES/34/145, 17 December 1979 (Measures to prevent international terrorism).

A/RES/32/147, 16 December 1977 (Measures to prevent international terrorism).

A/RES/31/102, 15 December 1976 (Measures to prevent international terrorism).

A/RES/3034(XXVII), 18 December 1972 (Measures to prevent international terrorism).

Other Documents at the Regional Level

1. European Union

All documents are available at: http://europa.eu.int/comm/justice_home/doc_centre/ criminal/terrorism/doc_criminal_terrorism_en.htm, last accessed: 23/11/2005.

1.1 Framework Decisions

Council Framework Decision of 13 June 2002 on combating terrorism, 22/06/2002, in *Official Journal L164,* 22/06/2002, pp. 3–7.

Council Framework Decision of 13 June 2002 on joint investigation teams, 20/06/2002, in *Official Journal L162,* 20/06/2002, pp. 1–3.

1.2 Joint Actions and Common Positions

Council Common Position of 12 December 2002 updating Common Position 2001/931/CFSP on the application of specific measures to combat terrorism and repealing Common Position 2002/847/CFSP, 12/12/2002, in Official Journal L337, 13/12/2002, pp. 93–96.

Council Common Position of 28 October 2002 updating Common Position 2001/931/CFSP on the application of specific measures to combat terrorism and repealing Common Position 2002/462/CFSP, 28/10/2002, in *Official Journal L295,* 30/10/2002, pp. 1–4.

Council Common Position of 17 June 2002 updating Common Position 2001/931/ CFSP on the application of specific measures to combat terrorism and repealing Common Position 2002/340/CFSP, 17/06/2002, in *Official Journal L160,* 18/06/2002, pp. 32–35.

Council Common Position of 27 May 2002 concerning restrictive measures against Usama bin Laden, members of the Al-Qaeda organisation and the Taliban and other individuals, groups, undertakings and entities associated with them and repealing Common Positions 96/746/CFSP, 1999/727/CFSP, 2001/154/CFSP and 2001/771/ CFSP, 27/05/2002, in *Official Journal L139,* 29/05/2002, pp. 4–5.

Council Common Position of 2 May 2002 updating Common Position 2001/931/ CFSP on the application of specific measures to combat terrorism, 02/05/2002, in *Official Journal L 116,* 03/05/2002, pp. 75–77.

Council Common Position of 12 December 2002 updating Common Position 2001/931/CFSP on the application of specific measures to combat terrorism and repealing Common Position 2002/847/CFSP, 27/12/2001, in *Official Journal L337,* 13/12/2002, pp. 93–96.

Directive of the European Parliament and of the Council of 4 December 2001 amending Council Directive 91/308/EEC on prevention of the use of the financial system for the purpose of money laundering – Commission Declaration (2001/97/ EC), 28/12/2001, in *Official Journal L344,* 28/12/2001, pp. 76–81.

Council Common Position of 27 December 2001 on combating terrorism, 27/12/2001, in *Official Journal L344,* 28/12/2001, pp. 90–92.

Council Common Position of 27 December 2001 on the application of specific measures to combat terrorism, 27/12/2001, in *Official Journal L344,* 28/12/2001, pp. 93–96.

Joint Action of 15 October 1996 adopted by the Council on the basis of Article K.3 of the Treaty on European Union concerning the creation and maintenance of a Directory of specialized counter-terrorist competences, skills and expertise to facilitate counter-terrorist cooperation between the Member States of the European Union (96/610/JHA), 25/10/1996, in *Official Journal L273,* 25/10/1996, pp. 1–2.

1.3 Decisions

Council Decision 2003/48/JHA of 19 December 2002 on the implementation of specific measures for police and judicial cooperation to combat terrorism in accordance with Article 4 of Common Position 2001/931/CFSP, 19/12/2002, in *Official Journal L016,* 22/01/2003, pp. 68–70.

Council Decision of 12 December 2002 implementing Article 2(3) of Regulation (EC) No 2580/2001 on specific restrictive measures directed against certain persons and entities with a view to combating terrorism and repealing Decision 2002/848/ EC (2002/974/EC), 12/12/2002, in *Official Journal L337,* 13/12/2002, pp. 85–86.

Council Decision of 28 February 2002 setting up Eurojust with a view to reinforcing the fight against serious crime (2002/187/JHA), 06/03/2002, in *Official Journal L063,* 06/03/2002, pp. 1–13.

Council Decision of 6 December 2001 extending Europol's mandate to deal with the serious forms of international crime listed in the Annex to the Europol Convention, 06/12/2001, in *Official Journal L063,* 06/03/2002, pp. 1–13.

Council Decision of 3 December 1998 instructing Europol to deal with crimes committed or likely to be committed in the course of terrorist activities against life, limb, personal freedom or property, 03/12/1998, in *Official Journal C026,*

30/01/1999, pp. 22–22.

1.4 Council Acts, Action Plans and Regulations

Council Regulation (EC) No 881/2002 of 27 May 2002 imposing certain specific restrictive measures directed against certain persons and entities associated with Usama bin Laden, the Al-Qaeda network and the Taliban, and repealing Council Regulation (EC) No 467/2001 prohibiting the export of certain goods and services to Afghanistan, strengthening the flight ban and extending the freeze of funds and other financial resources in respect of the Taliban of Afghanistan, 27/05/2002, in *Official Journal L139*, 29/05/2002, pp. 9–22.

Council Regulation (EC) No 2580/2001 of 27 December 2001 on specific restrictive measures directed against certain persons and entities with a view to combating terrorism, 27/12/2001, in *Official Journal L344*, 28/12/2001, pp. 70–75.

1.5 Commission Regulations

Commission Regulation (EC) No 244/2003 of 7 February 2003 amending for the 11th time Council Regulation (EC) No 881/2002 imposing certain specific restrictive measures directed against certain persons and entities associated with Usama bin Laden, the Al-Qaeda network and the Taliban, and repealing Council Regulation (EC) No 467/2001, 07/02/2003, in *Official Journal L033* , 08/02/2003, pp. 28–29.

Commission Regulation (EC) No 215/2003 of 3 February 2003 amending for the tenth time Council Regulation (EC) No 881/2002 imposing certain specific restrictive measures directed against certain persons and entities associated with Usama bin Laden, the Al-Qaeda network and the Taliban, and repealing Council Regulation (EC) No 467/2001, 03/02/2003, in *Official Journal L028*, 04/02/2003, pp. 41–42.

Commission Regulation (EC) No 145/2003 of 27 January 2003 amending for the ninth time Council Regulation (EC) No 881/2002 imposing certain specific restrictive measures directed against certain persons and entities associated with Usama bin Laden, the Al-Qaeda network and the Taliban, and repealing Council Regulation (EC) No 467/2001, 27/01/200327/01/2003, in *Official Journal L023* , 28/01/2003, pp. 22–23.

Commission Regulation (EC) No 2083/2002 of 22 November 2002 amending for the eighth time Council Regulation (EC) No 881/2002 imposing certain specific restrictive measures directed against certain persons and entities associated with Usama bin Laden, the Al-Qaeda network and the Taliban, and repealing Council Regulation (EC) No 467/2001, 22/11/2002, in *Official Journal L319*, 23/11/2002, pp. 22–23.

1.6 Reports from the Commission on implementing the Framework Decisions

Report from the Commission based on Article 11 of the Council Framework Decision of 13 June 2002 on combating terrorism (COM(2004/409 final)), 08/06/2004, in *Official Journal C321*, 28/10/2004, pp. 1–7.

2. Council of Europe

Most documents quoted below are available at: http://www.coe.int/T/E/Legal_ affairs/Legal_co-operation/Fight_against_terrorism/2_Adopted_Texts/default.asp

2.1 Committee of Ministers Acts
Rec(2005)10, *Recommendation of the Committee of Ministers to member states on 'special investigation techniques' in relation to serious crimes including acts of terrorism.*

Rec(2005)9, *Recommendation of the Committee of Ministers to member states on the protection of witnesses and collaborators of justice.*

Rec(2005)7, *Recommendation of the Committee of Ministers to member states concerning identity and travel documents and the fight against terrorism.*

Declaration on freedom of expression and information in the media in the context of the fight against terrorism (2005).

Guidelines on the Protection of Victims of Terrorist Acts (2005).

Guidelines on Human Rights and the Fight against Terrorism (2002).

Declaration on the Fight against International Terrorism (2001).

Rec(2001)11, *Recommendation concerning Guiding Principles on the Fight against Organised Crime.*

Tripartite Declaration on Terrorist Acts (1986).

Rec(1982)1, *Recommendation concerning International Co-operation in the Prosecution and Punishment of Acts of Terrorism.*

Declaration on terrorism (1978).

Resolution (1974)3 on international terrorism.

2.2 Parliamentary Assembly Recommendations and Resolutions

Recommendation 1687 (2004) on Combating terrorism through culture.

Recommendation 1677 (2004) on the Challenge of terrorism in Council of Europe member states.

Resolution 1400 (2004) on the Challenge of terrorism in Council of Europe member states.

Resolution 1367 (2004) on Bioterrorism: a serious threat for citizens' health.

Recommendation 1644 (2004) on Terrorism: a threat to democracies.

Recommendation 1584 (2002) on the Need for Intensified International Co-operation to Neutralise Funds for Terrorist Purposes.

Recommendation 1549 (2002) on Air Transport and Terrorism: how to enhance security.

Recommendation 1550 (2002) and Resolution 1271 (2002) on Combating Terrorism and Respect for Human Rights.

Recommendation 1534 (2001) and Resolution 1258 (2001) on Democracies facing Terrorism.

Recommendation 1132 (1997) on the Organisation of a Parliamentary Conference to reinforce Democratic Systems in Europe and Co-operation in the Fight against Terrorism.

Recommendation 1199 (1992) on the Fight against International Terrorism in Europe.

Recommendation 1170 (1991) on strengthening the European Convention on the Suppression of Terrorism.

Recommendation 1024 (1986) and Resolution No. 863 (1986) on the European Response to International Terrorism.

Recommendation 941 (1982) and 982 (1984) on the Defence of Democracy against Terrorism in Europe.

Recommendation 916 (1981) on the Conference on the Defence of Democracy against Terrorism in Europe – Tasks and Problems.

Recommendation 852 (1979) on Terrorism in Europe.

Recommendations 684 (1972) and 703 (1973) on International Terrorism.

2.3 European Ministers of Justice

26th Conference, Helsinki, 7–8 April 2005, *Resolution No. 3 on combating terrorism.*

25th Conference, Sofia, 9–10 October 2003, *Resolution No. 1 on combating terrorism.*

24th Conference, Moscow, 4–5 October 2001, *Resolution No. 1 on combating international terrorism.*

3. NATO

Partnership Action Plan against Terrorism, 22 November 2002 (available at: http://www.nato.int/docu/basictxt/b021122e.htm, last accessed 23/10/2004).

NATO's Military Concept for Defence against Terrorism, 21 November 2002 (available at: http://www.nato.int/ims/docu/terrorism.htm, last accessed 23/10/2005).

Statement by NATO Secretary-General Lord Robertson, on 2 October 2001 (available at: http://www.nato.int/docu/speech/2001/s011002a.htm, last accessed 23/10/2005).

Statement by the North Atlantic Council on 12 September 2001, Press Release (2001)124 (available at: http://www.nato.int/docu/pr/2001/p01-124e.htm, last accessed 23/10/2005).

The Alliance's Strategic Concept approved by the Heads of State and Government participating in the Meeting of the North Atlantic Council in Washington D.C., 23–24 April 1999, (Washington Strategic Concept), Press Release NAC-S(99)65 (available at: http://www.nato.int/docu/pr/1999/p99-065e.htm, last accessed 23/10/2005).

4. OAS

Work Plan of the Inter-American Committee against Terrorism, CICTE/doc.4/03 rev. 1, Adopted at the Sixth Plenary Session, 24 January 2003, (available at http://www.un.org/Docs/sc/committees/1373/IAC_wp.doc).

RC.23/RES.1/01, *Strengthening Hemispheric Cooperation to Prevent, Combat, and Eliminate Terrorism*, Meeting of Consultation of Ministers of Foreign Affairs, 21

September 2001 (available at http://www.oas.org/OASpage/crisis/RC.23e.htm, last accessed 27/10/2005).

AG/RES. 1650 (XXIX-O/99), *Hemispheric Cooperation to Prevent, Combat, and Eliminate Terrorism*, 7 June 1999 (available at http://www.oas.org/juridico/english/ ga-res99/eres1650.htm).

Commitment of Mar del Plata, Mar del Plata, Argentina on 23–24 November 1998 (available at http://www.oas.org/juridico/english/Docu1.htm, last accessed 27/10/2005).

5. OSCE

Report on Actions of OSCE Bodies and Institutions to Prevent and Combat Terrorism, including Implementation of the Bucharest Plan of Action for Combating Terrorism and the Bishkek Programme of Action (submitted to the 2003 Ministerial Council on 30 November 2003) (available at: http://www.un.org/Docs/sc/committees/1373/ masterfinal.doc, last accessed 27/10/2005).

Decision No. 6/03, Terms of Reference for the OSCE Counter-Terrorism Network, MC.DEC/6/03, Ministerial Council, 2 December 2003.

Decision No. 8/03, Man-Portable Air Defence Systems, MC.DEC/8/03, Ministerial Council, 2 December 2003 (available at: http://www.un.org/Docs/sc/ committees/1373/manpads.pdf, last accessed 27/10/2005).

Decision No. 7/03, Travel Document Security, MC.DEC/7/03, Ministerial Council, 2 December 2003 (available at: http://www.un.org/Docs/sc/committees/1373/travel_ docs.pdf, last accessed 27/10/2005).

OSCE Charter on Preventing and Combating Terrorism, MC(10).JOUR/2, 7 December 2002 (available at: http://www.osce.org/documents/odihr/2002/12/1488_ en.pdf, last accessed 26/10/2005).

Bishkek International Conference on Enhancing Security and Stability in Central Asia: Strengthening Comprehensive Efforts to Counter Terrorism – 'Programme of Action', 13–14 December 2001 (available at: http://www.osce.org/documents/ cio/2001/12/677_en.pdf, last accessed 26/10/2005).

Bucharest Plan of Action for Combating Terrorism, MC(9).DEC/1, 4 December 2001 (available at: http://www.osce.org/documents/cio/2001/12/670_en.pdf, last accessed 26/10/2005).

6. ECOWAS

Dakar Declaration Against Terrorism, Dakar 17 October 2001 (available at: http://www.unhcr.ch/cgi-bin/texis/vtx/home/opendoc.pdf?tbl=RSDLEGAL&id=3deb22b 14, last accessed 28/10/2005).

7. African Union

Decision on the Outcome of the Second High-Level Inter-Governmental Meeting on the Prevention and Combating of Terrorism in Africa, EX.CL/Dec.146 (VI) (available at: http://www.africa-union.org/Summit/jan2005/Executive%20Council/ Executive%20Council%20%20Decisions.pdf, last accessed 28/10/2005).

Declaration of the Second High-Level Inter-Governmental Meeting on the Prevention and Combating of Terrorism in Africa, Mtg/HLIG/Conv.Terror/Decl. (II) Rev. 2, Algiers, 13–14 October 2004 (available at: http://www.africa-union.org/Terrorism/ DECLARATION%20Algiers%20REV.pdf, last accessed 28/10/2005).

Report of the Chairperson of the AU Commission on the Implementation of the 1999 OAU Convention and the Plan of Action on the Prevention and Combating of Terrorism in Africa, Mtg/HLIG/Conv.Terror/2 (II), Second High-Level Intergovernmental Meeting on the Prevention and Combating of Terrorism in Africa, 13–14 October 2004, Algiers, (available at: http://www.africa-union.org/Terrorism/ REPORT%20OF%20THE%20CP.pdf, last accessed 28/10/2005).

8. Organization of the Islamic Conference

Resolution No. 51/31-P, On Combating International Terrorism, Istanbul, 26–28 Rabiul Thani, 1425H (14–16 June 2004), (available at: http://www.oic-oci.org/ english/fm/31/31%20icfm-pol2-eng.htm#RESOLUTION%20NO.51/31-P,   last accessed 28/10/2005).

Resolution No. 66/28-p, On the Convening of an International Conference under the auspices of the UN to define terrorism and distinguish it from peoples' struggle for national liberation, Bamako, 4–6 Rabiul Thani 1422H (25–27 June 2001) (available at: http://www.oic-oci.org/english/fm/28/28-ICFM-PIL4-en.htm#66/28-p, last accessed 28/10/2005).

Resolution No. 67/28-P, On the Follow-Up of the OIC Convention on Combating International Terrorism, Bamako, 4–6 Rabiul Thani 1422H (25–27 June 2001) (available at: http://www.oic-oci.org/english/fm/28/28-ICFM-PIL4-en.htm#67/28-p, last accessed 28/10/2005).

Resolution No. 65/27-P, On the OIC Convention for Combating International

Terrorism, Kuala Lumpur, 24–27 Rabi Ul Awal 1421H (27–30 June 2000) (available at: http://www.oic-oci.org/english/fm/27/27th-fm-political(3).htm#65, last accessed 28/10/2005).

Resolution No. 54/25-P, On the Follow-Up of the Code of Conduct for Combating International Terrorism, Doha, 17–19 Dhul Quida 1418H (15–17 March 1998) (available at: http://www.oic-oci.org/english/fm/25/resolutions25-p-3.htm#54, last accessed 28/10/2005).

Resolution No. 43/22-P, On the Preparation of a Code of Conduct for Combating International Terrorism and *Annex to Res.43/22-P, Code of Conduct for the Member States of the Organization of the Islamic Conference on Combating International Terrorism,* 8–10 Rajab 1415H (10–12 December, 1994) (available at: http://www.oic-oci.org/english/fm/22/resolution22-p.htm#43http://www.oic-oci.org/english/fm/22/resolution22-p.htm#43, last accessed 28/10/2005).

9. League of Arab States

Recommendations On Arab Regional Symposium on Combating Terrorism, Cairo, Egypt, 16-17/2/ 2005 (available at: http://www.arableagueonline.org/arableague/english/details_en.jsp?art_id=3664&level_id=219, last accessed 28/10/2005).

Bibliography[1]

Abi-Saab G., 'The Proper Role of International Law in Combating Terrorism', in *Chinese Journal of International Law*, 2002, pp. 304-312.

Alcaide Fernández J., *Las activitades terroristas ante el Derecho Internacional contemporanéo*, Madrid: Tecnos, 2000.

Alvarez J.E., 'The Security Council's War on Terrorism: Problems and Policy Options', in E. De Wet, A. Nollkaemper (eds), *Review of Security Council by Member States*, Antwerp/New York: Intersentia, 2003.

Alvarez J.E., 'The UN's War on Terrorism', in *International Journal of Legal Information*, vol. 31, 2003, pp. 238-250.

Arnold R., *The ICC as a New Instrument for Repressing Terrorism*, Ardsley: Transnational Publisher, 2004.

Arnold R., The Prosecution of Terrorism as a Crime Against Humanity, in *Zeitschrift für ausländisches öffentliches Recht und Völkerrecht (ZaöRV)*, vol. 64, 2004, pp. 979-1000.

Aust A., 'Counter-Terrorism – A New Approach', in *Max Planck Yearbook of United Nations Law*, Vol. 5, 2001, pp. 285-306.

Bâli A., 'Stretching The Limits of International Law: The Challenge of Terrorism', in *ILSA Journal of International and Comparative Law*, vol. 8, 2002, pp. 403-416.

Balkin K., *The War on Terrorism: Opposing Viewpoints*, Thomson Gale, Detroit, MI: Greenhaven Press, 2005.

Bantekas I., 'The International Law of Terrorist Financing', in *American Journal of International Law*, vol. 97, 2003, pp. 315-333.

Bassiouni M.C. (ed.), *International Terrorism. Multilateral Conventions (1937-2001)*, Ardsley, NY: Transnational Publishers, 2001.

Bassiouni M.C., 'Legal Control of International Terrorism: a Policy-Oriented Assessment', in *Harvard International Law Journal*, vol. 43, 2002, p. 83 ff.

Bassiouni, M.C. (ed.), *International Terrorism. A Compilation of U.N. Documents (1972-2001)*, Ardsley, NY: Transnational Publishers, 2001.

Benedek W. and Yotopoulos-Marangopoulos A. (eds.), *Anti-terrorist Measures and Human Rights*, Leiden, Nijhoff, 2004.

Bennoune K., '"To Respect and to Ensure": Reconciling International Human Rights Obligations in a Time of Terror', in *Proceedings of the American Society of International Law*, vol. 97, 2003, pp. 23-26.

---

1 By Valeria Santori. Among the very many scientific contributions on the various aspects of terrorism, this bibliography only lists (a) the most recent ones and (b) publications relating to one of the topics dealt with during the Trento meeting.

Benoit L., 'La lutte contre le terrorisme dans le cadre du deuxième pilier: un nouveau volet des relations extérieures de l'Union européenne', in *Revue Droit Union Européenne,* 2002, pp. 283-313.

Bianchi A. (ed.), *Enforcing International Law Norms Against Terrorism*, Oxford: Hart Publishing, 2004.

Bonanate L., 'Terrorism, International Conventions And Prevention Strategies After The Attacks Of 11 September 2001', in F. Cappè (ed.), *International Terrorism Prevention Strategies*, Turin: United Nations Interregional Crime & Justice Research Institute (UNICRI), 2002, pp. 11-26.

Bothe M., 'Terrorism and the Legality of Pre-Emptive Force', in *European Journal of International Law*, vol. 14, 2003, pp. 227-240.

Bothe M., 'The International Community and Terrorism', in Société Française pour le Droit International, *Les nouvelles menaces contre la paix et la sécurité internationales: journée franco-allemande*, Paris: Pedone, 2004, pp. 47-62.

Boulden J. and Weiss T.G. (eds.), *Terrorism and the UN: Before and after September 11*, Bloomington, Ind.: Indiana University Press, 2004.

Bribosia, Weyembergh A. (ed.), *Lutte contre le terrorisme et droits fondamentaux*, Bruxelles: Bruylant, 2002.

Buckley M.E.A., *Global Responses to Terrorism,* London: Routledge, 2003.

Byers M., 'Terrorism, the Use of Force and International Law after 11 September 2001', in *International and Comparative Law Quarterly*, vol. 51, 2002, pp. 401-414.

Cassese A., 'Terrorism is also Disrupting some Crucial Legal Categories of International Law', *European Journal of International Law*, Vol. 12, 2001, pp. 993-1001.

Charney J.I., 'The Use of Force Against Terrorism and International Law', in *American Journal of International Law*, vol. 95, 2001, pp. 835-839.

Chesterman S., 'Legitimacy and the Use of Force in Response to Terrorism: a Comment', in Paul Eden and Thérèse O'Donnell, *September 11, 2001: A Turning Point in International and Domestic Law?*, Transnational Publisher, Ardsley, NY: 2005, pp. 149-161.

Clark W.K., *Winning Modern Wars: Iraq, Terrorism, And The American Empire*, New York: Public Affairs, 2003.

Cohn M., 'Human Rights: Casualty of the War on Terror', in *Thomas Jefferson Law Review*, vol. 25, 2003, pp. 317-365.

Condorelli L., 'The Imputability to States of Acts of International Terrorism', in *Israel Yearbook on Human Rights*, vol. 19, 1989, p. 233 ff.

Condorelli L., 'Les attentats du 11 septembre et leur suites: où va le droit international?' *Revue générale de droit international public*, 2001, pp. 829-848.

Corten O. and Dubuisson F., 'Opération "Liberté immuable": une extension abusive du concept de légitime défense', in *Revue générale de droit international public*, vol. 106, 2002, pp. 51-77.

Council of Europe, *Guidelines on Human Rights and the Fight Against Terrorism: Adopted by the Committee of Ministers on 11 July 2002 at the 804th Meeting of the Ministers' Deputies*, Strasbourg: Council of Europe Publishing, 2002.

De Guttry A., Pagano F., *Sfida all'ordine mondiale: l'11 settembre e la riposta della comunità internazionale*, Roma: Donzelli, 2002.

De Jonge Oudraat C., 'The United Nations and the campaign against terrorism', in *Disarmament Forum*, issue 1, 2004, pp. 29-37.

De Sena P., 'Esigenze di sicurezza nazionale e tutela dei diritti dell'uomo nella recente prassi europea', in SIDI, *Ordine internazionale e valori etici. VIII Convegno, Verona, 26-27 giugno 2003*, Napoli: Editoriale Scientifica, 2004, pp. 195-268.

de Wet E., Nollkaemper A., 'Review of Security Council Decisions by National Courts', in *German Yearbook of International Law*, vol. 45, 2002, pp. 166-202.

Delbrück J., 'The Fight against Global Terrorism: Self-Defense or Collective Security as International Police Action? Some Comments on the International Legal Implications of the "War Against Terrorism"', in *German Yearbook of International Law*, 2002, pp. 9-24.

Delpech T., *Le terrorisme international et l'Europe*, Paris: Union Européenne, Institut d'Études de Sécurité, 2002.

Der Bagdasarian S.R., 'The Need For International Cooperation To Suppress Terrorism: The United States And Germany As An Example', in *New York Law School Journal of International And Comparative Law*, vol. 19, 1999, pp. 265-284.

Digest of Jurisprudence of the United Nations and Regional Organizations on the Protection of Human Rights While Countering Terrorism, compiled by the Office of the United Nations High Commissioner for Human Rights Geneva, New York and Geneva, 2003.

Dinstein Y., '*Ius ad bellum* Aspects of the "War on Terrorism"', in Heere P. W., *Terrorism and the Military: International Legal Implications*, The Hague: T.M.C. Asser Press, 2003, pp. 13-22.

Drumbl M., 'Self-defense in an age of terrorism', in *Proceedings of the American Society of International Law*, vol. 97, 2003, pp. 141-152.

Dupuy P-M., *The Law after the Destruction of the Towers*, at: http://www.ejil.org/forum_WTC/ny-dupuy.html.

Eden P. and O'Donnell T., *September 11, 2001: A Turning Point in International and Domestic Law?*, Ardsley, NY: Transnational Publisher, 2005.

'El orden internacional tras los atentados del 11 de septiembre de 2001' (symposium), in *Revista Española de derecho internacional*, 2001.

Fijnaut C., Wouters, J., and Naert F., *Legal Instruments in the Fight against International Terrorism. A Transatlantic Dialogue*, Leiden/Boston: Martinus Nijhoff, 2004.

Fitzpatrick J., 'Speaking Law to Power: The War Against Terrorism and Human Rights', *European Journal of International Law*, vol. 14, 2003, pp. 241-264.

Fletcher G.P., *Romantics At War: Glory and Guilt in the Age of Terrorism*, Princeton, NJ: Princeton University Press, 2002.

Franke V.C., *Terrorism and Peacekeeping: New Security Challenges*, Westport: Praeger, 2005.

Friedlander R.A. and Marauhn T., 'Terrorism', in Bernhardt R. (ed.), *Encyclopaedia of Public International Law*, Instalment 10, Amsterdam, New York, Oxford, Tokyo: Elsevier, 2000, vol. 4, p. 845 ff.

Friedman N., *Terrorism, Afghanistan, and America's New Way of War*, Annapolis: Naval Institute Press, 2004.

Fry J.D., 'Terrorism as a Crime Against Humanity and Genocide: The Backdoor to Universal Jurisdiction', in *UCLA Journal of International Law and Foreign Affairs*, vol. 7, 2002.

Gaja G., 'In What Sense Was There an Armed Attack?', in *European Journal of International Law Forum*, 2001, at: http://www.ejil.org/forum_WTC/ny-gaja.html.

Gaur M. (ed.), *Terrorism and Human Rights*, New Delhi: Anamika Publishers & Distributors, 2003.

Gearty C.A., 'Terrorism and Human Rights', in *European Human Rights Law Review*, vol. 1, 2005, pp. 1-6.

Gioia A., 'Terrorismo internazionale, crimini di guerra e crimini contro l'umanità', in *Rivista di diritto internazionale*, vol. 87, 2004, pp. 5-69.

Golder B. and Williams G., 'What is "Terrorism"?: Problems of Legal Definition', in *University Of New South Wales Law Journal*, vol. 27, 2004, pp. 270-295.

Greenwood C., 'International Law and the "War against Terrorism" ', *International Affairs*, vol. 78, 2002, p. 306.

Grote R., 'Between Crime Prevention and the Laws of War: Are the Traditional Categories of International Law Adequate for Assessing the Use of Force against International Terrorism', in C. Walter, S. Vöneky, V. Röben and F. Schorkopf (eds), *Terrorism as a Challenge for National and International Law, Security versus Liberty?*, Berlin-Heidelberg: Springer, 2004, pp. 951-985.

Guillaume G., 'Terrorism and International Law', in *The International and Comparative Law Quarterly*, vol. 53, 2004, pp. 27-548.

Halberstam M., 'The Evolution of the United Nations Position on Terrorism: From Exempting National Liberation Movements to Criminalizing Terrorism Wherever and by Whomever Committed', in *Columbia Journal of Transnational Law*, vol. 41, 2003, pp. 573-584.

Hedigan J., 'The European Convention on Human Rights and Counter-terrorism', in *Fordham International Law Journal*, vol. 28, 2005, pp. 392-431.

Heere P.W., *Terrorism and the Military: International Legal Implications*, The Hague: T.M.C. Asser Press, 2003.

Hoffman M.H., 'Quelling Unlawful Belligerency: The Juridical Status and Treatment of Terrorists under the Laws of War', in *Israel Yearbook of Human Rights*, vol. 31, 2002, pp. 161-181.

Hoffman M.H., 'Human Rights and Terrorism', in *Human Rights Quarterly*, vol. 26, 2004, pp. 932-955.

Howorth J., 'The European Union, Peace Operations and Terrorism', in T. Tardy, *Peace Operations after 11 September 2001*, London: Cass, pp. 80-97.

Hugues E., 'La notion de terrorisme en droit international: en quête d'une définition juridique', in *Journal du droit international*, vol. 129, 2002, pp. 753-771.

Human Rights Watch, 'Country Studies: The Human Rights Impact of Counter-Terrorism Measures in Ten Countries', in *In the Name of Counter-Terrorism: Human Rights Abuses Worldwide, A Human Rights Watch Briefing Paper for the 59th Session of the UN Commission on Human Rights, 25 March 2003*, at http://www.hrw.org/un/chr59/counter-terrorism-bck.htm.

Human Rights Watch, *Legal Issues Arising from the War in Afghanistan and Related Anti-Terrorism Efforts, 2002*, http://www.hrw.org/campaigns/september11/ihlqna.pdf.

Jekewitz J., 'The Action of the European Union to Combat Terrorism', in *Société française pour le droit international, Les nouvelles menaces contre la paix et la sécurité internationales: journée franco-allemande*, Paris: Pedone, 2004, pp. 77-94.

Johnstone I., 'The Plea of "Necessity" in International Legal Discourse: Humanitarian Intervention and Counter-terrorism', in *Columbia Journal of Transnational Law*, vol. 43, 2005, pp. 337-388.

Klabbers J., 'Rebel With a Cause? Terrorists and Humanitarian Law', in *European Journal of International Law*, vol. 14, 2003, pp. 299-312.

Knoops G., 'International Terrorism: The Changing Face of International Extradition and European Criminal Law', in *Maastricht Journal of European and Comparative Law*, vol. 10, 2003.

Koufa K., 'Human Rights and Terrorism in the United Nations', in G. Alfredsson and M. Stavropoulou (eds.), *Justice Pending: Indigenous Peoples and Other Good Causes: Essays in honour of Erica-Irene A. Daes*, The Hague: M. Nijhoff Publishers, 2002.

Koufa K., 'Human Rights and Terrorism in the United Nations', in Gudmundur Alfredsson and Maria Stavropoulou (eds.), *Justice Pending: Indigenous Peoples and Other Good Causes: Essays in honour of Erica-Irene A. Daes,* The Hague: Nijhoff, 2002, pp. 203-218.

Koufa K., 'Le terrorisme et les droits de l'homme', in *Le droit international face au terrorisme – Après le 11 septembre 2001*, CEDIN-Paris I, Cahiers internationaux No. 17, 2002, pp. 189-201.

La lutte contre le terrorisme: les normes du Conseil de l'Europe, Ed. du Conseil de l'Europe, Strasbourg, 2004.

Lansford T., *All For One: Terrorism, Nato and the United States*, Aldershot: Ashgate, 2002.

Laqueur W., *No End to War: Terrorism in the Twenty-First Century*, New York, NY: Continuum, 2003.

Lavalle R., 'The International Convention For The Suppression Of The Financing Of Terrorism', in *Zeitschrift für ausländisches öffentliches Recht und Völkerrecht (ZaöRV)*, vol. 60, 2000, pp. 491-510.

Lavalle R., Una pregunta sin respuesta cabal: ¿cómo ha de definirse, a nivel universal, el terrorismo?, in *Cuaderno de studio de la Universidad Rafael Landívar, Instituto de Investigaciones Jurídicas, Ciudad de Guatemala*, 2004.

Leurdijk D.A., 'NATO's Shifting Priorities: From Peace Support Operations to Counter-Terrorism', in Thierry Tardy, *Peace Operations after 11 September 2001*, London: Cass, London, pp. 58-79.

Lietzau W.K., 'Old Laws, New Wars: Jus ad Bellum in an Age of Terrorism', in *Max Planck Yearbook of United Nations Law*, vol. 8, 2004, pp. 383-455.

Lietzau W.K., 'Combating Terrorism: the Consequences of Moving from Law Enforcement to War', in David Wippman and Matthew Evangelista (eds.), *New Wars, New Laws? Applying the Laws of War in 21st Century Conflicts*, Ardsley, NY: Transnational Publishers, 2005, pp. 31-51.

Lowe V., 'Clear and Present Danger: Responses to Terrorism', in *The International and Comparative Law Quarterly*, vol. 54, 2005, pp. 185-196.

Luck E.C., 'Another reluctant belligerent: the United Nations and the war on terrorism', in Richard M. Price and Mark W. Zacher, *The United Nations and Global Security*, New York, N.Y.: Palgrave Macmillan, 2004, pp. 95-108.

Luck E.C., 'Tackling terrorism', in David M. Malone (ed.), *The UN Security Council: from the Cold War to the 21st Century*, Boulder: Rienner, 2004, pp. 85-100.

Lutz J.M., and Lutz B.J., *Terrorism: Origins and Evolution*, New York: Palgrave Macmillan, 2005.

Maogoto J.N., *Battling Terrorism: Legal Perspectives on the Use of Force and the War on Terror*, Aldershot: Ashgate, 2005.

Marschik, A., 'Legislative Powers of the Security Council', in R. St. John McDonald and D. M. Johnston (eds.), *Towards World Constitutionalism*, Leiden, Martinus Nijhoff, 2005, pp. 457-492.

McGinley G.P., 'The ICJ's Decision in the Lockerbie Cases', in *Georgia Journal of International Law*, vol. 22, 1992, pp. 577-580.

'Military responses to terrorism', *Proceedings of the American Society of International Law*, vol. 81, 1987, p. 287 ff.

Müllerson R., '*Jus Ad Bellum* and International Terrorism', in *Israel Yearbook on Human Rights,* vol. 32, 2002, pp. 1-51.

Murphy J.F., 'Terrorism and the Concept of "Armed Attack" in Article 51 of the U.N. Charter', in *Harvard International Law Journal*, vol. 43, 2002, pp. 41-51.

Murphy J.F., 'International Law and the War on Terrorism: the Road Ahead', in *Israel Yearbook on Human Rights*, vol. 32, 2002, pp. 117-163.

Murphy S.D., 'International Law, the United States, and the Non-Military "War Against Terrorism"', in *European Journal of International Law*, vol. 14, 2003, pp. 347-364.

Myer E.P.J. and White N.D., 'The Twin Towers Attack: An Unlimited Right to Self-Defence', in *Journal of Conflict and Security Law*, vol. 7, 2002, pp. 5-17.

Naert F., 'The Impact of the Fight against International Terrorism on the Ius ad Bellum after "11 September" ', in *Revue de droit militaire et de droit de la guerre*, vol. 43, 2004, pp. 55-107.

Nanda V.P., *Law in the War on International Terrorism*, Ardsley, NY: Transnational Publisher, 2005.

O'Connell M.E., 'Lawful Self-Defense to Terrorism', in *University of Pittsburgh Law Review*, vol. 63, 2002, pp. 889-908.

O'Connell M.E., 'Lawful and Unlawful Wars Against Terrorism', in Nanda V. P., *Law in the War on International Terrorism*, Ardsley, NY: Transnational Publisher, 2005, pp. 79-96.

Office for Democratic Institutions and Human Rights (ODHIR), 'Preventing and Combating Terrorism: The New Security Environment', in *Food for Thought Paper prepared for the 2nd OSCE Annual Security Review Conference*, Vienna 23-24 June 2004.

Osman M.A., *The United Nations and Peace Enforcement: Wars, Terrorism and Democracy*, Aldershot: Ashgate, 2002.

Pannick D., 'Human Rights in an Age of Terrorism', in *Israel Law Review*, vol. 36, 2002, pp. 1-18.

Patel King F., and Swaak-Goldman O., 'The Applicability of International Humanitarian Law to the "War Against Terrorism"', in *Hague Yearbook of International Law*, vol. 15, pp. 39-49.

Paust J.J., *Comment: Security Council Authorization to Combat Terrorism in Afghanistan*, 2001, in http://www.asil.org/insights/insigh77.htm#comment4.

Peers S., 'EU responses to terrorism', in *The International and Comparative Law Quarterly*, vol. 52, 2003, pp. 227-243.

Perera R., 'Suppression of Terrorism: Regional Approach to Meet the Challenges', in *Sri Lanka Journal of International Law*, vol. 16, 2004, pp. 19-26.

Posteraro C.C., 'Intervention In Iraq: Towards A Doctrine Of Anticipatory Counter-Terrorism, Counterproliferation Intervention', in *Florida Journal of International Law*, vol. 15, 2002, pp. 151-213.

Raymond G.A., 'Military Necessity and the War against Global Terrorism', in Hensel H.M. (ed.), *The Law of Armed Conflict: Constraints on the Contemporary Use of Military Force*, Aldershot: Ashgate, 2005, pp. 1-20.

'Responding to Terrorism: Crime, Punishment and War', in *Harvard Law Review*, 2002, pp. 1217-1238.

Rosand E., 'Security Council Resolution 1373, the Counter-Terrorism Committee, and the Fight against Terrorism', in *American Journal of International Law*, vol. 97, 2003, pp. 333-341.

Rosand E., 'The Security Council's Efforts to Monitor the Implementation of Al Qaeda/Taliban Sanctions', in *American Journal of International Law,* vol. 98, 2004, pp. 745-763.

Sandoz Y., 'Lutte contre le terrorisme et droit international: risques et opportunités', in *Revue suisse de droit international e de droit européen*, vol. 12, 2002, pp. 319-354.

Sassoli M., 'Use and Abuse of the Laws of War in the "War on Terrorism"', in *Law and Equality: A Journal of Theory and Practice*, vol. 22, 2004, pp. 195-221.

Schabas W.A., 'Is Terrorism a Crime against Humanity?', in *International Peacekeeping*, vol. 8, 2004, pp. 255-261.

Scharf M.P., 'Defining Terrorism as the Peacetime Equivalent of War Crimes: Problems and Prospects', in *Case Western Reserve Journal of International Law*, vol. 26, 2004, pp. 359-374.

Schmid A., 'Terrorism: the Definitional Problem', in *Case Western Reserve Journal of International Law*, vol. 36, 2004, pp. 375-419.

Schmitt M.N., 'Counter-Terrorism and the Use of Force in International Law', in *Israel Yearbook on Human Rights*, vol. 32, 2002, pp. 53-116.

Schmitt M.N., *Counter-Terrorism and the Use of Force in International Law*, Garmisch-Partenkirchen: George C. Marshall Center, 2002.

Schrijver N.J., 'Responding to International Terrorism: Moving the Frontiers of International Law for "Enduring Freedom"?', in Studievereniging voor Internationaal Recht, URIOS, Utrecht, *The Law on Terror: Terrorism and Human Rights*, Nijmegen: Wolf Legal Publishers, 2003, pp. 9-286.

Seiderman I.D., 'The Impact of Counter-Terrorism on Human Rights: towards an International Monitoring Mechanism', in *Yearbook of the International Commission of Jurists*, 2004, pp. 399-420.

Smith P.J., *Terrorism and Violence in Southeast Asia: Transnational Challenges to States and Regional Stability*, Armonk, N.Y.: Sharpe, 2005.

Sofaer A.D., 'Terrorism As War', in *Proceedings of the American Society of International Law*, vol. 96, 2002, pp. 254-259.

Stahn C., *Security Council Resolutions 1368(2001) and 1373(2001): What They Say and What They Do Not Say*, in *EJIL*, http://www.ejil.org/forum_WTC/ny-stahn.html.

Stein T., 'Preemption and Terrorism', in *International Peacekeeping*, vol. 9, 2005, pp. 155-171.

Stromseth J. E., 'The Security Council's Counter-Terrorism Role: Continuity and Innovation', in *Proceedings of the American Society of International Law*, vol. 97, 2003, pp. 41-45.

Symposium: 'A War against Terrorism': What Role for International Law? US and European Perspectives, in *EJIL*, vol. 14, 2003, p. 209 ff.

The Fight Against Terrorism: Council of Europe Standards, 2nd ed., Council of Europe Publishing, Strasbourg, 2004.

Torr J.D., *Is Military Action Justified Against Nations That Support Terrorism?*, San Diego: Greenhaven Press, 2003.

Travalio G.M., 'Terrorism, International Law, and the Use of Military Force', in *Wisconsin International Law Journal*, vol. 18, 2000, pp. 145-191.

United Nations, *International Instruments related to the Prevention and Suppression of International Terrorism*, New York, NY: United Nations Publications, 2001.

van de Rijt W., 'The EU and Terrorism After 11 September 2001', in F. Cappè (ed.), *International Terrorism Prevention Strategies*, Turin: United Nations Interregional Crime & Justice Research Institute (UNICRI), 2002, pp. 115-126.

van Krieken P.J., *Terrorism and the International Legal Order: with Special Reference to the UN, the EU and Cross-Border Aspects*, The Hague: T.M.C. Asser Press, 2002.

van Leeuwen M., *Confronting Terrorism: European Experiences, Threat Perceptions and Policies*, The Hague: Kluwer Law International, 2003.

Venneman N., 'Country Report on the European Union' in C. Walter, S. Voneky, V. Roben and F. Schorkopf (eds.), *Terrorism as a Challenge for National and International Security versus Liberty?*, Berlin-Heidelberg: Springer, 2004.

von Schorlemer S., 'Human Rights: Substantive And Institutional Implications of the War against Terrorism', in *European Journal of International Law*, vol. 14, 2003, pp. 265-282.

Walter C., *Terrorism As A Challenge For National And International Law: Security Versus Liberty?*, Berlin: Springer, 2004.

Warbrick C., 'The European Response to Terrorism in an Age of Human Rights', in *European Journal of International Law*, vol. 15, 2004, pp. 989-1018.

Warbrick C., 'The Principles of the European Convention on Human Rights and the Response of States to Terrorism', in *European Human Rights Law Reports*, vol. 7, 2002, pp. 287-314.

Ward C.A., 'The Counter-terrorism Committee: its Relevance for Implementing Targeted Sanctions', in P. Wallensteen and C. Staibano, *International Sanctions: Between Words and Wars in the Global System*, London: Frank Cass, 2005, pp. 167-180.

Wardlaw G., *Political Terrorism: Theory, Tactics and Countermeasures*, Cambridge: Cambridge University Press, 1982.

Weiss T.G., Crahan M.E., Goering J. (eds.), *Wars on Terrorism and Iraq: Human Rights, Unilateralism, and US Foreign Policy*, New York: Routledge, 2004.

Wouters J., Naert F., 'Of Arrest Warrants, Terrorist Offences and Extradition Deals: an Appraisal of the EU's Main Criminal Law Measures against Terrorism after "11 September"', in *Common Market Law Review,* vol. 41, 2004, pp. 909-932.

Yonah A., and Brenner E.H., *Terrorism and the Law*, Ardsley, NY: Transnational Publishers 2001.

Zaagman R., 'Terrorism and the OSCE: an Overview', in *Helsinki Monitor*, vol. 13, 2002, pp. 204-215.

Ziccardi Capaldo G., 'Fighting Global Terrorism: Through Global Enforcement Mechanisms Enforcement Mechanisms', in *The Global Community: Yearbook of International Law and Jurisprudence*, 2004, pp. 15-27.

Index

Note: numbers in brackets preceded by n are footnote numbers.